# Fieldwork in Tourism

The inherent mobility of tourists and consequent relative ephemerality of contact between the visitor and the visited tourism phenomenon have specific characteristics that challenge the usual fieldwork practices of the social and physical sciences. Such conditions create specific concerns for the tourism researcher in terms of their positionality, relationality, accessibility, ethics, reflexivity and methodological appropriateness.

*Fieldwork in Tourism* is the first book to focus on this extremely significant component of contemporary tourist research, and provides hands-on approaches to conducting tourism fieldwork in a range of settings, exploring the methodological considerations and offering strategies to mitigate these. The book also discusses how fieldwork affects researchers personally and what happens to field relationships. Divided into five sections, each with an introduction and a guide to further reading, the chapters cover the context of fieldwork, research relationships, politics and power, the position of the researcher in the field, research methods and processes, including virtual fieldwork, and the relationships between being a tourist and doing fieldwork. The concluding chapter suggests that the link between tourism and fieldwork perhaps offers greater insights into understanding creative fieldwork than may be imagined.

This book incorporates a rich and diverse set of fieldwork experiences, insights and reflections on conducting fieldwork in different settings, the problems that emerge, the solutions that were developed and the realities of being 'in the field'. *Fieldwork in Tourism* is an essential guide for Tourism higher level students, academics and researchers embarking on research in this field.

**C. Michael Hall** is Professor in the Department of Management, University of Canterbury, New Zealand; Docent in the Department of Geography, University of Oulu, Finland; and Visiting Professor at the Linnaeus University School of Business and Economics, Kalmar, Sweden. He is co-editor of *Current Issues in Tourism* and he has published widely in tourism, gastronomy and environmental history.

**Contemporary Geographies of Leisure, Tourism and Mobility**
Series Editor: C. Michael Hall Professor at the Department of Management,
College of Business & Economics, University of Canterbury, Private Bag
4800, Christchurch, New Zealand

The aim of this series is to explore and communicate the intersections and
relationships between leisure, tourism and human mobility within the social
sciences.

It will incorporate both traditional and new perspectives on leisure and
tourism from contemporary geography, e.g. notions of identity, representation and culture, while also providing for perspectives from cognate areas
such as anthropology, cultural studies, gastronomy and food studies, marketing, policy studies and political economy, regional and urban planning,
and sociology, within the development of an integrated field of leisure and
tourism studies.

Also, increasingly, tourism and leisure are regarded as steps in a continuum
of human mobility. Inclusion of mobility in the series offers the prospect to
examine the relationship between tourism and migration, the sojourner, educational travel, and second home and retirement travel phenomena.

The series comprises two strands:

**Contemporary Geographies of Leisure, Tourism and Mobility** aims to address
the needs of students and academics, and the titles will be published in
hardback and paperback. Titles include:

**The Moralisation of Tourism**
Sun, sand . . . and saving the
world?
*Jim Butcher*

**The Ethics of Tourism Development**
*Mick Smith & Rosaleen Duffy*

**Tourism in the Caribbean**
Trends, development,
prospects
*Edited by David Timothy Duval*

**Qualitative Research in Tourism**
Ontologies, epistemologies and
methodologies
*Edited by Jenny Phillimore and
Lisa Goodson*

**The Media and the Tourist
Imagination**
Converging cultures
*Edited by David Crouch,
Rhona Jackson and Felix Thompson*

**Tourism and Global Environmental Change**
Ecological, social, economic and political interrelationships
*Edited by Stefan Gössling and C. Michael Hall*

**Cultural Heritage of Tourism in the Developing World**
*Dallen J. Timothy and Gyan Nyaupane*

**Understanding and Managing Tourism Impacts**
*Michael Hall and Alan Lew*

Forthcoming:

**An Introduction to Visual Research Methods in Tourism**
*Tijana Rakic and Donna Chambers*

**Routledge Studies in Contemporary Geographies of Leisure, Tourism and Mobility** is a forum for innovative new research intended for research students and academics, and the titles will be available in hardback only. Titles include:

**Living with Tourism**
Negotiating identities in a Turkish village
*Hazel Tucker*

**Tourism, Diasporas and Space**
*Edited by Tim Coles and Dallen J. Timothy*

**Tourism and Postcolonialism**
Contested discourses, identities and representations
*Edited by C. Michael Hall and Hazel Tucker*

**Tourism, Religion and Spiritual Journeys**
*Edited by Dallen J. Timothy and Daniel H. Olsen*

**China's Outbound Tourism**
*Wolfgang Georg Arlt*

**Tourism, Power and Space**
*Edited by Andrew Church and Tim Coles*

**Tourism, Ethnic Diversity and the City**
*Edited by Jan Rath*

**Ecotourism, NGO's and Development**
A critical analysis
*Jim Butcher*

**Tourism and the Consumption of Wildlife**
Hunting, shooting and sport fishing
*Edited by Brent Lovelock*

**Tourism, Creativity and Development**
*Edited by Greg Richards and Julie Wilson*

**Tourism at the Grassroots**
*Edited by John Connell and Barbara Rugendyke*

**Tourism and Innovation**
*Michael Hall and Allan Williams*

**World Tourism Cities**
Developing tourism off the beaten track
*Edited by Robert Maitland and Peter Newman*

**Tourism and National Parks**
International perspectives on development, histories and change
*Edited by Warwick Frost and C. Michael Hall*

# Fieldwork in Tourism

## Methods, issues and reflections

**Edited by C. Michael Hall**

Routledge
Taylor & Francis Group

LONDON AND NEW YORK

First published 2011
by Routledge
2 Park Square, Milton Park, Abingdon, Oxon, OX14 4RN

Simultaneously published in the USA and Canada
by Routledge
270 Madison Avenue, New York, NY 10016

*Routledge is an imprint of the Taylor & Francis Group,
an informa business*

Typeset in Times New Roman by
RefineCatch Limited, Bungay, Suffolk

*British Library Cataloguing in Publication Data*
A catalog record for this book is available
from the British Library

*Library of Congress Cataloging in Publication Data*
Fieldwork in tourism / edited by C. Michael Hall.
        p. cm.
    Includes bibliographical references and index.
    1. Tourism – Research. I. Hall, Colin Michael, 1961–
    G155.A1F536 2010
    910.72′3 – dc22
    2010008240

ISBN 13: 978-0-415-58919-2 (hbk)
ISBN 13: 978-0-203-84551-6 (ebk)

# Contents

**PART II**

**Positionality: Researcher position in the field–practicalities, perils and pitfalls**

**PART III**

**Methods and processes**

# List of illustrations

# Contributors

**Malita Allan**, School of Social Sciences, La Trobe University, Melbourne, Victoria 3086, Australia.

**Jo Bensemann**, Department of Management, Massey University, Private Bag 11222, Palmerston North, New Zealand.

**Audrey Bochaton**, Paris Ouest Nanterre la Défense – Laboratory: Espace, santé et territoire (EST), Institute of Research for Development (IRD), 19 La Vionnaz, 74200 Thonon-les-Bains, France.

**Jenny Chio**, China Research Centre, Faculty of Arts and Social Sciences, University of Technology Sydney, PO Box 123, Broadway, NSW 2007, Australia.

**Stephanie Chok**, Asia Research Centre, Murdoch University, South Street, WA 6150, Australia.

**David Duval**, School of Business, University of Otago, Dunedin, New Zealand.

**Jörg Finsterwalder**, Department of Management, University of Canterbury, Private Bag 4800, Christchurch 8140, New Zealand.

**Jamie Gillen**, Department of Geography, Miami University, Oxford, Ohio 45056, USA.

**C. Michael Hall**, Department of Management, University of Canterbury, Christchurch 8140, New Zealand; Department of Geography, University of Oulu, Finland; and Linnaeus University School of Business and Economics, Kalmar, Sweden.

**Gijsbert Hoogendoorn**, Department of Geography, Rhodes University, PO Box 94, Grahamstown 6140, South Africa.

**Volker G. Kuppelwieser**, Schumpeter School of Business, Chair of Retail and Service Management, University of Wuppertal, Gaussstr. 20, 42097 Wuppertal, Germany.

**Raynard Harvey Lemelin**, School of Outdoor Recreation, Parks, and Tourism, Lakehead University, 955 Oliver Road, Thunder Bay, Ontario P7B 5E1, Canada.

**Bertrand Lefebvre**, University of Rouen – UMR IDEES, 6266-CNRS, France.

**Teresa Leopold**, Business School, University of Sunderland, Sir Tom Cowie Campus at St Peter's, St Peter's Way, Sunderland, SR6 0DD, UK.

**Alan A. Lew**, Department of Geography, Planning and Recreation, Northern Arizona University, Box 15016, Flagstaff, Arizona 86011-5016, USA.

**Chris McMorran**, Center for Asian Studies, Program for Teaching East Asia, University of Colorado, 595UCB, Boulder, CO 80309, USA.

**Noel B. Salazar**, Cultural Mobilities Research, IMMRC-Anthropology, Faculty of Social Sciences, University of Leuven, B-3000, Leuven, Belgium.

**Harng Luh Sin**, Department of Geography, Royal Holloway, University of London, Egham, Surrey, TW20 0EX, England.

**Emma Stewart**, Department of Geography, University of Calgary, Calgary, Alberta, Canada.

**David Tantow**, Department of Geography, National University of Singapore, Kent Ridge, Singapore 117570.

**Gustav Visser,** Department of Geography, University of the Free State, Bloemfontein Campus, Bloemfontein, 9301, South Africa.

**Sandra Wall Reinius**, Department of Tourism, Mid Sweden University, Kunskapens väg 1, SE-831 25 Östersund, Sweden.

**Melissa Wan Hassan**, Department of Hospitality and Recreation, Faculty of Economics and Management, Universiti Putra Malaysia, UPM Serdang 43400, Selangor, Malaysia.

**Elaine Wiersma**, Masters of Public Health, Lakehead University, 955 Oliver Road, Thunder Bay, Ontario P7B 5E1, Canada.

**Reiko Yamagishi**, Department of Japanese Studies, National University of Singapore, Singapore.

# Foreword

For many graduate students, as well as for many who have completed their graduate studies, fieldwork remains a major task in tourism research. However, despite the importance of fieldwork in tourism, especially those from a background in anthropology, development studies, environmental studies, geography, marketing and sociology, there is a relative dearth of analysis and reflection on fieldwork in tourism studies beyond what is contained in theses. This poses significant issues for those about to engage in fieldwork themselves, especially given that while many books which deal with research methods in tourism mention fieldwork or undertaking field-based studies, they often focus on what happens after the data are (hopefully) collected, not on the difficulties of getting the data in the first place nor of the profound methodological, philosophical, ethical and personal issues that the process raises. This volume therefore seeks to address this major gap in educating about the processes of tourism research by providing readers with a range of fieldwork experiences, issues and reflections so as to better equip researchers to engage in tourism fieldwork, the successful completion of their research projects and what comes afterwards.

The book had its genesis in a graduate workshop hosted by the Asian Research Institute at the National University of Singapore in partnership with the University of Otago on the topic of 'questions on methodology: researching tourism in Asia'. As a result of the formal and informal discussions at the workshop it was recognised that there was both a genuine interest and need from graduate students for better preparation for eventualities in the field and the implications that this had for their research and writing up. Revised versions of several of the excellent presentations from that workshop have found their way into the present volume. In addition, other contributors have provided their insights into fieldwork so as to give the book a wide thematic, methodological and geographical coverage. A number of authors have also provided the editor with suggestions for readings that they themselves found helpful in their work and a number of these are included in the introductions to each section.

One of the most exciting aspects of the book is that it brings together both 'old' and 'new' researchers with respect to their experiences in fieldwork. This allows both the immediate reflections of those who have completed their graduate studies relatively recently as well as those that finished in what their students probably deem to be 'ancient history'. In the case of the latter, their reflections allow insights into the advice they pass on to their own students as well as how they continue to deal with matters arising from fieldwork. Indeed, this is an issue pertinent to the editor as well, because when offered a 'research only' position at a supposedly leading Australian tourism programme in 2009 he was advised that the Dean would not support extended absence from campus to undertake fieldwork. Obviously when one reaches a certain age or seniority one is expected by some to only experience fieldwork vicariously through graduate students or to just do it at weekends!

In terms of acknowledgments the editor and many of the contributors would like to thank Chang Tou Chuang, Peggy Teo and Tim Winter for their efforts with the NUS graduate workshop, as well as David Duval, who not only contributed to the workshop but also served, as usual, as a sounding board for ideas that grew out of the meeting, including the development of the present volume. In addition, a number of colleagues with whom Michael has undertaken research and/or discussed fieldwork issues have also contributed indirectly to the development of the volume. In particular he would like to thank Tim Coles, Stefan Gössling, Anna Grundén, James Higham, Dieter Müller, Stephen Page, Jarkko Saarinen, Anna Dóra Sæþórsdóttir, Brian Springett, Sandra Wall and Allan Williams for their thoughts on being in the field over the years, as well as the stimulation of Jeff Buckley, Nick Cave, Bruce Cockburn, Elvis Costello, Stephen Cummings, Dimmer, Ebba Fosberg, Hoodoo Gurus, Ed Kuepper, Jackson Code, Don MacLashan, Vinnie Reilly, David Sylvian, Jennifer Warnes, Chris Wilson and BBC Radio 6 and World Service – without whom the four walls of many a hotel room would be much more confining. Emma Travis and the staff at Routledge also provided great support to the project, and the editing assistance of Sue Dickinson is also gratefully acknowledged. Finally, Michael would like to thank the many people who have supported his own fieldwork over the years and especially the Js and the Cs who often stay at home.

C. Michael Hall
Richmond
January 2010

# Introducing the contexts
# of fieldwork

Fieldwork is a vital part of research in the social and natural sciences. It is regarded by some as the core of cultural anthropology via the undertaking of ethnography, as Atkinson and colleagues (2001: 9) note: 'The conduct of ethnographic fieldwork – originally in "exotic" settings and more recently in a more diverse range of social worlds – has been the most distinctive character-istic of anthropology as a discipline.' As a method ethnography is also used in a large number of cognate fields such as cultural studies, sociology, cultural geography, education and communication, although 'This does not mean that ethnography always means exactly the same to all social scientists at all times or under all circumstances' (Atkinson *et al.* 2001: 5). Yet, such is the strength of ethnography that it is often regarded as virtually synonymous with field-work in the social sciences (Hobbs and Wright 2006). However, 'being in the field' can utilise a far greater range of social science research methods than ethnography including, but not exclusive to, content analysis, diaries, interviews, mental mapping, observation, participant observation, policy and programme evaluation, self-narrative, semiotic analysis and surveys, while fieldwork in the natural sciences such as biology, ecology and physical geo-graphy is also extremely important with respect to data collection and observa-tion of environmental processes (Reid 2003). Both social and natural science approaches to fieldwork are important in the understanding of tourism, particularly as a result of increased concerns over tourism's role in global change (Hall and Lew 2009).

So what is fieldwork? For Sunstein and Chiseri-Strater (2007: 1) 'The field is the site for doing research, and fieldworking is the process of doing it'. A more nuanced understanding of fieldwork is provided by McCall (2006), who identifies three different meanings of the term in a research context. First, it refers to primary research that occurs outside the controlled settings of the library or laboratory. It may involve 'field experiments' but field methods usually lean towards the non-experimental in approach and utilise observational studies, which can be either quantitative or qualitative in char-acter or a combination of the two. Second, it can refer to the period of time in a research period in which data collection and/or preliminary study occurs in a field setting. This period is then distinguishable from other phases such as design, analysis and writing up, which usually do not completely take place in the field, although some elements will as the researcher adapts to the field-work situation and/or writes while observations are 'fresh'. Finally, McCall (2006: 3) argues that there is a third meaning of fieldwork which is peculiar to the social sciences, and especially to anthropology and sociology, and stems from the phenomenon of reflexivity, 'inclusion of the observer in the subject matter itself' (although note Thorn [2003] with respect to the role of qualita-tive thought in the physical sciences). Interestingly, the elements of fieldwork identified by McCall (2006) fit very well with the definitions of fieldwork provided at a University of Southern Denmark graduate workshop (see Table 1.2 in Hall, Chapter 1, this volume).

The focus of this book is on the development of a better understanding of the challenges of fieldwork-based research in a tourism context. It does not aim to be a handbook of qualitative methods; there are already a number of books which do that job quite well (e.g. Phillimore and Goodson 2004; Denzin and Lincoln 2005) but it does seek to provide students of tourism, and graduate students in particular, with a much better understanding of the issues raised by fieldwork with respect to methods, positionalities and rela-tionships, and how they may be met. In order to do this the book is divided into five sections:

1 Introducing the contexts of fieldwork
2 Research relationships: Power, politics and patron–client affinities
3 Positionality: Researcher position in the field–practicalities, perils and pitfalls
4 Methods and processes
5 Future directions and new environments.

Each of these sections provides a brief outline of the issues raised in the section as well as an overview of each of the chapters. In addition, a guide to further reading relevant to the focus of each section is given; many of these readings have been recommended by the authors of the chapters as those that they found the most helpful with their own fieldwork and writing up. It should also be noted that a number of the readings suggested will be relevant to more than one section. Table 0.1 also provides an overview of the chapters in the volume with respect to the location of the field site, main methods used in the study (excluding the ubiquitous literature review!), and the key issues that each chapter addresses.

This first section consists of two chapters that aim to contextualise field-work as part of the broader context of undertaking research. Chapter 1 by Hall further introduces the reader to the idea of fieldwork and examines the relationship between tourism and fieldwork with respect to the notion of a journey. Hall argues that rather than denying or ignoring the relationship, it should instead be embraced as a way of helping to explain the various chan-ging positionalities and relationships that are inherent in much fieldwork. He

*Table 0.1* Outline of chapters by fieldwork location, methods and key issues

| Chapter | Author | Fieldwork locations | Methods noted | Key issues noted |
|---|---|---|---|---|
| 1 | Hall | N/A | • Framing of research and fieldwork | • Definitions of fieldwork<br>• Relationship between fieldwork and tourism<br>• Different spaces of fieldwork: location, time, regulation/power, ethics, social, theory/method |
| 2 | Lew | China, Singapore | • Framing of research | • Importance of developing a conceptual framework in undertaking research |
| 3 | Hall | N/A | • Elite interviews<br>• Power analysis<br>• Media analysis | • Definition and dimensions of power<br>• Relationship between power and method of analysis<br>• Author positionality with respect to power and actions<br>• Issues of access/role of gatekeepers and elite networks<br>• Academic capitalism |
| 4 | Chok | Singapore | • Covert research<br>• Interviews | • Power<br>• Responsibilities of researcher and ethics<br>• Activist research<br>• Accessibility and gatekeepers |
| 5 | Bochaton and Lefebvre | India, Thailand | • Elite interviews | • Accessibility and gatekeepers<br>• Working as a team in interview situations |
| 6 | Leopold | Thailand | • Ethnography<br>• Participant observation<br>• Interviews | • Positionality<br>• Reflexivity<br>• Time<br>• Power structures<br>• Participatory approaches |
| 7 | Yamagishi | Japan | • Ethnography<br>• Participant observation | • Reflexivity and relationality<br>• The role of emotions in the production of knowledge |
| 8 | Wan Hassan | New Zealand | • Snowball survey<br>• Interviews | • Reflexivity and positionality as a Muslim female with respect to undertaking fieldwork<br>• Researching hidden populations |
| 9 | Tantow | Singapore | • Ethnography<br>• Textual research | • Insiderness/outsiderness<br>• Reflexivity and positionality |
| 10 | Allan | Vietnam | • Ethnography | • Positionality<br>• Personhood and relationality |
| 11 | Bensemann | New Zealand | • Survey<br>• Interviews | • Reflexivity<br>• Feminist research<br>• Advantages and disadvantages of qualitative and quantitative approaches |

*(Continued overleaf )*

Table 0.1 Continued

| Chapter | Author | Fieldwork locations | Methods noted | Key issues noted |
|---|---|---|---|---|
| 12 | Salazar | Indonesia | • Ethnography | • Glocalisation |
| 13 | Hoogendoorn and Visser | South Africa | • Interviews<br>• Surveys<br>• Secondary data | • Accessing appropriate data<br>• Concept definition<br>• Positionality |
| 14 | Gillen | Vietnam | • Deconstruction<br>• Reconstruction of data into formal categories | • Use of information gained from the field<br>• Biography |
| 15 | Chio | China | • Visual media<br>• Ethnography | • Usable knowledge<br>• Relationality<br>• Participatory approaches |
| 16 | McMorran | Japan | • Participant observation | • Relationality and positionality<br>• Power relations |
| 17 | Wall Reinius | Sweden | • Surveys | • Undertaking field research in natural areas and trails<br>• Stakeholder and gatekeeper relations<br>• Communication<br>• Research planning |
| 18 | Finsterwalder and Kuppelwieser | New Zealand | • Survey | • Research planning<br>• Adaptation |
| 19 | Luh Sin | Cambodia / Singapore | • Participant observation<br>• Validity | • Issue of what can and cannot be used from discussions in the field<br>• Can we include in research those who reject participation?<br>• Relationality |
| 20 | Hall | Cyberspace | • Virtual ethnography<br>• Netnography<br>• Content analysis<br>• Online data characteristics and research methods | • Virtual fieldwork<br>• Computer Mediated Communication (CMC)<br>• Ethics<br>• Anonymity<br>• Co-presence and location<br>• Characteristics of qualitative online data |
| 21 | Lemelin et al. | Canada | • Environmental fieldwork<br>• Action research | • Working with indigenous communities<br>• Knowledge ownership and diffusion<br>• Ethics |
| 22 | Duval | Canada | • Ethnography<br>• Interviews | • Relationality<br>• Exiting the field |

then uses this approach to write of different spatialities of fieldwork and their implications: time, space (location), power/regulation, ethics, social/personal, theory/method.

Chapter 2 by Lew draws from recollection of his own doctoral studies and more recent research on tourism in China to argue for the importance of ensuring that fieldwork is undertaken with a clear conceptual framework. Such frameworks are regarded as extremely important to clarifying the goals and aims of undertaking fieldwork as well as the broader epistemological standpoint. According to Lew, conceptual frameworks have three roles to play in academic research. First, they are a reflection of the researcher's worldview, and should be intimately related to their self-identity. Second, they provide epistemological tools and paths. Third, they are a pedagogical tool. As Lew concludes, 'what is the conceptual framework for your current or next research project?' Does it 'relate to your epistemological beliefs about how we know what is true (revelation, observation, reasoning, and tacit knowledge)' and to your 'larger research paradigm (quantitative, qualitative, critical, or something else)? Answering these questions will make your field research more meaningful, useful and doable'.

## Suggested further reading

Atkinson, P., Coffey, A., Delamont, S., Lofland, J. and Lofland, L. (eds) (2001) *Handbook of Ethnography*. London: Sage.
For those engaged in ethnographic research, the handbook provides a very useful reference guide; there is no specific chapter on tourism ethnography, however.

Clifford, N.J. and Valentine, G. (eds) (2003) *Key Methods in Geography*. London: Sage. Although focused on geography the volume has a good range of chapters on field research methods from both the social and physical sciences.

De Laine, M. (2000) *Fieldwork, Participation and Practice: Ethics and Dilemmas in Qualitative Research*. London: Sage.
An excellent introduction to the difficulties that can be faced with respect to self in qualitative research, it provides a good discussion of some of the ethical dilemmas involved, the moral self and the performity of field research.

Hobbs, D. and Wright, R. (eds) (2006) *The Sage Handbook of Fieldwork*. London: Sage.
A very useful handbook for social scientific fieldwork, although there is no specific chapter on tourism.

Mauthner, M., Birch, M., Jessop, J. and Miller, T. (eds) *Ethics in Qualitative Research*. London: Sage.
Provides a good introduction to issues with respect to research ethics both in and out of the field.

Perry, J. (ed.) (2002) *Doing Fieldwork: Eight Personal Accounts of Social Research*. Sydney: University of New South Wales Press.
First published in 1989 and reprinted some four times since (a good indication that the

book has value to students or that they are forced to purchase it!), this book provides an excellent collection of reflections on identity, ethics, developing a research topic, writing, and revisiting the field.

Phillimore, J. and Goodson, L. (eds) (2004) *Qualitative Research in Tourism: Ontologies, Epistemologies and Methodologies*. London: Routledge.
A very good edited volume on qualitative research in tourism that brings together a range of different issues and perspectives.

Scheyvens, R. and Storey, D. (eds) (2003) *Development Fieldwork: A Practical Guide*. London: Sage.
Although focused on fieldwork in a development studies context, the lessons of many of the chapters apply well to studies in tourism, especially as Scheyvens' research on tourism and development means that there are a number of tourism examples that are referred to. The book is extremely user-friendly and most of the chapters provide excellent advice on doing fieldwork.

# References

Atkinson, P., Coffey, A., Delamont, S., Lofland, J. and Lofland, L. (eds) (2001) *Handbook of Ethnography*. London: Sage.

Denzin, N.K. and Lincoln, Y.S. (2005) *The Sage Handbook of Qualitative Research*. Thousand Oaks: Sage Publications.

Hall, C.M. and Lew, A.A. (2009) *Understanding and Managing Tourism Impacts: An Integrated Approach*, London: Routledge.

Hobbs, D. and Wright, R. (eds) (2006) *The Sage Handbook of Fieldwork*. London: Sage.

McCall, C.J. (2006) 'The fieldwork tradition', in D. Hobbs and R. Wright (eds), *The Sage Handbook of Fieldwork*. London: Sage.

Phillimore, J. and Goodson, L. (eds) (2004) *Qualitative Research in Tourism: Ontologies, Epistemologies and Methodologies*. London: Routledge.

Reid, I. (2003) 'Making Observations and Measurements in the Field: An Overview', in N.J. Clifford and G. Valentine (eds), *Key Methods in Geography*. London: Sage.

Sunstein, B.S. and Chiseri-Strater, E. (2007) *Fieldworking: Reading and Writing Research*, 3rd edn. Boston, MA: Bedford St Martins.

Thorn, C.E. (2003) 'The Critical Role of "Qualitative Thought" in Physical Geography and Geomorphological Research', in N.J. Clifford and G. Valentine (eds), *Key Methods in Geography*. London: Sage.

# 1 Fieldwork in tourism/touring fields

## Where does tourism end and fieldwork begin?

*C. Michael Hall*

## Introduction

Fieldwork is one of the defining approaches of academic research. Whether in the social or natural sciences, to get out of the office, lecture theatre or laboratory and study, 'the real world' is a vital component of the generation of knowledge. In the study of tourism too fieldwork has long been utilised not only to observe tourists and the interactions between tourists and destination communities but also to better understand the social, economic, political and environmental effects of tourism. Yet despite the long tradition of fieldwork in tourism studies and in cognate disciplines, such as anthropology, ecology, geography and sociology, that also place a high value on fieldwork, there is surprisingly little reflection on the role of fieldwork in tourism research (see Bruner [2005] as an exception).

Of course, studying tourism has often not been held favourably in other fields nor has it often been seen by other disciplines as providing anything unique or having its own body of knowledge (Hall 2005). Indeed, in the experience of the author, travel for tourism research purposes is often seen in disparaging terms by funding bodies and university research bodies as 'a subsidized holiday', while in a broader context travel for research is often viewed through an 'ironic lens' (Crick 1985). Hence, Mowforth and Munt (1998: 101) refer to 'academic tourism', Zeleza and Kalipeni (1999: 3) to 'academic tourists', Clifford (1997: 67) to 'research travelers', Kotarba (2002; 2005) to 'ethnographic tourism' encouraging the researcher to act like a stranger or a tourist in a foreign land and to treat the common as exotic and the taken-for-granted as unusual, while Stein (1998) uses the same phrase with reference to tourists 'armed with camcorders and a passion for local practices'! Of course, to separate 'academic travel' from 'popular travel' (Galani-Moutafi 2000) is an important concern for many researchers worried as they may be about being accused by university administrators, politicians, journalists or other academics who seek to purchase equipment (who all clearly never travel for work purposes) of misspending money for leisure purposes rather than serious research or paper presentations. Of course, as a result of processes of globalisation the increasing internationalisation of higher education, institutional collaboration and knowledge transfer does mean that academic work requires greater international travel than it did in the 1970s or 1980s. Clifford (1989: 177) stretches this point even further when he claims that, in order 'to theorize one leaves home', although, of course, like any act of travel, theory has to begin and end somewhere. Nevertheless, as Rojek and Urry (1997: 9) note, 'It is hard to justify just what makes academic travel a special source of academic authority. Where does tourism end and so-called fieldwork begin?'

In fact, for many people one of the features of fieldwork is the notion of working in a different environment or space. As Scheyvens and Storey (2003: 8) note, 'spatial differences are inherent in dominant conceptualisations of "the field".' Clifford (1997: 54) also observed that 'When one speaks of working in the field, or going into the field, one draws on mental images of a distant place with an inside and outside, reached by practices of physical movement'. The locational notion of the field, especially in contemporary studies of fieldwork in tourism which by itself often illicits ideas of 'otherness', strongly contributes to ideas of 'the field' being tied to cultural and environmental difference and 'the exotic'. Indeed, such is the strength of such ideas in anthropology that Clifford (1997: 55) noted; ' "Exotic" fieldwork pursued over a continuous period for at least a year has, for some time now, set the norm against which other practices are judged. Given this exemplar, different practices of cross-cultural research seem less like "real" fieldwork' (Clifford 1997: 55). Similarly, Gupta and Ferguson (1997: 1) comment that 'the single most significant factor determining whether a piece of research will be accepted as (that magical word) "anthropological" is the extent to which it depends on experience "in the field" ', thus, incorporating an expectation that the researcher will travel away from his or her normal home environment. Indeed, such has been the strength of this idea in ethnography, and to this we could also arguably add some of the research in other fields such as ecology, geography and sociology, that Gupta and Ferguson suggest the importance attached by some academics to the importance of a cultural, spatial and temporal distance between 'home' and 'the field' has resulted in a 'hierarchy of purity of field sites . . . After all, if "the field" is most appropriately a place that is "not home", then some places will necessarily be more "not home" than others, and hence more appropriate, more "fieldlike" ' (1997: 13). Yet, as they also note, notions of 'home' and 'away' should not just be understood in terms of geographic location or place, as they note with specific reference to ethnography, its 'great strength has always been in its explicit and well-developed sense of location, of being set here-and-not-elsewhere. This strength becomes a liability when notions of "here" and "elsewhere" are assumed to be features of geography, rather than sites constructed in fields of unequal power relations' (Gupta and Ferguson 1997: 35).

Nevertheless, while there is a familiar portrait or representation of ethnographic (and other fieldwork) which 'involves travel away, preferably to a distant locale where the ethnographer will immerse him/herself in personal face-to-face relationships with a variety of natives over an extended period of time . . . it is a rendering of . . . "fieldwork" that in one respect or another no longer suffices even as a serviceable fiction' (Amit 2000: 2; also see Caputo 2000). As in the case of Amit's (2000) edited work, the contributors to the present volume are not alone in their unease between the experience and archetype of fieldwork and they identify a number of paradoxes with respect to the realities and representations of fieldwork and its research outputs. To mirror Amit's (2000: 2) approach, such a situation represents epistemological, institutional and methodological variabilities that are not amenable to overly generalised solutions, but how we respond to them will affect whether we open up or limit the scope of tourism inquiry. And it is to the former orientation that the chapters in this volume are dedicated.

## Journeys of fieldwork

One way in which we can respond to Rojek and Urry's (1997) above semi-rhetorical question is to draw upon tourism theory itself. One of the most long-standing concepts of tourism is the 'stages' model of the travel process that was arguably originally proposed by Clawson and Knetsch (1966). As the seminal review on the stages of the travel experience by Fridgen (1984: 24) stated, tourism 'involves people moving from one environment through a range of other environments to a destination site and then home via a return trip . . . people not only act in their present setting, they also plan for subsequent settings. People prepare to arrive in another setting to carry out preplanned behaviors.' From this perspective travel can be recognised as having five distinct stages: (i) decision making and anticipation; (ii) travel to a tourism destination or attraction; (iii) the on-site experience; (iv) return travel; and (v) recollection of the experience (Hall 2005). From the tourist perspective each of these five stages has different psychological characteristics and, although not directly relevant to the personal perspective of the present chapter, it is useful to note that each stage also has different implications for production, management and impacts (Hall and Lew 2009). However, the stages of the tourist journey, and many dimensions of the experience, also reflect the stages of the fieldwork journey – both physical and metaphorical (Table 1.1). For both tourist and researcher relationships to significant others change as they pass through the journey and new relationships are developed (see Yamagishi, Chapter 7, this volume). Changing positionalities can also be a feature of the tourism journey as well as the research journey with respect to such matters as insider/outsider (see Tantow, Chapter 9, this volume), observer/observed (see Allan, Chapter 10, this volume), gender (see Bensemann, Chapter 11, this volume), and culture (see Wan Hassan, Chapter 8, this volume), while the fieldworker will also have the extra layer of positionality with respect to being a researcher (see Leopold, Chapter 6, this volume). Time spent in the field may also clearly create new issues of identity and positionality in relation to the people in the field

*Table 1.1* Stages of the travel experience/Stages of the fieldwork experience

| Stage | Stages of tourism | Tourist experience | Stages of fieldwork |
|---|---|---|---|
| 1 | Decision making and anticipation | Decision to visit, planning and thinking about the site visit | Decision to undertake study: goals, methods (fieldwork), theoretical grounding; anticipation |
| 2 | Travel to the site | Getting to the site, reflection on home and anticipation regarding the destination | Preparation – reading, risk assessment; anticipation |
| 3 | On-site behaviour | Behaviour on site or in the destination region, reflection on destination behaviour versus home behaviour | In the field – activities, relationships |
| 4 | Return travel | Travel from the site, reflection on the destination experience and anticipation of return home | Returning from the field/ re-entry issues (for longer periods in the field) |
| 5 | Recollection | Recall, reflection and memory of site visit. Precursor to possible return visit | Recollection, ongoing reflexivity, and possible reconnections and return visit |

location but even this bears similarities to the sojourner tourist/working holidaymaker who spends a significant period of time in a particular location, therefore often developing relationships with people in that area. Clearly, such a perspective does not make the task of separating tourism and fieldwork any easier. In fact, it is not the intention of this introductory chapter to separate them, but it is the goal of the chapter to stress, along with the experience of the authors of many of the chapters in this volume, just how important the multiple identities, positionalities and relationships of the researcher are when conducting fieldwork and the different spaces in which fieldwork occurs.

Spatiality is vital to our understanding of fieldwork. Table 1.2 lists a number of definitions of fieldwork provided by participants of a graduate workshop at the University of Southern Denmark in October 2009, to the author. The definitions were collected prior to the start of a presentation by the author on issues in tourism fieldwork. The notion of movement, whether away from the office or a laboratory or to somewhere in the 'real world', is clearly significant in these definitions. However, as the definitions also suggest, the mobility of the researcher undertaking fieldwork – as well as that of the tourist, for that matter – is more than just shifts in space or time. Rather than being isolated, separate entities, space and time are inextricably woven together to constitute social and economic relations. 'Space is created out of the vast intricacies, the incredible complexities, of the interlocking and the

*Table 1.2* Definitions of fieldwork provided at University of Southern Denmark workshop

---

- Fieldwork = applied, action research, empirical (Anonymous)
- Fieldwork is the art of getting out there, of talking to people, to try and understand their situation, attitudes, opinions, etc. Fieldwork requires a lot of skill from the researcher as regards sympathy, ethics, morals, questioning techniques, etc. (Jaqueline Nicolaisen, University of Southern Denmark)
- Work away from the office, i.e. non-desk research for collecting empirical material/data (Niels Christian Nielsen, University of Southern Denmark)
- The collection of data in real-world situations (Mats Carlbäck, Göteborg University)
- Collecting information by doing investigation in the 'real' world in order to transfer the data into a model (Thomas Lang, University of Graz)
- The researcher going into the actual field where a phenomenon he/she wants to research is present to collect data about the phenomenon. The researcher can also take part in actions happening – active research (Anonymous)
- Practical investigation/survey leading to collection of information/data (outside of a laboratory) (Anonymous)
- Participating and observing the object(s) researched in the relevant setting. Entering its network. Using tools adequate to register the data that is of interest (Bente Haug, Finnmark University College)

---

*Note:* Respondents had option of whether to self-identify or remain anonymous.

non-interlocking, and the network of relations at every scale from local to global' (Massey 1993: 155–6) (see also Allan, Chapter 10, this volume; Salazar, Chapter 12, this volume). Indeed, as Couclelis (1992) observes, it is appropriate to write of a variety of behavioural, experiential, political, physical and other spaces. This notion of movement and positionality in multiple spaces therefore lies at the heart of understanding the problems of undertaking fieldwork in tourism and is arguably more pronounced because of the inherent role of mobility within tourism phenomena (Hall 2005).

Tourism is integral to the increased mobility and connectivity (for many) wrapped within social and economic processes of contemporary globalisation, transnationalism and the development of new communications media. It both influences and is affected by such processes. Moreover, by its very nature as a form of temporary mobility (Hall 2005), the character of tourism and the socio-economic and technological systems within which it is embedded means that many of the social and economic relationships to which it contributes are temporary and ephemeral. Such a situation stands at odds with the 'traditional' ideas of socially and anthropologically oriented fieldwork occurring in relatively static and easily identifiable communities and social groupings (Hastrup and Hervik 1994). As Amit (2000: 14) anticipated:

> Episodic, occasional, partial and ephemeral social links pose particular challenges for ethnographic fieldwork. How do we observe interactions that happen sometimes but not necessarily when we are around? How do

we participate in social relations that are not continuous, that are experienced most viscerally in their absence? How do we participate in or observe practices that are enacted here and there, by one or a few? How do we take into account unique events that may not be recurring but still have irrevocable consequences [e.g. an event]? Where do we 'hang out' when the processes which we are studying produce common social conditions or statuses (freelance workers, peripatetic entrepreneurs, consultants, tourists) but not necessarily coterminous collectivities?

Indeed, from a tourism perspective one of the great weaknesses in tourism studies is the lack of research that traces the same group of individuals from their home environment, their travel to and from the destination, what occurs at the destination, and then what happens over time after they have returned to their home environment. This is not to suggest that fieldwork in tourism only studies tourists, but the fact that tourists are inherently short-term temporary visitors to a place outside of their home environment clearly has implications for the conduct of both physical and social scientific research with respect to assessing their affects on 'permanent' populations and structures. Nevertheless, for fieldworkers as for tourists the temporary stay in a specific location or destination can have long-term personal affects on both the visitor and the visited.

Six different types of interrelated spaces of fieldwork can be identified: temporal space, physical space, regulatory/political space, ethical space, social space and theoretical/methodological space. Such a position reflects Lorenz-Meyer's (2004) consideration that our physical and social location systematically shapes what we know and how, and that 'knowledge is always relative to (i.e. a perspective on, a standpoint in) specifiable circumstances' (Code 1993: 40). From a feminist standpoint, Lorenz-Meyer (2004) stresses that, structurally, a location is marked by parameters of social inequality such as gender, 'race', class, religion, sexuality and geopolitical location and their attending subject positions of identity, material conditions, privileges and emotions as well as 'conceptual resources . . . to represent and interpret these relations' (Wylie 2003: 31). However, it is vital to stress that these spaces are not mutually exclusive and instead overlap and interact with one another over time.

*Temporal space*

Fieldwork occurs in a given moment in time and is often part of a wider defined research project that has its own beginning and end, although the implications of the period of fieldwork can last long after it has been completed allowing for substantial recollection and reviewing of the time spent undertaking fieldwork. The time spent on fieldwork and the subsequent writing up is often set by the requirements of completing a graduate qualification or by an external body that is either funding the research project or which regulates access to the field in terms of time.

## Physical space

The field is a physical or virtual space with its own difficulties and challenges such as access and health and safety issues. Although historically exotic by virtue of geographical and cultural otherness, fieldwork is increasingly undertaken on local and popular cultural topics, of which leisure and tourism are a major part. Even the home environment can be simultaneously constructed as both a 'home' and fieldwork location. Yet the space of the field still has to be defined, even if just by virtue of making a research topic manageable. The boundary-making which is so critical to the successful undertaking of a research project will often have a physical component, while university research and ethics committees as well as funding bodies generally also require locational information, even if a virtual location (see Hall, Chapter 20, this volume) and even if just to ensure that health and safety requirements are met. In fact, from a university's perspective the location of research will often be a significant factor in influencing whether research will be supported and/or permitted, as many institutions conduct a risk assessment of locations for insurance and health and safety reasons. And it is generally not good publicity for a university if a graduate undertaking fieldwork is attacked, gored by wild animals, hijacked, kidnapped, injured, catches a rare disease or, at worst, dies in the field. (Note: it is hoped that the previous list reflects a set of low-risk mutually exclusive events!)

## Regulatory / political space

Gupta and Ferguson (1997) suggest that field areas should be conceptualised as political locations rather than as 'spatial sites' – a position that finds substantial support amongst feminist research. For example, Rich (1986: 212) argued that 'a place on the map is also a place in history within which as a woman, as a Jew, a lesbian, a feminist I am created and trying to create'. From a broad understanding of politics, locations are therefore positionings in time and space which have specific effects and consequences, or 'politics', that need to be analysed and historicised (Lorenz-Meyer 2004), while, from a narrower conceptualisation, fieldwork is also something that is subject to regulation and the exercising of power within the relations between fieldworkers and subjects/informants/gatekeepers both within the institution(s) of the researcher and of the subjects of research.

Institutional regulation occurs via the sponsoring body of the research, such as universities and funding bodies, which will often have guidelines as to what can and cannot be undertaken during fieldwork; this affects not only relations with subjects, but also selection of methods, questions that can be asked, protocols that must/should be followed, and even where research should/must occur. For example, via being a member of a PhD examination panel the author is aware of a case of a PhD student in New Zealand not being given permission by an ethics approval committee to ask direct questions on race in a survey on cultural attitudes and social distance with respect to tourism when, given the multicultural nature of New Zealand society, questions on race and ethnicity would seem to be extremely appropriate.

Regulation of fieldwork also occurs when research is conducted in other countries and jurisdictions in which the researcher is not a national or even a local. For instance, is it possible to get a visa and government permissions to undertake fieldwork? Certain locations and topics may be prohibited from being researched by outsiders or may be heavily monitored. Of course, the exertion of power and influence on a fieldwork topic or its conduct need not be done via formal regulatory structures but by key actors in gatekeeper organisations using informal means. In addition, the influence and actions of key stakeholders and gatekeepers will also affect fieldwork via relations to both the researcher and informants and subjects (e.g. see Chok, Chapter 4; Bochaton and Lefebvre, Chapter 5; Hoogendoorn and Visser, Chapter 13; all this volume). It is important to recognise that political/regulatory space in tourism fieldwork affects both social science and physical science research. Access to fieldwork sites for natural science and ecological research with respect to the impacts of tourism can be extremely controversial given that results can inform policy and decision making as well as potentially gain profile in the media. Arguably, given the growing concerns with tourism's role in environmental change there is potential for the physical science of tourism's effects on the environment as well as climate change to become even more politicised (Ruzza 2003).

### Ethical space

Ethical space occurs at the intersection between regulatory, social and theoretical spaces, as it includes both the formal and informal ethics generated by institutions and their cultures as well as the personal ethics of the researcher that develop out of social relationships developed in the field, and existing relationships. Ethics here should also not only be construed within the narrow framework of codes of conduct and what university ethics committees agree is permissible before research commences. Meta-ethical issues also includes consideration of even the 'right' to undertake such research as well as consideration of how the results will be used. In reflecting on positionality and feminist research, England (1994: 85) comments that 'fieldwork might actually expose the researched to greater risk and might be more intrusive and potentially more exploitative than more traditional [research] methods' (England 1994: 85), even noting that social 'Fieldwork is inherently confrontational in that it is the purposeful disruption of other people's lives. Indeed, anthropologists even speak of the "violence" of fieldwork, even if the violence is symbolic . . . In fact, exploitation and possibly betrayal are endemic to fieldwork' (England 1994: 85):

I am concerned that appropriation (even if it is 'only' textual appropriation) is an inevitable consequence of fieldwork. This possibility is uncomfortable for those of us who want to engage in truly critical social science by translating our academic endeavors into political action. Yet, as researchers we cannot escape the contradictory position in which we find ourselves, in that the 'lives, loves, and tragedies that fieldwork informants share with a researcher are ultimately data, grist for the ethnographic mill, a mill that has a truly grinding power'.

(Stacey 1988: 23, in England 1994: 86)

Given these observations it is therefore not surprising that she poses the question: 'can we incorporate the voices of "others" without colonizing them in a manner that reinforces patterns of domination?' (England 1994: 81).

Similarly, in discussing fieldwork in a development context Scheyvens and Leslie (2000) draw on the work of Elson (1991) to argue that 'what is essential is that those studied should not merely be seen as a source of data through which a researcher can further his or her career; the researcher should be accountable, reflexive and research should be a two-way process of interaction' (Scheyvens and Leslie 2000: 128–9). The latter, of course, also influences consideration of how the results will even be written up, how it is argued (which means considering who the audience is as it is they who will determine its suitability), what is left in and what is left out. The politics and ethics of fieldwork are well indicated by Kobayashi (1994: 78) when she states, 'the question of "who speaks for whom?" cannot be answered upon the slippery slope of what personal attributes – what color, what gender, what sexuality – legitimize our existence, but on the basis of our history of involvement, and on the basis of understanding how difference is constructed and used as a political tool'. Although it should be noted that debates over who has the right to research whom on the basis of culture, gender, sexuality, community or nationality, and therefore who has the right to speak for whom, has led some academics 'to withdraw completely from research that might place them in territory to which they have no social claim, or that might put in question their credentials for social representation' (Kobayashi 1994: 74).

*Social space*

The social space of research in terms of the interactions with informants/subjects and others as well as the experiences you have can have a profound effect on field research. As Devereux and Hoddinott (1992: 2) commented in introducing the various case studies in their book on fieldwork in developing countries, 'Anyone who has done research outside his or her home community knows that questions relating to lifestyle and personal relationships loom as large as narrowly defined technical issues.' The boundary between field and home which has so often been demarcated by the metaphor of travel has incorporated an assumption that, according to Amit (2000: 8), 'home is stationary while the field is a journey away. It is a presumption that is undone as much by the cognitive and emotional journeys which fieldworkers make in looking at familiar practices and sites with new ethnographic lenses as [it is] by the transnational organization of many academics' lives'.

The social spaces and personal relations of fieldwork are touched on in a number of chapters in this volume. Yamagishi's (Chapter 7) reframing of the concept of relational, Allan's (Chapter 10) reflections on her multiple positionalities, and Gillen's (Chapter 14) questions with respect to the role of informal discussion with informants in influencing his work all reflect the fact that the melding of personal and professional roles in participant and ethnographic fieldwork makes for 'a messy, qualitative experience in contrast to the positivist social-science vision of method' (Marcus and Fischer 1986: 22) that cannot readily or usefully be compartmentalised from other experiences and periods in our lives (Amit 2000).

### Theoretical/methodological space

The final form of spatiality in fieldwork is that of theoretical and methodological space. The identification of the role that theories and methods play in fieldwork is important as theories and methods frame and influence observations, interactions and experiences in the field (see Lew, Chapter 2, this volume). Reflections on theoretical space are required for just about everyone who ever writes a thesis (although, let's be honest, we do often write or at least alter them after the fieldwork 'facts' have come in!). Therefore, the theoretical lens that we apply, even if multiple in scope, affects what we leave in and what we take out or ignore or look for (sometimes even fail to see). This is not to suggest that our theoretical frames are unchanging or are rose-coloured glasses but they do affect how we define problems and our capacities to talk to other people who may have different frames with respect to what they see in the same physical or social space. This is not a place to write of those various theoretical and methodological spaces and how it affects our research, there are many books and articles that already do that, but it is to note how important an issue it is and how frequently it is mentioned in the various chapters in this volume.

### Conclusions

This first chapter has argued that tourism and fieldwork has many similarities which, rather than being treated ironically, may actually help shed light on the issues that many people face when undertaking field-based research, given that some of the issues of positionality over the journey that a tourist can face are reflected in the multiple positionalities and relations which the researcher can meet. More particularly, the challenged researcher, facing field-based research, also changes over time with respect to the particular stage of the research journey that he or she is on. Nevertheless, the spatialities of fieldwork are not just of location or even of time but, as the chapter has suggested, are also bound up in regulatory/political, ethical, social and theoretical/methodological spaces. In seeking to undertake successful field-work and production of an acceptable research output, it therefore becomes vital that these various spaces are reflected on, prior to entering the field, as a way of considering the stances and perspectives one may take, and their implications, as well as prepare for the public and personal journey of research. As with all travel or research, one can never anticipate all that one will face on a journey. After all, if you could, would there still be a point in going? But having a good idea of what one will face can only add to the excitement and anticipation of the journey to the field and the return home. Happy and safe travels.

## References

Amit, V. (2000) 'Introduction: Constructing the field', in V. Amit (ed.), *Constructing the Field: Ethnographic Fieldwork in the Contemporary World*. London: Routledge.

Bruner, E.M. (2005) 'Tourism Fieldwork', *Anthropology News* (May): 16, 19.

Caputo, V. (2000) 'At "Home" and "Away": Reconfiguring the Field for Late Twentieth-century Anthropology', in V. Amit (ed.), *Constructing the Field: Ethnographic Fieldwork in the Contemporary World*. London: Routledge.

Clawson, M. and Knetsch, J.L. (1966) *Economics of Outdoor Recreation*. Baltimore: Johns Hopkins Press.

Clifford, J. (1989) 'Notes on Travel and Theory', in J. Clifford and V. Dhareshwar (eds), *Traveling Theories, Traveling Theorists*. Santa Cruz: Group for the Critical Study of Colonial Discourse and the Center for Cultural Studies, University of California, Santa Cruz.

Clifford, J. (1997) *Routes: Travel and Translation in the Late Twentieth Century*. Cambridge, MA: Harvard University Press.

Code, L. (1993) 'Taking Subjectivity into Account', in L. Alcoff and E. Potter (eds), *Feminist Epistemologies*. New York: Routledge.

Couclelis, H. (1992) 'Location, Place, Region, and Space', in R.F. Abler, M.G. Marcus and J.M. Olson (eds), *Geography's Inner Worlds: Pervasive Themes in Contemporary American Geography*. New Brunswick: Rutgers University Press.

Crick, M. (1985) ' "Tracing" the Anthropological Self: Quizzical Reflections on Fieldwork, Tourism and the Ludic' *Social Analysis* 17: 71–92.

Devereux, S. and Hoddinott, J. (1992) 'The Context of Fieldwork', in S. Devereux and J. Hoddinott (eds), *Fieldwork in Developing Countries*. New York: Harvester Wheatsheaf.

Elson, D. (1991) 'Structural Adjustment: Its Effect on Women', in T. Wallace and C. March (eds), *Changing Perceptions: Writings on Gender and Development*. Oxford: Oxfam.

England, K. (1994) 'Getting Personal: Reflexivity, Positionality, and Feminist Research', *Professional Geographer* 46(1): 80–9.

Fridgen, J.D. (1984) 'Environmental Psychology and Tourism', *Annals of Tourism Research* 11: 19–40.

Galani-Moutafi, V. (2000) 'The Self and the Other: Traveler, Ethnographer, Tourist', *Annals of Tourism Research* 27(1): 203–24.

Gupta, A. and Ferguson, J. (1997) 'Discipline and Practice: "The Field" as Site, Method, and Location in Anthropology', in A. Gupta and J. Ferguson (eds). *Anthropological Locations: Boundaries and Grounds of a Field Science.* Berkeley: University of California Press.

Hall, C.M. (2005) *Tourism: Rethinking the Social Science of Mobility.* Harlow: Pearson.

Hall, C.M. and Lew, A.A. (2009) *The Impacts of Tourism.* London: Routledge.

Hastrup, K. and Hervik, P. (1994) 'Introduction', in K. Hastrup and P. Hervik (eds), *Social Experience and Anthropological Knowledge.* London: Routledge.

Kobayashi, A. (1994) 'Coloring the Field: Gender, "Race", and the Politics of Fieldwork', *Professional Geographer* 46: 73–80.

Kotarba, J.A. (2002) 'Rock 'n' Roll Music as a Timepiece', *Symbolic Interaction* 25(3): 397–404.

Kotarba, J.A. (2005) 'Rock 'n' Roll Experiences in Middle Age', *American Behavioral Scientist* 48(11): 1524–37.

Lorenz-Meyer, D. (2004) 'Addressing the Politics of Location: Strategies in Feminist Epistemology and their Relevance to Research Undertaken from a Feminist Perspective', in S. Štrbánová, I.H. Stamhuis and K. Mojsejová (eds), *Women Scholars and Institutions*, Volume 13b. Prague: Research Centre for History of Sciences and Humanities. Online. Available HTTP: <cec-wys.org> (accessed 10 January 2010).

Marcus, G.E. and Fischer, M.M.J. (1986) *Anthropology as Cultural Critique: An Experimental Moment in the Human Sciences*, Chicago: University of Chicago Press.

Massey, D. (1993) 'Politics and Space/Time', in M. Keith and S. Pile (eds), *Place and the Politics of Identity.* London: Routledge.

Mowforth, M. and Munt, I. (1998) *Tourism and Sustainability: New Tourism in the Third World.* London: Routledge.

Rich, A. (1986) 'Notes Towards a Politics of Location', in A. Rich (ed.), *Blood, Bread, and Poetry: Selected Prose, 1979–1985.* New York: W.W. Norton & Company.

Rojek, C. and Urry, J. (1997) 'Transformations of Travel and Theory', in C. Rojek and J. Urry (eds), *Touring Cultures: Transformations of Travel and Tourism.* London: Routledge.

Ruzza, C. (2003) 'Environmental Sustainability and Policy Networks in Tourist Locations', paper presented at Policies, Governance and Innovation for Rural Areas, International Seminar, 21–23 November 2003, Università della Calabria, Arcavacata di Rende.

Scheyvens, R. and Leslie, H. (2000) 'Gender, Ethics and Empowerment: Dilemmas of Development Fieldwork', *Women's Studies International Forum* 23(1): 119–30.

Scheyvens, R. and Storey, D. (2003) 'Introduction', in R. Scheyvens and D. Storey (eds), *Development Fieldwork: A Practical Guide.* London: Sage.

Stacey, J. (1988) 'Can there be a Feminist Ethnography?' *Women's Studies International Forum* 11: 21–7.

Stein, R.L. (1998) 'National Itineraries, Itinerant Nations: Israeli Tourism and Palestinian Cultural Production', *Social Text* 56: 91–124.

Wylie, A. (2003) 'Why Standpoints Matter', in R. Figueroa and S. Harding (eds), *Science and Other Cultures: Issues in Philosophies of Science and Technology.* New York: Routledge.

Zeleza, P.T. and Kalipeni, E. (1999) *Sacred Spaces and Public Quarrels: African Cultural and Economic Landscapes.* Trenton: Africa World Press.

# 2 Defining and redefining conceptual frameworks for social science field research

*Alan A. Lew*

Toward the end of my M.A. studies in geography at the University of Oregon, and when I was thinking about transitioning into the Ph.D. program at the same university, I happened to see an advertisement for a Fulbright award for graduate research in several countries, including Singapore. I had spent some time in Hong Kong as an undergraduate and had given lectures as a graduate student on the geographic similarities and differences between Hong Kong and Singapore. So I submitted an application with a proposal to do some kind of comprehensive study of tourism in Singapore. I read everything I could find on Singapore, which was not very much in the pre-Internet days of the early 1980s, managed to get a good interview review and was eventually granted the award.

Soon after I arrived in Singapore, in August 1983, I found that my original proposal was far too broad and not really possible. So I began in earnest to learn as much as I could about tourism in Singapore, while at the same time seeking to come up with a suitable focus for my research. In these efforts, Dr. P.P. Wong served as my advisor in my attachment to the Department of Geography at the National University of Singapore.

One question that Dr. Wong would ask me repeatedly during our meetings was: 'What is your conceptual framework?' I struggled with this question as I plowed ahead collecting as much data as I could get my hands on. Today, however, this is the same question that I ask all of the graduate students whose research I supervise and advise, because I now know that my efforts in Singapore could have been much more focused and efficient if I had been more clear about my own conceptual framework many years before.

So what is a conceptual framework, and why is it important? A conceptual framework, also known as a theoretical framework or an intermediate theory, is the general approach, perspective, or theory that will guide researchers as they try to understand their empirical research problem and their results (Shields and Tajalli 2006). Every research effort is based on a set of epistemological assumptions about what data are valid for inclusion in a study and what methods are appropriate for collecting and analyzing their data. Whether researchers are aware of their research epistemology or not, it is still there. The conceptual framework is a general or specific model or theory that is based on existing research literature and reflects the researcher's epistemology.

There are a great many different conceptual frameworks in the social sciences that researchers can draw upon to guide their fieldwork. Some definitions of what a conceptual framework or theoretical framework is include (MSCS 2003: 3; Borgatti 1999):

1    A set of coherent ideas or concepts that defines the overall context of the research question or problem;
2    An organized way of thinking about how and why a phenomenon takes place, and about how we understand it;
3    The basis for thinking about what we do and about what it means, influenced by the ideas and research of others;
4    An overview of ideas and practices that shape the way research is done in a field of study;
5    A set of assumptions, values, and definitions under which we conduct research;
6    A collection of interrelated concepts, like a theory, but not necessarily so well worked out.

Some of the conceptual frameworks that I have worked with in my own research include social theory, social capital, acculturation, semiotics, content analysis, and logical positivism. Some others that I think are interesting include game theory, post-colonialism, behaviorialism, and sequent occupance. To understand the significance and role of conceptual frameworks, I will first review issues involved in selecting a research topic, research epistemology, the scientific method, and research paradigms.

## Selecting a research topic

Academic researchers mostly approach their research in a linear manner (Crawford and Stucki 1990). The standard steps are to:

1    define a problem,
2    gather information and resources and identify research questions or formulate a hypothesis,
3    decide on a methodology and develop an appropriate research instrument,
4    perform the experiment or otherwise collect the data,
5    analyze data according to the predefined methodology,
6    interpret and draw conclusions and present the results,
7    retest the research question or hypothesis (usually done by other researchers).

Social science research problems often emerge from contemporary issues and debates related to changes in the realm of economics, sociology (including demography and culture), the built environment, politics, technology, and other human endeavors, many of which are also covered by the popular news media. They may also evolve from theoretical and methodological debates within academic disciplines, or the study of academic disciplines themselves (usually referred to as the 'philosophy of science,' 'history of science,' and 'sociology of science,' cf. Popper, 1959; Kuhn 1962, 1970). Research problems generally fall under the categories of applied research, which results in either recommendations for some type of policy or action to address a problem, or basic research, which has the goal of developing new insights into and perspectives on a problem, without necessarily solving it.

The process of developing research questions and hypotheses involves the framing of the problem in terms that can be addressed in a concise manner by the researcher. This is closely related to the methodology that is to be employed and, in fact, the methodology is often defined by the conceptual framework that is adopted. Most methodologies fall under the general categories of quantitative methods and qualitative methods (Creswell 2008). Quantitative methods typically focus either on hypothesis testing or on correlations between dependent and independent variables. Conclusions are often based on some form of statistical procedures. Qualitative data, on the other hand, are based more on narratives and naturalistic inquiry methods, including ethnography, phenomenology, case studies, and grounded theory.

Research instruments are developed to collect the data that will be assessed with the selected methodology. Instruments may include surveys, interview questions, digital recorders, and possibly specially designed instruments. The data (quantitative, qualitative or both) are then collected and analyzed, conclusions are made and the results are presented.

The steps described above are the model that most social science researchers aspire to – at least on paper. In the real world, however, most know that the research process is more often cyclical than linear. This is especially true when conducting field research, where variables and influences can be serendipitous and highly unpredictable.

While moving in a general step-by-step direction, researchers need to have a meta-awareness of the total project that allows continual revising of the research as new information is obtained and new opportunities arise. Thus, in total opposition to the linear scientific method, it is not uncommon to revisit the initial problem and research questions during the data analysis stage, and sometimes even in the data collection phase. And even more egregious, very different problems and conceptual frameworks can be applied to the same data that have been collected with very different objectives in mind.

*Meta* and *ex post facto* considerations and revisions to the initial research project can actually be indications of research competence, when they result in a large number of related and evolving publications in an individual's field of expertise. Therefore, even though a published research paper is usually written to give the appearance that a clearly defined, linear research process was pursued, it may or may not have actually been that way when the research was undertaken. The writing conventions in most areas of social science essentially require the delineation of a linear methodology.

Research moves in cyclical and unpredictable ways because the social sciences are not as easily predictable as are some of the physical sciences. The steps in a more cyclical research process may start with the formulation of a preliminary research question or questions, followed by an examination of the importance of the question(s) and an identification of the units of analysis or variables that would be needed to undertake a study. This is followed by an effort to understand the background of the problem or issue, which may include the collection of preliminary data, which in turn can be used to revise the research question(s).

Even though the finalization (more or less) of the research question(s) in a cyclical research design does not take place until one is well into the research effort, it is still very important to reach this point as soon as possible. This is because the research question is critical to (1) the conceptual framework and (2) final selection of the units of analysis or variables on which information or data will be collected. You cannot know what to collect if you do not know what you are studying . . . Or can you?

Based on my personal experience, as well as that of my students, it is actually quite common for graduate students who go to a foreign country to conduct fieldwork to have only a vaguely defined research question – no matter how much they have prepared beforehand. Unless one has previously lived for an extended period in a place, it is impossible to know the nuances of social relationships, of human interactions with the land, and of the political, cultural, and economic dynamics of the global–local nexus. These insights can be gained only through direct field observation, and this is one of the main reasons for doing fieldwork in the first place. The other reason is to collect primary data that can only be obtained through fieldwork.

In this type of fuzzy research situation, the research problem is often revised and refined at the same time that data collection takes place. This typically results in information and data collection that is actually superfluous to the research question(s) which eventually evolve(s) from the fieldwork. As new information is collected, the research question is refined, and new directions of information and data are explored, which further shifts the research question. Even when the fieldwork experience has ended, the final research question(s) may not be fully developed until data analysis is undertaken.

One advantage of this cyclical and shifting research experience is that it can result in large amounts of data, some of which can be used for the primary research question, and others of which can be assessed for different research questions and from different conceptual frameworks. Each approach to the data requires a good research question or problem. The goal is to define a problem that can be investigated by collection and analyzing a coherent set of data. The problem or question should have some theoretical or practical (applied) significance. If theory can be used to predict your results, then that is a good sign that the research has potential theoretical significance. In addition, it is important that the research question or problem is one that is interesting enough to motivate you to complete the study and share the research results. Research questions that are not well defined may be too vague to define appropriate units of analysis, too broadly defined to be finished in a timely manner, too narrow or superficial to offer meaningful insight, or too late to be useful or interesting.

While the field researchers are busy gathering information and data, and refining their research problem, they are also operating from a particular research or conceptual framework that they may or may not be fully aware of. The conceptual framework consists of the rules about which information is more important, beliefs about the fundamental nature of the research problem, and the concepts that define the relevant elements of the study. The conceptual framework is crucial, though it too is often poorly defined in the beginning and is subject to revision in a cyclical manner. To understand conceptual research frameworks requires an understanding of research epistemology (ways of knowing) and research paradigms (knowledge structures).

## Research epistemology, the scientific method, and research paradigms

Epistemology addresses the question of what truth is, and how we know it is true (BonJour 2002). It is the study of knowledge, including its nature (what knowledge is), its limitations, and its validity (truth). The question of epistemology (how truth is known) has been debated for thousands of years. Four basic ways of knowing (epistemologies) are: revelation, observation, reasoning, and tacit knowledge (Sell 2007).

*Revelation* is learning by being told what true knowledge is. Religion and much of formal, lecture-based education are examples of revelation. It requires a respect for authoritative knowledge givers, who are usually defined by socially accepted formal titles, such as 'minister' or 'professor.' Its methods have been mostly associated with rote or didactic learning. In addition to religious leaders and teachers, there are many other authorities and key informants who are important sources of information for researchers. We have faith that these experts in local and other specialized forms of knowledge are sources of truth through their life experiences.

*Observation* is learning through personal experience, which includes both observing what you see and what you experience. The basic assumption is that something is true if we experience it. Experiential learning, or learning by doing, is an example of this approach to knowledge. For researchers, observations can also be recorded through surveys, interviews, and recordings (including audio, photography, video, and diaries). Observation is the basis of both phenomenology and the scientific method. The scientific observation and measurement of phenomena or events are also referred to as empirical knowledge.

*Reasoning* is learning by thinking, usually using logic to move from one reference to the next (e.g., 'I think, therefore . . .'). Inductive reasoning starts with specific observations and moves to more general hypotheses or theories. Deductive reasoning starts with a structure based on generalizations or theories, and applies them to specific case instances (Liehr and Smith 2001). Comparative case studies, which are common in social science field-work, are often inductive, with the case example providing lessons to expand knowledge and theory. Controlled experiments are usually derived from deductive reasoning, where a theory can be examined and applied to new cases. In social science fieldwork, using economic and social theories, such as structuralism or social capital, to explain case studies is a deductive reasoning approach.

*Tacit knowledge* refers to skills that we acquire by using our physical body, and which we are typically unaware of (Polanyi 1958). This has also been called 'muscle memory' and 'body-subject' (Seamon 1980). It includes knowing how to walk, throw a ball, draw a portrait, perform a dance, and build a house. While it is possible to read about these, or to be told how to do them, mastery can be achieved only by doing them – often repeatedly over time. Education through apprenticeships is still common in many professions, including medicine and engineering. Tacit knowledge as a way of learning truth is also common in the arts and humanities, but is much less common in the social sciences. Phenomenology, which was discussed above under 'Observation,' could also be a form of tacit knowledge research, as could the participant-observation methodology, depending on the research objectives.

When thinking about epistemology, the major question that needs to be addressed is: how will you know what is true in what you see in the field? Each of the four basic approaches to epistemology outlined above will result in a different type of data when applied to similar research questions. And each has its advantages and disadvantages. Recognizing this situation, it has become increasingly popular for field researchers to address more than one epistemology by adopting a *mixed method* approach (Greene *et al.* 1989; Johnson and Onwuegbuzie 2004). Thus a study may include interviews with key and expert sources, a survey of different population groups, a preferred theoretical context, and direct participant-observation. As with the cyclical redefining of the research problem, this results in both a greater understanding of the breadth of the research problem and opportunities for publishing different perspectives on the collected data.

The epistemology that has had the most significant impact on the development of modern science, including the social sciences, is the scientific method. The scientific method is a belief that truth is only knowable through observation and logic. This approach is also known as logical positivism: if something can be positively shown to occur (usually by being measured in a repeatable manner) and it is logically associated with what is known (related to a theoretical framework), then it is accepted as true. Conversely, if something cannot be measured and logically fit within a theory, then it cannot be understood using the scientific method, and a different epistemology (and associated methodology and theoretical framework) needs to be adopted.

The scientific method is a way of achieving group consensus by using methodologies and assumptions that are agreed upon by other researchers. For the scientific method, the methodology should be so exact that it can be repeated (observed) by any other scientist with the same results (truth). As such, the scientific method cannot study unique events, such as miracles, or anything else that cannot be measured repeatedly by scientific instruments (including survey questionnaires). A scientific finding that is accepted by most scientists becomes a 'fact.' Facts can be assembled into theories and laws that conceptualize and summarize the scientific view of reality and truth.

The scientific method has also been the most influential and dominant scientific paradigm since the Enlightenment, and as such has been a point of considerable critique (e.g., Polanyi 1958; Kuhn 1962; Feyerabend 2002). A paradigm is a coherent set of epistemological beliefs that are predominant in a scientific discipline at a particular period of time. This is often referred to as a *scientific paradigm* to distinguish it from other uses of the word paradigm. According to Kuhn (1962), a scientific paradigm is a social agreement that defines what is appropriate for observation and analysis, what kinds of questions are considered valid, how these questions are formulated and structured, and how the results are interpreted and shared.

A scientific paradigm, in other words, is a belief system and an image of reality that is held by a consensus of scientists. And in that sense, it has characteristics that are similar to political and religious belief systems. Observations that contradict the dominant scientific paradigm(s) are often ignored until they reach a point that forces a change in the paradigm, and a *paradigm shift* occurs. Examples of paradigm shifts include the Copernican Revolution (putting the sun rather than the earth at the center of the solar system), Darwin's Theory of Evolution, Einstein's Theory of Relativity, and the Theory of Plate Tectonics. Through paradigm shifts, science evolves incrementally over time as new knowledge structures are developed to better explain the world around us.

Table 2.1 shows three major scientific paradigms that are widely used in the social sciences in general, and in human geography in particular: logical positivism/quantitative geography, qualitative interpretivism/cultural ecology, and critical theory/critical geography. In fact, Kuhn's concept of scientific paradigms (1962; 1970) itself is an example of a critical theory approach to understanding, knowledge, and truth. The scientific paradigms model, as a way of understanding scientific inquiry, is a structuralist analysis that assumes dominance by an agreed-upon set of socially defined rules that are identified through historical deconstruction.

Considerable divisions exist not only among the three paradigms in Table 2.1, but also within each of them. Each of Marxism (a type of stucturalism), semiotics, and post-structuralism, for example, has its strong proponents and internal debates. It is not unusual that avid proponents of one of these

*Table 2.1* Three major social sciences paradigms used in human geography

| PARADIGMS: | *Logical positivism*<br><br>*(Quantitative geography)* | *Qualitative/ interpretivism* *(Cultural ecology)* | *Critical theory/ postmodernism* *(Critical geography)* |
|---|---|---|---|
| Assumptions | Objective world – can be mirrored by science | Intersubjective world – represented by concepts | World structured by ideologies and exploitations |
| Key focus | Measurable variables | Patterns of meaning | Hidden contradictions and silent voices |
| Key theories | Systems theory, ecology | Symbolic interaction, phenomenology | Marxism, semiotics, post-structuralism |
| Goals | Uncover truths and facts as quantitative relationships among variables | Describe meanings and subjective understandings; how these produce realities | Expose hidden interests; displace ideology with scientific insights |
| Nature of knowledge | Verified hypotheses; valid, reliable, and precise variables | Abstract descriptions of meanings and members | Structural and historical insights |
| Criteria for assessing research | Predictions that match explanations; methodology rigor | Trustworthiness, authenticity | Theoretical consistency, transcendent interpretations |
| Research methods/ analysis | Experiments, surveys, primary and secondary data, statistics, content analysis | Ethnography, interviews, case studies, participant-observation, textual analysis | Field research, historical analysis, deconstruction, textual analysis, interviews |

*Source:* Based on Gephart (1999).

research perspectives belittle research conducted under the assumptions of another paradigm perspective. This is especially true for scientists whose entire research lives have been defined by a dominant paradigm or theory, and whose personal worldview sees, understands, and interprets the world through the image of the reality that their research paradigm presents.

## The conceptual framework

The scientific paradigm may serve as conceptual frameworks for a specific research effort. But paradigms are more likely to provide a large context for a more specific theory that guides the research. While the scientific paradigm defines how a researcher views the world, the conceptual framework defines how the researcher views the specific research problem(s) before them. The conceptual framework may be referred to as 'theoretical framework' when a clearly defined theory forms the basis of the research. However, not all conceptual frameworks are theory driven. Instead, conceptual frameworks in social science fieldwork are more likely to be defined by a more or less coherent set of ideas, concepts and definitions, research methods, and examples derived from published research by others (Crawford and Stucki 1990). Whereas a paradigm requires a consensus among a relatively large group of scientists, the conceptual framework requires consensus only between the researcher and either a funding agency or, for students, an academic advisor or committee of advisors.

It is somewhat important to know the scientific paradigm that defines a researcher's worldview, because it helps us to understand what the researcher's focus will be on, and what might be ignored or unseen. However, the conceptual framework is much more important to the research effort itself. A conceptual framework is absolutely required for deductive, theory-testing studies, in which a theory is applied to a specific case study (Borgatti 1999). The theory is the conceptual framework, and it must be well understood with a methodology that is clearly thought out.

A conceptual framework is also very important for inductive, exploratory studies. As discussed above, all research is formulated and structured by basic preconceived notions, even though they may not be consciously identified. Having an awareness of our research paradigm and conceptual framework tells us where our attention is and, more important, what we are ignoring. Not knowing our conceptual framework can result in two problems: we may miss important information that is required by the framework we are using; and we may needlessly collect superfluous information that is not required by our framework. The latter is a common problem in field research, as discussed above, in part because the conceptual framework is often shifting as the research progresses. Thus, for an inductive, exploratory research project, the conceptual framework may be seen as an intermediate theory that guides and connects all aspects of a research project, including the problem statement and purpose of the study, the literature review, the methodology, data collection and analysis.

Shields and Tajalli (2006), in discussing public administration research, suggested five types of conceptual frameworks, depending on the nature of the research question or problem (Table 2.2). While their model may not encompass the full range of potential conceptual frameworks across the diversity of the social sciences and humanities, their categories do provide a useful starting point toward defining and narrowing an initial research interest. A researcher may find a particular topic or problem of compelling interest. Narrowing that compelling topic to one of the categories in Table 2.2 could make the research more manageable and lead to similar studies upon which the methodology could be modeled and modified.

More specifically, many of the conceptual frameworks that social scientists

*Table 2.2* Types of conceptual frameworks and research questions in public administration

**Formal hypotheses** – applying and verifying theories that explain or predict outcomes and behaviors, usually based in logical positivism; addresses research questions on the validity of a theory

**Working hypotheses** – cautiously exploring a hypothesis or idea with the realization that knowledge is limited and, as a result, the idea will likely change over time; mostly used for exploratory research questions

**Descriptive categories** – working with, or developing new, ideographic typologies that can be used to understand social and geographic patterns; for research questions that attempt to describe pattern variations

**Practical ideal type** – comparing real world cases to theoretical model to gauge, measure, or otherwise assess case sample(s); allows research questions that compare specific case studies to broader models

**Models of operations research** – deconstructing and assessing the decision making, organizational, and political processes; for research questions exploring underlying structures and assumptions

*Source:* Based on Shields and Tajalli (2006).

*Table 2.3* Common conceptual theoretical dualisms in the social sciences

| | |
|---|---|
| Authentic, real | Inauthentic, contrived |
| Modern | Traditional, historic |
| Modern | Postmodern |
| Science, physical, objectivity | Religion, spiritual, subjectivity |
| Structure | Agency |
| Nature | Nurture |
| Relativism | Absolutism |
| Public | Private |
| Insider, hosts | Outsider, guests |
| Globalization | Localization |
| Production | Consumption |
| Quantitative | Qualitative |
| Sustainability, conservation | Development |
| Known | Unknown |
| Self | Other |
| East, South, periphery | West, North, center |
| Good, right | Evil, wrong |
| Formal | Informal |
| Political liberalism, socialism | Political conservativism, capitalism |

*Source:* Lew (2006).

work with can be conceptualized as dualism (Table 2.3). Most of the theoretical debates that surround these dualisms exist somewhere in the middle ground between the dualistic extremes. However, proponents of the extreme positions also exist, making for stimulating analysis and discussions. The quantitative–qualitative split, discussed above, is an example of a dualism, and the mixed-methods approach (using both quantitative and qualitative methods) is an example of a middle-ground response.

While apparently simplistic, thinking in terms of dualisms is a powerful social science research tool that can unearth the worldviews that shape the behavior of individuals and groups. They can also be used to challenge research paradigms and conceptual frameworks, and, in so doing, to further refine the definition and focus of our research efforts.

## Examples of conceptual frameworks

A definitive list of conceptual frameworks that may be used in the social sciences is not possible because of continual incremental changes and advancements that occur with each refereed publication, and because of the different goals and problems that researchers themselves define. In my own research, as well as that of my graduate students, I have explored and used a number of conceptual frameworks over the past couple of decades, including Maslow's hierachy of needs (Lew 1998), social capital (Lew and Wong 2004), existential authenticity (Lew and Wong 2005), postmodernism (Lew 2007), long tail economic theory (Lew 2009), and logical positivism (Ng and Lew 2009). Most of my publications, however, have been from a less formal, somewhat structuralist-influenced, Descriptive Categories approach (see Table 2.2).

One example that shows the use of different conceptual frameworks applied to the same field research data is a series of articles that I published on overseas Chinese tourists to China. Being half Chinese I have had a long, personal interest in overseas Chinese tourism to China. Although I studied in Hong Kong as an undergraduate student from 1974 to 1976, learning Cantonese, I was not allowed to visit China due to restrictions on who was allowed into China at that time (Lew 1987). It was a decade later, in 1984, that I made my first short trip to Guangzhou, while passing through Hong Kong on my return to the US from Singapore where I had spent a year doing doctoral research funded by the Fulbright program.

For me, Hong Kong, Singapore, and Guangzhou were each an existential experience, connecting me back to my Chinese roots in its own way. But it was not until 1990 that I was able to make a trip back to my ancestral village, accompanying my father, who was born there. The village is in Taishan (Toisan in the local dialect) County, Guangdong Province, and is a relatively small one that was accessible at the time only by bicycle and motorcycle on a narrow trail. The visit included a banquet for the entire village and two whole roast pigs for my great-grandfather's grave, all paid for by my father, of course. I made one more trip to the village with my father in 1996, and made two more trips there on my own in later years.

My doctoral research in Singapore focused on the historical evolution of the city-state's tourism landscape, and tourism gradually came to dominate my academic research focus. Based on my personal experience, I had long had an interest in the phenomenon of overseas Chinese travel back to China.

With limited opportunity to travel there myself in the 1980s and early 1990s, I relied entirely on secondary material to write my first article on the topic, 'Overseas Chinese and Compatriots in China's Tourism Development,' which was published in 1995 (Lew 1995).

That article reviewed the history of the Chinese diaspora, the relationship between Communist China and ethnic Chinese living overseas, the role of overseas Chinese investment in contemporary China, and some discussion of the overseas Chinese experience. It was an exploratory study, with an informal structuralist perspective, arguing that historical perspectives could reveal influences that shape contemporary relationships and experiences. My personal goal was to understand what I had experienced in my travels to my ancestral village. This first article was a step in that direction, based on the data that I had access to, but it did not satisfy that need to know.

It was not until I spent time at the Hong Kong Polytechnic University during a sabbatical in 2000 and 2001 that I was finally able to pursue my interests in overseas Chinese tourism to China to its full extent. This was enabled by my being in Hong Kong, which made China more accessible, and my collaboration with a Hong Kong colleague who was born in Macao and who shared my interest in this topic. Together we researched, wrote, and published four articles on overseas Chinese tourism in China.

The research included three field trips to major sources of ethnic Chinese residing outside of China: Taishan County and Zhongshan County in Guangdong Province, and Xiamen (historically known as Amoy) in Fujian Province. The Taishan County visit included a stop at my ancestral village, interviews with local Overseas Chinese Affairs Office officials, and the collection of a variety of publications produced about and for overseas Taishanese. The Zhongshan field trip included similar interviews, along with a focus on efforts by a Fijian-Chinese to find her village and remaining relatives in China. The Xiamen trip included visits to the city's Overseas Chinese Museum, interviews with museum officials and administrators, the collection of publications about overseas Chinese, and visits to overseas Chinese-funded tourist sites in the Xiamen area.

The first of the articles to emerge from this research effort (Lew and Wong 2002) was essentially an update of the 1995 publication. This was necessary due to the new data that we had collected, including new statistics published by local-level government agencies, and expanded by insights into the structure of the overseas Chinese tourism phenomenon that we had gained from the fieldwork.

The second article was a content analysis of magazines that are produced by two Overseas Chinese Affairs Offices in Taishan County for overseas Chinese readers (Lew and Wong 2003). These types of magazines are common throughout Guangdong and Fujian Provinces, which is where the majority of overseas Chinese have originated from historically. The content of these magazines included stories of overseas Chinese visits to their ancestral villages, of successful overseas Chinese from the regions covered by the magazines, lists of donations made by visitors, and related local development news and stories. There were even occasional announcements of overseas Chinese searching for long-lost relatives. The research used the content analysis methodology and the analysis deconstructed the content to understand the motivations of local officials and their efforts to manage the visitor experience for achieving local social and economic development.

The third article to come from this collaborative research effort focused on the role of social capital in the overseas Chinese tourism experience in China (Lew and Wong 2004). Social capital in the Chinese context is closely related to *guangxi*, or prescribed rules of reciprocal social debt. This is very closely related to the relationship between overseas Chinese and their ancestral villages, and motivates both sides to make an effort to create strong social ties that can sometimes be leveraged into financial relationships. Social capital (Halpern 2005) provided a very coherent conceptual framework for exploring new avenues and insights into the data we collected.

The fourth and final article was a post-structuralist or postmodern focus on the existential experience and place seduction that is evident in the overseas Chinese experience in traveling back to China (Lew and Wong 2005). Tourism to ancestral homelands is one form of existential tourism that transcends most of the traditional tourism experience (Cohen 1979; Steiner and Reisinger 2006). This article used the conceptual framework of existential tourism to focus on elements that help make an ancestral homeland visit transcendental, and those that do not, at least in the Chinese context. In general, existential experiences in travel and tourism are fleeting, although they are what many people seek in their travels. Ancestral homeland visits can be more likely to enable existential experiences, but they cannot guarantee them for every visit and for every individual.

These examples show how different conceptual frameworks can be applied to the same set of collected fieldwork data. Each conceptual framework provides a different set of questions and answers that together help fill out a picture of the topic of interest. By the time I finished the last of these articles, I personally felt that I had satisfied all of my own curiosity about what I had experienced as an overseas Chinese tourist – at least for now.

## Conclusions

What is the conceptual framework of your research? Along with the research question or problem, this is the most important issue that needs to be addressed early on in a research effort because it is directly related to both the larger research paradigm (and epistemology) and the more narrow research methodology. In fact, identifying a research topic is easy when compared to identifying a conceptual framework. However, it is especially important to address this question in a field research situation to keep the research focused and manageable. At the same time, the conceptual framework is subject to the cyclical revisions that are a natural part of the research process.

Conceptual frameworks have three roles to play in academic research. First, they are a reflection of the researcher's worldview, and should be intimately related to their self-identity. This is important to keep the researcher interested and up to date on the debates, concepts, and theories related to the conceptual framework that has been adopted. In relation to this, the conceptual framework generalizes and simplifies the complexity of the real world by offering one perspective on it. This also makes the research effort more manageable.

Second, the conceptual framework provides epistemological tools and paths. When the research question and the conceptual framework are aligned, the choice of methodology and type of analysis will often become self-evident. In particular, research produced by others using the same or similar conceptual frameworks can be borrowed, adapted, and applied to the new research project. This is one of the major objectives of the traditional literature review. However, because research questions and cases in the social sciences usually vary from one instance to the next, there will be some variation in the epistemological assumptions that underlie the research. This results in a need to renew, reinvent, re-question, and re-conceptualize our methods and theories over time, and this is what advances scientific knowledge.

The third major use of conceptual frameworks is as a pedagogical tool. Understanding the debates and discourses that surround every research paradigm, theory, and idea can help us to better critique our own research and that of our colleagues, students, and mentors. Learning is advanced through such discussions, as alternative and new perspectives are uncovered and considered. Thus it may be useful to take an extreme position (being the 'devil's advocate') to educate others in a Socratic manner.

So what is the conceptual framework for your current or next research project? How does your conceptual framework relate to your epistemological beliefs about how we know what is true (revelation, observation, reasoning, and tacit knowledge)? How does your conceptual framework relate to your larger research paradigm (quantitative, qualitative, critical, or something else)? Answering these questions will make your field research more meaningful, useful, and doable.

## Acknowledgment

The author thanks Dr. James Sell, Northern Arizona University, for assistance with a portion of this chapter.

## References

BonJour, L. (2002) *Epistemology: Classic Problems and Contemporary Responses*. Lanham, MD: Rowman & Littlefield.
Borgatti, S.P. (1999) *Elements of Research*, Online. Available HTTP: <http://www.analytictech.com/mb313/elements.htm> (accessed 2 May 2009).

Cohen, E. (1979) 'A Phenomenology of Tourist Experiences,' *Sociology* 13(2): 179–201.

Crawford S. and Stucki, L. (1990) 'Peer review and the changing research record,' *Journal of the American Society for Information Science* 41: 223–8.

Creswell, J.W. (2008) *Research Design: Qualitative, Quantitative, and Mixed Methods Approaches*. Thousand Oaks, CA: Sage.

Feyerabend, P. (2002) *Against Method*, 3rd edn. New York: Verso.

Greene, J.C., Caracelli, V.J. and Graham, W.F. (1989) 'Toward a Conceptual Framework for Mixed-method Evaluation Designs,' *Educational Evaluation and Policy Analysis* 11(3): 255–74.

Halpern, D. (2005) *Social Capital*. Cambridge: Polity Press.

Johnson, R.B. and Onwuegbuzie, A.J. (2004) 'Methods Research: A Research Paradigm Whose Time has Come,' *Educational Researcher* 33(7): 14–26.

Kuhn, T. (1962) *The Structure of Scientific Revolutions*. Chicago: University of Chicago Press.

Kuhn, T.S. (1970) *The Structure of Scientific Revolutions*, 2nd edn. Chicago: University of Chicago Press.

Lew, A.A. (1987) 'The History, Policies and Social Impact of International Tourism in the People's Republic of China,' *Asian Profile* 15(2): 117–28.

Lew, A.A. (1995) 'Overseas Chinese and Compatriots in China's Tourism Development,' in A.A. Lew and L. Yu (eds), *Tourism in China: Geographical, Political, and Economic Perspectives*. Boulder, CO: Westview Press.

Lew, A.A. (1998) 'Tourism and Quality of Life in Cities: Friend or Foe? (The Singapore model),' in *Proceedings of the First International Conference on Quality of Life in Cities – Issues and Perspectives*, 4–6 March 1998, Singapore. Singapore: National University of Singapore, School of Building and Real Estate.

Lew, A.A. (2007) 'Pedestrian Shopping Streets in the Restructuring of the Chinese City,' in T. Coles and A. Church (eds), *Tourism, Power and Place*. London: Routledge.

Lew, A.A. (2009) 'Long Tail Tourism: New Geographies for Marketing Niche Tourism Products,' *Journal of Travel and Tourism Marketing* 25(3/4): 409–19.

Lew, A.A. and Wong, A. (2002) 'Tourism and the Chinese Diaspora', in C.M. Hall and A.M. Williams (eds), *Tourism and Migration: New Relationships between Production and Consumption*, pp. 205–19. Dordrecht: Kluwer Academic.

Lew, A.A. and Wong, A. (2003) 'News from the Motherland: A Content Analysis of Existential Tourism Magazines in China,' *Tourism Culture and Communication* 4(2): 83–94.

Lew, A.A. and Wong, A. (2004) 'Sojourners, Guangxi and Clan Associations: Social Capital and Overseas Chinese Tourism to China,' in D. Timothy and T. Coles (eds), *Tourism, Diasporas and Space*. London: Routledge.

Lew, A.A. and Wong, A. (2005) 'Existential Tourism and the Homeland Seduction: The Overseas Chinese Experience,' in C.L. Cartier and A.A. Lew (eds), *The Seduction of Place: Geographical Perspectives on Globalization and Touristed Landscapes*. London: Routledge.

Liehr, P. and Smith, M.J. (2001) *Frameworks for Research*, Online. Available HTTP: <http://homepage.psy.utexas.edu/HomePage/Class/Psy394V/Pennebaker/Reprints/Liehr%20Class.doc, posted 16 Oct 2001> (accessed 2 May 2009).

Mujer Sana Comunidad Sana (MSCS) (2003) *Healthy Women – Healthy Communities Project*. Online. Available HTTP: <http://www.mujersana.ca/msproject/framework 1-e.php> (accessed 2 April 2009).

Ng, P.T. and Lew, A.A. (2009) *Quantile Regression Analysis of Visitor Spending: An Example of Mainland Chinese Tourists in Hong Kong*. Flagstaff: W.A. Franke College of Business Working Papers Series, Northern Arizona University,

Polanyi, M. (1958) *Personal Knowledge: Towards a Post-Critical Philosophy*. Chicago: University of Chicago Press.

Popper, K. (1959) *The Logic of Scientific Discovery*. New York: Basic Books.

Seamon, D. (1980) 'Body-subject, Time-space Routines, and Place-ballets,' in A. Buttimer and D. Seamon (eds), *The Human Experience of Space and Place*. London: Taylor and Francis.

Sell, J. (2007) 'Epistemology and paradigms.' Unpublished document, Flagstaff: Department of Geography, Planning and Recreation, Northern Arizona University.

Shields, P. and Tajalli, H. (2006) 'Intermediate theory: The missing link in successful student scholarship,' *Journal of Public Affairs Education* 12(3): 313–34. Online. Available HTTP: <http://ecommons.txstate.edu/polsfacp/39/> (accessed 2 May 2009).

Steiner, C.J. and Reisinger, Y. (2006) 'Understanding Existential Authenticity,' *Annals of Tourism Research* 33(2): 299–318.

# Part I

# Research relationships

## Power, politics and patron–client affinities

Issues of power and politics are a major theme running through the various chapters in this volume. This section provides three chapters that set the context for such issues and which also allow reflection on some of the ethical issues involved not only in the undertaking of fieldwork and the communication of results but also with respect to the selection of topics.

In Chapter 3, Hall provides a discussion of how the concept of power can be understood at different levels of analysis and its relationship to the politics of tourism. He notes that much commentary on power and politics in tourism tends to be undertaken in a relative theoretical vacuum that is divorced from the well-established debates on power in political science and community studies and with little detailed analysis. Although there is a small but significant body of literature on power in the tourism literature (e.g. Church and Coles 2007a; Macleod and Carrier 2010) the situation still reflects that described by Church and Coles (2007b: 270): 'Given the tourism academy contains many researchers with backgrounds in anthropology, geography and sociology it is still curious that power, a core concept in social sciences generally and more importantly very recently, has not become a more prominent issue in tourism research.' Hall argues that research is where knowledge meets power and provides a number of macro- and micro-scale cases for consideration of how power affects fieldwork and the broader research process. He concludes by observing that although we can recognise that 'constructing informants as adversaries, or the fields they occupy as hostile terrain, is crude and problematic' (Hanson Thiem and Robertson 2010: 5), it does nevertheless reinforce the notion that at certain times and places the construction of research and its communication will serve some interests and not others, and that researchers need to be aware of this situation. As part of this process Hall suggests that tourism research is also being increasingly influenced by the development of 'academic capitalism' in which market-like behaviour and the principle of performity are regarded as crucial for economic competitiveness (Slaughter and Leslie 1997, 2001; Hall, 2010) and, as Paasi (2005: 773) notes, such measures 'will transform, reposition, and regulate the activities of researchers'. At issue is the ethical question which each researcher must address (Heaney 1996): not whether to serve political interests, but which political, economic, cultural, and class interests do we serve?

Chapter 4 by Chok examines issues with respect to ethics and politically sensitive research by drawing upon her experiences in undertaking labour relations and human rights research in Singapore. Two key themes run through this chapter – visibility and invisibility. Labour relations is a controversial issue (see also McMorran, Chapter 16, this volume) and the challenges of conducting politically sensitive research in an authoritarian state are multi-dimensional. Conducted in phases, her fieldwork included covert research, i.e. research in which her identity as a researcher was hidden. But her research also indicated that other areas of the labour experience were difficult to access. Her fieldwork also entailed investigative visits to determine recruitment processes for hospitality workers that were generally low-risk but still 'deceptive' in that intentions were concealed. Her research revealed how unethical practices have become 'normalized' within a large segment of the recruitment and private hospitality education industry. Nevertheless, she recognised that she faces a major dilemma in her study: How is one to be an 'ethical researcher' when investigating unethical practices? As she noted, institutional requirements for 'ethical research' place demands on her to be explicit about research objectives and methods, yet this presupposes strong stakeholder support for the research project to succeed. What does a researcher do when such support is not available?

In Chapter 5 Bochaton and Lefebvre discuss the issues they encountered, as well as their responses, with respect to interviewing elites during their study of medical tourism in India and Thailand. They outline their preparations for the interviews, the different strategies used to access interviewees, as well as the power relations issues that emerged from the process of interviewing. As in the chapter by Chok, the authors identify concerns over positionality and the ethics of the fieldwork process.

## Suggested further reading

Church, A. and Coles, T. (eds) (2007) *Tourism, Power and Space*. London: Routledge. Edited volume which examines issues of power in tourism.

Conti, J.A. and O'Neil, M. (2007) 'Studying power: Qualitative Methods and the Global Elite', *Qualitative Research* 7(1): 63–82.
Discussion of the issues involved in studying power using feminist methodologies.

Davis, D. (2003) 'What did you Do Today?: Notes from a Politically Engaged Anthropologist', *Urban Anthropology* 32(2): 147–73.
Examines some of the issues arising out of politically committed fieldwork and research with respect to social change.

Fine, G.A. (1993) 'Ten Lies of Ethnography: Moral Dilemmas in Field Research', *Journal of Contemporary Ethnography* 22(3): 267–94.
The article described the compromises that fieldworkers continually have to make

against idealised ethical standards. The focus is on three clusters of moral dilemmas: the classical virtues (the kindly ethnographer, the friendly ethnographer, and the honest ethnographer), technical skills (the precise ethnographer, the observant ethnographer, and the unobtrusive ethnographer), and the ethnographic self (the candid ethnographer, the chaste ethnographer, the fair ethnographer, and the literary ethnographer).

Hall, C.M. (1994) *The Politics of Tourism*. Chichester: John Wiley.
One of the standard works with respect to political issues in tourism. Also available in Arabic.

Lukes, S. (2005) *Power: A Radical View*, 2nd edn. London: Palgrave Macmillan in association with the British Sociological Association.
This revised edition of one of the classic works on power, which was first published in 1974, highlights the relationship between how power is defined and what is identified with respect to power relationships. Provides a very good overview of the power literature.

Macleod, D. and Carrier, J. (eds) (2010) *Tourism, Power and Culture: Anthropological Insights*. Bristol: Channel View Publications.
Edited volume that examines the interplay between power and culture with chapters that are authored mainly by anthropologists.

Richards D. (1996) 'Elite interviewing: Approaches and pitfalls', *Politics* 16(3): 199–204.
A seminal paper with respect to the issues of elite interviewing.

# References

Church, A. and Coles, T. (eds) (2007a) *Tourism, Power and Space*. London: Routledge.
Church, A. and Coles, T. (2007b) 'Tourism and the Many Faces of Power', in A. Church and T. Coles (eds), *Tourism, Power and Space*. London: Routledge.
Hall, C.M. (2010) 'Academic Capitalism, Academic Responsibility and Tourism Academics: Or, the Silence of the Lambs?' *Tourism Recreation Research* 35(3): in press.
Hanson Thiem, C. and Robertson, M. (2010) 'Editorial. Behind Enemy Lines: Reflections on the Practice and Production of Oppositional Research', *Geoforum* 41: 5–6.
Heaney, T. (1996) 'Politics of Explanation: Ethical Questions in the Production of Knowledge', *The Researcher* 11(2): 27–34.
Macleod, D. and Carrier, J. (eds) (2010) *Tourism, Power and Culture: Anthropological Insights*. Bristol: Channel View Publications.
Paasi, A. (2005) 'Globalisation, Academic Capitalism, and the Uneven Geographies of International Journal Publishing Spaces', *Environment and Planning A* 37: 769–89.
Slaughter, S. and Leslie, L. (1997) *Academic Capitalism: Politics, Policies and the Entrepreneurial University*. Baltimore: Johns Hopkins University.
Slaughter, S. and Leslie, L. (2001) 'Expanding and Elaborating the Concept of Academic Capitalism', *Organization* 8: 154–61.

# 3 Researching the political in tourism

## Where knowledge meets power

*C. Michael Hall*

## Introduction: The politics of tourism

For many people tourism is perhaps the antithesis of politics. The word 'tourism' conjures up images of leisure, free-time and play. Far away from the association with the electioneering, revolutions and power-plays that many seem to associate with politics. Yet tourism and tourism research is inextricably linked to issues of politics. Decisions affecting the location and character of tourism development arise out of politics as does, of course, whether an individual is even allowed to travel or whether certain locations, subjects or communities are available for study. For example, despite the association of travel and tourism with 'freedom' nowhere in international law is there enshrined a right to enter foreign spaces. Even the non-binding Universal Declaration of Human Rights postulates a right only of exit and entry to one's own country (Article 13).

In its broadest sense politics is about power: who gets what, where, how and why (Lasswell 1936). The conception of politics and the political is important because it will shape the questions that researchers do or do not consider as well as assumptions made when undertaking research. Donahue (2009) identifies seven different classes of conceptions of what constitutes politics: power-seeking conceptions, power-distributing conceptions, struggle-and-competition conceptions, collective decision and action conceptions, group and social order-production conceptions, authority-asserting conceptions, and shaping values and arrangements conceptions. Some of the most widely used definitions of politics are: Politics is the exercise of power. Politics is the public allocation of things that are valued. Politics is the resolution of conflict. Politics is the competition among individuals and groups pursuing their own interests. Politics is the determination of who gets what, when and how. All of these definitions share the central idea that the political process involves the values of actors (individuals, interest groups and public and private organisations) in a struggle for power (Danziger 2001).

Politics is also closely related to public policy given that politics is concerned with both the exercise of power and influence in a society and in specific decisions over public policy. A common element in definitions is that 'public policies stem from governments or public authorities . . . A policy is deemed a public policy not by virtue of its impact on the public, but by virtue of its source' (Pal 1992: 3). Public policy is therefore what officials within government decide to do or not to do about issues and problems that require government intervention. 'Government' is a term that refers to the legitimate institutions and associated political processes through which public policy choices are made. Unfortunately, the language used to discuss public policy is often confusing. Policy is more than just a written document, although that may represent an important output of a decision- and policy-making process. Instead, public policy is an extremely broad concept that covers such matters as:

- the purpose of government action;
- the goals or ends that are to be achieved;
- the means to achieve goals, usually referred to as plans, proposals or strategies;
- the programmes that are established to achieve goals, these are the government-sanctioned means; and
- the decisions and actions that are taken with respect to policy, including implementation.

In addition, it is also important to differentiate between public policy outputs: which are the formal actions taken by government with respect to policy from public policy outcomes, what are the effects government policy outputs actually have. As a result public policy can be defined as 'a course of government action or inaction in response to public problems' (Kraft and Furlong 2007: 5). Yet the division between politics and public policy is arguably something related more to Anglo-American discourse as many languages do not really distinguish between politics and policy (Hall and Jenkins 1995).

As noted in numerous chapters throughout this volume, as individuals researchers are also engaged in dealing with the politics of fieldwork. The politics of fieldwork may be overt in that researchers are deliberately aiming to uncover political elements in their study in that issues of power, public policy and/or governance are central to their research questions. However, more often than not politics is an indirect though significant element in the capacity to undertake fieldwork. This can include such matters as permission to enter particular countries or field locations; access to archives, institutions and elite actors; institutional and regulatory oversight of fieldwork and its results; concern that respondents may not be able to engage in certain discussions with the researcher because of authorities' perceptions of what should or should not be reported; and even the capacity to ask certain research questions at all (e.g. Tehindrazanarivelo 1997; see also Chok, Chapter 4, this volume; Yamagishi, Chapter 7, this volume).

Unfortunately, much commentary on power and politics in tourism, if it is discussed at all, tends to be undertaken in a theoretical vacuum and with little detailed analysis. Although there is a small but significant reaction to this in the tourism literature (e.g. Burns and Novelli 2006; Church and Coles 2007a; Macleod and Carrier 2010) the situation still reflects that described by Church and Coles (2007b: 270): 'Given the tourism academy contains many researchers with backgrounds in anthropology, geography and sociology it is still curious that power, a core concept in social sciences generally and more importantly very recently, has not become a more prominent issue in tourism research.' Several reasons may be posited as to why this situation may have occurred (Hall 1994; 2010a):

- the subject occupies a range of theoretical locations and is highly contested, meaning that there is no consensus over definitions of key concepts or the application of theoretical frameworks;
- tourism studies, at least in business schools, are strongly dominated by managerialism and economism, which has led to the dominance of rationalist and apolitical conceptualisations of tourism-related decision making and management;
- given the role of government and, to a lesser extent, the tourism industry in funding tourism research and education, researchers may not wish to 'bite the hand that feeds' as a result of the production and circulation of 'critical' studies;
- The politics of political ethnography and participant observation may itself act as a discouragement to some students of tourism to undertake research in the area while also being concerned at the long-term effects that the selection of subject matter for graduate research may have on a career.

Ironically, some of the reasons provided above for not studying power may in themselves be regarded as occurring because of the actualisation of power by particular interests. To silence a debate even before it can start is surely evidence of power operating in institutional forms? But, of course, even that type of assertion would be regarded by some tourism scholars as being little more than a conspiracy theory. Regardless, the connection between the ideas of power and responsibility that arise in the value-dependence of the analysis of power arguably highlights the importance of understanding the morality of power and the political and ethical space of what we study.

## Power

The concept of power is grounded in broader questions as to how power is conceptualised and how it can be studied. Addressing the issue of power is therefore intrinsically 'messy'. Key questions with respect to power structure research include: (1) what organisation, group or class in the social structure under study receives the most of what people seek and value (*who benefits*)? (2) which organisation, group or class is overrepresented in key decision-making positions (*who sits*)? (3) which organisation, group or class wins in the decisional arena (*who wins*)? and (4) who is thought to be powerful by knowledgeable observers and peers (*who has a reputation for power*)? (Domhoff 2007). These are questions that reflect Lasswell's (1936) comment about politics: politics is about power, i.e. who gets what, where, how and why. Unfortunately, in tourism studies such questions are often never asked (Hall 1994; 2007; 2010).

Power is always present in relationships between individual and institutional actors. Power is exercised every time a group or individual is dependent upon someone else for carrying out a role or task. Political leaders and followers, managers and employees, communities and citizens, bureaucrats and clients, tour guides and parties, university departments and their students all exercise power through the forms of cooperation and conflict they enact. This relational view of power is a key element of understanding its exercise and nature. Giddens (1979: 93) noted that power is always a two-way process, 'even if the power of one actor is minimal compared to another'. Such a relational understanding of power is inherent to Lukes' (1974) seminal work on power in which power was conceptualised as 'all forms of successful control by A over B – that is, of A securing B's compliance' (Lukes 1974: 17). However, the very notion of 'power', one of the cornerstones of political analysis, is an 'essentially contested' concept (Gallie 1955–6) by which there is no universal agreement as to exactly how the concept should be understood and therefore analysed. Indeed, Lukes (1974; 2005) has stressed that the use of the concept of power is inextricably linked to a given set of value assumptions held by researchers which predetermine the range of its empirical application. We all have different assumptions about values, power and interest.

Guzzini (2001), for example, notes that any neutral definition of 'power', such as that proposed by Oppenheim (1981), seems elusive, exactly because power is used as an explanatory variable and there is no neutral concept of power for the dependence of theory, empirical and conceptual analyses, on meta-theoretical commitments. Similarly, Gray (1983: 94) compared individualist (voluntarist) and structuralist (determinist) positions and concluded that 'since judgements about power and structure are theory-dependent operations, actionists and structuralists will approach their common subject-matter – what goes on in society – using divergent paradigms in such a fashion that incompatible explanations (and descriptions) will be produced'.

Given the issues involved in its application, the question may therefore be asked as to why it is important to study power, especially within the context of tourism studies where it has drawn only extremely limited attention as a subject of direct study (Hall and Jenkins 2004)? According to Morriss (1987), it is because of the practical, moral and evaluative contexts. First, we are interested in power because we want to know how things are brought about. Second, through the assessment of power, moral responsibility for the use of power can be attributed. Third, people are not just interested in the judgement of individuals but in the evaluation of society. All of these issues emerge in studying tourism, with the connection between the ideas of power and responsibility that arise in the value-dependence of the analysis of power arguably highlighting the importance of understanding the morality of power and the political and ethical space of what we study.

> When we see the conceptual connection between the idea of power and the idea of responsibility, we can see more clearly why those who exercise power are not eager to acknowledge the fact, while those who take a critical perspective of existing social relationships are eager to attribute power to those in privileged positions. For to acknowledge power over others is to implicate oneself in responsibility for certain events and to put oneself in a position where justification for the limits placed on others is expected. To attribute power to another, then, is not simply to describe his or her role in some perfectly neutral sense, but is more like accusing him or her of something, which is then to be denied or justified.
>
> (Connolly 1974: 97)

For Connolly (1974) the notion of power therefore implies counterfactuals, i.e. it could be done differently. Indeed, Lukes (1974) indicated that Bachrach and Baratz's (1962; 1970) conceptualisation of power with respect to the importance of non-decision making (confining the scope of decision making so as to deliberately exclude other decision options) served to redefine what counts as a political issue in the sense that what is not done is as important as what is done, and often more so. this issue is raised in several chapters in the present volume (e.g. Chok, Chapter 4 in relation to employment rights in the tourism industry; Leopold, Chapter 6, with respect to community tourism research; and Bensemann, Chapter 11, with respect to gender issues in rural entrepreneurship). To be 'political' therefore means to be potentially changeable (Hoffmann 1988). For Guzzini (2000; 2001) this provides a constructivist dimension to the analysis of power as concept formation is part of the social construction of knowledge; and the defining and assigning of power is therefore a power or 'political' exercise in itself and hence part of the social construction of reality. Therefore, the study of power, in and of itself, runs counter to those who seek to 'depoliticise' policy and research fields and present them as 'rational' exercises in decision making and analysis. Such a perspective may also be applied to discussion in much of tourism studies about the inherent value of 'collaboration', 'partnership' and 'networks' without there being any consideration of the power dimensions of such social relationships.

Although not being as fashionable in tourism research with notions of power as the work of Foucault, one of the most influential students of power (including on the present author) is the work of the political and social theorist Steven Lukes. In his review of the concept of power Lukes (1974; 2005) identified three different approaches, or dimensions, in the analysis of power, each focusing on different aspects of the decision-making process:

- a *one-dimensional view* emphasising observable, overt behaviour, conflict, and decision making;
- a *two-dimensional view* which recognises decisions and non-decisions, observable (overt or covert) conflict, and which represents a qualified critique of the behavioural stance of the one-dimensional view, especially with respect to recognition of values and institutional practices in political systems that favour the interests of some actors over others; and
- a *three-dimensional view* which focuses on decision making and control over the political agenda (not necessarily through decisions), and which recognises observable (overt or covert) and latent conflict.

Each of the three dimensions arises out of, and operates within, a particular political perspective as the concept of power is value-dependent (Lukes 1974; 2005). For example, a pluralist conception of the tourism development process, such as that which underlies the notion of community-based tourism, including its more recent applications in terms of ecotourism and pro-poor tourism, will focus on different aspects of the decision-making process than structuralist conceptions of politics which highlight social relations within the consumption of tourist services. These distinctions are extremely significant for the understanding of tourism. However, given the need to understand the dominant interests and ideologies operating within the political and administrative system which surrounds indigenous tourism, it seems reasonable to assume that the use of a wide conception of power, capable of identifying decisions, non-decisions and community political structure, will provide the most benefit in the analysis of the political dimensions of tourism (Hall 2007).

## One-dimensional views

Much of the writing in tourism that discusses issues of collaboration, participation and decision making often fails to recognise the role of power relations between actors. Where this occurs it may well reflect a rather naïve perspective on tourism development that holds that everyone has equal access to power and representation. To an extent this has been one of the driving elements behind utilising the community approach as an appropriate conceptual framework for tourism planning since there appears to be an inherent assumption that it is somehow 'closer to the people' (see Leopold, Chapter 6, this volume). However, public participation in tourism development has long been recognised as imperfect (Hall 2008). Nevertheless, a one-dimensional view of power in communities suggests that, even though imperfect, the community decision-making process is at least observable, as it operates through the overt action of pluralist interests (Dahl 1961; Debnam 1984). In addition, political issues are regarded as coming into existence when they command 'the attention of a significant segment of the political stratum' (Dahl 1961: 92). This concept of power has the advantage that it can be relatively easily operationalised. As Lukes (1986: 2) observes, when B seeks to resist the power of A it is 'relevant in the sense that, if it is actualised, it provides the test by which one can measure relative power, where parties conflict over an issue'. The latter observation is significant in that power relations shift according to the issue (Lukes 1986: 8). The one-dimensional view of power therefore reinforces that power is not evenly distributed within a community and some groups and individuals have the ability to exert greater influence over tourism than others through the access to financial resources, expertise, public relations, media, knowledge and time to put into contested situations (Hall and Jenkins 1995).

## Two-dimensional views: the two faces of power

Bachrach and Baratz (1970) identified two major weaknesses in the pluralist approach to power. First, it did not provide for the fact that power may be exercised by confining the scope of political decision making. Second, they argued that the pluralist model provided no criteria for determining the significant issues. Therefore, two-dimensional views of community decision making focuses on decision making and non-decision making and observable (overt and covert) conflict (Bachrach and Baratz 1962; 1970). Bachrach and Baratz (1970: 44) defined a non-decision as 'a decision that results in suppression or thwarting of a latent or manifest challenge to the values or interests of the decision-maker'. A non-decision is a means by which demands for change in the existing allocation of benefits and privileges in the community can be suffocated before they are even voiced; or kept covert, or killed before they gain access to the relevant decision-making arena; or, failing all these things, maimed or destroyed in the implementation stage of the policy process (Lukes 1974). Non-decision making exists 'to the extent that a person or group – consciously or unconsciously – creates or reinforces barriers to the public airing of political conflicts, that person or group has power' (Bachrach and Baratz 1970: 8). The role of non-decision making is now widely acknowledged in the political literature given that political actors, and organisations, 'can leave selected topics undiscussed for what they consider their own advantage' (Holmes 1988: 22).

   With respect to problems of the one-dimensional version of power in identifying key issues, Bachrach and Baratz (1970: 11) also stress the importance of an analysis of the 'mobilization of bias', which is 'the dominant values and the political myths, rituals, and institutional practices which tend to favor the vested interests of one or more groups, relative to others'. Non-decision making is also the 'primary method for sustaining a given mobilization of bias' (Bachrach and Baratz 1970: 43–4). A variation of non-decision making is the concept of non-implementation in which, though policy is developed or regulation enacted, it is not actually enforced (Mokken and Stokman 1976).

   Within the political studies literature the role of institutional arrangements has been long recognised as important, although studies in a tourism context are extremely limited. As Schattsneider (1960: 71) commented, 'All forms of political organisation have a bias in favour of the exploitation of some kinds of conflict, and the suppression of others, because organisation is the mobilisation of bias. Some issues are organised into politics while some others are organised out.' Those who benefit from tourism may well be placed in a preferred position to defend and promote their interests through the structures and institutions by which communities are managed. Significantly, the influential models of community tourism promoted by Murphy (1985) and more recently developed into the concept of 'pro-poor tourism' clearly fail to address issues of the distribution of power and representation in communities. Indeed, Hall (2008) argues that there is a wider tendency in tourism studies to romanticise the collective capacity of local communities to undertake participative decision making, quoting Millar and Aiken (1995: 629): 'Communities are not the embodiment of innocence; on the contrary, they are complex and self-serving entities, as much driven by grievances, prejudices, inequalities, and struggles for power as they are united by kinship, reciprocity, and interdependence. Decision-making at the local level can be extraordinarily vicious, personal, and not always bound by legal constraints.'

Bachrach and Baratz's (1970) method for empirical application of the concept of non-decision making consists of three stages. First, the study of the actual decision-making process within the political arena and the resultant outcomes; second, the determination of the remaining overt and covert grievances of the apparently disfavoured group; and finally, the determination of 'why and by what means some or all of the potential demands for change have been denied an airing' (Bachrach and Baratz 1970: 49).

## Three-dimensional views

The three-dimensional view of power (Lukes 1974) incorporates the first dimension of observable power in decision making and Bachrach and Baratz's (1962; 1970) power through non-decision making, but adds to these the dimension of institutional bias and the manipulation of preferences. The three-dimensional view of power 'allows for consideration of the many ways in which potential issues are kept out of politics, whether through the operation of social forces and institutional practices or through individuals' decisions' (Lukes 1974: 240). Lukes (1974: 22) argues that Bachrach and Baratz (1970) did not recognise that the phenomenon of collective action is not necessarily 'attributable to particular individual decisions or behaviour, nor that the mobilisation of bias results from the form of *organisation*, due to "systemic" or organisational effects'. He then goes on to emphasise the role that power has in shaping human preferences, arguing, 'to assume that the absence of grievances equals genuine consensus is simply to rule out the possibility of false or manipulated consensus by definitional fiat' (Lukes 1974: 24): 'A may exercise power over B . . . by influencing, shaping or determining his very wants' (Lukes 1974: 23). To Lukes (1974: 23), such an approach is 'the most effective and insidious use of power'.

At first glance, examination of a three-dimensional view of power in tourism studies may appear to be quite problematic. After all, 'how can one study, let alone explain, what does not happen?' (Lukes 1974: 38). Nevertheless, the way 'things do not happen' is as important as what does: 'the proper object of investigation is not political activity but political inactivity' (Crenson 1971: vii). Indeed, Lukes (1974) argued that third-dimensional power may be recognised when it is not in accordance with an individual or group's 'real interests'. Lukes (1974: 24–5) therefore recognises a *'latent conflict*, which consists in a contradiction between the interests of those exercising power and the *real interests* of those they exclude'. This means that we can arrive at a slightly broader definition of power based on notions of interest in which 'A exercises power over B when A affects B in a manner contrary to B's interests' (Lukes 1974: 27). Lukes (2005) argues that what counts as 'real interests' are a function of explanatory purpose, framework and methods, 'which in turn have to be justified' (2005: 148). The notion of interests can therefore be argued from a number of perspectives including material, rational choice and environmental well-being approaches as well as understood as a way of identifying 'basic' capabilities which existing arrangements preclude. In the case of the latter, Lukes (2005) cites the work of Nussbaum on Indian women's collectives, who argued that the seclusion of women in the north of India who 'just peep out of their houses and don't take any action in the world' is 'incompatible with fully human functioning' (Nussbaum 2000: 43).

Non-decisions and latent conflicts provide evidence for the existence of the third dimension of power. The third dimension of power is also related to the analysis of structural dominance in the restriction of human agency. However, some critics (e.g. Giddens 1979; Hyland 1995) argue that such structural domination is beyond the scope of any focus on intentionally exerted power of individual actors. Nevertheless, Lukes (2005: 12) has more recently commented that it was a mistake to define power by 'saying that A exercises power over B when A affects B in a manner contrary to B's interests'. Instead, Lukes argues that power is a capacity rather than the exercise of that capacity (which may never even have to be exercised). Instead, power is the imposition of internal constraints, with those subject to such constraints being 'led to acquire beliefs and form desires that result in their consenting or adapting to being dominated, in coercive or non-coercive settings' (Lukes 2005: 13).

Lukes' (2005) approach to the third dimensions of power recalls Bourdieu's (2000 (1997)) ideas with respect to how the maintenance of 'habitus' appeal to the workings of power, 'leading those subject to it to see their condition as "natural" and even to value it, and to fail to recognise the sources of their desires and beliefs' (Lukes 2005: 13). Such domination is, according to Bourdieu,

> exerted not in the pure logic of knowing consciousness but through the schemes of perception, appreciation and action that are constitutive of

habitus and which, below the level of the decisions of consciousness and the controls of the will, set up a cognitive relationship that is profoundly obscure to itself.

(Bourdieu 2000 (1997): 37)

Lukes' third dimension also intersects with Foucault's (1972; 1980) power/knowledge framework, which also acknowledged the relational nature of power: 'in reality power means relations, a more-or-less organised, hierarchical, co-ordinated cluster of relations' (Foucault 1980: 198). To Foucault knowledge and power are inseparable. Power can be assessed through knowledge because knowledge itself has a function of power. 'Once knowledge can be analysed in terms of region, domain, implantation, displacement, transposition, one is able to capture the process by which knowledge functions as a form of power and disseminates the effects of power' (Foucault 1980: 69). In this power–knowledge relationship, power in turn impacts the formation of knowledge. According to Foucault (1980: 51, 59), 'the exercise of power itself creates and causes to emerge new objects of knowledge and accumulates new bodies of information . . . Far from preventing knowledge, power produces it.' However, perhaps significantly for the study of power in a tourism context, Lukes (2005: 91) downplays the potential explanatory contribution of Foucault in understanding the structure of power, noting that his idea of power, 'in its non-overstated and non-exaggerated form, is simply this: that if power is to be effective, those subject to it must be rendered susceptible to its effects'.

According to Foucault (1987: 11), 'the subject constitutes himself in an active fashion, by the practices of self'. These practices are not invented by the individuals, but are derived from 'patterns that he finds in the culture and which are proposed, suggested and imposed on him by his culture, his society and his social group'. Yet, as Lukes (2005) suggests, what is therefore so supposedly radical about the Foucauldian notion of power (referred to by Digesser (1992) as the fourth face of power)? Instead, it restates some elementary sociological understandings that would be known to any first-year student.

> Individuals are socialized: they are oriented to roles and practices that are culturally and socially given; they internalise these and may experience them as freely chosen; indeed, their freedom may, as Durkheim liked to say, be the fruit of regulation – the outcomes of discipline and controls. Of course, it restates these truths in a distinctively Foucauldian way. . . .
>
> (Lukes 2005: 97)

Indeed, Lukes goes on to note that Foucault's notion that power is 'productive' through the social construction of subjects therefore actually makes no sense in terms of understanding how the various modern forms of power actually succeed or fail in securing compliance. Nevertheless, it is apparent that Foucault's writings have had a wide impact (e.g. Macleod and Carrier 2010), leading Lukes (2005: 98) to suggest that 'Foucault's writings thereby themselves exhibit an interesting kind of power: the power of seduction'.

Lukes' (2005) approach is therefore not to deny that 'false consciousness' does not exist, but to suggest that rather than being understood as some sort of assertion that one has privileged access to truths denied to others, it needs to be understood as the cognitive power to mislead (Lukes 2005). Such power can be witnessed in censorship and disinformation as well as in the denial of other ways of thinking and doing. However, such power is not all-embracing, cracks do appear in walls, and power's third dimension is partial at best over time, as power does meet resistance (Hall 2010a).

In seeking to operationalise the concept of power, we therefore arrive at the importance of locating issues of power within particular issue and locational contexts, even though we must also acknowledge that such loci of power relations will be connected to the myriad of other issues and sets of interests. Indeed, the value of a Lukesian approach to power is highlighted in the multi-layering of observations of power occurring in the three dimensions in that it provides an empirical strength often missing in Foucauldian analyses which, while they acknowledge the role of structural dominance, often fail to record the actions of individual actors in relation to specific issues and interests (e.g. Cheong and Miller 2000). Indeed, arguably there is a substantial amount of such writing in tourism where authors have exhorted the notion of a tourist gaze without interrogation of the concepts of power and knowledge on which it is grounded and given little thought to the role that individual actors play with respect to power relations from a decision- and non-decision-making perspective. Nevertheless, such criticisms aside, tourism potentially provides a number of good examples that illustrate the various dimensions of power with respect to knowledge and interests.

## Fieldwork, research, power and knowledge

Research is where knowledge meets power. Overt interests are often hidden and may be difficult to determine in general. Economic, political and social systems ascribe 'interests' to participants in those systems in subtle ways. According to Heaney (1996: 29), 'The "disinterestedness" of traditional research represents such a systemic interest nurtured and sustained by academics in order to maintain a position of privilege and protect their monopoly over the production and legitimation of knowledge.'

One of the most obvious ways in which tourism research is bound up in the various dimensions of power at the micro-scale is with respect to such matters as access to elite respondents and the interview process that is undertaken with them. As Cormode and Hughes (1999: 299) note, undertaking research on

'the powerful' presents very different methodological and ethical challenges from studying 'down'. The characteristics of those studied, the power relations between them and the researcher, and the politics of the

research process differ considerably between elite and non-elite research
... When studying elites, the scholar is a supplicant.

Such issues apply not only to studying elite networks (see Bochaton and
Lefebvre, Chapter 5, this volume) but also the role of gatekeepers in allowing
access to particular fieldwork sites, locations and, in some situations, research
topics. These issues are often little discussed and, when they are, are usually
placed in the context of trying to undertake research in another country
or jurisdiction from where the research usually resides. Yet, in the author's
experience, there are also significant institutional gatekeeping roles with
respect to ethics committees, research granting bodies, and directed funding
for research projects that also reflect the exercise of power and affect what
does and does not occur in the field.

At a more macro-scale level, fieldwork and tourism research is also being
increasingly influenced by the development of 'academic capitalism' in which
market-like behaviour and the principle of performity are regarded as crucial
for economic competitiveness (Slaughter and Leslie 1997; 2001) and, as Paasi
(2005: 773) notes, such measures 'will transform, reposition, and regulate the
activities of researchers'. The growth of academic capitalism means that academic knowledge production is governed to an increasing degree through
practices based on market-like operations. This situation has been strengthened by the rise of scaling, which often means simply rankings (Paasi 2005)
of publication forums by various bodies and individuals that serve not only
to bestow academic kudos but also influence reward systems and human
resource management within universities and research institutions as well
as the trajectories of knowledge construction and its promotion. As Paasi
(2005: 774) observes, 'The current culture of competition may transform
centre–periphery relations in academic markets on all spatial scales from
individual researchers and departments to international constellations of
academic fields and the movement of people and ideas.' The growth of
scaling programmes, such as the Research Assessment Exercise/Research
Excellence Framework (RAE/REF) and the Performance Based Research
Fund (PBRF) in New Zealand, along with the development of journal
rankings that are used as an evaluation metric in the allocation of research
performance and hence funding, may serve to drive publishing and adoption
of research topics in some directions over others (Hall 2005; 2010b).

Furthermore, there is increased recognition that the research and publishing
which some regard as credible and 'detached' is undertaken within dominant
discourses as well as within institutional arrangements (e.g. publishers, journal
editors, universities, public–private partnerships, research councils, tourism
organisations and non-government organisations) and networks. Research
on tourism is inherently part of the tourism discourse that it is trying to understand. There are therefore institutional incentives and drivers for research to
be undertaken in some directions and not others. Indeed, discourses of tourism may be driven like other academic discourses, such as the creative city or

the experience economy, by the credibility of the academic celebrity and perhaps the discourse itself is embedded in the machinations of the academic fashion cycle, 'which plays out through a particular industrial actor-network of academic knowledge production, circulation and reception' (Gibson and Klocker 2004: 425), within which 'favoured academic personalities' are

> Swept up into international circuits of academic celebrity, a move that is dependent less upon internal disciplinary modes of evaluation than on the shifting imperatives of knowledge dissemination . . . Dedicated followers of fashion hurry to buy the new . . . book, an act of discernment and discrimination that starkly reveals the truism that identity is constructed in and through the consumption of commodities.
>
> (Barnett 1998: 388)

## Locating self in power relationships

The above discussion of power and the positionality of research highlight the importance of understanding not only the selection of what we research but also the reasons why. Research is grounded in autobiography, even if usually unacknowledged (though see Hall 2004), or, where it is, it may be subject to substantial opposition with respect to its publication (e.g. Hall 2010c). Personally, this author takes the perspective that research – the systematic and rigorous examination of experience – begins with the systematic and rigorous examination of political and social commitment and should lead us to ask questions such as: For whom do we work? Whose interests are served by our explanations of the world? What questions do we include and what questions do we exclude in order to focus on those interests? However, I realise that such questions may not be acceptable to some supervisors, institutions or individuals and the very notion of oppositional or counter-institutional research would be anathema to those who believe in the 'objectivity' of research. Although we can recognise that 'constructing informants as adversaries, or the fields they occupy as hostile terrain, is crude and problematic' (Hanson Thiem and Robertson 2010: 5) it does nevertheless reinforce the notion that at certain times and places the construction of research and its communication will serve some interests and not others, and that researchers need to be aware of this situation. Furthermore, it should be recognised that this is an occurrence not just in social scientific research but also in the natural sciences, especially with respect to the undertaking of research in such politically charged areas as climate and environmental change.

Understanding the role of power in influencing field research and the communication of research results therefore means paying attention to key ethical issues and concerns, such as the relative weighting of personal versus institutional ethics in research method and knowledge production. This will then affect decisions with respect to such matters as:

- the use of media in the field;
- the possibilities of undertaking 'illegal' research in some situations (this is actually relatively common with respect to the number of graduate students who undertake fieldwork in foreign countries on tourist visas as opposed to work, student or research visas);
- the capacity or willingness to undertake covert research;
- reporting on knowledge gained outside of the methodological parameters approved by ethics committees and codes of conduct;
- selection of venue for publication or even the decision on whether to publish some information at all;
- selection of where we travel to do research or travel for leisure; for example, the decision by some people to travel to do research or give presentations in authoritarian states.

Understanding how we as researchers fit into networks and structures of power and their associated relationships means that we need to know ourselves. But to know ourselves is not necessarily to change behaviour. Reflexivity might leave us conscious, as well as conscientious, servants of a world order which provides us with sufficient income, privilege and security. Professors and students alike might continue to ignore the political implications of their research, no longer because of adherence to academic 'neutrality' or a homogenistic notion of 'truth,' but rather because of the decision to avoid conflict with those who provide salaries, grades or status. At issue is an ethical question which each researcher must address (see Heaney 1996): not whether to serve political interests, but which political, economic, cultural and class interests we serve.

## References

Bachrach, P. and Baratz, M.S. (1962) 'Two Faces of Power', *American Political Science Review* 56: 947–52.

Bachrach, P. and Baratz, M.S. (1970) *Power and Poverty: Theory and Practice*. New York: Oxford University Press.

Barnett, C. (1998) 'The Cultural Turn: Fashion or Progress in Human Geography?' *Antipode* 30: 379–94.

Bourdieu, P. (2000 [1997]) *Pascalian Meditations* (R. Nice, trans.). Stanford: Stanford University Press.

Burns, P.M. and Novelli, M. (eds) (2006) *Tourism and Politics: Global Frameworks and Local Realities*. Oxford: Elsevier Science.

Cheong, S. and Miller, M. (2000) 'Power and Tourism: A Foucauldian Observation', *Annals of Tourism Research* 27(2): 371–90.

Church, A. and Coles, T. (eds) (2007a) *Tourism, Power and Space*. London: Routledge.

Church, A. and Coles, T. (2007b) 'Tourism and the Many Faces of Power', in A. Church and T. Coles (eds), *Tourism, Power and Space*. London: Routledge.

Connolly, W.E. (1974) *The Terms of Political Discourse*. Oxford: Martin Robertson.

Cormode, L. and Hughes, A. (1999) 'Editorial: The Economic Geographer as a Situated Researcher of Elites', *Geoforum* 30: 299–300.

Crenson, M.A. (1971) *The Un Politics of Air Pollution: A Study of Non-decisionmaking in the Cities*. Baltimore: The Johns Hopkins Press.

Dahl, R.A. (1961) *Who Governs? Democracy and Power in an American City*. New Haven, CN: Yale University Press.

Danziger, J.N. (2001) *Understanding the Political World*, 5th edn. New York: Longman.

Debnam, G. (1984) *The Analysis of Power: A Realist Approach*. London: Macmillan.

Digesser, P. (1992) 'The Fourth Face of Power', *Journal of Politics* 54(4): 977–1007.

Domhoff, G.W. (2007) 'C. Wright Mills, Floyd Hunter, and 50 Years of Power Structure Research', *Michigan Sociological Review* 21: 1–54.

Donahue, T.J. (2009) Research Note: 46 1/2 Conceptions of Politics (18 September, 2009). SSRN. Online. Available at HTTP: <http://ssrn.com/abstract=1151265> (accessed 1 January 2010).

Foucault, M. (1972) *The Archeology of Knowledge*, trans. A.M. Sheridan Smith. New York: Pantheon.

Foucault, M. (1980) *Power/Knowledge: Selected Interviews and Other Writings 1972–1977*. New York: Pantheon Books.

Foucault, M. (1987) 'The Ethic of Care for the Self as a Practice of Freedom: An Interview with Michel Foucault on 20 January 1984', in J. Bernauer and D. Rasmussen (eds), *The Final Foucault*. Cambridge, MA: MIT Press.

Gallie, W.B. (1955–6) 'Essentially Contested Concepts', *Proceedings of the Aristotelian Society* 56: 167–98.

Gibson, C. and Klocker, N. (2004) 'Academic Publishing as "Creative" Industry, and Recent Discourse of "Creative Economies": Some Critical Reflections', *Area* 36(4): 423–34.

Giddens, A. (1979) *Central Problems in Social Theory: Action, Structure and Contradiction in Social Analysis*. London: Macmillan.

Gray, J. (1983) 'Political Power, Social Theory and Essential Contestability', in D. Miller and L. Siedentop (eds), *The Nature of Political Theory*. Oxford: Clarendon Press.

Guzzini, S. (2000) 'A Reconstruction of Constructivism in International Relations', *European Journal of International Relations* 6(2): 147–82.

Guzzini, S. (2001) 'The Significance and Roles of Teaching Theory in International Relations', *Journal of International Relations and Development* 4(2): 98–117.

Hall, C.M. (1994) *The Politics of Tourism*. Chichester: John Wiley.

Hall, C.M. (2004) 'Reflexivity and Tourism Research: Situating Myself and/with Others', in J. Phillimore and L. Goodson (eds), *Qualitative Research in Tourism: Ontologies, Epistemologies and Methodologies*. London: Routledge.

Hall, C.M. (2005) 'Systems of Surveillance and Control: Commentary on "An Analysis of Institutional Contributors to Three Major Academic Tourism Journals: 1992–2001".' *Tourism Management* 26(5): 653–6.

Hall, C.M. (2007) 'Tourism, Governance and the (Mis-)location of Power', in A. Church and T. Coles (eds), *Tourism, Power and Space*. London: Routledge.

Hall, C.M. (2008) *Tourism Planning*, 2nd edn. Harlow: Pearson.

Hall, C.M. (2010a) 'Power in Tourism: Tourism in Power', in D. Macleod and J. Carrier (eds), *Tourism, Power and Culture: Anthropological Insights*. Bristol: Channel View Publications.

Hall, C.M. (2010b) 'Academic Capitalism, Academic Responsibility and Tourism Academics: Or, the Silence of the Lambs?' *Tourism Recreation Research* 35(3): in press.

Hall, C.M. (2010c) 'The life and opinions of C. Michael Hall, Gent: A Shandy or Full Beer? Volume the First', in S. Smith (ed.), *The Discovery of Tourism*. Bingley: Emerald Publishing Group.

Hall, C.M. and Jenkins, J.M. (1995) *Tourism and Public Policy*. London: Routledge.

Hall, C.M. and Jenkins, J.M. (2004) 'Tourism and public policy', in A. Lew, C.M. Hall and A.M. Williams (eds), *Companion to Tourism*. Oxford: Blackwell.

Hanson Thiem, C. and Robertson, M. (2010) 'Editorial. Behind Enemy Lines: Reflections on the Practice and Production of Oppositional Research', *Geoforum* 41: 5–6.

Heaney, T. (1996) 'Politics of Explanation: Ethical Questions in the Production of Knowledge', *The Researcher* 11(2): 27–34.

Hoffmann, J. (1988) *State, Power and Democracy: Contentious Concepts in Practical Political Theory*. New York: St. Martin's Press.

Holmes, S. (1988) 'Gag Rules or the Politics of Omission', in J. Elster and R. Slagstad (eds), *Constitutionalism and Democracy*. Cambridge: Cambridge University Press.

Hyland, J.L. (1995) *Democratic Theory: The Philosophical Foundations*. Manchester: Manchester University Press.

Kraft, M.E. and Furlong, S.R. (2007) *Public Policy: Politics, Analysis, and Alternatives*, 2nd edn. Washington, DC: CQ Press.

Lasswell, H.D. (1936) *Politics: Who Gets, What, When, How?* New York: McGraw-Hill.

Lukes, S. (1974) *Power: A Radical View*. London: Macmillan.

Lukes, S. (1986) 'Introduction', in S. Lukes (ed.), *Power*, Oxford: Basil Blackwell.

Lukes, S. (2005) *Power: A Radical View*, 2nd edn. London: Palgrave Macmillan in association with the British Sociological Association.

Macleod, D. and Carrier, J. (eds) (2010) *Tourism, Power and Culture: Anthropological Insights*. Bristol: Channel View Publications.

Millar, C. and Aiken, D. (1995) 'Conflict Resolution in Aquaculture: A Matter of Trust', in A. Boghen (ed.), *Coldwater Aquaculture in Atlantic Canada*, 2nd edn. Moncton: Canadian Institute for Research on Regional Development.

Mokken, R.J. and Stokman, F.N. (1976) 'Power and Influence as Political Phenomena', in B. Barry (ed.), *Power and Political Theory: Some European Perspectives*. London: John Wiley.

Morriss, P. (1987) *Power: A Philosophical Analysis*. Manchester: Manchester University Press.

Murphy, P. (1985) *Tourism: A Community Approach*. New York: Methuen.

Nussbaum, M.C. (2000) *Women and Human Development: The Capabilities Approach*. Cambridge: Cambridge University Press.

Oppenheim, F.E. (1981) *Political Concepts: A Reconstruction*. Oxford: Basil Blackwell.

Pal, L.A. (1992) *Public Policy Analysis: An Introduction*. Toronto: Nelson Canada.

Paasi, A. (2005) 'Globalisation, Academic Capitalism, and the Uneven Geographies of International Journal Publishing Spaces', *Environment and Planning A* 37: 769–89.

Schattsneider, E. (1960) *Semi-sovereign People: A Realist's View of Democracy in America*. New York: Holt, Rinehart and Wilson.

Slaughter, S. and Leslie, L. (1997) *Academic Capitalism: Politics, Policies and the Entrepreneurial University*. Baltimore: Johns Hopkins University.

Slaughter, S. and Leslie, L. (2001) 'Expanding and Elaborating the Concept of Academic Capitalism', *Organization* 8: 154–61.

Tehindrazanarivelo, E.D. (1997) 'Fieldwork: The Dance of Power', *Anthropology and Humanism* 22(1): 54–60.

# 4 The visible/invisible researcher

## Ethics and politically sensitive research

*Stephanie Chok*

## Introduction

A day after my first (and only) shift as a night kitchen cleaner for a five-star hotel, the skin on my right hand starts to peel. This is the direct result of cleaning with industrial strength chemicals without gloves – which I was not given; neither were the two other women I was working with. For a seven-hour night shift (11pm–6am), the wages were US$2.30 per hour (at the time of writing, the exchange rate was SGD1.00 to US$0.65; the wage in Singapore dollars was SGD3.50 per hour), of which US$6.50 was to be deducted for the contracting company's T-shirt (it was mandatory for all cleaners to wear it).

Our selection 'interview' took place at a public space in a central area of town. From the group that showed up, there appeared to be a clear gender and ethnic composition with regard to 'this sort of work'. The 'contract', which we were given about five minutes to read and sign on the spot, was two pages long and requested information like our race, contact details, identity card numbers and the occupations of our immediate family members. The contract offered no protection or benefits to the workers – it basically listed our obligations as contract workers for this cleaning company, including its right to reassign us to other duties if deemed appropriate. The salary was also lower than that advertised in the newspapers – an additional US$32.50 per week 'incentive' was for only those who could work six days a week.

From that one night of work, I not only gained information in quantitative terms (e.g. wages, contract terms, gender ratio) but was also enriched with qualitative insights on subcontracting recruitment processes and modes of interaction between supervisors and contract workers and among contract workers themselves. Experientially, the term 'invisible workers' was brought to life – dressed in our dark blue company T-shirts, black pants and black rubber boots, we navigated our way through the back entrances, kitchens and winding hallways of the large hotel as people slumbered, never once seen or greeted by a single hotel guest.

Two themes run through this chapter – visibility and invisibility. Labour relations is a controversial issue and the challenges of conducting politically sensitive research in an authoritarian state are multi-fold. Conducted in phases, my fieldwork included covert research, i.e. research in which my identity as researcher was hidden. Frustrated attempts to gain physical access prompted me to apply for a job in the industry but the actual experience revealed other dimensions of access closed off to me – namely social access (Johnson, Avenarius and Weatherford 2006: 117) and mental access (Okumus, Altinay and Roper 2007). Operating in a hierarchical society where social stratification is pronounced meant overcoming socio-cultural barriers was difficult. This was the case when I was 'studying up' power elites and equally pervasive when I was interacting with low-income workers.

My fieldwork also entailed investigative visits to determine recruitment processes for hospitality workers. This was generally low-risk but still 'deceptive' in that intentions were concealed. These interactions revealed how unethical practices have become 'normalized' within a large segment of the recruitment and private hospitality education industry. The heart of my dilemma, though, is this: How is one to be an 'ethical researcher' when investigating unethical practices? Institutional requirements for 'ethical research' place demands on me to be explicit about my research objectives and methods. This, however, presupposes strong stakeholder support for the research project to succeed.

Another aspect of 'invisibility' refers to attempts to *appear* a 'neutral observer' on controversial issues. Researching 'elites' – both business and political elites – with a low tolerance for public criticism requires some manner of strategic 'political identity management'. Yet, as Whitfield and Strauss (1998: 26) point out, industrial relations is a highly controversial area, with relations between labour and management typically adversarial. Under such charged circumstances, 'professed neutrals are often suspect' and researchers who make such claims may end up being attacked by both sides (Whitfield and Strauss 1998: 26). Complicating the issue is the reality that many industrial relations researchers are committed to one side, having worked previously for one or other parties. Therefore, 'both actual and perceived objectivity may be difficult' (Whitfield and Strauss 1998: 27).

At the final stages of my fieldwork, continued interactions with 'informants' – low-wage migrant workers in distressed situations – led to an accelerated shift into activist mode. This meant abandoning the cloak of 'neutrality' under politically charged situations as I shifted from observer/facilitator to interventionist mode. Witnessing workers' thwarted attempts to access justice led me to publish accounts of the situation, including naming and shaming the companies involved. Visibility was sought after as a tool to exert pressure, both directly and indirectly, on companies and authorities. In some ways, I abandoned a 'myth' because it was probably evident from the start where my empathies lay. Abandoning the *pretence* of political neutrality, however, no matter how poorly maintained, did lead to some negative consequences as well as rewards.

## Access to organizations: work your way in?

From their experience of researching international hotel groups, Okumus and colleagues (2007) note that gaining and maintaining access is a key issue for in-depth qualitative case studies and requires considerable time, effort and patience. With the tourism industry, 'the interdependence of different sectors . . . generally smaller scale of many operators . . . fragmentation of markets . . . [as well as] spatial separation of origins and destinations . . . make the task of facilitating and maintaining entry into its organizations more complex' (Okumus *et al.* 2007: 8). Moreover, 'organizations are dynamic and complex places and outsiders are not always welcome, particularly those asking what may be perceived as sensitive and awkward questions about firms and managerial actions' (Okumus *et al.* 2007: 9).

Academics like Grey (1999) gained access to a meat-packing plant – a rare feat – as a consultant. He also notes that previous studies in meat-packing plants similarly involved anthropologists hired as consultants as well as another anthropologist who was hired for a packing job without identifying herself as a researcher. Camacho (1996), who did an ethnographic study on hotel workers in Mexico, spent two months working in a five-star hotel in Huatulco. As she also conducted interviews with hotel upper- and middle-level management, it would appear they were aware of her research position.

However, strategies for access 'are not always appropriate for every situation and for academics at different stages in their careers' (Okumus *et al.* 2007: 8). Consultancies are generally awarded to academics with established careers and contacts. Progressive organizations may see the value in allowing acess to independent researchers but this has generally not been the case in Singapore, my field study site, where 'closed-door' approaches are preferred. Negotiating access, therefore, has been a crucial determining aspect of my fieldwork, causing frustrating delays and requiring much patience and flexibility.

Fortunately, I finally obtained approval from my university ethics committee to undertake covert research, framed as 'direct participant observation'. It was also couched as a 'complementary component' rather than the principal research method (Chok 2007: 1). Strict confidentiality was emphasized and actions to mitigate potential risks outlined. These included the imperative for the researcher to be 'alert and discreet', in terms of note-taking and interview venues (Chok 2007: 1). The main argument for direct immersion emphasized the importance of observation methods in certain fields, for example, industrial anthropology, sociology, employment relations and human resource management. As stated in my application:

These methods have been important in presenting 'worker truth' – in so doing, they have the potential to help those in vulnerable positions and yield rich insights into workplace relations in ways that would be impossible if written consent were first required.

(Bamber and Sappey 2007: para 9)

It has been pointed out that the pursuit of truth as a research objective must also include the interests of the vulnerable – in the case of suspected exploitative workplaces, it may sometimes be necessary to bypass powerful gatekeepers with vested interests in maintaining the status quo in order to present a richer and more truthful picture.

It soon became clear, however, that gaining physical access is just one aspect of participant observation. As noted by Johnson and colleagues (2006: 113), a major difficulty facing an ethnographer in the field is 'his or her status as a stranger or outsider to the social system under study'. This 'outsider's status' can severely limit access to information and 'the success or failure of a project may hinge on the ethnographer's ability to deemphasize such a status' (Johnson *et al.* 2006: 113). Other problems facing the fieldworker in a particular setting include residence patterns, production constraints, environment, geographical isolation, regional conflicts, language, social stratification, degrees of social homogeneity, government influences, need to establish working relationships with tribes or ethnic groups, intellectual property rights and the cultural groups' experience of previous scrutiny (Johnson *et al.* 2006).

In my case, I was denied access to informal banter and gossip (the 'hidden transcripts' of the workers) due to my inability to understand the ethnic language most of the workers communicated in. While most of them spoke (at least) a basic level of English, the preference to chat in their ethnic tongue meant I could gain verbal information only by asking them specific questions. Further thwarting my imperative to be an 'unobtrusive' observer was my demographic misfit. Among the other local workers, I was a bit of a curiosity by virtue of my race (Chinese), manner of speaking (English-educated) and even address (a middle-class suburb). During our coffee break, I received stares and a similar series of questions in the staff canteen: 'Chinese?'/ 'Married?'/'What you do?' [*sic*]/'Where you stay?' [*sic*]. I was also asked questions I could not answer convincingly – for example, 'Why don't you work in a factory?'; 'You're studying tourism – your English must be very good, right?'

Ironically, my clumsy efforts to 'de-emphasize' my outsider status only served to re-emphasize how class-conscious and socially stratified we were as a society. Filling in the application form entailed creative 'omissions' – I did *not* state that my highest educational qualification was an MA. When co-workers pressed me for where I lived, I 'tweaked' my address to include an adjoining suburb (which would not immediately betray my middle-class background). I was honest about my age (then 34) and admitted I was a student (not untrue) – unfortunately, this made me even more of a curiosity. When questioned further, I mentioned being in a private school doing 'tourism' (a partial truth). After a while, there seemed to be some tacit understanding that a person who does menial work for minimal pay must need the money and the questions ceased (until a new worker joined in the conversation). However, the lies created a barrier to rapport-building with other workers. Ultimately, the strain of secrecy made me nervous. I decided to discontinue until I had worked out a longer-term strategy for not just gaining access, but maintaining it. I also felt a need to consider how to 'ethically' manage personal relations during the process of covert research to avoid any sense of betrayal.

Another major concern was the 'worst possible outcome' of researching working conditions – having a worker lose their job as a result of sharing information (Barrientos 2002: 72). This is a very real and troubling dilemma. A researcher who volunteered for an overseas organization campaigning for a living wage related an incident where a service worker was dismissed after her involvement in the campaign was discovered. The organization in question was unable to compensate for this and the researcher, disillusioned, has decided not to continue a working relationship with them. Another researcher with many years of experience doing covert research believes that this is an unfortunate consequence but, nonetheless, the contribution of the dismissed worker can indirectly benefit the plight of many others. The issue, in the latter researcher's opinion, is whether the risks were properly explained and whether the interviewee was willing rather than coerced into participation. Ultimately, worker safety was the top priority and anxiety about risks was a constant companion.

## Playing detective-researcher: The ethics of investigating unethical practices

Investigating employment conditions and codes of conduct through value chain mapping in a globalized economy is 'a complex process, [involving] piecing together a wide range of information from diverse sources, and much of it informal or anecdotal' (Barrientos 2002: 61). It therefore requires 'the skills of a detective as much as a researcher' (Barrientos 2002: 61).

As my fieldwork continued, evidence was growing that unscrupulous practices in the largely unregulated and transnational recruitment industry were exacerbating vulnerabilities for migrant workers. It was also an industry notorious for its lack of transparency and whispers of links to criminal syndicates in sending countries made the prospect of investigating it particularly daunting. However, as defensiveness or denial are common responses to suggestions of unethical practices, it was important to verify that any reported violations were neither 'hearsay' nor 'isolated incidents'.

I tried to confirm anecdotal information as directly as I could by visiting stakeholders involved in recruitment, often without revealing my research interests. In such cases, the less I revealed the better. Not only were there admissions of rights violations, but also I was encouraged to either ignore employment laws or engage in unethical practices. In two instances, I was offered, without prompting, financial incentives to recruit students/workers. Generally, patterns indicate poor ethical standards in the recruitment industry and an informal 'normalization' of such practices.

There were limits, though, to how long this investigation could be sustained.

It required a somewhat different skills set (Drama 101 would have been useful), wardrobe changes and creative note-taking. Despite my commitment to uncovering 'worker truth', there were residual guilt and some nervousness at deception. On several occasions, I was greeted with mild to overt suspicion, limiting interactions. There was also concern about impacts for future researchers, as 'researchers also have obligations to those who may come after them' (Whitfield and Strauss 1998: 28). Was I, as Whitfield and Strauss (1998: 28) put it, 'fouling the collective nests' of researchers?

There was a constant tussle between almost contradictory impulses: to determine 'the truth' about accounts of unethical practices, but in as 'ethical' a way as possible. In general, interactions were kept brief and I avoided language that could be viewed as entrapment. At a later stage, I did manage to locate an 'ethical' agent who was willing to speak to me and give me an overview of the industry. It was a relief to have an open discussion and I was transparent about my interests. However, this was facilitated by the fact that we both identified ourselves as sharing similar values – a commitment to ethical recruitment practices. In instances where there is a clear values clash, transparency of motives may result in the withholding or altering of information, or even outright hostility. In one instance, I did attempt to have a conversation with an employer who was withholding the salaries of large numbers of workers and had refused to report workplace injuries. Voices were raised and the phone was hung up on me.

It may appear ironic that some level of dishonesty is required to uncover 'truth'. Yet the practical reality is that certain types of 'truth' cannot be uncovered 'truthfully'. The way an unethical recruitment agent 'markets' a worker to a potential employer will be a marked difference from how that same agent relates to an investigative reporter, researcher or enforcement officer. That is why investigative reporters often 'pretend' – they pretend to be potential customers, clients, employers or employees (see Ehrenreich 2001; Wynhausen 2005) Practical concerns, in such instances, may range from 'blowing one's cover' to personal safety and libel. Such undercover research is generally accepted as 'justifiable' for it is done in the name of wider consumer/community interest – reporters take risks to 'expose' a ruse. Are these, however, legitimate approaches for academic researchers and how do regulatory boundaries or 'codes of conduct' differ?

In 'Ten lies of ethnography: moral dilemmas in field research', Fine (1993: 289) argues that 'all trades develop a body of conceits that they wish to hide from those outside the boundaries of their domain; so it is with ethnographers'. As Fine (1993: 271) points out, 'the illusion of being more sympathetic than we are aids research but is deceptive'. Investigative research further limits informed consent – the information provided is often less than what subjects would wish to know, and what researchers recognize they should report (Fine 1993: 271).

According to Bello (2008: 438), 'to really do good research, you sometimes have to break the law'. Bello's ground-breaking underground bestseller

*Development Debacle: The World Bank in the Philippines* was based on documents he and colleagues stole from the World Bank offices in the Philippines. According to Bello (2008: 437), the World Bank was 'non-transparent. When you tried to figure out what this giant institution was up to, all you got were sanitized press releases'. In the end, Bello and some colleagues resorted to breaking into the offices, taking documents over a three-year period. The book has been credited, says Bello, for mobilizing the middle class against Marcos.

Tunnell (1998: 212), who undertook research on convicted felons, points out that 'deception, which is central to the sociology of crime, is two-pronged: it involves misleading participants and duping those with only peripheral affiliation to the research'. The 'do no harm' imperative is central, regardless of where one stands on deception, and participants' interests are paramount. Tunnell, however, comes from a position where his participants are viewed as vulnerable and requiring protection. In his view, deception of the second group, those with 'peripheral affiliation' to his research, is sometimes 'not only necessary but also laudable' (Tunnell 1998: 212). These include those 'whose positions of official power allow them to adversely affect participants, researchers, and researchers' work', such as prison guards, university administrators, bureaucrats and attorneys (Tunnell 1998: 212). The crucial element in both cases, according to Tunnell (1998: 212), is power differentials, 'and in both scenarios, participants, in the final analysis, are those most at risk and with the most to lose'.

Tunnell's case study was certainly more extreme, involving lying to attorneys involved in a death row case. What the discussion does bring up is how messy, value-laden and political research can be. Power relations between a researcher and the 'researched' always require contemplation. However, research ethics has been predominantly concerned with researchers exploiting vulnerable 'Others' (and rightly so). It is less clear how certain rules governing issues such as informed consent and transparency of motives can or should be 'bent' when power relations shift such that the researcher, in certain cases, may be the more vulnerable subject. Moreover, does the possibility of certain ends (e.g. fairer outcomes for exploited workers) justify the means? Such means could include some level of deception.

While certainly not suggesting theft or duping authorities, it remains unclear to me what practical 'ethical' strategies exist for extracting 'truthful' information from those with vested interests to keep such information hidden, particularly when they remain protected by those in positions of power. In cases where exploitation and oppression are allowed to persist due to censorship of information, a broader question should also be asked: *Whose* interests remain protected if risks are not taken to gain such information? Is it really theft when we strive to obtain evidence that should not be kept secret in the first place? In such situations, ethical considerations should strive equally for fairness and justice as balancing principles, as well as an acute awareness of uneven power relations that exist between those 'in-the-know' and those 'trying-to-know'.

## Losing focus or gaining perspective? From participant observation to political action

Doing fieldwork 'at home' led me to believe, somewhat naïvely, that there would be greater levels of control and predictability over the process. While I expected 'surprises', I was little prepared for 'fire-fighting', as I got deeper and further drawn into the battlefield.

Through a chance encounter, I got to know a number of workers who were being intimidated by unscrupulous employers and whose attempts to seek justice for salary disputes, unlawful deductions and workplace injuries were unsuccessful. I also found out they were subcontracted workers of a large casino developer building a high-profile tourism project backed by the state government. As contacts were shared informally between workers, more cases started to emerge. Soon, I was meeting workers in distress several days a week, often more. They were mostly male workers from China and could not speak English (we conversed in Mandarin). Most had not been paid in months and were living in filthy, overcrowded conditions. All of them ate poorly, some irregularly. A number were injured and denied adequate medical treatment or compensation. Delays in mediation were aggravating their distress, along with poor treatment when they sought assistance from authorities. No longer 'neutral observer', I intervened when authorities either neglected their duties or did not do enough to ensure mediation outcomes were just and fair. I updated a local non-governmental organization (NGO) on the cases and sought their assistance to apply pressure on authorities to recover wages. At some point, I ended up at the central police station in an attempt to locate two missing workers taken against their will from their dormitory.

My 'well-planned' three-month field trip was extended to four and I applied for a temporary suspension. When it became clear that the companies involved were shirking responsibilities and authorities were not moving swiftly enough to prosecute them, I decided to sharpen the tool I knew best – the pen. I wrote about the situation and publicly named the companies involved (Chok 2009). I shared information with the news media (both main-stream and alternative), which displeased the authorities. I also ended up spending a lot more time with many of the men, construction workers from various provinces in China, than I had ever imagined.

The accelerated shift into activist mode during the last phase of my field-work was less a conscious leap than a commitment to seeing justice done. Witnessing the men's daily indignities and thwarted attempts to gain justice for an extended period of time gave me invaluable insights into not just entrenched structural problems but also the socio-cultural barriers many migrant workers face in my country. Driving the persistence was a sense of loyalty and deep concern for 'informants' who had become friends, men whose names and numbers I stored on my mobile phone, whose idiosyncrasies I grew familiar with. Over time, and with each new 'adventure' – e.g. a night in the lock-up – mutual trust grew and endless waiting times allowed spaces for unexpected conversations and sharing.

The issue of getting close to participants and the impacts on our research is another 'offside' topic that should, perhaps, be discussed more openly. For Tunnell (1998: 212), 'getting close to participants means confronting, with head and heart, the myth of value-free sociology, for it was no longer possible to be simply objective toward this participant. He had become nonnegotiable.' The decision made to safeguard a participant-turned-friend was 'not based on some rational standard of scientific evaluation' but on 'emotion work'. For Tunnell (1998: 212), protecting his friend from those in positions of power was 'the only choice. There was no calculation, no debate. The decision was a simple one.'

As 'scholars', the relational and emotional aspects of our work are rarely emphasized. Milton (2005: 198), an anthropologist with a special interest in exploring the relationship between human emotions and environmentalism, believes 'emotions are fundamental to human life; they define its quality and motivate action.' This extends to the research experience as well: our emotional responses to our research subjects, the landscapes we explore and conditions we work under influence the dynamics of our fieldwork experience, inadvertently influencing our subsequent interpretation of it. In the last four months of my fieldwork, I experienced incredible highs and lows. There was deep frustration and despair as group after group of men were repatriated without their rightful salaries, returning home to huge debts and disappointed families. I learnt how complex the web of exploitation is, and the callousness of a development model that spares little time or resources for those gasping in the undertow. I have also been enriched and marked by the experience, in the bonds that were nurtured through shared relief and empathy, as much as I encountered sorrow.

My growing involvement also led me to reevaluate the obligations and responsibilities of researchers who confront daily injustices and require 'data' from persons in distress. Davis (2003: 147), for example, takes the view that 'when research agendas address issues of inequity, there is a responsibility to use the information in the service of social change'. Identifying herself as a 'politically engaged anthropologist', Davis (2003: 149) seeks to 'link thought, research and action' in her work, or what she terms 'pracademics' (2003: 153). This clearly situates academics as active participants in the research process and encapsulates our multiple roles and dimensions in which we are 'critics and scholars in the academic world; we work for communities, movements and operational institutions . . . and we are linked to direct action as members of a community or social movement' (Davis 2003: 153). It is an honest description that diminishes the false binary of academics as 'scholars' and activists as 'actors', and any suggestion that the two are mutually exclusive.

In terms of doing research with vulnerable populations, Brennan (2005: 45) says 'it is . . . incumbent upon researchers to explain what we do *not* do'.

Brennan conducts research with trafficked persons in the United States and explains that ex-captives tell their stories to two general groups – those in the criminal justice system (e.g. attorneys, law enforcers) and service providers (e.g. social workers, health practitioners). Researchers fall into a third group and 'must emphasize that there are no similar sets of tangible benefits to speaking with us' (Brennan 2005: 45). She recommends transparency in explaining our work as scholars and, possibly, advocates (including the different kinds of writing, duration before publication, audiences for publications) and reflection on how our writing can be used for such a politicized issue.

I read Brennan's article before I left for fieldwork and prepared a 'script' with clumsy explanations of my 'work' in Mandarin. The script was soon forgotten. In practice, the significance of my research was of little importance to men living on the fringes, desperate for justice and a hot meal. In instances where workers were generally satisfied or unwilling to make formal complaints, I left an NGO helpline card with them. When it came to workers embroiled in disputes, I broke Brennan's rule constantly. While making it clear I could not ensure outcomes would be to their expectations, I interacted with them less as researcher than as helpline volunteer, someone with an active interest in seeing their case resolved as swiftly and fairly as possible. There was no formal 'interview', semi-structured or otherwise. Direct immersion rewarded me with greater insights, both in depth and in breadth, than I had ever hoped. It needs to be noted that I had undergone helpline training with a local NGO on a previous field trip, which included information about local employment laws and places to direct workers in distress. This decision facilitated my fieldwork and allowed me to alleviate, to some degree, concerns about reciprocity between researchers and their participants. Thankfully, my supervisors were supportive of my involvement and did not see a conflict with my research objectives.

This does not mean it was unproblematic. As DeLyser (2001: 443) notes, 'when insider researchers choose topics in which they are deeply embedded in their personal lives, the entanglements can become difficult to unravel'. The overlap of roles can be strenuous, as researchers divide their time between the pursuit of longer-term academic achievements and, in most cases, the shorter-term goals of justice movements. Admittedly, life in the field was severely imbalanced and, at points, highly stressful. Physical exhaustion did mean I lagged behind in consistent organization of data and chasing up on other appointments. Being engaged in a multi-stakeholder study meant juggling various 'roles', sometimes in a single day. Towards the end, my 'visibility' as a migrant worker advocate made it difficult for me to secure interviews with political and business elites. This will no doubt influence my analysis, but I still have 'data'. In fact, every twist and turn in the fight for justice is a unit for analysis.

### Researching elites: The art of 'political identity management'

My multi-stakeholder study entailed 'studying up' industry and government elites, for political change involves contestation and it is important to understand the values of those in power. This component of my research presented a different set of challenges.

The problems associated with researching elites may include 'locating and funding travel to interview a hyper-mobile social group, gaining entrée into elite settings, modifying dress and appearance, and mastering specialized forms of knowledge in order to successfully complete interviews' (Conti and O'Neil 2007: 63). Conti, who interviewed influential 'experts' from the World Trade Organization, grappled with 'the strategic contest over authority during the research process and the feelings of despondency that resulted from being "talked down to" by informants' (Conti and O'Neil 2007: 63).

Marshall (1984: 236), in discussing her experiences of research in policy settings, warned: 'Elites, people in high positions, may keep tight control of information and access.' Moreover, bureaucrats, 'whose livelihood requires them to protect agency goals, may invoke rules that frustrate researchers'. In high-powered environments where spin, manipulation and applying pressure to meet outcomes is common, Marshall (1984: 236–7) says that a researcher 'must know what is sacred, sensitive and valued in this environment to avoid violating trust'.

It is known that researchers sometimes 'manipulate' respondents in 'harmless' ways in order to gain information – for example, through appearing more naïve (Marshall 1984), sympathetic (Fine 1993) or 'a-political' (Conti and O'Neil 2007) than one is. Conti and O'Neil (2007: 75) use the term 'political identity management' to refer to the strategy of hiding personal politics, the visibility of which could lead to an early end of an interview or else provoke a defensiveness in the respondent. By containing the perception of the interviewer as a 'threat' to the organization (in this case the World Trade Organization), Conti subtly manipulated the interviewee by distancing himself from anti-WTO protesters and couching his work as 'sociological' (rather than political) in nature. Marshall (1984) similarly dispenses with strategies to deal with reluctant and suspicious elites, some of which include strategic behavioural changes throughout different stages of the research process.

To gain physical access, I resorted to a currency readily accepted in the corporate world – cash. I paid to attend industry-run courses and forums, which allowed me access to situations where clusters of business as well as government elites 'networked' and discussed issues related to corporate social responsibility. I consider this the 'business ethnography' component of my work. Ethnographic richness comes not only from what is said or presented, but from visible omissions, bodily inflections and responses to agitation – the surprises that serve as a reward for being present. Question-and-answer sessions, as well as conversations along the buffet line, proved to be quite insightful – much more than slick PowerPoint presentations and grandiose opening speeches.

I also realized that despite my best attempts, on a student budget, to 'dress the part', there was a social system in place that I could not penetrate just by donning a collared shirt and high heels. Power relations remain marked in a generally hierarchical society. VIPs often lunched separately and both entered and left the rooms before 'normal' attendees. There was sometimes a veneer of suspicion or guardedness when I mentioned my research, which led me to formulate a variety of vague responses, depending on whom I was being introduced to. In general, there was reluctance among the business community to engage with politically sensitive issues or questions.

Generalized stereotypes were both a tool and a bane. As a 'young' female student, I could, to a certain degree, probe in the name of 'social inquiry' and feigned naïvety. Language as well as demeanour was important. There was little space for rights-based discourse in de-politicized settings and network-ing necessitated adopting 'soft terms' (e.g. 'employee relations' rather than labour rights) and a non-confrontational stance. Generally, upholding a false veneer of political neutrality was a strenuous and clumsy process, with vary-ing degrees of success. Pay-offs included some useful contacts that could be followed-up post-forum and a greater contextualizing of stakeholder values. I shared Conti's (Conti and O'Neil 2007) experience of being talked down to or otherwise dismissed, and found it necessary to take frequent breaks – both physical and mental – to maintain sufficient goodwill for the diplomacy required.

Over time, it grew increasingly difficult to divorce myself from involvement with migrant worker advocacy locally, particularly after publishing an article calling for greater corporate responsibility – and naming the errant com-panies. I did manage to secure a small number of interviews after that with industry representatives, but there was also a gaping silence and repeated refusals from others, particular government elites. Timing, clearly, is crucial. By then I had mostly completed my 'studying up' component, so was not heavily dependent on these interviews. On a more positive note, speaking up generated spaces for new modes of interaction with other stakeholders (such as civil society activists) and enlarged my research experience in unpredictable and invaluable ways. In fact, the top-down responses to agitation now form part of my analysis on the nature of political contestation.

## Conclusion

This chapter shares some of the key dilemmas generated from investigating a politically sensitive topic in a strictly controlled environment. As such, it is an attempt to examine the 'micropolitics of research' (Conti and O'Neil 2007: 66) through critical reflexivity. The ethical dilemmas of conducting research of this nature are significant but not insurmountable. Doyle (1999: 245), who conducted research on homeless women, admits the intractability of some of the issues but maintains that 'reflexive research on socially excluded groups that is aware of power relations is better than no research at all' (Doyle 1999: 245). Desmond (2004: 268), who also encountered challenges in 'researching up' an elite field, says a 'reflexive approach to fieldwork demands . . . acknowledgment of the researcher's positionality, the "experiences" of "others" and the demands of the research project itself'. It also means acknowledging that 'the knowledge produced by the research exercise cannot be understood as objective, pure or innocent' (Desmond 2004: 268).

As Hyndman (2001: 262) notes, 'Fieldwork is at once a political, personal and professional undertaking.' These are not clearly defined roles; neither do such interwoven undertakings occur within neatly defined spaces. My research journey has been one of unintended shifts – including changes in topic and case study site – and untold penalties in flight changes. Certain conditions made it possible though no less challenging. I benefited from being an 'insider' in practical ways. I had a rent-free place to live indefinitely (my parents) and as a citizen, did not have to worry about visas expiring. I was competent in Mandarin and my previous involvement with migrant worker activism allowed me a familiarity with the issues as well as access to contacts. Living at home while doing my fieldwork also meant access to support networks – friends and family were a great buffer during periods of high stress and frustration. Researchers who endure geographical as well as emotional isolation over prolonged periods will have to find ways to balance the difficulties of this sometimes lonely though rewarding period.

Other factors facilitated or inhibited my research choices. General institutional constraints govern items such as timelines and funding. I would have preferred to spend more time in the field, but the imperative to complete before funding runs out has cut this short. Fortunately, throughout the twists and turns this doctoral project has taken, I have benefited greatly from not just the intellectual stewardship but also the encouragement and trust from supervisors who believed in my work and what it is striving to achieve.

The challenge now remains for me to weave these disparate 'bits and pieces' of observations, conversations and unexpected 'adventures' into 'a coherent story with a conceptual purpose' (Friedman and McDaniel 1998: 124). It is a task that both excites and overwhelms me. Despite warning that ethnography can be 'an extremely time-consuming and high-risk way to do research', Friedman and McDaniel (1998: 125) believe it plays an important role in warding off 'collective deafness' in the workplace, where we become 'unhealthily enamored of our own theories, and overconfident that our surveys and regressions have conveyed complete and unbiased truth'.

Being honest about our collective conceits (Fine 1993) as researchers poses necessary challenges to any moral high ground we claim. There is a need for self-reflexivity and deep concern, because the problematic methodological and ethical issues contemplated and debated globally from conference rooms to coffee shops won't be amicably 'solved' by the next field trip or project. They are constant companions on our journeys as social scientists, academic or otherwise. Much like inquisitive children who ask inappropriately direct questions, they attempt to keep us honest – or, at the very least, acutely uncomfortable at the fact that we are not.

## Acknowledgments

I extend my appreciation to the Asia Research Centre, Murdoch University and the Sustainable Tourism Co-operative Research Centre (STCRC) for supporting my research. I am also indebted to the continued intellectual as well as emotional support of my supervisors, Associate Professor Jim Macbeth and Associate Professor Carol Warren.

## References

Bamber, G. and Sappey, J. (2007) 'Consenting Adults and the Path to Truth', *The Australian*, Higher Education Supplement, 21 February.

Barrientos, S. (2002) 'Mapping Codes through the Value Chain: From Researcher to Detective', in R. Jenkins, R. Pearson and G. Seyfang (eds), *Corporate Responsibility and Labour Rights: Codes of Conduct in the Global Economy*. London: Earthscan.

Bello, W. (2008) 'Why am I engaged?', *Antipode* 40(3): 436–41.

Brennan, D. (2005) 'Methodological Challenges in Research with Trafficked Persons: Tales from the Field', *International Migration* 43(1/2): 35–54.

Camacho, M.E.M. (1996) 'Dissenting Workers and Social Control: A Case Study of the Hotel Industry in Huatulco, Oaxaca', *Human Organization* 55(1): 33–40.

Chok, S. (2007) HREC Application: Attachment for Form A2, unpublished form, Murdoch University, Perth.

Chok, S. (2009) 'Mega Development Projects and Labour Supply Chains – Whose Responsibility is it?' *CSR Asia Weekly*, CSR Asia, Singapore, Online. Available HTTP: <http://theonlinecitizen.com/2009/01/mega-development-projects-and-labour-supply-chains-%E2%80%93-whose-responsibility-is-it/> (accessed 23 February 2009).

Conti, J.A. and O'Neil, M. (2007) 'Studying Power: Qualitative Methods and the Global Elite', *Qualitative Research* 7(1): 63–82.

Davis, D. (2003) 'What did you do Today?: Notes from a Politically Engaged Anthropologist', *Urban Anthropology* 32(2): 147–73.

DeLyser, D. (2001) ' "Do you really live here?" Thoughts on Insider Research', *Geographical Review* 91(1/2): 441–53.

Desmond, M. (2004) 'Methodological Challenges Posed in Studying an Elite in the Field', *Area* 36(3): 262–9.

Doyle, L. (1999) 'The Big Issue: Empowering Homeless Women Through Academic Research?', *Area* 31(3): 239–46.

Ehrenreich, B. (2001) *Nickel and Dimed: On (Not) Getting by in America*. New York: Metropolitan Books.

Fine, G.A. (1993) 'Ten lies of ethnography: Moral Dilemmas in Field Research', *Journal of Contemporary Ethnography* 22(3): 267–94.

Friedman, R.A. and McDaniel, D.C. (1988) 'In the Eye of the Beholder: Ethnography in the Study of Work', in K. Whitfield and G. Strauss (eds), *Researching the World* of Work: Strategies and Methods in Studying Industrial Relations. New York: Cornell University Press.

Grey, M.A. (1999) 'Immigrants, Migration, and Worker Turnover at the Hog Pride Pork Packing Plant', *Human Organization* 58(1): 16–27.

Hyndman, J. (2001) 'The Field as Here, and Now, not There and Then', *Geographical Review* 91(1/2): 262–72.

Johnson, J.C., Avenarius, C. and Weatherford, J. (2006) 'The Active Participant-observer: Applying Social Role Analysis to Participant Observation', *Field Methods* 18(2): 111–34.

Marshall, C. (1984) 'Elites, Bureaucrats, Ostriches, and Pussycats: Managing Research in Policy Settings', *Anthropology and Education Quarterly* 15(3): 235–51.

Milton, K. (2005) 'Emotion (or Life, the Universe, Everything)', *Australian Journal of Anthropology* 16(2): 198–211.

Okumus, F., Altinay, L. and Roper, A. (2007) 'Gaining Access for Research: Reflections from Experience', *Annals of Tourism Research* 34(1): 7–26.

Tunnell, K.D. (1998) 'Honesty, Secrecy and Deception in the Sociology of Crime – Confessions and Reflections from the Backstage', in J. Ferrell and M.S. Hamm (eds), *Ethnography at the Edge: Crime, Deviance, and Field Research*. Boston, MA: Northeastern University Press.

Whitfield, K. and Strauss G. (eds) (1998) *Researching the World of Work: Strategies and Methods in Studying Industrial Relations*. New York: Cornell University Press.

Wynhausen, E. (2005) *Dirt Cheap: Life at the Wrong End of the Job Market*. Sydney: Pan Macmillan.

# 5  Interviewing elites

## Perspectives from the medical tourism sector in India and Thailand

*Audrey Bochaton and Bertrand Lefebvre*

## Introduction

From culture, to cookery, and to eco-tourism, the holiday experience is becoming more and more diverse. Since the Asian financial crisis of 1997, medical tourism has increasingly contributed to this trend, particularly in Thailand and India. The main motivation of our project was to undertake a research study on medical tourism which has hitherto been almost exclusively approached from the point of view of media representation. Indeed, medical tourism has been widely commented on by the press, which presents the 'sea, sun, sand and surgery' (Connell 2005) phenomenon as 'the' answer for patients living in developed countries and having to deal with long consultation waiting lists, and high medical costs. At the time of undertaking the research, few articles had placed medical tourism in perspective and therefore we wanted to go a little further than the headline story that the media and the medical tourism stakeholders keep selling. Through a comparison between India and Thailand, our objective was to better assess medical tourism, its development, its impacts. Medical tourism takes place in different parts of the world today and emphasises well the globalisation in the field of healthcare. In this context, we thought that the mirroring effect between the two countries would be very effective to deepen our understanding of the phenomenon, and to bring out the main elements constituting this trend.

During our research project we had to conduct many interviews with medical professionals, marketing and operation managers of corporate hospitals, and key members of different ministries or professional organisations in India and Thailand. Following Herod (1999: 313) in his effort to define foreign elite, we can identify our interviewees as 'foreign nationals who hold positions of power within organisations such as corporations, governments'. In India and Thailand, the corporate hospitals, the professional organisations (e.g. the Confederation of Indian Industry) and the ministries of health and tourism are instrumental in the growth of medical tourism. There is a growing literature about the specificity of elite interview (e.g. Herod 1999; Sabot 1999; Welch *et al.* 2002; Desmond 2004; Smith 2006). Though not exclusive to the process, interviewing elites raises various methodological issues such as access to informers, the unbalanced power relations during the interview, and the reliability of information. Herod (1999) even considers that conducting research on foreign elites creates very specific issues of cultural positionality that do not exist in the case of study of non-foreign elites.

The objective of this chapter is to address the methodological issues we faced as French PhD students interviewing a foreign elite. How did we interact with the main actors of medical tourism both in India and Thailand? How did we deal with interviewees who are mastering the art of communication and marketing? What strategies were adopted to get the right information during the interview?

In the following sections of this chapter, we will discuss the preparation of our fieldwork and remember how it is essential before interviewing an elite's members. Then, we will present the different strategies we used to access our interviewees. We will also document the process of interviewing and the related power-relation issue. In conclusion, we would like to discuss the significance of cross-border fieldwork.

## Preparing the fieldwork

### *Approaching a global phenomenon: medical tourism*

In order for the comparison to become both useful and effective, we needed to choose some methods which could be applied in both Thailand and India. With a common framework being used in two different contexts, we aimed to discern similarities and differences in the way medical tourism has emerged in Thailand as well as in India. The first phase of our research relied heavily on secondary quantitative and qualitative sources. It involved the collection of many figures, articles, public speeches and interviews on medical tourism in the research reviews, the news magazines, the daily press and the professional magazines from both countries. We extended this work to the international and Western media. These different sources of information gave us a broad perspective on a topic which was not that familiar to us.

We quickly found out that if we talk about medical tourism generally, it takes different forms through the context. For example, India receives among its 'medical tourists' Non-Resident Indians (NRI) who live abroad and who travel for medical treatment to their 'homeland' during their holidays. In Thailand, there is no typical medical tourist but a mix of nationalities among the patients and interviewees were cautious in separating medical tourists from foreign patients. The private hospitals in India have more difficulties in drawing such a distinction. The medical tourist and the expatriate can be counted as foreigner patients, while the NRI coming for a health check-up can be counted as a local patient. As noted by Connell (2005), measuring and assessing the exact number of patients involved in medical tourism is rather tricky. How do you differentiate a patient coming for care in Thailand or India from an expatriate or a tourist who uses local health infrastructure following an illness? Similarly, how do you differentiate those who have no quality hospital system in their countries from those who are looking for cheaper treatments? The problem of the definition of a 'medical tourist' and the dissimilarities between the Thai and Indian systems of counting them meant that we had to be careful with the figures that we used and called into question the appellation of 'medical tourism' itself. The further we looked, the more we became sceptical to the stock phrase 'medical tourist', as the expression refers today to a reality which cannot be precisely measured.

We also collected and analysed in a detailed manner, the communication of the corporate hospitals involved in medical tourism. We collected brochures and visited their websites on various occasions. The concept of the brochures and the websites is similar for both countries: they are a well-thought-out mix of reassuring pictures, texts, patients' testimonials and international certifications. The ultimate purpose is to seduce the potential medical tourist into going to this particular facility in the same way as a leisure tourist would choose this or that resort from a holiday brochure. This information gave us an idea of the manner in which the patients are perceived and medical tourism is heralded. All this documentation and the information previously collected in the media was analysed in order to outline the discourses produced by the various stakeholders of medical tourism and to identify the key arguments for or against medical tourism and their variation from one country to another. We then realised that discourses on medical tourism, particularly in mass media, are coming from a limited number of sources and are controlled by certain groups and organisations.

### In defence of medical tourism

In an enlightening paper about the development of biotechnology in Ireland, Desmond wrote (2004: 267): 'During this early period the industry was embroiled in a society-wide discourse regarding its general safety and appropriateness. To counter these accusations, the sector actively attempted to discursively re-construct this image around claims of sound science and the national economic interest.' In a similar manner, medical tourism's stakeholders are producing discourses and ready-to-think ideas to justify and reassess their activity. This group of actors can be identified as an elite as they have a great control over medical tourism, from its creation to the discourses pertaining to the sector. In India, most of them are affiliated to the Healthcare branch of the Confederation of Indian Industry (CII). In Thailand they are affiliated to the Private Hospital Association (PHA). These lobbies are instrumental in the implementation of medical tourism and in the interactions with the public authorities and political sphere. In 2002 the release by the CII of a joint report with the audit agency McKinsey on the future of Indian healthcare (Confederation of Indian Industry 2002) gave them the opportunity to market the idea that medical tourism was paving the way for a profitable future for the all nation. The information on Indian healthcare is often fragmented and outdated; this report has been praised as a thorough attempt to fill such gap. It has been heavily over-quoted and is now at the base of many articles or figures on medical tourism in Indian and international media. It is on the evidence of this report that Indian central government gave more support to medical tourism and began to work with the corporate hospitals to frame and market medical tourism. In its National Health Policy 2002 (NHP-2002) paper (Government of India 2002) the government stated that: 'To capitalize on the comparative cost advantage enjoyed by domestic health facilities in the secondary and tertiary sectors, NHP-2002 strongly encourages the providing of such health services on a payment basis to service seekers from overseas.'

Interestingly, the arguments supporting medical tourism used in India and Thailand were slightly different. We noticed that Indian communication is well focused on the benefits of medical tourism for the whole nation as a means to justify this trend in their country and also to prevent criticism of the phenomenon. As one brochure of the Indraprastha Apollo Hospital of Delhi claims after the hospital received the Joint Commission International accreditation, they are: 'Carrying the Indian Flame High'. This nationalist aspect does not appear at all in Thailand. Thai communication lays more stress on the medical hub, gentleness of Thai people, the leisure infrastructure and the good time you can get after your treatment. The Thai Authority of Tourism is creating confusion, mixing medical tourism and wellness tourism (spa, traditional Thai massage, etc.) in its communication campaigns, and thus concealing the medical procedures that made the reputation of Thailand at the international level (plastic surgery, sex change, etc.).

### Who? What? How? Preparing the interview

After assimilating all this different information, it was time for us to pre-pare for interviews. We first identified three different types of interviewees: the hospital managers, the medical staff and the public authorities. We were interested in tracing the history of medical tourism, the diffusion of this concept and the network of actors involved in the birth of medical tourism. The most important thing for us was to collect their views on medical tour-ism, on the future of medical tourism, on the impact on local healthcare systems, on their marketing strategies, on the links between private and public players, on architectural design and on the way the hospital as a place is envisioned. As in any elite or organisation, the official voice, heavily repro-duced in the media, may be undermined by some clashing voices from the inside. We were therefore very much interested in collecting the views of the medical staff.

We used a semi-structured questionnaire and designed a list of all the issues we wanted to discuss. By doing so, our objective was to create a confident climate between participants and interviewers based on a discussion more than just simply asking direct questions from a ten-page questionnaire. It was regarded as the best way to adapt to the, sometimes, limited time that the interviewees could give to us; it was also a way of staying close to the interviewees' vision of medical tourism. The issues were structured according to their importance for us. We did not ask for too much detailed information on the hospital or the quality of the offer (i.e. medical equipment, staff) when time was limited, as it was available in the brochures and the annual reports that the corporate hospitals publish for their shareholders. By doing so we have been able to extract the main elements constituting medical tourism trends globally but also underline differences in the way of broaching the phenomenon.

## Accessing the elite

Through selected examples, we will present the different ways we accessed the elite constituted by the managers, the medical practitioners and the ministries' representatives.

### Thai fieldwork

We conducted fieldwork in Bangkok over a period of two weeks in June 2006. Bangkok is a common gateway for international tourists to Southeast Asia. And, as the representatives of the main private hospitals based in the city used to repeat, Bangkok is now 'the healthcare hub' for Southeast Asia: this is where all the biggest healthcare facilities, the best standards, the best skilled and trained staff in the country are concentrated. We conducted interviews in the hospital sector and in the public authorities.

We interviewed a doctor working in the International Patient building of the Bangkok Hospital (BH). Audrey previously met him for her own PhD research and arranged a meeting with him at the Bangkok Hospital. At the end of the interview we asked him how we could access and interview somebody from the marketing department. He called the marketing department and managed to arrange an appointment for us. Half an hour later, to our own surprise and without any prior appointment, we were having a long and in-depth interview with the head of the marketing department.

Audrey contacted the head of the marketing division of the Bumrungrad Hospital through email on various occasions but never got any reply from his side. Once we were together in Bangkok, we just decided to go the hospital and try to get an appointment with this person. We briefly introduced ourselves and our project at the reception office of the hospital and asked if it was possible for us to meet somebody from the marketing department. An employee asked us to wait and went to make an inquiry. She came back to us saying it was not possible for us to meet somebody from the marketing department as they were all in a meeting. We insisted, saying that we were ready to wait or to come back later. We reminded her that Audrey had tried to contact the head of the marketing division on many occasions without receiving any reply. We told her that Bertrand was coming directly from India. We also pointed out that we already had an interview with their opposite number from the Bangkok Hospital. The employee went again with all this new information to check with the marketing division. Surprisingly, she came back to us with a cheerful demeanour, saying the head of the marketing departmentwas ready to meet us at the end of the meeting.

### Indian fieldwork

The interviews in Delhi, conducted by Bertrand only, were slightly different. The choice of Delhi was well justified given other than practical advantages. With its international airport, a mushrooming corporate hospital sector (Apollo, Max, Fortis), and the rather good level of infrastructure compared to the rest of India, Delhi is a 'hot spot' for medical tourism in the country.

In the case of this research on medical tourism he mostly interviewed contacts he had already met on previous occasions for his own PhD research. Since 2004, Bertrand has been conducting PhD research on the corporate hospitals in India. When he started, some Indian scholars were pessimistic about his chances to get information and interviews with marketing and operations managers from the corporate hospitals of Delhi.

Apparently, an MPhil student from the Jawaharlal Nehru University had tried to work with Apollo Hospitals for six months, until she realised it was not possible due to their lack of cooperation. He faced the same kind of difficulties during his first fieldwork period. It took a long time to get an appointment in hospitals or at the Confederation of Indian Industry. Some people simply did not want to bother with a junior student in geography ('Why are you studying the hospital sector? Geographers should study relief and landscape', as one person said to him once on the phone) coming from an unknown university and struggling while speaking English. He shared these difficulties with one of the heads of the Economic Mission of the French Embassy, who kindly prepared a letter of introduction for him, requesting the interviewees to be kind enough to cooperate as Bertrand was supposedly preparing a report on the corporate hospitals for the Economic Mission. Thanks to this letter and this faked identity, people were suddenly keener on taking some of their precious time to answer to his questions; it gave more credibility to his study. With this experience in mind, he is now emphasising his affiliation not to his research centre in India, which is a division of the French Embassy, nor his remote French university, but simply to the French Embassy in India to gain an easier access to any new contact he wants to meet.

### Is accessing the elite so difficult?

With regard to these experiences, it seems difficult to assess which method is better than another. From being introduced by an insider to the use of a letter of introduction, there are various possibilities to access the interviewees. We can thus consider two important issues out of our own limited experiences.

As Desmond (2004) notes, the question of time to access elite members is extremely important. Medical tourism is actually a booming sector and the managers are ready to open their doors to herald the story of their success. As the marketing manager of the Bumrungrad Hospital told us, we were not the first students to visit him. His hospital is actually receiving a great amount of interest from the media (e.g. CBS 60 minutes). We have been able to access, sometimes very easily, some top managers because we are now at a significant moment for medical tourism. It is no longer a marginal phenomenon, be it by the number of patients involved or by the potential impact on the local healthcare sector. The use of marketing and branding is indeed a double-edged sword; While Bumrungrad Hospital or Apollo Hospitals position their brand at the international level in order to attract more international patients, it also positions them as potential targets for public campaigns against medical tourism. There is an urgent need for the actors of this sector to legitimate their activity in face of local and international public opinion. In an international activity like medical tourism, researchers, even juniors, can also be used to herald the success of medical tourism and disseminate the information abroad. For example, Audrey was in contact with a TV journalist preparing reportage on medical tourism in Thailand. In 2005, Bertrand was interviewed for a French travel magazine (*Match du Monde*) on medical tourism in India. It is somehow flattering for the managers to receive some interest from abroad.

Another important issue was our positionality. We sometimes manipulated our identity to gain easier access to the interviewees. For example, we never insisted too much on the fact we were both geographers, in order to avoid the confusion and the reservation that goes with the typical question: 'Why are geographers studying medical tourism?' In the case of Bertrand, we can see how his status improved drastically in the eyes of his potential interviewees, thanks to the French Embassy's label. The researcher's position is defined by not only what he or she is (e.g. a white, French, male/female researcher in geography) but also what he or she represents in the eyes of the interviewees. This position evolves with time and there is space for revealing more of your identity later. Being friendly with your contacts can become beneficial in the long term; the interview is a defining moment in the evolution of your identity.

## The moment of the interview

### Foreigners, junior researchers . . . the different faces of the interviewers

Being a foreigner was certainly of great help to conduct our interviews. A foreigner is probably perceived as being less threatening than the local researcher by any elite. At the local level medical tourism raises some controversy with respect to the increasing inequality in term of access to healthcare. A foreign researcher is not here to stay. Because we travelled such a long way, coming from abroad, the foreign researcher is often welcomed by the interviewee with a lot of curiosity: 'How long have you been in Thailand?' 'Do you like Indian food?' 'My daughter is going to study in France.' This empathy helped on many occasions to engage the interviewee in a positive and warm atmosphere. On certain occasions, particularly with Western managers, we also faced a rather cold welcome, probably because there was a sense of disappointment at the sight of two junior scholars. We could feel from the start that the interview would require a lot of patience and humility on our side because our interviewee was making us understand that he was busy and was doing us a favour by receiving us.

One, clear advantage of being a foreigner and a junior scholar is that you are allowed to ask stupid questions. You are not aware of the local situation or all the details. You can genuinely ask challenging questions or point out some contradictions in the discourse but without too much damage because, in the end, 'I did not know'. Our experience was rather similar to what Sabot (1999: 334) describes when writing about the foreign researcher: 'S/he is also able to circumnavigate cultural taboos whereas the local researcher is tied by his/her own culture. In effect, the reception given to foreign researchers becomes a sort of public relations exercise at an international level; thus the foreigner researcher is allowed to ask almost anything.'

### Who is controlling the interview?

During an interview the power balance between the interviewee and the interviewers is evolving. This issue is very important while interviewing an elite group because elites have a strong sense of their own importance (Richards 1996). In our case we were interviewing marketing directors and operations managers who are trained for this type of exercise. During our interviews in both countries, the message delivered was that medical tourism is positive for the country, its economy and its healthcare system. Whoever is doubtful of this positive impact is 'an outsider who has misconceptions on what is really medical tourism', as one of the interviewees explained to us. It was important for the managers of the corporate hospitals we interviewed to deliver the proper message, to emphasise certain points and to legitimise their opinion. As the marketing director of Bumrungrad Hospital put it: 'Regarding Medical Tourism, I am THE source.' It gives them more power over the interviewer, who always has to be extremely careful if he or she wants some rewarding information. We had our own agenda for the interview, but so had our interviewees.

In face of such specialists, it was sometimes difficult for us to keep control over the interview. Some interviews were somehow turning into a public relations operation. Probably because we were junior researchers, some of the interviewees even took a paternalistic attitude, trying to advise us on what we

should write and think or what part of their report was 'particularly important to understand our activity', and that all the information we needed 'is in
the report'. Because we prepared our interviews well beforehand, studying the
marketing discourses, we were able during the interview to separate original
information from communication material. Although we remained extremely
humble during every interview, we also tried to make our interviewees
understand that we were not that new to the field of healthcare.

Being together during our fieldwork in Bangkok was indeed of great help
to gain more information from our interviewees. If one forgot to ask a question, the other could carry on the interview. Facing the same answer, we could
have a different interpretation and thus push the interview in different directions. During this fieldwork, Audrey was familiar with the Thai healthcare
system and affiliated to a Thai university, while Bertrand, coming straight
from India, was a complete alien to the local context; we had different levels
of foreignness to the situation. We experienced what Herod (1999) describes as
different degrees of 'outsiderness'. The interviews were ultimately very rich.
Doing her PhD between Laos and Thailand, Audrey was very much aware of
the local context, while coming from India, without any prior knowledge
about the local trends, Bertrand was asking very naïve questions. This strange
combination was probably confusing for the interviewees and thus helped us
to regain more control over the interview.

## Of decentring and reciprocity

Because we felt our position during the interview was fragile, we tried to
broaden the perspective of the interview. Instead of addressing certain sensitive issues too directly, we used such formulas as 'People are saying that . . .'
'We read on your website that . . . can you tell us more?' or 'The X hospital is
doing that. What about you in Y hospital?' That way we gained information
on not only certain sensitive issues (or those we perceived as sensitive) but
also their perception of their competitors in medical tourism. While in
Bangkok, the general atmosphere at least in conversations was more of 'The
medical tourism cake is big enough to be shared' or 'Their hospital is very
different from ours. They are working their ways, we are working ours',
whereas in Delhi we could feel a strong sense of concurrence from every side:
'We will always remain first because we invented everything in the field of
hospital care in India. They are just followers and had previously nothing to
do with this sector. They are just considering health as a business'; or 'In this
hospital, they are talking too much about medical tourism. What about the
Indian patients? They are my real concern.'

An interesting aspect from our fieldwork in Bangkok was the use of India
as a decentring point: 'In India, they are doing . . .' or 'It is the same in India'.
It was again a way to avoid blunt questions on the use and misuse of marketing, for example. By relating some information collected previously in India
or about the Indian experience, we have been able to build a confident

exchange. Bertrand explained to some of our interviewees what the situation was in the Indian hospital sector. The interview became then more like an exchange of information. The reciprocity of information, the exchange of opinion, was of great help in building confidence among the interviewees. As the interviews were going on, the interviewees in Thailand were becoming franker, even sometimes very straightforward, the charitable activity being merely cosmetic and a tool for communication, as has been clearly explained to us. There was the same frankness regarding the surprising lack of cooperation between private players and the public authorities in Thailand. Similarly in India, interviewees were very keen on learning something about European or French healthcare. They were very curious about the French or other European health systems and were asking precise questions on the insurance systems, the public–private partnership or the potential for India to attract medical tourists. It was not unusual that an interview supposed, at the start, to last only fifteen minutes in fact lasted more than an hour.

## Conclusion

We approach medical tourism from different points of view, dealing with mainly private actors in the hospitals and some important public actors in both countries. As it is a first step in the running of this study, we tried to focus the approach on the way the medical tourism phenomenon was being established in both countries, the political aspects of the trend, and the levels of implications of different actors. But during this first stage, we did not have the chance or the time to examine the point of view of the medical tourists themselves; how do they perceive the treatment and the global experience in these 'Five-Star Hospitals'? What about their satisfaction? Of course, some of these patients' comments are available in the media, hospital websites or brochures but they are embedded in the discourse built on medical tourism as the 'perfect answer' today in the field of healthcare. It will be very necessary to interview the medical tourists in order to balance the discourse from the main actors and to get a less 'polished' vision of medical tourism.

The use of a comparative study allowed us to go beyond a general description of the medical tourism trend and put the phenomenon into better perspective. The comparison between India and Thailand sheds light, for example, on the misconceptions of the 'Thai model' as it is perceived and explained by the Indian medical tourism stakeholders. Thailand is seen as the country ahead of the rest regarding the various aspects of medical tourism (marketing strategy, infrastructure, management of the medical staff). In India, during the professional summits on medical tourism or in the interviews given to the media, Thailand is praised as the model to follow and to beat. What is particularly stressed is the need for strong joint action between public authorities and private actors to market medical tourism abroad and to develop this activity (e.g. Express Healthcare Management 2005). The interviews in Thailand have qualified this vision as idealistic. The managers we met at the Bangkok Hospital (BH) and Bumrungrad Hospital have both stressed that the connections with Thai public authorities were very recent and still very weak. They both agreed that on this point Thailand was lagging behind Singapore and even India. Indian stakeholders of medical tourism seem to use Thailand as an idealistic model to pressure Indian public authorities to get more support. During the 2004 Health Summit organised by the Confederation of Indian Industry, the managers of the main corporate hospitals were requesting the central government to create a medical visa, as in Thailand. At the next Health Summit in 2005, the same managers were proud to announce that the medical visa had been launched a couple of months previously. It seems also that constantly referring to the successful medical tourism in Thailand is a good means to try and influence public opinion, justify the development of this trend in India and prevent possible criticism. Comparison, and the necessary multi-sited fieldwork we conducted, gave us some interesting information on medical tourism. It also showed us how a global phenomenon is embedded in local societies and how certain elites are manipulating facts and discourses in their own interest.

## References

Confederation of Indian Industry (2002) *Health Care in India: The Road Ahead*, A report by CII-McKinsey and Company, October. New Delhi: Confederation of Indian Industry.

Connell, J. (2005) 'Medical tourism: Sea, Sun, Sand and . . . Surgery', *Tourism Management* 27(6), 1093–100.

Desmond, M. (2004) 'Methodological Challenges Posed in Studying an Elite in the Field', *Area* 36(3): 262–9.

Express Healthcare Management (2005) 'Integrated Approach by All Stakeholders Needed for Developing Medical Tourism,' *Express Healthcare Management* 1–15 February. Online. Available HTTP: <http://www.expresshealthcaremgmt.com/20050215/interview01.shtml> (accessed 31 December 2009).

Government of India (GOI) (2002) *National Health Policy – 2002*, New Delhi: Government of India. Online. Available HTTP: <http://mohfw.nic.in/np2002.htm> (accessed 20 April 2006).

Herod, A. (1999) 'Reflections on Interviewing Foreign Elites: Praxis, Positionality, Validity, and the Cult of the Insider', *Geoforum* 30(4): 313–27.

Richards, D. (1996) 'Elite Interviewing: Approaches and Pitfalls', *Politics*, 16(3): 199–204.

Sabot, E.C. (1999) 'Dr Jekyll, Mr H(i)de: The Contrasting Face of Elites at Interview', *Geoforum* 30(4): 329–35.

Smith, K.E. (2006) 'Problematising Power Relations in "Elite" Interviews', *Geoforum* 37(4): 643–53.

Welch, C., Marschan-Piekkari, R., Penttinen, H. and Tahvanainen, M. (2002) 'Corporate Elites as Informants in Qualitative International Business Research', *International Business Review* 11(5): 611–28.

# Part II

# Positionality

## Researcher position in the field– practicalities, perils and pitfalls

Positionality is a major theme in qualitative fieldwork (e.g. England 1994; Rose 1997; Mohammad 2001; Valentin 2002; Humberstone 2004; Hopkins 2007) and is also a key concern for many researchers undertaking their graduate studies and/or dealing with sensitive research issues. The collection of chapters in this section brings a variety of perspectives on single and multiple positionalities in relation to dimensions such as gender, insiderness/ outsiderness, religion, and various forms of risk.

Ethnography has become a flexible research approach which allows for adjustments of research projects in light of experiences made and knowledge gained by the researcher in the field. Chapter 6 by Leopold discusses ethnography as an applied research framework for community tourism, with an emphasis on dilemmas and problems encountered in the community of Koh Phi Phi, Thailand, which was heavily damaged by the Indian Ocean tsunami in December 2004, and their influence on the development of research. To illustrate this, particular attention is given to four methodological challenges encountered during the researcher's time in the island community: the time duration spent in the community of Koh Phi Phi, Thailand; the exploration of existing power structures within the community; community attachment and ethical research concerns. The author argues that the key strength of ethnographic research is its assimilation with reflexivity as it offers the possibility to position and acknowledge the power of the researcher over the project design. Ethnographic research conducted in the community provided insights into the complex stakeholder interaction and their roles and influences on the reconstruction of the community, while reflexivity guided the author's ontological and epistemological development during the study. Thus, the author draws on her own reflexive and ethnographic research in the tourism community of Koh Phi Phi and elaborates on personal paradigms to illustrate the possibilities of the dual approaches.

Chapter 7 by Yamagishi provides a highly personal narrative of reflexity and relationality with reference to her fieldwork that investigated the growth and nature of the Japanese 'host club' industry where young heterosexual men provide 'companionship' to women, who are predominantly sex workers. While many of the chapters covered in this book focus on international tourism phenomena, her topic deals with a unique form of Japanese domestic tourism – the sex industry. Adult entertainment activities, including a host club, have been conceptualised as a site of 'leisure', providing clients with a liminal space to temporarily escape from their mundane routines (Frank 2003; Ryan and Martin 2001; Takeyama 2005; Yamagishi 2006). It is within this context that she discusses methodological issues arising out of her fieldwork held in Kabukichō – the largest red-light district in Japan – from July 2004 to June 2005.

The question of departure for discussion in her chapter is asked by many undertaking fieldwork: Where does a researcher's private life and emotions lie during the course of the fieldwork? In order to have objectively sound research, do they, or should they, exist independently outside of the research without interfering in it? Although discussion of the reflexive methodology in qualitative research often focuses on relational aspects between the researcher and his other subjects, this chapter demonstrates how our very personal relationships, though seemingly unrelated to research, can impact on the way our fieldwork is shaped, particularly in studies that bear sensitive issues and risky environments. This chapter suggests that having a critical recognition is important to a wider range of relational aspects, including one's emotions, in the production of knowledge and when teaching qualitative research courses.

In Chapter 8 Wan Hassan provides insights into the positionalities of a female Muslim researcher working on halal food issues in a primarily non-Muslim country. Her New Zealand research provides a fascinating insight into some of the research practices that can be adopted to manage religious and cultural relations between the researcher and informants as well as the manner in which 'hidden' populations may need to be approached. The success of the approach highlights the value for carefully planned research practices and the development of appropriate fieldwork practices so as to maximise information returns.

A key issue for many researchers engaging with respondents in the field is that of insider versus outsider perspectives. Tantow recounts some of these issues in Chapter 9 when he reflects on his experiences in undertaking doctoral research in heritage tourism in Singapore. Tantow brings two major issues to the reader. First, he argues that 'objective outsideness' is a valid approach when selecting specific field sites. While absolute neutrality might be illusionary, a non-biased selection and a first round of observation of these sites can clarify whether they demonstrate the research problem well. In contrast, a selection which is openly based on personal ties can in some cases be distorting if the subjective inclination towards a particular place supersedes its actual suitability as a selection criterion. Second, researchers who lack any kind of initial insider connection to the researched could be discouraged from engaging in ethnographic research at the start. According to Tantow, self-reflection in feminist literature describes respective situations in which academics withdraw from research not because of harmful implications to the researched, but because of a subtle feeling of being not 'close enough' to them to undertake ethnographic fieldwork. Instead, academics would retreat to textual research where their 'outsideness' would matter less, and potential valid insights would never been gained. He therefore argues that although prior personal ties and connections can be helpful, they should not serve as preclusion from engagement in fieldwork for other 'outside' researchers. The latter's initial outsider perspective is complementary to those of the local researcher, not superfluous. Thus, he suggests that inviting outsiders in to undertake research is important for gaining fresh perspectives.

In Chapter 10 Allan takes issues of positionality even further by noting the multiple and shifting relationships that occur through undertaking ethnography over time. As she suggests at the outset of her chapter, ethnographic method involves the researcher 'participating, overtly or covertly, in people's everyday lives for an extended period of time, watching what happens, listening to what is said [and] asking questions' (Hammersley and Atkinson 1995: 1), in relation to the issues that are the focus of the research. As such, personhood is one of the most important methodological 'tools' of anthropologists. As with Tantow in Chapter 9, Allan notes that in her ethnographic fieldwork on ethnic tourism in Tai villages in Vietnam she felt torn between insider and outsider. However, she also notes that she was embedded within a web of relationships, with the multiple identities she experienced often being ambiguous, overlapping and shifting at different times with various people (see Kahn 2003). Nevertheless, being an 'in-between' person also had its benefits and challenges, reminding her that she could not take things for granted. Her identities as researcher, tourist, Tay, friend, villager, family member, and as a fellow traveller (with tourists), all provided different and contradictory outcomes and enabled her to straddle both insider and outsider viewpoints.

In Chapter 11 Bensemann uses a study of tourism copreneurship in rural New Zealand to develop a broader discussion of the competing problems which exist in fieldwork in tourism. The first part of the chapter provides a brief overview of the interpretivist approach and its validity for this type of research. The importance of reflexivity is raised and the relevant significance of situating herself as researcher is presented because critical reflexivity or consideration of the researcher as a research instrument is an important principle of tourism fieldwork, which inevitably involves talking with: 'real' people. The research is contextualising within a feminist approach as this is regarded as providing a pathway to understanding the lived experiences of others. Significantly, the broader philosophical issues of the research are seen as providing a secure base on which to develop different methodological approaches which provide insights into different dimensions of copreneurship. The quantitative research dimension of the study provided information about descriptions of the owners and the businesses, and what happens within the business (the reality of *who does what*?), while the qualitative part of the research offered insights into women's experiences of this – not *what happens, but how it is experienced*. The interview part of the research meant that the gendered nature of work in and on the business became real and expressed. Exploring both 'realities' of copreneurship within rural tourism therefore ended up showing that any perception of copreneurship as a tool for enabling women to become freed from traditional gender roles may not equal the reality.

## Suggested further reading

Alvesson, M. and Sköldberg, K. (2000) *Reflexive Methodology: New Vistas for Qualitative Research*. London: Sage.
An influential book with respect to reflexivity in qualitative research.

Denzin, N.K. and Lincoln, Y.S. (2005) *The Sage Handbook of Qualitative Research*. Thousand Oaks: Sage Publications.
An excellent sourcebook for qualitative research throughout the social sciences.

Faugier, J. (1997) 'Sampling hard to reach populations', *Journal of Advanced Nursing* 26(4): 790–7.
This article, which reviews literature on snowball sampling and link-tracing methodologies, explores the advantages and limitations of snowball sampling. It is recommended because of the scarcity of literature discussing the difficulties of fieldwork or problems of data sampling in the study of hidden populations. Even accepted authoritative textbooks on research methods seldom devote more than a paragraph to sampling issues in unknown populations, making Faugier's article a useful source.

Feldman, M.S., Bell, J. and Berger, M.T. (2003) *Gaining Access: A Practical and Theoretical Guide for Qualitative Researchers*. New York: Altamira Press.
An extremely useful book for those considering issues of access to desired informants and populations.

Gardner, K. (1999) 'Location and relocation: Home, "the Field" and Anthropological Ethics (Sylhet, Bangladesh)', in C.W. Watson (ed.), *Being There: Fieldwork in Anthropology*. London: Pluto Press.
A very good reflective chapter on the issues associated with being 'home' and 'away' and the personal challenges it brings as well as the relational concerns it can create. The book as a whole also provides a number of insights into fieldwork practice, processes and adaptation.

Hall, C. M. (2004) 'Reflexivity and tourism research: Situating myself and/with others', in J. Phillimore and L. Goodson (eds), *Qualitative Research in Tourism: Ontologies, Epistemologies and Methodologies*. London: Routledge.
A highly personal piece on reflexivity in tourism research.

Jacobs, B.A. (2006) 'The case for dangerous fieldwork', in H. Hobbs and R. Wright (eds), *The Sage Handbook of Fieldwork*. London: Sage.
While the whole book is useful, this particular chapter is important reading both for those thinking of undertaking risky fieldwork and for their research and ethics committees who might otherwise not support such endeavours.

Kleinman S. (1991) 'Field-workers' feelings: What we Feel, Who we Are, How we Analyze', in W. Shaffir and R. Stebbins (eds), *Experiencing Fieldwork: An Inside View of Qualitative Research*. London: Sage.

Not enough has been written about the fieldwork experience. The whole book is a useful read with respect to 'being there' and dealing with returning to the 'home' environment, but this chapter is one of the best in also addressing some of the multiple roles that researchers can assume and how to be aware of them.

O'Reilly, K. (2005) *Ethnographic Methods*. London: Routledge.
An extremely solid introduction to ethnographic methods, with applications throughout the social sciences.

Phillimore, J. and Goodson, L. (eds) (2004) *Qualitative Research in Tourism – Ontologies, Epistemologies and Methodologies*. London: Routledge.
One of the most widely read advanced-level books on qualitative research in tourism, which brings together a range of different perspectives and approaches.

Roald, A.S. (2001) *Women in Islam: The Western Experience*. New York: Routledge.
In this book the author discusses her positionality as a Muslim female researcher. As a European convert to Islam, Roald positions herself as being in between the insider/outsider or research participant/researcher divide. Her book is recommended because academic studies examining the positionality of Muslim female researchers in the study of male Muslims is currently almost non-existent.

Tucker, H. (2003) *Living with Tourism*. London: Routledge.
A well-cited, detailed and reflexive fieldwork-based qualitative study on tourism in Turkey that provides a useful 'model' for similar tourism studies.

## References

England, K. (1994) 'Getting Personal: Reflexivity, Positionality and Feminist Research', *The Professional Geographer* 46: 80–9.
Frank, K. (2003) 'Just Trying to Relax: Masculinity, Masculinizing Practices, and Strip Club Regulars', *The Journal of Sex Research* 40: 61–75.
Hammersley, M. and Atkinson, P. (1995) *Ethnography: Principles in Practice*. New York: Routledge.
Hopkins, P.E. (2007) 'Positionalities and Knowledge: Negotiating Ethics in Practice', *ACME: An International E-Journal for Critical Geographies* 6: 386–94.
Humberston, B. (2004) 'Standpoint Research: Multiple Versions of Reality in Tourism Theorizing and Research', in J. Phillimore and L. Goodson (eds), *Qualitative Research in Tourism: Ontologies, Epistemologies and Methodologies*. London: Routledge.
Kahn, J.S. (2003) 'Anthropology as Cosmopolitan Practice?' *Anthropological Theory* 3(4): 403–15.
Mohammad, R. (2001) '"Insiders" and/or "Outsiders": Positionality, Theory and Praxis', in M. Limb and C. Dwyer (eds), *Qualitative Methodologies for Geographers: Issues and Debates*. London: Arnold.
Rose, G. (1997) 'Situating Knowledges: Positionality, Reflexivities and Other Tactics', *Progress in Human Geography* 21: 305–20.
Ryan, C. and Martin, A. (2001) 'Tourists and Strippers: Liminal Theater', *Annals of Tourism Research* 28(1): 140–63.
Takeyama, A. (2005) 'Commodified Romance in a Tokyo Host Club', in M. McLelland and R. Dasgupta (eds), *Genders, Transgenders and Sexualities in Japan*. London: Routledge.

Valentin, G. (2002) 'People Like Us: Negotiating Sameness and Difference in the Research Process', in P. Moss (ed.), *Feminist Geography in Practice: Research and Methods*. Oxford: Blackwell Publishers.

Yamagishi, R. (2006) 'When an Emotional Labourer serves another Emotional Worker: The Works and Leisure Activities of Male Heterosexual Sex Workers and their Clients in Japan', paper presented at Research Institute 5th Graduate Student Workshop on Question of Methodology, National University of Singapore, Singapore, September 2006.

# 6 Reflexivity and ethnography in community tourism research

*Teresa Leopold*

## Introduction

The growing recognition of the inadequate application of quantitative methods for some research problems has resulted in an increased acknowledgment and exploration of qualitative research tools of other disciplines within tourism projects (Echtner and Jamal 1997). Thus, social science research approaches are frequently applied, theorised and critically reflected upon within tourism studies and epistemology and ontology, positivism and non-positivism, self-reflectivity and self-reflexivity, ethnography and auto-ethnography are regularly discussed within a tourism context (e.g. Sandiford and Ap 1998; Echtner 1999; Galani-Moutafi 2000; Botterill 2001; Jamal and Hollinshead 2001; Palmer 2001; Rogelja 2002; Tucker 2003; Phillimore and Goodson 2004). It seems that tourism researchers are finally attempting to claim their role within the 'ongoing search for a more satisfactory epistemological solution in the social science' (Botterill 2001: 212). However, the complex nature of qualitative research complicates the development of a universal philosophical framework (if such a thing is actually necessary). Thus, while qualitative research has been increasingly applied within social science projects, its contextual standing is perceived along the lines of 'messy, experimental and multi-layered texts, cultural criticism, new approaches to the research text, new understandings of old analytic methods, and evolving research strategies' (Denzin and Lincoln 2002: xi). Nevertheless, project-specific philosophical and contextual frameworks are possible and necessary for individual qualitative projects. Generally speaking, 'qualitative research has become an umbrella term encompassing a wide range of epistemological viewpoints, research strategies, and specific techniques for understanding people in their natural contexts' (Denzin and Lincoln 2002: 3; see also Denzin 1997; Cresswell 1998; Willis and Trondman 2002; Hobbs and Wright 2006; McCall 2006).

Ethnography is often discussed as a flexible research approach of qualitative inquiry for community tourism. O'Reilly (2005: 3) reflects on different definitions of ethnography and summarises them as an 'iterative-inductive research', which develops in design through the progress of the study. Ethnography enables the application of different methods which are characterised through constant and direct contact with human agents within their daily lives through observation and communication (Willis and Trondman 2002; O'Reilly 2005). Thus, ethnographically collected research data produce 'a richly written account that respects the irreducibility of human experience' through acknowledgment of theory, the researcher and humans within the study design (O'Reilly 2005: 3). In other words, ethnography is the attempt to construct the community itself or a community-related matter as the main research component of a study. It could almost be argued that the researched (human agents) are producing and personifying the research output and thus become the 'objects of knowledge', while the researcher rather acts as the 'knowledge producer' (Butz and Besio 2004: 354). Thus, applying ethnography offers the possibility to step beyond the passive designer's position and become an active component within a cultural interpretation approach (Wolcott 1980; Sandiford and Ap 1998).

## Ethnography applied

The author's ethnographic research into tourism and natural disaster recovery of the community of Koh Phi Phi, Thailand which was undertaken as part of doctoral study is subject to the search for understanding the reconstruction of a post-disaster tourism destination. Choosing ethnography, a traditionally anthropological technique, as an appropriate research methodology was based on its nature of evolving in design during the research process to provide an 'insightful source' for the social understandings of a disaster community (Hewitt 1995: 326). Thus, community studies which are conducted over a longer period and with consideration of the wider social and environmental context are seen as being more significant for disaster processes, such as vulnerability (Hewitt 1995). As ethnography comprises research which is carried out in people's everyday setting, it acknowledges the research problem within the complex cultural and historical system in which it actually occurs (Hammersley and Atkinson 1995; Savage 2000; Willis and Trondman 2002; O'Reilly 2005). Given that the main focus of the study is the recovery period of a post-disaster community, this involved analysing the ways in which different stakeholders relate both to and with the community and place. Thus, the aim was to employ different research methods that enabled the researcher to develop an understanding of the reconstruction of the community by searching for underlying themes. It therefore follows Quarantelli (1994) and Taylor's (1978) call for the application and exploration of more sociological research techniques and methodologies within the field of disaster research. As Hammersley and Atkinson (1995: 231) illustrate: 'Ethnography often involves a combination of techniques and thus it may be possible to assess the validity of inferences between indicators and concepts by examining data relating to the same concept from participant observation, interviewing, and documents.'

Hence, methods were employed to discover patterns of thinking and to discover commonalities in what is presented and what is not presented (Billig 1992). A key feature of the research is the identification of different constructions and formations of vulnerabilities inherent in the reconstruction of a community that was affected by a natural disaster. The island of Koh Phi Phi Don, which was heavily damaged by the Indian Ocean tsunami, represents a specific social setting in which research was conducted as it was rebuilt through the interaction and involvement of different stakeholders. It is through observation and recording of the communal internal action and external influences upon the community, against the background setting within which the community is situated, that the reconstruction of a post-disaster tourist destination was examined.

Ethnography was therefore chosen as it further allows the application of different research methods (interviews, participant observation, written sources) while simultaneously living and experiencing people's daily lives and cultures (fieldwork on Koh Phi Phi). This served to develop a critical focus and gain an understanding (which ultimately is the researcher's under-standing) of the complex structures and dilemmas that underlined the phys-ical and social reconstruction of a tourist destination within its natural context: Koh Phi Phi (O'Reilly 2005). Wax (1980: 272) argues that 'the task of the fieldworker is to enter into the matrix of meanings of the researched, to participate in their system of organized activities, and to feel subject to their code of moral regulation'. In other words, ethnography and fieldwork are forms of methodological inquiries in which the researcher him- or herself becomes part of the social activities and knowledges of a researched group (Wolcott 2005), while simultaneously partly inflicting his or her opinion upon a researched subject. This is clearly applicable to this research study, as the researcher was able to take on different roles (e.g. volunteer, tourist) and carry out different activities (research, teaching, physical reconstruction work) within the community structure of Koh Phi Phi. Butz and Besio (2004: 354) argue that this process 'inevitably establishes or enacts a power relationship', which is reflected in one scenario where a local asked the researcher to approach a hotel owner regarding concerns about a newly built hotel resort. This caused a dilemma for the researcher as, on the one hand, the author wanted to feel part of the community and show her appreciation by thus pursuing the request. On the other hand, in her role as researcher the author felt it was inappropriate to take such a clear stance within communal power relations. Thus, ethical discussion within ethnographic work which centres on finding a balance between giving and taking (O'Reilly 2005) was also evident within this research. This characterises the notion of betweenness, which in turn has been identified as a constructionist metaphor within reflexivity (Cunliffe 2003; Butz and Besio 2004). Correspondingly, the research project is dominated by a self-critical attitude of the search for an adequate contribu-tion to the community. Wolcott (2005) refers to fieldwork as the dark arts, highlighting that no matter how tolerant and ethically correct a researcher acts, a certain level of superficiality, obviousness, self-serving attitude, lack of independence, deception and betrayal, and clandestine observation prevails, reflected in the scenario above.

## Methodological questions

The foundation of an ethnographic research project lies in the interactions, observations and conversations that take place between the researcher and community members (O'Reilly 2005). Multiple factors influence the interactions between both parties. With reference to a researcher, these range from the personal background (i.e. German nationality, first-time fieldworker) to the ethnographic reluctance or compliance in relation to a study (Ely *et al.* 1993). Differently, communities, e.g. Koh Phi Phi, are subject to numerous social, economic, political and cultural matters, all of which are interconnected through existing power relations and subcultures. The challenge lies in drawing together the interests of both parties in an acceptable, respectable and ethical manner (O'Reilly 2005). However, such a statement immediately brings with it questions regarding the meaning of the word 'acceptable' – acceptable for whom, to what standard? Through continuous questioning of the researcher's role and integration of positive and negative experiences, the researcher engaged with different questions of methodology (discussed as Challenges 1–4 below) that arose during the fieldwork process.

Much has been written about the conduct and dilemmas of ethnographic fieldwork from a researcher's perspective. Daniels (1983: 195) discusses issues of self-deception and self-discovery in fieldwork and placed his work within 'a developing tradition of reminiscence about the personal difficulties encountered while doing fieldwork'. Twenty years and many related articles later, researchers are still confronted with situational challenges and complexities deriving from the research process. While acknowledging these fundamental discussions, four main questions of methodology or challenges emerged as a consequence of the ethnographic studies conducted: first, the length of time spent on Koh Phi Phi; second, the challenge of recognising numerous knowledges and truths within the Koh Phi Phi community system; third, the growing attachment to the community of Koh Phi Phi and consequent challenges of acknowledging this development; and, fourth, the author's individual role in and gain from the project from an ethical perspective. Underlining these issues was the attempt to find a balanced approach between giving to and taking from the community. Researchers have struggled with these kinds of questions within the complexity of ethnographic research projects (e.g. Daniels 1983; Stacey 1988; Strauss and Corbin 1998; Smythe and Murray 2000; Waldrop 2004; Christians 2005; Holmes and Marcus 2005; Foley and Valenzuela 2005; O'Reilly 2005; Hargreaves 2006). Consequently, the following sections explore the main four challenges encountered during the conduct of the research project.

### Challenge 1: The time factor

The challenge of deciding upon an appropriate length of time spent on Koh Phi Phi was dominated by issues of, initially, homesickness and unease within a new culture, time restriction based on study commitments and the personal judgement call regarding the adequate and sufficient amount of information and knowledge gained for the scope of this research project (discussed as Challenge 2). Traditionally, ethnography is seen as a research methodology that requires time (Hicks 1984; Burns 1999; O'Reilly 2005). This is based on three main reasons: first, it gives a researcher time to settle in and become acquainted with a community's daily life; second, with time a researcher 'begins to understand the society better' (O'Reilly 2005: 12); and, third, initial unformed research strategies and design can be created (Malinowski 1922; O'Reilly 2005). In other words, the time after the immediate arrival provides an important view to a researcher within a community, while with time deeper subcultures are revealed, which shows the importance of spending longer time in a community (O'Reilly 2005). In contrast Spradley (1980: 62) argues that 'the less familiar [researchers] are with a social situation, the more [they] are able to see the tacit cultural rules at work'. Considering these opposing views it seems rather difficult to pronounce set time periods for research. This dilemma is reflected in the experience made on Koh Phi Phi. Thus, even though with time (approximately two weeks) deeper communal structures and difficulties regarding the reconstruction of the island were noted, as O'Reilly (2005) suggested, the author also agrees with Spradley (1980), as after approximately seven weeks spent on Koh Phi Phi only minor information regarding substructures and problems were noted and collected within the scope of the thesis. Thus, within the discussion on length of time it seems essential to give weight to the research context itself, the community culture as well as any preparations carried out prior to arriving in a community. As Palmer (2001: 302) argues, 'ethnography and participant observation do not have to entail long periods of time living with another community, it all depends on the nature of the research topic and the amount of detail required'. This is particularly true, as the social setting of a community is an essential component of ethnography (Palmer 2001; O'Reilly 2005). Given the nature of this research, which explores different stakeholder involvement within the reconstruction of a post-disaster community, the central focus on the community is slightly lessened. Thus, with the collection of research information in the form of observations, interviews, conversations and photographs, a period of three months emerged as adequate length.

By interviewing a range of stakeholders the attempt was made to create an all-encompassing piece of research and portrait of the community, which offered a number of different viewpoints on major issues regarding its recovery. The personal disapproval regarding an initial lack of awareness of specific local traditions and customs was quickly overcome and with time a close contact with members of the community and participants was formed.

Nevertheless, an awareness of being a Western academic carrying out research in Asia prevailed throughout the research period.

### Challenge 2: Power structures within the community

The second challenge is closely interlinked with Challenge 1, as the length of time period was based on the personal judgement call regarding the adequate and sufficient amount of information and knowledge gained for the scope of this thesis. This decision was made once information observed and gained no longer contributed to the researcher's knowledge of underlying communal substructures within the recovery process of Koh Phi Phi. Many issues have to be considered when carrying out research in a post-disaster community. Research has to acknowledge a community (itself a dynamic and developing entity), which is characterised through changes and developments in the environment and the societal structure of a region. Past disastrous events and subsequent developments especially impact upon a community's structure and subculture. Developing an understanding for a post-disaster community's subculture and vulnerability is therefore essential when carrying out research within its structure.

Different substructures were encountered during the researcher's time on Koh Phi Phi, such as governmental involvement in the community, inter-action with and influence of community internal recovery organisations and other international influences (e.g. global aid, volunteers) upon the community. The challenge was to become familiar with all relevant sub-structures that were important to the research study, which was met through observation and participation in communal activities, for example teaching at school, and volunteer work, i.e. rubbish collection. In addition, pre-fieldwork research was carried out in the form of literature, media and news reports; however, it provided only minor insights into communal structures on Koh Phi Phi. According to O'Reilly (2005) and Malinowski (1922), the initial lack of knowledge of existing subcultures and substructures within fieldwork communities can, however, be quickly overcome upon arrival in the research community but is of course dependent on the particular situation. Bearing in mind that, especially during and directly after times of disasters, the struc-tures, networks, social orders or disorders and alliances within a community or region are more strongly revealed, O'Reilly's (2005) and Malinowski's (1922) argument applied to the research setting. Conducting an ethnographic research study thus offered the possibility to adjust the research process to this situational challenge and finalise the length of time spent on Koh Phi Phi according to the research information gained.

### Challenge 3: Community attachment

The third question of methodology concerns the dilemma of growing increas-ingly attached to the community of Koh Phi Phi and finding an appropriate way of incorporating this community attachment into the research project. Conducting ethnography in a post-disaster tourism community greatly influenced the researcher's attachment to the community of Koh Phi Phi. This was based on not only relationships formed with community members but also the actual physical work carried out within the recovery phase of the community. Thus, volunteer work and living arrangements resulted in a feeling of belonging. The challenge of acknowledging this personal development was overcome through the application and adoption of reflexivity within the study. Coming back to the point made above, the longer the time spent carrying out an ethnographic research project, the more familiar a researcher becomes with the communal setting (Malinowski 1922; O'Reilly 2005). This then becomes part of the researcher's identity – consciously and subconsciously. Authors have acknowledged the immersion of qualitative researchers into a researched population, while still carrying out observations and data collection (Ely *et al.* 1993; Padgett 1998; Strauss and Corbin 1998; Waldrop 2004). Clearly, the necessity exists for researchers to acknowledge their changing role within the research process (Fine *et al.* 2000; Lincoln 2005). With regard to reflexivity, this means that collected research information and presentation should be acknowledged as in-process realities rather than fixed realities and truth claims, influenced by a researcher's knowledge and viewpoints before, during and after the research process (writing and reflection) (Punch 1998; Ceglowski 2002). However, 'many practitioners complain that participants' involvement often stops at the analysis stage' (Cornwall and Pratt 2003: 4), which would make research less community-dominant and, supposedly, more subjective. Thus, the researcher embraced reflexivity as a way of overcoming this challenge and making herself part of the research project, e.g. through the acknowledgment of different roles and subsequent influence on participants.

### Challenge 4: Personal ethical considerations

The final question which emerged during the research process relates to the interpretation of personal research ethics in light of situational challenges, which was largely overcome through the adaptation of research questions. Research preparation is essentially dually designed by the development of a research project itself and a continuous acknowledgment regarding any possible ethical concerns that might emerge. While acknowledging that ethical concerns are prevalent throughout all research projects (e.g. Smythe and Murray 2000; Hall 2004, 2006 [see also Chapter 3, this volume]; Waldrop 2004; Christians 2005), it has to be recognised that they are experienced on different levels according to a researcher's personal consideration. At the outset, the research aim was to explore feelings of safety and security within the recovery process of a post-disaster tourist destination. However, upon arrival in the community the researcher felt it was morally wrong to inquire about the disaster experience of people for two main reasons: First, shortly upon arrival a general feeling of wanting to move on was discovered based on initial observations and conversations. The tsunami had happened more than a year beforehand and, upon inquiring, an unwillingness to discuss past experiences was sensed. With regard to qualitative research with high-risk populations, Waldrop (2004: 236) argues:

> Some of the discoveries made in the field can generate moral ambiguity (Weiss, 1994) and uncertainty, but I would argue that this discomfort is an important and even desirable component of the qualitative research experience. Being uncomfortable makes us more aware and alert, stretches our thinking, and enriches our insight about the very struggles and experiences of the . . . populations we study.

Second, the researcher did not feel comfortable to research people's perceptions of safety and security issues based on the feeling of guilt aroused by causing additional pain through reference made to horrible experiences people had had in the close past. While a certain level of wariness towards exploring the perceptions of people who experienced the disaster at close hand was expected, the complete discomfort with the inquiry process was not anticipated. Various concepts of removing or suppressing personal feelings during the time of data collection have been proposed, e.g. neutralisation of own feelings (Weiss 1994) or bracketing (Ely *et al.* 1991). As mentioned above, ethnography enables the researcher to progressively develop an appropriate research design based on situational challenges and developments (O'Reilly 2005). This approach was adopted for this research as not only the time period was finalised but also the research question was adjusted upon arrival and an initial time period spent on Koh Phi Phi. Crick (1989: 25) illustrates:

> Despite all the methodological texts which inform one on how to create a 'research design' – setting out hypotheses, significant variables, and so on – and despite the necessity of setting out such matters for grant-awarding bodies, it is a matter of common knowledge that much anthropological fieldwork is a process of 'playing things by ear'.

Thus, ethnography enabled a progressive development of the project during the actual research conduct on Koh Phi Phi, which eventually resulted in the final study.

Most institutional ethical guidelines emphasise four prevalent basic tenets for directing and conducting research, all of which were considered within this project: informed consent; avoidance of deception; privacy and confidentiality; and accuracy (Christians 2005). Ethical approval was received from the institutional ethics committee regarding the outlined methodology and consent was given by all interview partners based on initial explanation provided before the interview and an information sheet which outlined the overall purpose of the study (Padgett 2004; O'Reilly 2005). Confidentiality was ensured to all participants, collected information was treated with respect for privacy and transcription kept in secure storage during and after the study process (Weiss 1994; O'Reilly 2005).

## Conclusion

This chapter discusses ethnography as qualitative method and places it within current discussion on reflexivity and ethical considerations as well as traditional anthropological problems surrounding ethnographic research studies. The appropriateness of ethnography to carry out fieldwork in tourism is discussed as it offered a flexible approach to the research progress, which allowed for adjustments of research questions and time duration to be made in light of the author's experiences and knowledge gained on the island of Koh Phi Phi. It further enabled the research project to be conducted in people's everyday setting and thus offered the researcher the possibility to gain a deeper understanding of different stakeholders that played a role in the reconstruction of the community while having to overcome four major challenges – the issue of time duration; the depth of possible knowledge; community attachment; and ethical concerns. Special attention is given to exploring the power of the researcher within the research to illustrate that 'social researchers do not and cannot observe neutrally' (O'Connell-Davidson and Layder 1994: 55).

Reflecting on the doctoral fieldwork, it can be concluded that the discussed challenges dominated and directed much of the research process. That said, the question arises whether there is an actual need to master these challenges. As much as they hinder and complicate research, they also encourage researchers to think beyond the standard paradigms of conducting research and to re-question actions carried out underneath the umbrella of doing research. Thus, on the one hand, dealing with questions of uncertainty and discomfort can be perceived as difficulties or biases resulting from the process of fieldwork, and on the other hand it can be argued that it is exactly these challenges that increase a researcher's involvement within a study and encourage critical thinking.

## References

Billig, M. (1992) *Talking of the Royal Family*. London: Routledge.

Botterill, D. (2001) 'The Epistemology of a Set of Tourism Studies', *Leisure Studies* 20: 199–214.

Burns, P. (1999) *An Introduction to Tourism and Anthropology*. London: Routledge.

Butz, D. and Besio, K. (2004) 'The Value of Autoethnography for Field Research in Transcultural Settings', *The Professional Geographer* 26(3): 350–60.

Ceglowski, D. (2002) 'Research as Relationship', in N.K. Denzin and Y.S. Lincoln (eds), *The Qualitative Inquiry Reader*. Thousand Oaks: Sage Publications.

Christians, C.G. (2005) 'Ethics and Politics in Qualitative Research', in N.K. Denzin and Y.S. Lincoln (eds), *The Sage Handbook of Qualitative Research*. Thousand Oaks: Sage Publications.

Cornwall, A. and Pratt, G. (eds) (2003) *Pathways to Participation*. London: ITDG Publishing.

Creswell, J. (1998) *Qualitative Inquiry and Research Design: Choosing Among Five Traditions*. Thousand Oaks: Sage Publications.

Crick, M. (1989) 'Shifting Identities in the Research Process: An Essay in Personal Anthropology', in J. Perry (ed.), *Doing Fieldwork: Eight Personal Accounts of Social Research*. Geelong: Deakin University Press.

Cunliffe, A.L. (2003) 'Reflexive Inquiry in Organizational Research: Questions and Possibilities', *Human Relations* 56(8): 983–1003.

Daniels, A. (1983) 'Self-deception and Self-discovery in Fieldwork', *Qualitative Sociology* 6(3): 195–214.

Denzin, N.K. (1997) *Interpretive Ethnography: Ethnographic Practices for the 21st Century*. Thousand Oaks: Sage Publications.

Denzin, N.K. and Lincoln, Y.S. (2002) *The Qualitative Inquiry Reader*. Thousand Oaks: Sage Publications.

Echtner, C.M. (1999) 'The Semiotic Paradigm: Implications for Tourism Research', *Tourism Management* 20: 47–57.

Echtner, C.M. and Jamal, T.B. (1997) 'The Disciplinary Dilemma of Tourism Studies', *Annals of Tourism Research* 24: 868–83.

Ely, M., Anzul, M., Friedman, T., Garner, D. and McCormack-Steinmetz, A. (1991) *Doing Qualitative Research: Circles within Circles*. London: The Falmer Press.

Ely, M., Anzul, M., Friedman, T., Garner, D. and McCormack-Steinmetz, A. (1993) *Doing Qualitative Research: Circles within Circles*, 2nd edn. London: The Falmer Press.

Fine, M., Weis, L., Weseen, S. and Wong, L. (2000) 'For Whom? Qualitative Research, Representations, and Social Responsibilities', in N.K. Denzin and Y.S. Lincoln (eds), *Handbook of Qualitative Research*. Thousand Oaks: Sage Publications.

Foley, D.E. and Valenzuela, A. (2005) 'Critical Ethnography: The Politics of Collaboration', in N.K. Denzin and Y.S. Lincoln (eds), *The Sage Handbook of Qualitative Research*. Thousand Oaks: Sage Publications.

Galani-Moutafi, V. (2000) 'The Self and the Other: Traveler, Ethnographer, Tourist', *Annals of Tourism Research* 27(1): 203–24.

Hall, C.M. (2004) 'Reflexivity and Tourism Research: Situating Myself and/with Others', in J. Phillimore and L. Goodson (eds), *Qualitative Research in Tourism: Ontologies, Epistemologies and Methodologies*. London: Routledge.

Hall, C.M. (2006) 'Studying the Political in Tourism: Ethics, Issues, Methods and Practicalities', Paper presented at Graduate Workshop on Researching Tourism in Asia, National University of Singapore, September.

Hammersley, M. and Atkinson, P. (1995) *Ethnography: Principles in Practice*. London: Routledge.

Hargreaves, J. (2006) 'Hidden Identities and Personal Stories: International Research about Women in Sport', in D. Hobbs and R. Wright (eds), *The Sage Handbook of Fieldwork*. London: Sage Publications.

Hewitt, K. (1995) 'Excluded Perspectives in the Social Construction of Disaster', *International Journal of Mass Emergencies and Disasters* 13(3): 317–39.

Hicks, D. (1984) 'Getting into the Field and Establishing Routines', in R. Ellen (ed.), *Ethnographic Research: A Guide to General Conduct*. London: Academic Press.

Hobbs, D. and Wright, R. (eds) (2006) *The Sage Handbook of Fieldwork*. London: Sage Publications.

Holmes, D.R. and Marcus, G.E. (2005) 'Refunctioning Ethnography: The Challenge of an Anthropology of the Contemporary', in N.K. Denzin and Y.S. Lincoln (eds), *The Sage Handbook of Qualitative Research*. Thousand Oaks: Sage Publications.

Jamal, T.B. and Hollinshead, K. (2001) 'Tourism and the Forbidden Zone: The Underserved Power of Qualitative Inquiry', *Tourism Management* 22: 63–82.

Lincoln, Y.S. (2005) 'Institutional Review Boards and Methodological Conservatism: The Challenge to and from Phenomenological Paradigms', in N.K. Denzin and Y.S. Lincoln (eds), *The Sage Handbook of Qualitative Research*. Thousand Oaks: Sage Publications.

McCall, G.J. (2006) 'The Fieldwork Tradition', in D. Hobbs and R. Wright (eds), *The Sage Handbook of Fieldwork*. London: Sage Publications.

Malinowski, B. (1922) *Argonauts of the Western Pacific: An Account of Native Enterprise and Adventure in the Archipelagoes of Melanesian New Guinea*. New York: Dutton.

O'Connell-Davidson, J. and Layder, D. (1994) *Methods, Sex and Madness*. London: Routledge.

O'Reilly, K. (2005) *Ethnographic Methods*. London: Routledge.

Padgett, D.K. (1998) *Qualitative Methods in Social Work Research: Challenges and Rewards*. Thousand Oaks: Sage Publications.

Padgett, D.K. (ed.) (2004) *The Qualitative Research Experience*. South Bank, VA: Thomson Learning.

Palmer, C. (2001) 'Ethnography: A Research Method in Practice', *International Journal of Tourism Research* 3: 301–12.

Phillimore, J. and Goodson, L. (2004) 'Progress in Qualitative Research in Tourism', in J. Phillimore and L. Goodson (eds), *Qualitative Research in Tourism: Ontologies, Epistemologies and Methodologies*. London: Routledge.

Punch, M. (1998) 'Politics and ethics in qualitative research', in N.K. Denzin and Y.S. Lincoln (eds), *The Landscape of Qualitative Research*. Thousand Oaks: Sage Publications.

Quarantelli, E.L. (1994) *Draft of a Sociological Disaster Research Agenda for the Future: Theoretical, Methodological and Empirical Issues*. University of Delaware – Disaster Research Center, Delaware, Preliminary Paper 228.

Rogelja, N. (2002) *The Ethnography of Local Tourism*. Maritime Studies. Online. Available HTTP: <http://www.marecentre.nl/mast/documents/NatasaRogelja.pdf> (accessed 20 April 2007).

Sandiford, P.J. and Ap, J. (1998) 'The Role of Ethnographic Techniques in Tourism Planning', *Journal of Travel Research* 37(1): 3–11.

Savage, J. (2000) 'Ethnography and Health Care', *British Medical Journal* 321: 1400–2.

Smythe, W.E. and Murray, M.J. (2000) 'Owning the Story: Ethical Considerations in Narrative Research', *Ethics and Behavior* 10(4): 311–36.

Spradley, J. (1980) *Participant Observation*. New York: Holt, Rinehart and Winston.

Stacey, J. (1988) 'Can there be a Feminist Ethnography?' *Women's Studies International Forum* 11(1): 21–7.

Strauss, A. and Corbin, J. (1998) *Basics of Qualitative Research: Techniques and Procedures for Developing Grounded Theory*. Thousand Oaks: Sage Publications.

Taylor, V. (1978) 'Future Directions for Study', in E.L. Quarantelli (ed.), *Disasters: Theory and Research*. Beverly Hills: Sage Publications.

Tucker, H. (2003) *Living with Tourism*. London: Routledge.

Waldrop, D. (2004) 'Ethical Issues in Qualitative Research with High-risk Populations', in D.K. Padgett (ed.), *The Qualitative Research Experience*, South Bank, VA: Thomson Learning.

Wax, M.L. (1980) 'Paradoxes of "Consent" to the Practice of Fieldwork', *Social Problems* 27(3): 272–83.

Weiss, R.S. (1994) *Learning from Strangers: The Art and Method of Qualitative Interview Studies*. New York: The Free Press.

Willis, P. and Trondman, M. (2002) 'Manifesto for Ethnography', *Cultural Studies – Critical Methodologies* 2(3): 394–402.

Wolcott, H.F. (1980) 'How to Look Like an Anthropologist Without Really Being One', *Practicing Anthropology* 3(6–7): 56–9.

Wolcott, H.F. (2005) *The Art of Fieldwork*. Walnut Creek, CA: AltaMira Press.

# 7    Doing 'risky' and 'sexy' research

## Reframing the concept of 'relational' in qualitative research

*Reiko Yamagishi*

## Introduction

My fieldwork investigated the growth and nature of the Japanese 'host club' industry where young heterosexual men provide 'companionship' to women, who are predominantly sex workers (according to my informers, 70–90 per cent of clients visiting their clubs engage in some form of adult entertainment businesses). Adult entertainment activities, including a host club, have been conceptualised as a site of 'leisure', providing clients with a liminal space to temporarily escape from their mundane routines (Ryan and Martin 2001; Frank 2003; Takeyama 2005). It is within this context that I wish to discuss methodological issues of my fieldwork undertaken in Kabukichō – the largest red-light district in Japan – from July 2004 to June 2005.

The departure of my discussion in this chapter is as follows: Where do a researcher's private life and emotions lie during the course of the fieldwork? In order to have objectively sound research, do they, or should they, exist independently outside of the research without interfering in it? Although discussion of the reflexive methodology in qualitative research often focuses on relational aspects between the researcher and his or her subjects, this chapter will demonstrate how our very personal relationships, though seemingly unrelated to research, can impact on the way our fieldwork is shaped, particularly in studies that bear on sensitive issues and risky environments. This chapter suggests the importance of having a critical recognition of a wider range of relational aspects, including one's emotions, in the production of knowledge and when teaching qualitative research courses.

## Reframing the concept of 'relational'

In contrast to the positivist's epistemology that recognizes a researcher as an 'objective' observer, the interpretivist approach understands that the construction of realities is not a value-free activity. Given the unavoidable involvement of a researcher in the entire course of research, including writing, an anti-essentialist acknowledges and highlights collaborative, or 'relational', aspects between the researcher and the participants involved in the research, as Alvesson and Sköldberg (2000: 6) state:

> The research process constitutes (re)construction of the social reality in which researchers both interact with the agents researched and, actively interpreting, continually create images for themselves and for others: images which selectively highlight certain claims as to how conditions and processes – experiences, situations, relations – can be understood, thus suppressing alternative interpretations.

It is this complex collaborative aspect of the researcher and research subjects that requires researchers to have a critical assessment of their subjective positionalities. And this is where reflexive methodology, a critical analysis of the self as the researcher, comes into play as an instrument to gain trust-worthiness in their interpretation (Behar 1993; Alvesson and Sköldberg 2000; Feldman *et al.* 2003; Gergen and Gergen 2003; Lincoln and Guba 2003; Tedlock 2003; Gray 2004). As Wasserfall (1993: 24) notes, 'reflexivity has become one of the most important tools for controlling the acquisition of knowledge, by providing a monitor over the problem of subjective influences of the researcher on her topic'.

However, what seems to be missing in the discussion is recognition of the researcher's personal emotions and other relationships within her or his pri-vate life. The predominant focus in the concept of reflexivity has been the relationship between the researcher and his or her subjects, even in some former studies dealing with sex workers that contain intensive emotional and sensitive issues (Lerum 2001; Sanders 2006). Other scholars have extended the concept of reflexivity to include the impact of readers' interpretation of the knowledge production process. Thus Gergen and Gergen (2007: 14) define 'relational' to be 'a set of relations among researcher, participants, and audiences' and state:

> In our view, the most important of these alternatives may be termed *relational*. As our methodologies become increasingly sensitive to the rela-tionship of researchers to their subjects as dialogical and co-constructive, the relationship of researchers to their audiences as interdependent, and the negotiation of meaning within any relationship as potentially ramify-ing outward into the society, individual agency ceases to be our major concern. We effectively create the reality of relational process.
>
> (2000: 603)

In both cases, the aspects of 'reflexivity' seem to be narrowly understood, implying that research is relational and dialogical mainly with the people 'directly' involved in our research. Other relationships in the researcher's private life are externalised. It is maybe because personal attributes are considered to be insignificant or irrelevant in academia, or as Kleinman and Copp (1993: 10) remind us, it is regarded as 'unprofessional' since 'the conventional image of a researcher is someone who neutralises his or her "irrelevant" identities and viewpoints while conducting research'. However, my fieldwork proved differently. This chapter elucidates how various 'other' relationships, especially private ones, actually had considerable impact on my fieldwork on host clubs in Kabukichō. Three significant relationships, (1) the researcher – the parents; (2) the researcher – the boyfriend; and (3) the researcher – the self, will be examined subsequently.

## Outlining the fieldwork

Known as a country with a patriarchal social order, Japan has conventionally accepted the practice of male consumption of women's body (Allison 1994; Aikawa and New business kenkyūkai 2005). However, since the end of the 1990s, there has been a rapid growth of a form of adult entertainment business called a 'host club' (*hosuto kurabu*). Young Japanese men known as 'hosts' provided Japanese women 'companionship', such as talking, drinking and singing karaoke inside of a host club and/or going on a date or having an intimate relationship outside of the host club upon mutual agreement.

The first host club was launched in 1965 in Tokyo, but since the mid- to late 1990s, the scale of this industry particularly in its mecca, Kabukichō, grew rapidly from fewer than 50 clubs in early 1990s to nearly 300 in 2003. The goal of my fieldwork was to examine the nature of this business and factors behind its phenomenal success from micro (motivations of hosts/clients), meso (organizational characteristics) and macro (social factors) perspectives. As such, the methods employed in this research comprised: (1) conducting interviews with hosts, host club owners, female clients, renowned owners of adult entertainment businesses and business organisations which worked with host clubs; (2) conducting participant observation in which I observed the hosts' work and clubs' events; (3) employing participant observation as I adopted the role of a client and made visits to clubs; (4) participating in internet forums about the host clubs; (5) going on a date with a host; and (6) conducting document analysis of media materials and legal documents.

## The research site

Kabukichō was selected as the research site because of its highest concentration of host clubs and the greatest attention paid by the media on hosts working in this region. Kabukichō is, however, historically known for the highest concentration of adult businesses, providing visitors 3,950 adult entertainment venues and 3,656 establishments of food and beverage (Ieda 2004). Every night, an estimated average of half a million people visit this *fuyajoo* – 'sleepless castle' (Akō 2001).

Consequently, despite the government's continuous efforts, a broad range of criminal and illegal activities are evident in Kabukichō, and yakuza (the organised syndicate) forms the backbone of such activities (Bozono 1998; Lee 2002, 2003). In 1997, the Anti-Yakuza law (*booryokudan taisakuhoo*) was greatly tightened to give authorities more power to regulate their activities (Bozono 1998). In 2002, in order to enhance the security system, the Tokyo Metropolitan Government spent 220,000,000 yen (US$ 1,900,000) to set up 50 high-powered street cameras to monitor the area for 24 hours (Ieda 2004). Additionally, in 2004, the Metropolitan Government has launched the new project entitled the 'Kabukichō Renaissance' to cleanse the district of illegal activities and build a cinematic zone instead.

The crime rate in this district has been the highest in Japan while the concentration of yakuza is the greatest. In Kabukichō, the crime rate is 40 times higher than in other areas of Tokyo. Consequently, the total number of police in Kabukichō is also 26 times higher than that in any other districts in Tokyo (Akou 2001). Foreigners are greatly visible in this zone. About 20 to 30 per cent of the population in Kabukichō are foreigners coming from over 70 different countries and the majority of them are illegal residents (Segawa 2003). Foreign prostitutes from 30 different countries work here (Kitashiba 2002). The total number of yakuza in this area is over 10,000, comprising one-ninth of the total members in Japan (Kitashiba 2002). Over 100 different yakuza groups and the recently developed Chinese and Korean mafias are in constant territorial battle (Ieda 2004). The majority of businesses in Kabukichō are associated with a yakuza group, as they have to pay *mikajime ryou* (the fee for being 'protected' by yakuza) to keep their business running (Kitashiba 2002).

These conditions made it difficult for me to do research and it was research that had potentially great risks. Some writers had been killed or hurt while doing research on people involved in Kabukichō. For example, prior to my research, a freelance writer who published an article about a business in Kabukichō was found dead in Tokyo Bay and, in June 2006, the son of a writer who wrote about yakuza was stabbed while the writer himself was also nearly killed in 1990. Although Kabukichō as I had imagined it, through social discourses and media representation, was so much more frightening than my actual experiences of it during my fieldwork, I was not risk-free. I started this research without having any connection with people in the Kabukichō's sex industry, and I in fact faced threats from one of my informants. Gaining access and determining how far I should get involved in the field thus was an extremely difficult task. And both the topic (host clubs) and the location of the research (Kabukichō) created various complex relations during my fieldwork.

## 'Occupational stigma' of the subjects in the research context

A researcher's role is, after all, 'more than just a researcher' (Kleinman and Copp 1993). We have emotions and carry on with a life beyond that of a researcher, despite our training. And a study on topics that is deemed socially deviant often puts a strain on the researcher's private life. In *Doing Research on Sensitive Topics*, Lee (1993: 9) argues:

> Where deviant groups or individuals are being studied research can become problematic for the researcher. This seems to be true in particular for researchers on human sexuality, who have not infrequently remarked on their stigmatization by colleagues, university administrators and students . . . the *'occupational stigma'* which attaches to research (or teaching) on sexual behaviour produces *personal and professional* risks.

(italics added by the author)

During my research, I had also experienced extensively both *personal and professional* 'risks' that were caused by the 'occupational stigma' of the people I was studying – the hosts. In the Japanese society, as my informants said, hosts are perceived to be 'parasites', deceiving women and extorting every single penny from them. When they are introduced in the West, hosts are often viewed as 'male *geishas*', making their living with women's financial support. Such negative occupational stigmas attached to their work affected my overall personal life during the fieldwork, such as my relationship with my Japanese friends, parents, Canadian boyfriend, and even foreign acquaintances who knew about my research. Although they were not directly involved in my fieldwork, their perceptions towards me began to significantly impact on my involvement in the research.

## The researcher – the parents: Our daughter goes to Kabukichō?!

My parents had never disagreed with any of my decisions in my life. They have always been supportive, understanding and rather liberal. They are parents who say things like, 'Oh, it's fine with us if you are a lesbian, if that is what makes you happy.' However, when I told them about my dissertation topic in May 2004, they were horrified, confused and angry. I asked them if I could stay with them during my fieldwork, but their answer was: 'Absolutely not.' Yet, after doing some research, I concluded that I would not have sufficient funds to conduct a year-long research in Tokyo – one of the most expensive cities to live in. I desperately needed to stay with my parents, whose house was within commuting distance from Kabukichō. Selfishly, I also needed them for security purposes. The majority of host club businesses were not legally run and my subjects were involved in activities occurring in Kabukichō. So I needed someone who could keep a lookout for my safety. Thus, prior to my fieldwork, I had tried negotiating with my parents many times, but they never approved of my staying with them.

There were two main reasons behind their rejection. First, it was dangerous. For the Japanese, the yakuza have always been viewed with fear, more so than any other authority. Yet the common social understanding is that as long as one does not step into their territory, they would do nothing to hurt us. Never go to Kabukichō – this is what I heard while growing up in Japan. My research, however, was concentrated in the middle of Kabukichō. My parents then had a very difficult time understanding why I had to put my life at risk, and possibly their lives too, 'for this "nonsense" research topic', as my father called it.

Secondly, they were worried about the consequential negative gossip about me in their neighbourhood. If that happened, it would become difficult for my parents to maintain the same 'harmonious' relationship with their neighbours, something which the Japanese community valued. At the time of conducting fieldwork, the host clubs opened after 1 a.m. and closed around 8 a.m. and peak business was after 3–4 a.m., when the top-ranked hosts come to work. (The Tokyo Metropolitan Government has since enacted new regulation to restrict host clubs and other adult entertainment businesses in Tokyo. As a result, host clubs stopped operating their business after legalized business hours, which are between midnight and sunrise.) Therefore, doing this research required me to take the last train from home and come back in the morning. My parents and their neighbours assume only women who are 'sex workers' would work in these hours. So I grew up hearing neighbours' gossip about such women in their community who leave at night and come back home in the early morning. They are stigmatized. I knew how hard my parents have tried to maintain peace with their neighbours. But then my research could ruin their reputation. 'You could always go back to your nest after this research, but we have to be here', my mother said.

Despite understanding their fears, without informing them, I decided to extend my stay at their house from the initial approved three months to the entire course of my fieldwork – one year. Money was an issue, but more importantly, after talking to several people, I concluded that living too close to the people I studied in Kabukichō was not so safe for my case. Thus I continued to live with my parents. However, this decision created an implicit hierarchy between us, necessitating me to modify the way I conducted research to minimise conflict with my parents. In order to continue to stay at the unwelcoming home, I varied my research time while my visits grew infrequent. Though the host clubs' business hours were between 1 a.m. and 8 a.m., hosts could still be found in Kabukichō at any time except during the early afternoon. Therefore, for some days I would leave home at 3 a.m. and be back at noon. On other days, I would leave at 9 p.m. and be back at 10 a.m. or went straight to a host club after my part-time job and then back in the morning. During other days, I would be there during the day. I also avoided being there on consecutive days so that my neighbours would not suspect my activity.

Another hidden intention of staying with them was to 'use' my parents as guardians of my safety, against their will. However, it was unsuccessful and, instead, aggravated the situation further. I was contacting people who were, according to my informants, 'the people in the world of night' (*yoruno sekai no ningen*) – the sex industry. By stating so, they distinguished themselves from 'the people in the world of day' (*hiruno sekai no ningen*) who lived and worked in the daytime and who are considered to be *katagi* (respected) citizens in society. When I started interviewing my informants, I 'casually' informed my mother about my interview schedule: who I was meeting that day, what he does, where I was meeting him and what time I would return home. Yet, a month later, my parents began to be upset because of the people I was meeting. One night, my quiet father became furious with me and said, 'After all these risks that you are taking, where is this research leading you in your career or in your future?' I had no answer. Because of such challenging fieldwork, I had my own doubts too. Since then, I have stopped telling my parents anything about my research, while they also never asked me what I was doing every day. In the following nine months, it was as if my parents were in denial, imagining that their daughter was doing something else, but not going to Kabukichō. I sensed their unspoken concern and fear, so I did everything behind their backs. I could not let them worry any more.

'*Occupational stigma*' of the people in Kabukichō was evident in my parents' reaction. They regarded this research as dangerous and socially stigmatized. Under this condition, though living with my parents was financially helpful, it constrained my involvement in the fieldwork not only physically, such as altering times and days of conducting fieldwork in Kabukichō, but also emotionally. Caring for their feelings and maintaining their social reputation became an integral part in my planning and the conducting of my research.

### The researcher – the boyfriend: 'My girlfriend is a "client" of a host'

Another significant relationship which led to tension during my fieldwork was with my Canadian ex-boyfriend, who was working in Japan. If 'danger' and 'social stigma' towards sex workers were the main concern for my parents, his was 'sex'. He thought I was having sex with a host whenever I visited a host club or interviewed my informants.

This kind of treatment was nothing new to me. Since I had decided on my research topic, my body had suddenly become a topic, being greatly sexualized. Sexualization and stigmatization of a female researcher's body, when she deals with topics relating to sexualities, has been widely reported (Alison 1991; Hart 1997; Malam 2004; Yamaga 2006; Yamagishi 2006a). In my case, this was particularly clear in my interaction with Western men, who were unable to understand that some adult entertainment businesses, in Japan at least, were geared to sell 'fantasy' or 'pseudo-romance', but not necessarily leading to sexual intercourse. Some Western men treated me as if I were a prostitute or an easy woman simply because I was involved in research on men working in the sex industry (Yamagishi 2006a). My ex-boyfriend would be one of these men.

At the beginning he seemed to be accepting. But his complaints gradually surfaced six months after I started my fieldwork. The situation escalated and he began to sound more offensive, humiliating and even abusive towards the end of our two-year relationship. He was more than just angry or jealous. What upset me the most was his demeaning sexualization of my body. And he doubted my loyalty towards him because of my 'happiness'. According to him, I was getting happier whenever I returned from visiting a host club. This was true to an extent, but for different reasons. As I was having a difficult time gaining access in my fieldwork, any kind of data I got meant a great deal to me. This satisfaction was a source of my 'happiness', something my ex-boyfriend could never understand.

The more he sexualized me, the more I contested it. I remember that over two years I kept repeating to him, 'This is just a research', 'This will end soon', 'I am not that type of person that you might think of me as'. But these words did not reassure him because, to him, his 'bias' was somewhat confirmed by my long engagement in the study of the host clubs. After six months in my fieldwork he began to say things like: 'Are you still "collecting" data?' 'When will you stop going to meet "your man"?' 'Will you ever stop your "research"?' and in the second year, the comments came to be: 'How were your men today?' and, 'Oh well, you are just going there because you love sex.' His criticism and acts of humiliation intensified and I was tired of being reassuring to one who had never seemed to be supportive or even tried to understand my situation.

Some may wonder why I continued to stay with him. The problem was that his stigmatization towards me was also evident in the reactions of my Japanese friends and co-workers where I took a part-time job. These people, though they had known me even before this research, had started describing me as 'a woman going to a host club'. They were not sexualizing my body, but they ridiculed me and were worried that I was losing myself because, to them, visiting a host club is not something expected of an educated woman. 'What is wrong with you? What happened to you, Reiko?', one of my male best friends asked me one night.

All these people seemed to forget who I used to be. I was suddenly given a new identity and forced to live with it. When many people around me reacted negatively at the same time, it became an overwhelming force. And because they were not in favour of my involvement in this research, it made me feel guilty towards my boyfriend. Several Western men, including an academic, mentioned that they could not allow their girlfriends to conduct such research. These comments made me unsure if it was my fault or his lack of understanding. Eventually, as with my parents, I stopped telling him anything about my research although I continued doing it.

Unlike the case of living with my parents, the problem with my ex-boyfriend seemed to increase my emotional attachment to my research. One day, one of my gatekeepers who knew about my struggles with my boyfriend told me that I seemed to be more emotionally involved in visiting host clubs because of my 'unhappiness'. Incidentally, hosts are said to help meet the emotional needs of women. My feeling of confusion and anger towards my ex-boyfriend began to make me appreciate what hosts could offer me, even though I was a 'researcher'. In March 2005, I wrote to my key informant, a host club owner, that I felt I finally understood why women paid so much money to visit host clubs. This was initially difficult for me to understand. When the *occupational stigma* of hosts invaded my personal sphere, a host club became like an oasis to me because there was no issue about my body, neither was there the label of me as 'a woman visiting a host club'. It was a place where I did not have to contest against an unpleasant label. During my visits, I found myself feeling refreshed and happily smiling. With their good sense of humour and skills in listening to the problems of others, the hosts helped me to forget my troublesome life, even though this was a temporary relief. This was re-energizing, and I became a researcher who personally began to enjoy visiting a host club.

Methodologically, then, the *occupational stigma* of hosts made my positionality as a researcher indistinct and ambivalent, or even problematic if 'objectivity' is discussed in the conventional term. In this fieldwork, I was a 'female' researcher who performed as a 'client' as part of my method. I incessantly travelled between a host club in Kabukichō and my 'private' sphere where my socially expected roles changed from a 'trained' female researcher to a 'good' daughter and a 'loyal' girlfriend. In this context, I struggled to isolate the boundaries that each role would have expected of me, and to separate my emotions completely. And when I failed to do so, there was a sense of being a failure as a 'professional' researcher. Despite my effort to stay 'objective', when I was sitting on a sofa in a host club, complaining about my boyfriend to the hosts, was I a researcher or a client?

These ambivalent positionalities that I experienced during the fieldwork required me to ask this question: Do subjective qualities and my feelings interfere with achieving an objective research? I found that the more I struggled to reconcile these conflicting personal vs professional positionalities, the more I became aware of and critical about the overall process of knowledge production. Furthermore, it helped me to shift my standpoint of looking at hosts from my own world to one from theirs. As mentioned above, hosts often separated themselves from 'the people in the world of daytime'. Because of the negative reactions of the people in my private life, emotionally I felt somewhat closer to the hosts than the people in the world of daytime where I supposedly belonged, although I was never considered to be a member of the world of night. This incident then enabled me to become an in-between, appreciating the social stigmas surrounding the hosts and understanding, or at least feeling, how their lives as hosts would be.

## The researcher – the self relationship: fears

Although my parents and ex-boyfriend complicated my fieldwork, the relationships with them were not the hardest to deal with. I was, in fact, my own worst enemy in the fieldwork. I was caught up with my own fears.

The Kabukichō community, which has a closed, complex, knitted hierarchical social network of power, does not welcome strangers to do research. Bodily violence in host clubs and in Kabukichō was reported widely in the media. These already provided me enough fear when starting my research but then, unfortunately during my fieldwork, the authorities began a clamp-down on host clubs in Kabukichō, continuing to tighten regulations over the following years. People within the host club industry became more suspicious of strangers. Sometimes I was mistakenly identified as a female undercover police agent by the hosts. A few people I contacted warned me not to continue this research, especially after the authorities got involved. Then, one of my informants, who wanted to use me for his personal revenge on the hosts, began to threaten my life. This particular incident was so complex and dangerous that, in the end, all these amplified 'delusional fears' caused me to nearly give up doing this research.

In such circumstances, it was evident that what I learned from seven qualitative courses I took during my postgraduate years was not so helpful after all. The training focused exclusively on 'the subjects' rather than the researcher and we learned how to care for the feelings of the former but not the latter. Ethics, safety matters and human rights of the people we study are central to the training, but that of the researchers have been neglected. Prioritizing my subjects became so engraved in me that even when my informant implied his connection with yakuza and threatened my life, with his fingers pointing to me as if killing me with a gun, what I heard myself saying to him, while feeling a chill of fear, was that 'I cannot give you my data because I am an academic. I am responsible for protecting my informers.' How about *my* safety?

One might argue that fear is more or less 'constructed' so it will be reduced once a researcher gains familiarity with the site, obtaining insider's perspectives. Some scholars even warn that a researcher 'must not include fear', particularly in dangerous fieldwork, because people can sense fear and take advantage of it (Williams *et al.* 1992). But my experiences show that it was not that simple. More importantly, can we really eliminate fears or any other emotions? Or, is it necessary? Scholars on reflexive methodology often stress that our research is based on negotiation with the subjects. But with my fieldwork experiences, I discovered that the person with whom I had to negotiate the most with was actually myself and my fears. Fear was like a creature living inside me, shaping the way this research was conducted, slowing down the process, skewing my views sometimes, and making me hesitant to get involved in the field. In this sense, my emotions regulated and played a very influential part in determining the overall landscape of my fieldwork, much as Hockey (1996) reported when discussing the emotional aspects of his research.

> The research I have described was not just an intellectual journey but also fundamentally an emotional one. Feelings were prime movers in the selection of the research initially, they were involved in the definition of its scope and the level of analysis chosen. They influenced the questions I asked and how I asked them, and they saturated the habitual interaction which is the essence of doing participant observation.
>
> (1996: 25)

Yet emotion is not all that negative. Recently scholars have contested the conventional qualitative research that hides researchers' emotions (Kleinman and Copp 1993; Dupuis 1999; Frohlick 1999; Lerum 2001; Jacobs 2006; Yamaga 2006). Lee (1993) argues that, particularly in research dealing with sexualities, concealing one's emotions and private life can be hard to achieve. Moreover, a concealment of our emotions might actually cause epistemological problems. Kleinman (1991: 184) argues: 'Managing our emotions by putting them aside neglects how "feelings become resources for understanding phenomena" and if emotions are not analysed they "will still shape the research process, but you will not know how".' Recognizing emotions is thus 'a fundamental feature of well-executed research' (Frohlick 1999: 158–9). And such subjectively engaged research does not necessarily neglect aims of 'objectivity', as Lerum (2001: 480) argues:

> In fact, without being rooted in highly subjective and emotionally engaged experiences, objective knowledge has no hope of being critical. Thus, I argue that the best objective knowledge is rooted in subjective experiences, publicly acknowledged and reflected on by authors, which are then augmented by, contrasted with, and verified against a number of analytic levels and validity checks.

## Conclusion

This chapter has reassessed the conventional concept of reflexivity and suggests drawing more attention to a wider range of relational aspects other than just the researcher–researched relationship. By doing so, it would be possible to gain more critical and richer reflexive assessments. However, exclusion of a researcher's private attributes, including emotions, does not seem to be the only epistemological issue. It also impacts on how method courses are taught. As Thomas (2004: 212) uses the analogy of 'journey' to describe the process of qualitative research, fieldwork exists in real life, being subjected to encounters full of challenges, surprises and excitements. But the researchers' wisdoms and their vulnerable strategies in their journeys often disappear in their writings, although these were what I wished to read before heading to my fieldwork. Students seem to be hardly exposed to the real-life experiences of researchers simply because those researchers are barely given a chance to write them. Then what we need to reassess might not be just the concept itself but also the institutionalization of the reflexivity, as Sanders (2006: 203) discusses:

> In my own work to date, like others, reporting the findings had been prioritized, leaving little time for reflection on the intricacies of the sexual field. However, such prioritizing is an excuse for admitting that the real barriers to critical methodological evaluation stem from the constraints of institutional expectations that favour a less subjective approach to presenting data, as well as a subtle masculine research culture where reflexivity sits uncomfortably at the margins.

## References

Aikawa, M. and New Business Kenkyūkai (2005) *Yoruno shihonshugi [Capitalism at Night]*. Tokyo: Nihonbungei-sha.

Akō, R. (2001) *Kabukichō underworld*. Tokyo: Dōhōsha.

Alison, A. (1994) *Nightwork: Sexuality, Pleasure, and Corporate Masculinity in a Tokyo Hostess Club*. Chicago: The University of Chicago Press.

Alvesson, M. and Sköldberg, K. (2000) *Reflexive Methodology: New Vistas for Qualitative Research*. London: Sage.

Behar, R. (1993) *Translated Woman*. Boston, MA: Beacon Press.

Bozono, S. (1998) 'Yakuza on the Defensive', *Japan Quarterly* 45: 79–82.

Dupuis, S.L. (1999) 'Naked Truths: Towards a Reflexive Methodology in Leisure Research', *Leisure Sciences* 21(1): 53–69.

Feldman, M.S., Bell, J. and Berger, M.T. (2003) *Gaining Access: A Practical and Theoretical Guide for Qualitative Researchers*. New York: Altamira Press.

Frank, K. (2003) 'Just trying to relax: Masculinity, Masculinizing Practices, and Strip Club Regulars', *The Journal of Sex Research* 40: 61–75.

Frohlick, S. (1999) ' "Home has Always been Hard for Me": Single mothers' narratives of identity, home, and loss,' in R. Bridgman, S. Cole and H. Howard-Bobiwash (eds), *Feminist Fields: Ethnographic Insights*. Peterborough: Broadview Press.

Gergen, M.M. and Gergen, K.J. (2003) 'Qualitative Inquiry: Generative Tensions', in N.K. Denzin and Y.S. Lincoln (eds), *Handbook of Qualitative Research*. 2nd edn. Newbury Park: Sage.

Gergen, M.M. and Gergen, K.J. (2007) 'Qualitative Inquiry: Tensions and Transformations', Kenneth J. Gergen Homepage. Online. Available HTTP: <http://www.swarthmore.edu/SocSci/kgergen1/web/printer-friendly.phtml?id=manu31> (accessed 24 January 2007).

Gray, D.E. (2004) *Doing Research in the Real World*. London: Sage.

Hart, A. (1997) *Buying and Selling Power: Anthropological Reflections on Prostitution in Spain*. Boulder, CO: Westview.

Hockey, J. (1996) 'Putting down smoke: Emotion and Engagement in Participant Observation', in K. Carter and S. Delamont (eds), *Qualitative Research: The Emotional Dimension*. Aldershot: Avebury.

Ieda, S. (2004) *Kabukichō Sinogino Hitobito [People Milling around in Kabukichō]*. Tokyo: Syufutoseikatsu-sha.

Jacobs, B.A. (2006) 'The Case for Dangerous Fieldwork', in H. Hobbs and R. Wright (eds), *The Sage Handbook of Fieldwork*. London: Sage.

Kleinman, S. (1991) 'Field-workers' Feelings: What we Feel, Who we Are, How we Analyze', in W. Shaffir and R. Stebbins (eds), *Experiencing Fieldwork: An Inside View of Qualitative Research*. London: Sage.

Kleinman, S. and Copp, M. (1993) *Emotions and Fieldwork*. Newbury Park: Sage.

Kitashiba, K. (2002) *Kabukichōga moshi 100hitono muradattara [If Kabukichō Was the Village with 100 People]. Tokyo: Long Sellers*.

Lee, R.M. (1993) *Doing Research on Sensitive Topics*. London: Sage.

Lee, X.M. (2002) *Kabukichō annainin [The guide of the sleepless town]*. Tokyo: Kadokawa.

Lee, X.M. (2003) *Kabukichō Underworld Guide*. Tokyo: Nihonbungeisha.

Lerum, K. (2001) 'Subjects of Desire: Academic Armor, Intimate Ethnography, and the Production of Critical Knowledge', *Qualitative Inquiry* 7: 466–83.

Lincoln, Y.S. and Guba, E.G. (2003) 'Paradigmatic Controversies, Contradictions, and Emerging Confluences', in N.K. Denzin and Y.S. Lincoln (eds), *The Landscape of Qualitative Research*. 2nd edn. London: Sage.

Malam, L. (2004) 'Embodiment and Sexuality in Cross-cultural Research', *Australian Geographer* 35: 177–83.

Ryan, C. and Martin, A. (2001) 'Tourist and Strippers: Liminal Theater', *Annals of Tourism Research* 28(1): 140–63.

Sanders, T. (2006) 'Researching Sex Work: Dynamics, Difficulties and Decisions', in H. Hobbs and R. Wright (eds), *The Sage Handbook of Fieldwork*. London: Sage.

Segawa, K. (2003) *Kabukichō Dream*. Tokyo: Shinchōsha.

Takeyama, A. (2005) 'Commodified Romance in a Tokyo Host Club', in M. McLelland and R. Dasgupta (eds), *Genders, Transgenders and Sexualities in Japan*. London: Routledge.

Tedlock, B. (2003) 'Ethnography and Ethnographic Representation', in N.K. Denzin and Y.S. Lincoln (eds), *Strategies of Qualitative Inquiry*. London: Sage.

Thomas, K. (2004) 'The Research Process as a Journey: From Positivist Traditions into the Realms of Qualitative Inquiry', in J. Phillimore and L. Goodson (eds.), *Qualitative Research in Tourism: Ontologies, Epistemologies and Methodologies*. London: Routledge.

Wasserfall, R. (1993) 'Reflexivity, Feminism and Difference', *Qualitative Sociology* 16: 23–41.

Williams, T., Dunlap, E., Johnson, B.D., and Hamid, A. (1992) 'Personal Safety in Dangerous Places', *Journal of Contemporary Ethnography* 21: 343–74.

Yamaga, C. (2006) 'Showing my Heart for Writing "Our" Stories: Questions of Ethnographer Self in Researching Romance, Love and Sex on Tourism', paper presented at Asia Research Institute 5th Graduate Student Workshop on Question of methodology, Singapore, September 2006.

Yamagishi, R. (2006a) 'Trying to Explain "Host Club" to Western Men: What Reiko Yamagishi has Learned about Language, Culture, and Power', *Kyoto Journal* 64. Online. Available HTTP: http://www.kyotojournal.org/kjcurrent/kjcurrent.html (accessed 6 September 2007).

# 8 Studying halal restaurants in New Zealand

## Experiences and perspectives of a Muslim female researcher

*Melissa Wan Hassan*

## Introduction

New Zealand is a country that is increasingly placing marketing emphasis on attracting visitors from countries and regions with significant Muslim populations. Furthermore, as a major exporter and producer of halal slaughtered meat in the world, New Zealand is believed to be well positioned as an attractive destination for Muslim travellers. Approximately 98 per cent of the lambs and sheep, 60 per cent of the cattle, as well as 85 per cent of the deer grown in New Zealand, are halal slaughtered every year (NZIMM 2007; MIA 2007; MAF 2007). However, perhaps somewhat surprisingly, although halal meat production is high, research has shown that Muslims find it difficult to obtain halal food while travelling in the country, with many having to prepare their own meals (Wan Hassan and Hall 2003).

A study was subsequently conducted to investigate how halal food is managed and promoted in New Zealand restaurants. Among the aims of the study was an examination of the awareness that restaurant managers have towards halal dietary standards and practices, as well as to determine whether or not they regard Muslim travellers as a significant market for their business.

In this chapter, the objectives of the study will first be examined before discussing the significance of the study and the rationale behind its research design. The advantages and disadvantages of being a Muslim female researcher in this study will also be reflected on in addition to other research difficulties encountered during the fieldwork. The chapter then concludes with some thoughts and lessons that can be taken from the researcher's experiences and perspectives.

## Research objectives

The aim of the study undertaken was to examine the management and promotion of halal food in restaurants and other types of food service establishments such as cafés, food courts and takeaway outlets. The following research questions were established for the study:

1   What are the characteristics of food service managers and restaurants in this study?
2   Do halal restaurants regard Muslim tourists as a significant market for their business?
3   Are restaurant managers aware of halal dietary standards and practices?
4   How do restaurants in the study advertise their halal food?
5   Would restaurants in the study consider applying for halal certification in the future?

## Significance of study

Although the issue of halal food is important for Muslims, academic literature and research regarding halal food in the hospitality and tourism industry is almost non-existent. At the time of undertaking the study (2004–7) there was not a single research article on halal food in hospitality books and journals written in the English language. Academic articles on halal food are extremely sparse and the little that has been written mainly comes from academic areas such as marketing and consumer studies (Ahmed 2008; Bonne and Verbeke 2006, 2008a, 2008b; Bonne *et al.* 2007), food science and technology (Regenstein *et al.* 2003; Riaz and Chaudry 2003), nutrition and dietetics (Lawrence and Rozmus 2001), sociology (Bergeaud-Blackler 2004; 2007) and cultural anthropology (James 2004).

In all the academic literature available, no one has addressed the importance of halal food in hospitality and tourism in the same way that the significance of kosher food, for example, has been addressed (Desser 1979; Hall and Sharples 2003; Malka and McCool 2003; Blech 2004). At present, even schools of culinary arts and hospitality pay little or no attention at all to the cultural and religious dimensions of food. The majority of cookery books that display the recipes of certain Muslim cuisines (e.g. Salloum and Peters 1997; Morse 1998; Başan 2002; Jamal 2003; Zaouali 2007) would similarly not even address the meaning of halal. Occasionally, however, when cookery books do give a description of halal food production, the information provided may either be too simplistic or would be flawed by inaccuracies.

Considering the dearth of information available on halal food in Muslim cultures, this study of halal food in hospitality and tourism is therefore significant as it seeks to reduce the ignorance prevailing in the industry towards food laws observed by a growing consumer segment, not only in the East but also in the West.

### Increasing population of Muslims

The Western world is becoming home to growing Muslim communities, especially in Western Europe where their numbers have tripled since the 1970s (Osnos 2004). In New Zealand alone, the Muslim population increased by 52.6 per cent between 2001 and 2006 (Statistics New Zealand 2007). At the time of writing there is an estimated 53 million Muslims in Europe, including 16 million who live in the European Union (Islamic Population 2009; CIA World Factbook 2009). The rapid growth of Muslim population in Europe is mainly due to the massive influx of workers and migrants from the Middle East and former colonial territories in Africa, Asia and the Carribean region. Although Muslims are still a small minority in Europe, demographers predict that their number will increase significantly within the next few decades, to up to 10 per cent of the EU's population as early as 2020 (The Pew Forum on Religion and Public Life 2005).

The burgeoning population of Muslims emphasises the significance of this study, which examines halal food in the hospitality industry. Westerners, although generally familiar with the Jewish kosher diet, still know little about the requirements of halal slaughter or the food restrictions observed by Muslims. Yet the need to be aware about halal food has never been more crucial for businesses, considering the population of Muslims worldwide.

Globally, there are between 1.5 and 1.8 billion Muslims who form at least a fifth of the world's population (Islamic Population 2009). Islam is today the second largest religion in the world after Christianity (CIA World Factbook 2009) and it is also growing faster numerically than any other major world religions (World Network of Religious Futurists 2006).

### Growth of inbound Muslim travellers

The growth of the world's Muslim population, however, is not the only factor contributing to the significance of this study. The potential for countries to receive more inbound Muslim tourists also brings the need for increased awareness concerning halal food in hospitality and tourism. New Zealand, for example, has in recent years been targeting countries with significant Muslim populations, such as Saudi Arabia and the United Arab Emirates, for inbound tourism. In fact, the 'Middle East' region has been identified by Tourism New Zealand (TNZ) (2008) as being important for long-term tourism growth. Visitors from the Arabian Gulf, who are among the highest-spending travellers in the world, are welcomed in New Zealand because they undertake long-haul travel in the months of June, July and August, when the number of international visitor arrivals in New Zealand is lowest (Meikle 2001).

Apart from the Middle East, New Zealand has also been targeting other countries with significant Muslim populations, such as Malaysia, India and Singapore, for inbound tourism. There is consequently potential for New Zealand to receive more inbound Muslim tourists in the future. The implication is that tourism marketers and the hospitality industry will need to be aware of the cultural sensitivities and inhibitions of Muslims, especially with regards to food. They need to understand some of the basic teachings of Islam concerning food, and food production represents another significant subject of exploration in this study.

## Research design

Exploratory studies are called for when very little is known about a particular product, respondent group or when the researcher wishes to expand the current state of knowledge (Mariampolski 2001). In social scientific research, exploratory studies are essential whenever a researcher is breaking new ground or seeking to yield new insights into a topic for research (Mariampolski 2001; Stebbins 2001; Maxwell 2005).

The exploratory approach has been chosen for this study to satisfy the researcher's desire for a better understanding of the way that halal food is managed in New Zealand restaurants. The approach has also been selected because it meets the demands of the objectives set for this study. Although the main shortcoming of this approach is that it seldom provides satisfactory answers to research questions, it nevertheless can hint at the answers and give insights into the research methods that could provide definitive answers (Babbie 1998).

Considering the limits of the questionnaire as a data collection instrument, other qualitative methods such as fieldwork observation and in-depth interviews were also used in exploring the phenomenon under study. As it was difficult to disclose each answer's context in a questionnaire, the involvement of interviews and field observations provided additional insights and explanation for why certain patterns of answering occurred in large numbers in the questionnaire. It was through in-depth interviews, for instance, that the researcher was able to find explanations as to why the majority of participants were reluctant to advertise their halal food or put up the halal sign in front of their shop. Having questionnaires administered through face-to-face interviews was also appropriate in this study given the diverse ethnic backgrounds of participants and the language barrier that some of them faced with English as a medium of communication.

## Sample selection

This study is unique not only in terms of its research focus but also because it is among the few to have sampled a 'hidden population' within the restaurant sector. Indeed, past studies using the snowball sampling techniques have mainly been conducted to locate 'deviant populations'. As Watters and Biernacki (1989: 1) observe, the snowball sampling technique has been used to 'help researchers study health or social problems that exist among populations that are difficult to reach because of their attributed social stigma, legal status and consequent lack of visibility'. Studies with snowball samples of peripheral or hard-to-locate restaurants are very uncommon. Besides this research, another example would be the ethnographic study of Chinese restaurants in rural Western Canada (Smart 2003).

In this study, the locations that were chosen for sample selection were Auckland, Wellington, Christchurch and Dunedin, because of the high population of Muslims living in those cities and the fact that they are also major tourist destinations in New Zealand.

The sampling process began with only three lists of halal restaurants; the first list, taken from the FIANZ (Federation of Islamic Associations of New Zealand) website, was that of halal certified restaurants and takeaways in Auckland; the second list consisted of halal restaurants in Wellington and Christchurch, which was taken from the IMAN (International Muslim Association of New Zealand) website; the third and final list was taken straight from the New Zealand Yellow Pages® website. In all the three lists gathered, there were a total of 24 halal restaurants, of which nine were franchises of the Nando's restaurant.

After searching for halal restaurants on the Yellow Pages® website, advertisements in the Yellow Pages® book were also referred to. A handful of them advertised the availability of halal food on their menus. Several restaurants listed in the White Pages® (business directory), serving mainly Asian and Middle Eastern cuisine, were also contacted, with those offering halal food being invited to participate in the survey. Apart from the telephone directories, the Restaurant Association of New Zealand was also contacted to see if they had a list of restaurants serving halal food and they replied saying that they had no such list.

As mentioned above, the snowball sampling technique was chosen for the survey since the total population of halal restaurants in New Zealand is unknown. The sample was thus identified and selected from various sources of information including direct, face-to-face contact with restaurant managers and local Muslims (see Table 8.1). In each of the cities selected for sample selection, the researcher had Muslim friends who would introduce her to the other people they knew in the Muslim community. As she got to know more people, who then informed her of the names and locations of restaurants serving halal food, the research sample grew.

Muslim customers were the first group of people whose views were sought after to locate and obtain the research sample. Generally, each Muslim customer spoken to would not know of more than five halal restaurants in the city they were living in. They were commonly unaware of halal restaurants except for the ones they had visited or had been told about by friends and relatives. As noted above, very few restaurants in New Zealand advertise their halal food, with halal signage or labels in front of shops being hard to come by. Additionally, many restaurants have very small halal signage that cannot easily be seen from the street. While these restaurants were hard to locate, Muslim consumers typically admit that they were mistrustful of restaurants that were not halal certified. Yet, more than half of the restaurants sampled said they would not consider applying for halal certification in the future.

Leaders and members of various Islamic organisations in New Zealand were also interviewed during fieldwork, as indicated in Table 8.1. The researcher spoke to three halal certifiers in Auckland who work for FIANZ

*Table 8.1* Groups interviewed during fieldwork

| Group interviewed | Number interviewed | Why their views were sought |
| --- | --- | --- |
| Restaurant managers | 99 | Restaurant managers represent the research sample of this study. |
| Muslim customers | 47 | Information from customers was sought to identify and locate halal restaurants. Generally, halal restaurants are not advertised in New Zealand and are mainly promoted by word of mouth. |
| Halal certifiers | 6 | Halal certifiers are able to provide the names of restaurants that have been halal certified by their organisation. They would also be aware of some restaurants that claim to sell halal food but have not applied for halal certification. |
| Leaders and/or members of Islamic organisations | 21 | This group's awareness of halal may be slightly higher than other consumers. They may also act as non-profit and non-affiliated watchdog groups that monitor the halal industry. |
| Halal meat suppliers | 15 | Halal meat suppliers readily know of the restaurants which purchase halal meat. Suppliers deal directly with business establishments that market themselves as halal restaurants or food service outlets. |
| Retailers of speciality food stores | 4 | Some speciality food stores sell halal meat and food products imported from overseas. They are aware of halal food suppliers, wholesalers and distributors in their locality. An Asian food store in Auckland also distributes free booklets advertising New Zealand Indian businesses (such as restaurants, bakeries and butcheries) selling halal food. |

on a voluntary basis. On one occasion, the researcher was invited to the home of one of the halal certifiers, who supplied her with the names of nine (non-certified) halal restaurants in Auckland. On another occasion, the researcher came across a group of Muslim students at the hall of residence where she was staying. They were all committee members of a Malaysian student organisation which had just finished holding a gathering for the Malaysian community. As they were cleaning up and were just about to leave, the researcher quickly sat with about six or seven of them, including the association's President, and from that meeting alone gathered the names of 14 halal food service outlets in Auckland.

Other than the Muslim customers, the researcher also interviewed Muslim food retailers or owners of speciality food stores selling Asian and Middle Eastern spices, imported manufactured products, frozen foods, vegetables and halal meat. Halal meat butchers, suppliers or wholesalers were spoken to and asked about restaurants which were supplied with their meat. Speaking to halal meat suppliers was often very helpful, because they knew at least the names, if not the exact location, of restaurants purchasing halal meat. In Auckland, for example, one supplier provided a list of 11 restaurants while another gave the names of 19 halal restaurants.

For various reasons, the researcher was not able to interview each and every restaurant that she was informed about. This was because arranging for appointments was sometimes difficult due to time and financial constraints. Finding the phone number or address of some of the restaurants was also difficult, either because they were not listed in the phone directory or had already gone out of business. A few of the managers or restaurant owners who were approached were also evasive and not keen to participate in the research. One restaurant owner, for example, told the researcher to return another day but refused to talk to her when she did because the owner was allegedly too busy and could not leave a new staff member working alone in the kitchen. However, about fifteen minutes later, the restaurant owner was seen leaving the restaurant while her staff continued to mind the shop alone. In another incident, a restaurant manager asked the researcher to return the next day specifically at a time when he was scheduled to be on duty at another branch.

When pre-arranged interviews failed, the researcher would walk up to other restaurants and ask whether they served halal food. If they did, an appointment would be made with the manager or restaurant owner for an interview. At times, however, the researcher was able to interview participants immediately on the spot.

## Questionnaire

Following sample selection, data were collected using a questionnaire that was administered through face-to-face interviews. The questionnaire consisted primarily of closed-ended questions but some had open-ended responses to accommodate answers that did not fall into specific categories. The questions were divided into three sections. The first section had 11 questions which covered information such as the location and type of restaurant, number of employees and customer seats, the type of food or cuisine served, the environment in which the restaurant operated and the media or places of advertisement that were used to promote the restaurant. The second section had 13 questions examining special diets. In this section, restaurants were asked about the type of special diets they could cater for and whether or not they saw a difference between the halal and kosher diets. They were also asked to indicate how often Muslims and tourists dined in their restaurants and how significant these markets were to their business. In the third and final section, participants were asked 30 questions concerning the management and promotion of halal food in their restaurants. This section also included six questions that were designed to measure the level of awareness that participants have toward halal dietary standards and practices.

## Reflections on the research process

In some cultures 'the gender, age, religion, status or political beliefs of the researcher may be very important and may facilitate or restrict access to the community being researched' (Donohoue Clyne 2001: 2). Merriam and colleagues (2001), for example, suggest that a researcher working within her own culture is able to interpret meanings because of familiarity with that culture and an understanding of how events may be perceived. The researcher working within another culture, however, does not have this knowledge and may not know, for example, what meaning is attached to being interviewed. 'Is the interviewer a government investigator, agent of the police, undercover journalist planning television exposure or an academic undertaking serious research?' Muslims in Australia, for example, have been subject to all of these (Donohoue Clyne 2001).

As a researcher who was working within her own religious culture, I had several advantages. First, I was generally trusted by the Muslims I approached, except for restaurant owners, who would often be wary of me regardless of whether or not they were Muslims. As a relative insider, I had access to key figures in the Muslim community through the introduction of friends and acquaintances. I was invited into the homes of people I hardly knew and was treated with great kindness and hospitality. Many of them expressed interest in my research and felt it was going to be a significant contribution to Muslims' life in New Zealand.

Secondly, another advantage I had was that I understood what it meant to be a Muslim in New Zealand and I was aware of some of the racist stereotypes of Muslims presented in the media (Musa 2006). This made it easier for research participants to express any fears or concerns they have about being Muslim or being known as operators of restaurants serving halal food in a Western non-Muslim country.

Thirdly, I was free from many misconceptions that some non-Muslims have about Muslims. I knew, for instance, that in New Zealand there was no segregation between the Sunnis and Shi'as. In New Zealand, just as in any other Western country, Sunnis and Shi'as pray together in the same mosque, celebrate religious festivals together and send their children to the same Islamic schools or Sunday classes at the mosque. Westerners, however, are often obsessed with the division between Sunnis and Shi'as. As a Muslim, I find it strange whenever I am asked by Westerners 'Are you a Sunni or Shi'a?', because this is a question that Muslims in New Zealand and many countries around the world would not care to ask one another.

Although female Muslim researchers have some advantages over non-Muslim researchers when doing research in the Muslim community, her access to male Muslim participants, however, would be more restricted if she was conducting the research without a *mahram*.

*Mahram* refers to the group of people whom it is unlawful for a Muslim woman to marry due to marital or blood relationships. A Muslim woman's *permanent mahrams* due to blood relationship are her father, her son (who passed puberty), her brother, her uncle from her father's side, her brother's son, her sister's son, and her uncle from her mother's side. Apart from permanent *mahrams*, a Muslim woman may also have *radha' mahrams* due to sharing the nursing milk when she was an infant. Thus, when a woman breastfeeds an infant who is not her own child for a certain amount of time with certain conditions, she becomes the child's *radha'* mother and the same applies to her husband and children, who become the child's *radha'* father, brothers and sisters respectively. The status of *radha' mahrams* is similar to the status of permanent *mahrams*, which is one that remains throughout one's life. Additionally, as a result of marriage, a Muslim woman may also acquire in-law *mahrams* who specifically are her husband's father (father-in-law), her husband's son (stepson), her mother's husband (stepfather) and her daughter's husband. These categories of people, along with the woman's husband, form the group of allowable escorts for a Muslim woman when she travels (Abdul-Rahman 2004).

In 2002, when I was doing a survey on Muslim travellers in New Zealand, I discovered that for religious and cultural reasons some Muslim men would not feel comfortable being interviewed by a woman unless her *mahram* was present. Having spent most of my life in Malaysia, I was at first offended by this behaviour displayed by some Muslim men in New Zealand. However, as I got to know more immigrants from the Middle East and South Asian countries, I began to understand why the men behave that way towards women. In many Muslim countries, men and women do not intermingle or socialise as freely as people do in non-Muslim societies. In such cultures, a Muslim woman would be shy to socialise with men outside her family while Muslim men similarly feel the same way in the company of a woman who is not with her *mahram*. For this reason, I felt that it was necessary to be accompanied by my father while I was travelling and interviewing people for my survey on restaurants.

Interestingly, while being female may create some restrictions for the Muslim researcher, Flores-Meiser (1983) nevertheless had a different experience when researching Muslims in the Philippines. She found that being female and Christian enabled her to have a different research relationship, as she was permitted to sit and converse with the men at public feasts or in front of the mosque after Friday prayer, unlike other women in the community. According to Warren (1988), honorary maleness and foreignness facilitate cross-gender access in some cultures. Papanek (1982: 160) similarly contends that in some cultures non-Muslim female researchers have greater 'role flexibility'.

Role flexibility has enabled non-Muslim female researchers like Donohoue Clyne (2001) and Haw (1996) to speak directly with Muslim men. At a Muslim education conference, for example, Donohoue Clyne (2001) observed that, although women and men were seated separately and had different areas for meals, she was nevertheless approached several times by male participants not known to her, who wanted to know why she was there and why she was interested in Muslim education. Each of them provided her with valuable, unsolicited information and some also suggested potential interviewees. Haw (1996), another non-Muslim female researcher who studied the educational experiences of Muslim girls, also found that as a white non-Muslim female who was an academic, she was treated with respect by Muslim men. She says, 'It was not difficult to negotiate access. I was positioned by them in the space normally given to Muslim men so that in a parents' meeting at the Muslim school, where the males were separated from the women, I was given a seat in the room with the men' (Haw 1996: 328). We can therefore conclude that the female non-Muslim researcher may have certain advantages over the female Muslim researcher in certain circumstances (Mirza 1995).

Fortunately, during my research I did not face any significant problems with wearing the *hijab* (headscarf or head-covering that is fastened and opaque, as well as loose and large, covering my head, neck and chest). Apart from one non-Muslim female participant who asked me to explain why wearing the *hijab* was necessary in a Western country, the rest of my research participants did not at all seem to make an issue of it. Initially (with *hijab*), I tried to dress in a fashion similar to that of the people I was going to interview as I came to understand that the 'richly dressed interviewer will probably have difficulty getting good cooperation and responses from poorer respondents' and 'a poorly dressed interviewer will have similar difficulties with richer respondents' (Babbie 1998: 265). Nevertheless, I later found that it was not always possible for me to match my outfit with the people that I interviewed, because the restaurants I visited on any day could range from a small takeaway outlet to a large fine dining restaurant. Additionally, because I travelled around all the cities I visited by bus and had to do a few miles of walking each day, I also had to be simple and practical when it came to what I wore. I thus kept to apparel that was clean, neat and modest. According to Babbie (1998), although middle-class neatness and cleanliness may not be acceptable to all sectors of society, they remain the primary norm and are the most likely to be acceptable to the largest number of respondents.

The short amount of time I had with each participant was another difficulty that I had to cope with during the survey. I usually had between 20 and 30 minutes to interview each respondent. The majority of them typically became restless after 15 minutes of being interviewed, with most preferring not go beyond 20 minutes. Restaurant owners and managers were often interviewed while they were working, cooking or preparing food. Some of them also spoke to me in between serving customers. Due to their hectic and tense working environment, every now and then I had to deal with employees who were under stress or unhappy in their jobs.

Along with time constraints, there was also the difficulty of arranging interview appointments. It was not possible to get restaurant managers operating in the same suburb or location to be interviewed on the same day. Additionally arranging for appointments was also difficult because it was sometimes not possible to estimate the length of time it would take to get from one suburb to the other due to my unfamiliarity with the city's traffic patterns. There was one day in Auckland, for example, when I missed three appointments because of the pouring rain and the horrendous traffic jam. It took an hour for the bus I was riding to get from Ponsonby to Newmarket when it should have taken only 15 minutes.

Finally, another difficulty I had to cope with while doing research on restaurants was with managers asking me whether I was interested to purchase food or meal items from their restaurant either before or after interviews. In any case, I would always feel obliged to turn myself into a customer in order to encourage cooperation and participation, especially before interviews.

## Conclusion

My research on halal food in New Zealand restaurants has indeed been challenging. Based on observations I made while carrying out a survey on Muslim travellers in 2002, I first began this study thinking that there could possibly not be more than 30 halal restaurants throughout New Zealand. During my fieldwork I was surprised to learn that the number of halal restaurants has increased so rapidly that there are now over a hundred halal restaurants operating in New Zealand. However, due to time and financial constraints, I only managed to interview 99 restaurants and food service establishments serving halal food in the country. Although there are many halal restaurants operating in New Zealand, they are still few and far between. Since the majority of these restaurants do not advertise or promote their halal food, the task of searching for them has been difficult and time-consuming.

I think the two months I spent searching for halal restaurants served me well. Perhaps the most valuable lesson I learned came from just 'being there', observing restaurants, people and the way they responded to me when I approached them or interviewed them. Certainly, this strategy has provided much useful information. However, it was also through further communication and in-depth interviews that I began to understand the needs of restaurant owners and the circumstances they were operating under, as well as the serious situation that customers of halal food are now faced with.

On a final note, I must say that I do not envy non-Muslim female researchers, who are less restricted in their access to male Muslim respondents. Even with the seemingly greater access they have to Muslim men in some situations, non-Muslim female researchers could never really be 'positioned . . . in the space normally given to Muslim men' just because they are sitting in the same room with them (Haw 1996: 328). Men will always behave differently in the company of other men compared to when they are in the company of women.

Roald (2001), who researched attitudes about gender among first- and second-generation Arabic-speaking Sunni Islamists living in Europe, recognised the significance of her gender to her fieldwork and explained how her husband legitimated her research. She writes,

> I was accompanied by my husband who not only functioned as a bridge between the interviewees and myself, but who was also active in posing questions . . . without his (my husband's) help I would not have penetrated the issues to the same extent and would probably not have been given such honest answers
>
> (Roald 2001: 76).

In retrospect, I think my father's presence was also an advantage for me as a researcher. My father spoke to some of my respondents either before or after I had interviewed them. Although he did not participate in the interviews, I observed that both Muslim and non-Muslim male respondents were often more obliging and more comfortable talking to me in my father's presence. Through my father, who has a jovial and friendly character, I had the privilege of seeing many of my male respondents becoming relaxed and being more of themselves during and/or after interviews. Given the invisible barrier segregating men and women in very traditional Muslim communities, it may therefore be an acceptable solution for female researchers to be accompanied by a male supporter or colleague when interviewing male Muslims.

## References

Abdul-Rahman, M.S. (2004) *Jurisprudence and Islamic Rulings: General and Transactions – Part 4*, MSA Publication Ltd.

Ahmed, A. (2008) 'Marketing of Halal Meat in the United Kingdom: Supermarkets versus Local Shops', *British Food Journal* 110(7): 655–70.

Babbie, E.R. (1998) *The Practice of Social Research*, 8th edn. Belmont: Wadsworth Publishing Company.

Başan, G. (2002) *Classic Turkish Cookery*. London: Tauris Parke Books.

Bergeaud-Blackler, F. (2004) 'Social Definitions of Halal Quality: The Case of Maghrebi Muslims in France', in M. Harvey, A. McMeekin and A. Warde (eds), *Qualities of Food*. Manchester: Manchester University Press.

Bergeaud-Blackler, F. (2007) 'New Challenges for Islamic Ritual Slaughter: A European Perspective', *Journal of Ethnic and Migration Studies* 33(6): 965–80.

Blech, Z.Y. (2004) *Kosher Food Production*. Ames: Blackwell Publishing.

Bonne, K. and Verbeke, W. (2006) 'Muslim Consumers' Motivations towards Meat Consumption in Belgium: Qualitative Exploratory Insights from means–end chain analysis', *Anthropology of Food*, 5, May 2006, Food and Religion/Alimentation et religion. Online. Available HTTP: <http://aof.revues.org/document90.html> (accessed 22 July 2008).

Bonne, K. and Verbeke, W. (2008a) 'Muslim Consumer Trust in Halal Meat Status and Control in Belgium', *Meat Science* 79: 113–23.

Bonne, K. and Verbeke, W. (2008b) 'Religious Values Informing Halal Meat Production and the Control and Delivery of Halal Credence Quality', *Agriculture and Human Values* 25: 35–47.

Bonne, K., Vermeir, I., Bergeaud-Blackler, F. and Verbeke, W. (2007) 'Determinants of Halal Meat Consumption in France', *British Food Journal* 109(5): 367–86.

CIA World Factbook (2009) *World Factbook*. Washington, DC: CIA. Online. Available HTTP: <https://www.cia.gov/cia/publications/factbook/geos/xx.html> (accessed 1 January 2009).

Desser, M. (1979) 'Kosher Catering: How and why', *Cornell Hotel and Restaurant Administration Quarterly* 20(2): 83–91.

Donohoue Clyne, I. (2001) 'Educating Muslim Children in Australia', in A. Saeed and S. Akbarzadeh (eds), *Muslim Communities in Australia*. Sydney: University of New South Wales Press.

Flores-Meiser, E.P. (1983) 'Field Experience in Three Societies', in R. Lawless, V.H. Sutlive and M.D. Zamora (eds), *Fieldwork: The Human Experience*. New York: Gordon & Breach Science Publishers.

Hall, C.M. and Sharples, L. (2003) 'The Consumption of Experiences or the Experience of Consumption?', in C.M. Hall, L. Sharples, R. Mitchell, B. Cambourne and N. Macionis (eds), *Food Tourism Around the World: Developments, Management and Markets*. Oxford: Butterworth-Heinemann.

Haw, K.F. (1996) 'Exploring the Educational Experiences of Muslim Girls: Tales Told to Tourists: Should the White Researcher Stay at Home?' *British Educational Research Journal* 22(3): 319–30.

Islamic Population (2009) *European Muslim Population*, Islamic Population, Online. Available HTTP: <http://www.islamicpopulation.com/europe_general.html> (accessed 7 January 2009).

Jamal, S. (2003) *Arabian Flavours: Recipes and Tales of Arab Life (Aroma Arabe: Recetas y Relatos)*, trans. Elfreda Powell. London: Souvenir Press.

James, R. (2004) 'Introduction: Halal Pizza: Food and Culture in a Busy World', *The Australian Journal of Anthropology* 15(1): 1–11.

Lawrence, P. and Rozmus, C. (2001) 'Culturally Sensitive Care of the Muslim Patient', *Journal of Transcultural Nursing* 12: 228–33.

MAF (The Ministry of Agriculture and Forestry) (2007) *Situation and Outlook for New Zealand Agriculture and Forestry (August 2007)*, MAF Online. Available HTTP: <http://www.maf.govt.nz/mafnet/rural-nz/statistics-and-forecasts/sonzaf/2007/page-17.htm#P1591_102554> (accessed 27 August 2008).

Malka, O. and McCool, A.C. (2003) 'Kosher Airline Food: A Logistical Challenge', *FIU Hospitality Review* 21(1): 67–82.

Mariampolski, H. (2001) *Qualitative Market Research: A Comprehensive Guide*. Thousand Oaks: Sage.

Maxwell, J.A. (2005) *Qualitative Research Design: An Interactive Approach*. Thousand Oaks: Sage.

Meikle, S. (2001) 'Middle Eastern Growth', *Tourism News*, September.

Merriam, S.B., Johnson-Bailey, J., Lee, M.Y., Kee, Y., Ntseane, G. and Muhamad, M. (2001) 'Power and Positionality: Negotiating Insider/Outsider Status within and across Cultures', *International Journal of Lifelong Education* 20(5): 405–16.

MIA (Meat Industry Association of New Zealand) (2007) *About Us*, MIA, Wellington, Online. Available HTTP: <http://www.mia.co.nz/about_us/index.htm> (accessed 19 September 2007).

Mirza, M. (1995) 'Some ethical dilemmas in field work: Feminist and Antiracist Methodologies', in M. Griffiths and B. Troyna (eds), *Anti-Racism, Culture and Social Justice in Education*. Stoke-on-Trent: Trentham Books.

Morse, K. (1998) *Recipes from my Moroccan Kitchen: Cooking at the Kasbah*. San Francisco: Chronicle Books.

Musa, M. (2006) 'Market, Media and Representations: A Study of New Zealand media coverage of Muslims', unpublished text of a paper for the 'Muslim of New Zealand' symposium, University of Canterbury, Christchurch, 18–19 February.

NZIMM (New Zealand Islamic Meat Management) (2007) *New Zealand Meat Processing Industry*. Wellington: Muslim League of New Zealand (Inc.). Online. Available HTTP: <http://www.muslimleague.org.nz/modules/wfchannel/index. php?pagenum=4> (accessed 19 September 2007).

Osnos, E. (2004) 'Islam Shaping a new Europe', *Chicago Tribune*, 19 December.

Papanek, H. (1982) 'Purdah: Separate Worlds and Symbolic Shelter', in H. Papanek and G. Minault (eds), *Separate Worlds: Studies of Purdah in South Asia*. Delhi: Chanakya Publishers.

Regenstein, J.M., Chaudry, M.M. and Regenstein, C.E. (2003) 'The Kosher and Halal food laws', *Comprehensive Reviews in Food Science and Food Safety* 2: 111–27.

Riaz, M.N. and Chaudry, M.M. (2004) *Halal Food Production*. Boca Raton, FL: CRC Press.

Roald, A.S. (2001) *Women in Islam: The Western Experience*. New York: Routledge.

Salloum, H. and Peters, J. (1997) *From the Lands of Figs and Olives: Over 300 Delicious and Unusual Recipes from the Middle East and North Africa*. London: I.B. Tauris Publishers.

Smart, J. (2003) 'Ethnic Entrepreneurship, Transmigration, and Social Integration: An Ethnographic Study of Chinese Restaurant Owners in Rural Western Canada', *Urban Anthropology and Studies of Cultural Systems and World Economic Development* 32(3–4): 311–32.

Statistics New Zealand (2007) *QuickStats about Culture and Identity – 2006 Census*. Statistics New Zealand. Online. Available HTTP: <http://www.stats.govt.nz/NR/ rdonlyres/5F1F873C-5D36-4E54-9405-34503A2C0AF6/0/quickstatsaboutculture andidentity.pdf> (accessed 30 October 2007).

Stebbins, R.A. (2001) *Exploratory Research in the Social Sciences*. Thousand Oaks: Sage.

The Pew Forum on Religion and Public Life (2005) *An Uncertain Road: Muslims and the Future of Europe*. Washington, DC: The Pew Forum on Religion and Public Life.

Tourism New Zealand (2008) *Background: Gulf Region Market Overview*, Tourism New Zealand. Online. Available HTTP: <http://www.tourismnewzealand.com/ tourism_info//events/arabian-travel-market-2006/background.cfm> (accessed 27 June 2008).

Wan Hassan, W.M. and Hall, C.M. (2003) 'The Demand for Halal Food among Muslim Travellers in New Zealand', in C.M. Hall, L. Sharples, R. Mitchell,

B. Cambourne and N. Macionis (eds), *Food Tourism Around the World: Developments, Management and Markets*. Oxford: Butterworth-Heinemann.

Warren, C.A.B. (1988) *Gender Issues in Field Research*. Newbury Park: Sage Publications.

Watters, J.K. and Biernacki, P. (1989) 'Targeted Sampling: Options for the Study of Hidden Populations', *Social Problems* 36(4): 416–30.

World Network of Religious Futurists (2006) *Trends in Religion*. World Network of Religious Futurists. Online. Available HTTP: <http://www.wnrf.org/news/trends.html> (accessed 1 August 2006).

Zaouali, L. (2007) *Medieval Cuisine of the Islamic World: A Concise History with 174 Recipes*, trans. M.B. DeBevoise. Berkeley: University of California Press.

# 9 Researching heritage tourism in Singapore

## An outsider perspective as an asset?

*David Tantow*

## Introduction

This chapter deals with my dissertation on heritage tourism in Singapore. Stating my position as a newly arrived first-time foreigner to Singapore in January 2006, I attempt to undertake a comprehensive evaluation of Singapore's tourism strategies. I am interested in exploring how heritage has been represented and marketed as a tourism asset in the Southeast Asian context, in a country that has achieved a life standard comparable to most nations in Europe within the past decades. A further research question is how those representations have materialized in the physical landscape. Thirdly, heritage sites are of fundamental significance for both locals and tourists, albeit possibly to varying degrees. That is why I would like to identify how different people consume and interpret these representations in Singapore, operating from an outside perspective, being neither local nor tourist.

This situation and its implications are twofold, offering both chances and risks: on the one hand I had imagined operating from a position of 'objective outsideness' (Relph 1976). On the other hand I needed to compensate for my lack of background information in Singapore, with which an 'insider' (e.g. a researcher born and educated in Singapore) would be arguably more equipped. Hence, there would definitely be a need to leverage this lack of expertise by dint of acquiring a detailed understanding of local processes and possible problems, thus aiming for a perspective of 'empathic insideness' (Relph 1976). While undertaking graduate studies overseas certainly is a common phenomenon, the choice to collocate my research area within the immediate surrounding of my new alma mater was considered unusual. As a European freshly graduated from the University of Trier, Germany's oldest city and a UNESCO World Heritage Site, I was often approached for tips on cultural tourism to the 'old continent', while my ability to conduct research in Singapore was frequently, and I think legitimately, put into question.

Acquiring more detailed knowledge about methodology in fieldwork, stemming from literature as well as from informal discussion with fellow researchers, initially rather discouraged than encouraged me: Can an outsider perspective ever be an asset? Is not any similarity with the researched community an indispensable virtue? Did not most of my colleagues choose field sites they were long-term familiar with? Indeed, many texts about methodologies in fieldwork decidedly denounce the notion of objectivity and neutrality (see Rose 1997; Chari 2003; Tembo 2003). The post-positivist researcher has to immerse him- or herself in the field. One main challenge is to acknowledge subjectivity, positionality and the irreconcilable limitations to the attainment of a full insider status (see Rose 1997). This impossibility of becoming a true insider is a fact that is not only discussed but at times is also openly regretted (see England 1994). In feminist literature, this uneasiness is frequently addressed, up to the point where the researcher feels incompetent to work on certain topics. For example, England (1994) discussed a personal example, i.e. herself being a straight female academic and not feeling fully qualified to do research on lesbians. In turn, every aspect of similarity with the researched and every bit of prior familiarity with the research area is stressed to legitimate the research process (see Tembo 2003). There certainly are other threads in literature and many of my colleagues have been encouraging, yet I was imbued to reflect upon my consciously chosen 'outsider'-approach over again. This chapter revisits 'objective outsideness', discussing its applicability in ethnographic fieldwork.

## Objective outsideness revisited

According to post-positivist literature neutrality and objectivity are illusionary (Rose 1997). Any researcher would have a specific stand on the prospective research topic, no one would 'parachute into the field with [an] empty head' (England 1994: 84). Claiming to be truly objective in ethnography is frequently dismissed as the 'god-trick'. Respectively, the most recommended way out of the dilemma would be a very early familiarization and identification with the research area, the subsequent acknowledgment of this positionality and the immediate embarkation on a journey to insider status (see Katz 1994). However, it should be noted that the notion of 'positioning' oneself as a researcher in the 'landscape of power' of the field has also been critiqued within feminist literature as a simplification (see Rose 1997). It is acknowledged that multiple identities of the researcher and the reflexivity of the research process do not allow for a 'once and for all' positioning. Nevertheless, many researchers choose a field site they have cultural or personal connections with, allegedly to get a 'head start'. I would like to share two interrelated critical thoughts on this procedure, stemming from my own research in Singapore which started off as a total alien to local culture. First, I argue that 'objective outsideness' is a valid approach when selecting specific field sites from a broader area. While absolute neutrality might be illusionary, a non-biased selection and a first round of observation to these sites can clarify whether they demonstrate the research problem well. In contrast, a selection which is openly based on personal ties can in some cases be distorting if the subjective inclination towards a particular place supersedes its actual suitability as a selection criterion. In this case acknowledging subjectivity and positionality would not help to balance out this fundamental flaw. Second, researcher personalities who lack any kind of initial insider connection to the researched could be discouraged from engaging in ethnographic research to begin with. Self-reflection in feminist literature describes respective situations in which academics withdraw from research not because of harmful implications to the researched, but because of a subtle feeling of being not 'close enough' to them to undertake ethnographic fieldwork. Instead, academics would retreat to textual research where their 'outsideness' would matter less, and potential valid insights would never have been gained. I argue that, although prior personal ties and connections can be helpful, they should not serve as preclusion from engaging in fieldwork for other 'outside' researchers. The latter's initial outsider perspective is complementary to those of the local researcher, not superfluous. Thus, I argue that on a general level academic institutions should not hesitate to invite outsiders to undertake research even within their local domain in order to gain fresh perspectives.

## Choosing a field site

I certainly agree that positionality matters and that there is inevitably a good degree of subjectivity involved in qualitative research. In my own case, I researched on tourism at the Upper Middle Rhine Valley World Heritage landscape before I left Europe for Singapore. Clearly I have long since shaped a personal idea of how a heritage site should or should not be represented, marketed and consumed. I agree that the parameters of heritage tourism in Europe may be quite different from the Asian context, but even the few fundamental parallels could serve to bias my observation. Even if I try hard not to impose my standards, I will inevitably have a perception of a state of 'normality' in tourism landscapes and of deviations from it anywhere in the world, which will influence my judgements (see Rose 1997).

In so far as it is certainly true that 100 per cent objectivity is unobtainable, the crucial question arising is thus how to deal with this unachievability, and opinions about adequate reactions differ. One common reaction is the abandonment of objectivity and neutrality as an aim altogether. This is combined with acknowledging subjectivity and building upon the fruitfulness of pre-existing personal ties to the research area (see Chari 2003; Tembo 2003). Upon my arrival in Singapore, I pursued a different strategy by initially trying to minimize a personal attachment to a particular area. I value my colleagues' approaches which often build upon personal bonds with a specific area or field. However, I do not think the embracing of the personal is the only way to position oneself correctly in the field. I argue that a first round of nearly objective observation of the prospective field site is an equally valid start for ethnographic fieldwork in tourism studies.

I would like to suggest three steps to familiarize oneself with the research locality. The steps characterize distinct stages in the transition from 'objective outsideness' to 'empathic insideness', each embodying specific assets on the way to reaching the overall research goal. In the following section, I shall begin by describing the 'tourist stage'. I argue that researchers should feel free to undertake initial observations without a massive load of background information. This is followed by the 'literature stage'. Almost all possible research localities will have been covered to some degree in existing literature. In this second step, the focus lies on identifying major debates concerning the research area and to evaluate their usefulness for my personal research. The impressions gained in the initial 'tourist stage' can help to determine the relevance of these literature findings. In most cases, the influx of detailed local knowledge can contribute to more targeted research in subsequent stages. Thus, the third stage is a synthesis of the observations gained as an 'outsider' with the findings of textual research. The synthesis shall serve to choose one particular field site which demonstrates the research problem without being previously 'over-studied'.

### *Living the tourist experience: Objectivity for field site selection?*

In regard to these circumstances, I limited myself to general enquiries from a local senior tourism researcher about heritage venues in Singapore, sans the pros and cons of respective conservation efforts. Instead, I perused Singapore Tourism Board (STB) brochures which feature basic information about the sites, but do not elaborate on respective urban redevelopment issues or related themes. Likewise, I avoided casual *ex ante* information from popular newspapers, magazines, etc. about specific sites. I intentionally did not ask my new colleagues about possible hotspots for recent tourism developments. I aimed to remain as neutral and objective as possible to avoid foregone conclusions.

I spent my first months in Singapore visiting local heritage sites, consisting of ethnic districts like Chinatown, Little India and Kampong Glam. I also looked at the Civic and Cultural District (CCD) and the 'quays strip' at Singapore River, both of them representing centrally located, non-ethnic tourist attractions. I wrote down notes and took pictures of what I believed to be 'characteristic' features.

I quickly became intrigued by the three ethnic heritage districts I visited, whereas the CCD and the two 'quays' did not appeal to me. While the warehouses of these trading hubs of the colonial era showcase the local commercial heritage of entrepôt trading, the urban design of both sites possibly overemphasizes global connections. Adoptive reuse has completely reshaped the areas, which are presently active spots for nightlife.

I had not read up academic literature about possible inauthenticity or commodification processes in these particular districts. Yet, I could not help but notice the uniformity of these two Singaporean waterfronts and their resemblance to their North American and European counterparts.

Likewise the Civic and Cultural District, with its beautifully refurbished

colonial era buildings, lacked a touch of uniqueness. Its pompous representation of the grand administrative tradition of the Commonwealth seemed
to be disregarding of local and vernacular culture. In contrast to that, my
impressions of ethnic heritage were more favourable. Let me provide extracts
of my notes about the three ethnic historic districts as an example:

*Chinatown* appears to be a lively downtown area, popular both among
tourists and locals. Staged activities and shops exclusively catering to tourists
seemed to be limited to the pedestrianized area adjacent to the Mass Rapid
Transit (MRT)-station overpass. Other parts of the district are much diversi-
fied in their function, ranging from the food haven of Smith Street and the
nightlife hub of Club Street to quieter areas on the edges of the district which
are serving residential purposes. Some posh shops and bars stand in contrast
to more traditional less upscale venues. The variety of shopping, drinking
and dining options obviously cater to a wide range of customers.

In *Little India* the architectural ensemble is more fragmented than Chinatown, with huge apartment blocks truly overshadowing the heart of the
neighbourhood. In this respect the physical appearance of the area is quite
a disappointment. On the other hand, quite a few authentic Indian shops
provided a rich insight into the subcontinent's every day culture. Numerous
temples and vegetarian restaurants contributed to the uniqueness and
attractiveness of the district, which features a vibrant commercial and cultural life.

*Kampong Glam* on Arab Street is the center of the Malays and the Muslim
community in Singapore. It is a small conservation area featuring two main
attractions, the Sultan Mosque and the Malay Cultural Center. A short
pedestrian street leading to the Mosque's main entrance is one major retail
centre of the area. The other less upscale commercial strip is located on North
Bridge Road, a thoroughfare to downtown. The refurbished area makes a
pleasant impression, but it seems to lack a minimum centre of attractions to
draw tourists. There are a lot of commercial vacancies in non-refurbished
buildings right beside the core area. Yet, the district features a distinct character. The area exhibits tourism potential, but in contrast to most other conservation districts, there are also some problems with the physical condition of
the built heritage.

When I looked at my first comments after a couple of weeks, I was quite
taken aback by what I had put down. I had come to Singapore to pursue
tourism research and to broaden my horizons to another continent. Yet my
notes read like simple travel writing. I wondered whether I had glorified the
'Exotic Other' in the atmosphere of the ethnic districts. I therefore had possibly dismissed all Western influences which were more prevalent along the
riverfront.

This perception was disillusioning because I had counted on the highest
possible degree of objectivity, only to notice that I might have subconsciously
worked along a scheme of Western-centric thought. It seemed that I had so
far produced travel records from a neo-orientalist perspective, deeming signs

of economic progress in the destination as deviant from the 'authentic' local culture. On the other hand I still did not have any background information, so my complaint about the loss of uniqueness in certain areas might be justified. Ultimately, I could only detect my own biases when comparing my initial judgements with the findings of other tourism researchers.

## Embracing local expertise: Striving for insider information

Immediately after gathering and evaluating these first impressions I returned to discuss with my supervisor and look through secondary data. My aim was to go through key readings about local heritage sites and to learn which issues they focus upon. Having conducted my first round of 'outsider observations', I was eager to know whether my personal perceptions of achievements and possible problems at heritage tourism sites were in line with issues highlighted in relevant literature.

Heritage tourism is a major theme in the growing literature on tourism in Singapore (see Yeoh and Kong 1995; Chang 1996; Teo and Yeoh 1997; Saunders 2004). The extensive coverage is mainly due to two factors: first, the Singapore government has previously identified the multiracial environment and cultural heritage of the city as one of the main potentials for tourism (see Leong 1997; Chang 2000; Woon *et al.* 2000; Henderson 2002). More specific-ally, the STB recognized multiracialism as a 'tourism asset'. Thus, 'its current strategy, dating from the mid-1990s, incorporates ethnicity as a vital com-ponent to be marketed as a "celebration of diversity" ' (Henderson 2003: 36). I found that my inclination towards the ethnic districts tallied with the strong role of multiracialism in local tourism discourse which the Singapore government stressed. It was therefore not necessarily a manifestation of a Eurocentric perspective.

The second factor for extensive coverage is rooted in the fact that the building stock of Singapore was radically 'rejuvenated' in the last couple of decades, resulting in a built environment with a perceived 'antiseptic atmosphere' (Chang and Yeoh 1999: 104). As a consequence, the remaining heritage is regarded as very precious and has thus become a focal point of literature. As Chang (2000: 350–1) notes 'ethnic neighborhoods were [since the 1980s] considered repositories of the nation's fast diminishing heritage which give a sense of place and identity to the country and its citizens', so 'what were once local residential and commercial sites have now been elevated to national importance as civic and tourism assets'. These findings are not only in line with my observations about the fragmented character of built heritage in Singapore but they also explain why especially the ethnic heritage districts seemed to be attractive venues for tourism in Singapore. The local tourism board emphasizes them for its economic aims and other government agencies promote them for raising local historical awareness and for nation-building purposes (see STB 1996). This combined focus of international marketing and inward promotion on ethnic heritage put high pressure on both state agencies and tourism brokers to display it well in designated areas. Thus, conservation efforts have been concentrated on ethnic districts like Chinatown, Little India and Kampong Glam (see URA 1991 for the latter). It is therefore no wonder those areas stand out as picturesque in contrast to the rest of the predominantly functional cityscape. Non-ethnic tourism areas such as the Civic and Cultural District and the Singapore Riverfront have also undergone conservation. However, I still perceived them as overly globally orientated. This ostensible contradiction is explained by Chang (2005: 251), who states that they indeed stand out as two of Singapore's most inauthentic urban landscapes, 'where the excessive redevelopment plans . . . seem to rob rather than restore the distinctive sense of place'.

Summing up, the study of local tourism literature had reinforced my confidence that my outsider approach had produced some valuable results. With my first step of field observations I had identified the ethnic heritage districts as enjoyable tourism landscapes. Local tourism researchers had elaborated on those districts' special combined role as tourism venues and places of symbolic value for nation building. I was intrigued by the incidental complexity of this combination. Admittedly, I had not fully grasped these multiple functions upon my first visit. Nor did my notes contain a clear statement of the district which is of most appeal or which bears witness to most tourism-related problems. However, I recalled my ambiguous judgment about the Malay/Muslim heritage district of 'Kampong Glam' as displaying both a lot of potential for tourism and visible problems of heritage presentation. I still intended to focus on one specific field site for my research on heritage tourism in Singapore and certainly wanted to avoid an 'over-researched' area. Hence, I felt compelled to study local literature exclusively on ethnic heritage tourism over again, relating it closer to my notes and photo material. Let me describe how this process eventually led to the choice of Kampong Glam as my field site in the following section.

## Synthesis: An agenda for ethnographic fieldwork on a particular site

Revising my personal findings and interpretations of literature, I would like to elaborate why I did *not* choose Chinatown or Little India as a field site first. Let me then demonstrate how the combined results of my outsider observation and the textual studies inspired me to take a closer look at Kampong Glam, representing the Malay and Islamic heritage of Singapore. Being initially unaccustomed to Southeast Asian Muslim culture, it would still be a long way to go to become an 'empathetic insider'. While a true insider status would be unachievable for me, I will elaborate on my strategies to gain a better understanding of local tourism-related problems in the area.

Singapore's population is predominantly Chinese, and Chinese heritage would thus be the 'mainstream' heritage of the city state. Accordingly, local tourism practitioner Pamelia Lee (2004: 122) states that 'of all the historic zones in Singapore, Chinatown is always chosen to be studied first'. She further discusses the loss of vibrancy in the area, arguing that the area lacks originality. Her quite drastic analysis represents a common point of view in literature. Many local researchers agree with these findings and call for sensitive action by the government (see also Yeoh and Kong 1994; Woon *et al.* 2000), accounting for the voices of locals. However, other authors argue that urban redevelopment was a necessity and that adequate concessions had been made to Chinese heritage (Chang 1997). Henderson (2002) also cautions not to romanticize the poor living conditions of the past and to accept changes in lifestyle. My personal notes mentioned both commodified tourism hotspots and remaining places of predominantly local significance within Chinatown. Hence I could easily see where both sides were coming from. Chinatown has been intensively studied since the very onset of conservation. Even though I was fascinated by the district, I felt that there was nothing much to add to the intense discourse which has been equally informed by pro-redevelopment and critical voices.

In contrast to Chinatown, local tourism literature commonly describes Little India as a commercial hub for both locals and tourists (see Begam 1997; Chang 1999, 2000). Furthermore the area always remained popular among many locals and there was no severe economic downturn in the district. The potential area of conflict between the district's function as a traditional local shopping area and its role as a globally marketed destination for heritage tourism has been analysed in a previous dissertation (Chang 1996) and subsequently intensely discussed (see Chang 1999, 2000). Referring to my personal notes, I had also gained the impression that potential tensions between locals and tourists have been bridged sufficiently well, making it a relatively unproblematic heritage site. Furthermore the existing research on tourism in the area has addressed almost all the existing problematic issues. I therefore decided against Little India as a field site.

Kampong Glam as the Malay/Muslim heritage district was by no means my last consideration as a prospective field site. I was intrigued by the unique appeal of the area upon my first visit. At the same time it clearly showcased problems with the presentation of heritage. The refurbished core area is small in size and its surrounding bears witness to relatively severe urban decay, which is unusual by Singapore standards (see Sim 1996). The combination of the high tourism potential but quite problematic reality heightened my curiosity about the area.

In terms of textual sources, there is quite a remarkable gap in literature concerning Kampong Glam. Apparently, tourism research in the district has had to fight off many constraints in recent years since 'urban restoration was underway' until the end of the 1990s, and the place was thus 'devoid of visitors' (Chang 1996: 79). Therefore, tourism researchers had previously shied away from the locality, with the notable exception of Sim (1996) and Yeoh and Huang (1996). Both texts constitute an interim evaluation of conservation policies. The former work is a comparative approach, implicitly stating that Kampong Glam lagged behind the two other historic ethnic districts in terms of adaptive reuse. Tourism is not directly addressed but Kampong Glam can be identified as lacking attractiveness due to the highest number of 'unrestored and vacant' building units and other flaws in heritage presentation (Sim 1996: 404). While Sim discusses problematic points *within* the conservation area, the latter work precisely raises the interesting questions of how its boundaries have been drawn. Yeoh and Huang (1996) argue that an historic Islamic school (Madrasah) as allegedly problematic heritage had been deliberately excluded from the conservation area, whose boundaries had been defined very tightly. 'A bigger zone' could have been saved (Lee 2004: 123) in the case of Kampong Glam. Tourism potential had been lost because of the undesirability of specific built heritage and its subsequent removal. From my own observations, I could see that an apparently well-frequented brand new Malay Heritage Centre had opened in the heart of the district. I concluded that heritage presentation must have improved overall in recent years, but that efforts have been selective.

As I became aware of these details of heritage representation, I realized that 'objective outsideness' would be impossible to keep up for the subsequent stages of research. I had to gain some sort of insider status in order to underline my expertise on Malay and Muslim heritage in Singapore. As a first step, I subscribed to Malay classes in university and I started to attend university forums on the position of Malays in Singapore society. I got in touch with researchers working on Malay and Muslim identity, and the respective groups' struggles for adequate representation. I learnt that Singapore's Malays are the racial group with the most socio-demographic problems, for instance with the lowest median income and lowest rate of tertiary degrees, being on the edge of marginalization (see Chua 1995, 1998; Hill and Fee 1995). Interestingly, I could see this fact reflected in problems with heritage representation, i.e. in the discussion on the tight boundaries of 'their' ethnic historic district and the remaining problems with the built heritage within. Clearly, I had to position myself now as a researcher personality interested in Malay and Muslim Identity in Singapore and the adequate representation of their heritage. Continuously claiming objectivity as an 'outsider' would not be truthful and would make me vulnerable to legitimate criticism. Yet, I was ultimately content with the results of my initial 'objective outsider' approach. Summing up that 'objective outsideness', despite all limitations that apply, has enabled me to find an interesting field site, which demonstrates problems of heritage representation well. Furthermore, it showcases both opportunities (economic uplifting) and risks (alienation of locals) of tourism development, as redevelopment efforts have only been completed recently.

Having elaborated on the selection process for a field site, I will now turn to reflections on the researcher personality when thriving for 'empathetic insideness'. Starting off with general statements about positionality, I would like to share my personal experiences. I argue that becoming a 'full' insider can only be a utopian vision for both researchers with and without prior exposure to the researched place and people. Hence, I would like to emphasize that it is not a must to be accustomed to this research setting beforehand. I will conclude by highlighting the importance of outside academicians for the advancement of local research.

## 'Empathetic insideness' – reflections on the researcher personality

I agree that post-positivist, i.e. feminist, literature has good reasons to stress the importance of close ties of a researcher with the researched. First, ethnographic research requires personal involvement, so the perpetuation of objectivity throughout the research process is indeed illusionary (see Rose 1997). Secondly, the ambition for gaining insider status in the course of the process can be useful because it enables and, to a certain degree, enforces a deeper understanding of the researched. Certainly, this emphasis on 'insiderization' is in part a reaction to historical proceedings in research. In the past, the relatively uninformed and rushed travel writing of 'busy' researchers has in many instances reinforced prejudices rather than contributed to the spread of knowledge (see Othman 2002; Kahn 2006). In a colonial context, and with the regional focus on Southeast Asia, this general statement also applies to research done in collaboration with the British Colonial government in Malaysia. For instance, Alatas (1977) discusses the erroneous assumptions about Malay people and their attitude to religion and Islamic culture. Other than feminism, the postcolonial discourse has therefore taken in the postulation of insiderization as a reaction to the Euro- or Western-centric ethnographic works of the colonial era. Such sensitivities are natural and they persist to date. Upon my initial presentation on possible assets of an outsider perspective, I was confronted with a critique which highlighted the ability of local academics to do rigorous research in their own surrounding. While I certainly do not doubt this fact, I would argue against an imperative of 'insiderization'. I reacted by trying to reach out for 'empathetic insideness' in learning the language and attending cultural forums of the researched.

However, there are certainly limits to the engagement as an 'empathetic insider', especially when one considers the historical background of the researched in question. In my case, for example, it will never be entirely possible to understand what exactly the locals feel about the redevelopment of Kampong Glam. For instance, I never witnessed the literal function of its Istana ('Palace') as the seat of Malay Royalty. I only perceived it as an enjoyable tourism venue, when it had already been converted into a heritage centre. The descendants of the Sultan had already been evicted. Having read critiques of gentrification in Singapore's central city, including Kampong Glam, I have an understanding that older Malays feel critical about it, but I still cannot fully empathize with them because I lack their level of emotional attachment (Rose 1997).

This fact, however, does not disqualify me as an ethnographic researcher on the topic of Malay/Muslim heritage and tourism. Personality matters in any case; and Singapore's population has been rigorously subdivided into four races: Chinese, Malay, Indian and 'Others' (CMIO) as a residual category (see Chua 1995). Even local researchers could not escape the consequences of being categorized in this so-called CMIO scheme: a Singaporean Malay researcher would most likely have to face reproaches of being biased towards his or her own ethnic group. A Singaporean Chinese would represent the dominant culture and thus work out of a delicate position when researching on the allegedly marginalized Malays and their heritage, while the 'usual' outsider constraints might apply to a Singaporean Indian researcher. Most importantly, we should not define personal suitability as a researcher along racial lines to begin with. In an ironic twist to the Eurocentric travel writing of the colonial area, potentially interested researchers from abroad could be discouraged from entering their host universities' local research domain because of their different, non-local origins or affiliations. The consequence can thus be to support only those researchers, regardless of race or gender, who are willing to indulge in the culture of the researched.

Despite some shortcomings there is no alternative for universities but to host alien research scholars for local projects, as long as these scholars acknowledge their initial outsider perspective. 'Foreign research talents' can never reach 100 per cent insider status, just as 'home-grown' researchers probably never will, since positionality matters for them too. However, it is necessary for research institutions to draw on outside expertise for local problems in order to engage in a comparative perspective. The host institution should help the outside researcher on his or her way to gain 'empathetic insideness', by means of providing literature sources as well as personal encouragement. This 'intensive care' will pay off for them via gaining new insights from a fresh and unconsumed perspective.

## Conclusion

Both complete 'objective outsideness' and unmitigated 'empathetic insideness' should be understood as utopian visions rather than academic practicalities. However, they can serve as valid aims to strive for in different stages of research. In the initial step of choosing a field site, practising as objective as possible observations on a number of possible locations can be a valuable approach. In my case, I identified ethnic heritage as being a key component of tourism in Singapore. Despite initial doubts about the validity of my outsider observations, I found many aspects conformed to previous research works on local tourism. Thus I argue that researchers who are alien to their field site could engage in this approach instead of making a choice based on prior affiliation.

In the subsequent steps of research, the ethnographic fieldworker will attempt to acquire an insider status, knowing that 100 per cent insideness is unobtainable. Based on the synthesis of my fieldwork notes and information about tourism-related problems derived from local academic literature, I chose the Malay/Muslim ethnic district as my field site since it bears witness to both a high potential and severe risks of tourism development. Subsequently, I embarked on a journey to empathetic insideness, learning the local language and attending gatherings of the researched community.

Clearly, it is the motivation to become an 'empathetic insider' which is welcome, even though full insider status is utopian. Therefore, I caution not to discriminate against researchers who have to bridge a wider cultural gap and whose journey to any degree of 'empathetic insideness' thus is a longer one compared to equivalent efforts of local academics. In order to gain a variety of perspectives in research, it is necessary to enable researchers from diverse cultural background to engage in fieldwork. This would include research done by cultural 'outsiders' on 'subjects' and localities which have previously been considered a domain of a particular local university or department. For Singapore, I also argue that local researchers face limitations – and often bias – on account of their personal ethnicity. Therefore, problems of positionality are not just restricted to outside researchers. This fact demonstrates that cultural aliens are equally qualified to undertake research in new surroundings. 'Objective outsideness' therefore can serve as a valid starting point for initial research steps, given the researchers' willingness to identify with the researched area and people in subsequent stages.

## References

Alatas, S. (1977) *The Myth of the Lazy Native*. London: Cass.

Begam, N.B. (1997) 'The Making of a Place: History, Community and Identity of Little India'. Unpublished academic exercise thesis, National University of Singapore, Singapore.

Chang, T.C. (1996) 'Local Uniqueness in the Global Village: Heritage Tourism in Singapore'. Unpublished PhD Thesis, McGill University, Montreal.

Chang, T.C. (1997) 'Heritage Tourism as a Commodity: Traversing the Tourist–local Divide', *Singapore Journal of Tropical Geography* 18(1): 46–68.

Chang, T.C. (1999) 'Local Uniqueness in the Global Village: Heritage Tourism in Singapore', *Professional Geographer* 51(1): 91–103.

Chang, T.C. (2000) 'Singapore's Little India: A Tourist Attraction as a Contested', *Urban Studies* 37(2): 343–66.

Chang, T.C. (2005) 'Place, Memory and Identity: Imagining "New Asia"', *Asia Pacific Viewpoint* 46: 247–53.

Chang, T.C. and Yeoh, B. (1999) 'New Asia–Singapore: Communicating Local Cultures through Global Tourism', *Geoforum* 30(2): 101–15.

Chari, S. (2003) 'Marxism, Sarcasm, Ethnography: Geographical Fieldnotes from South India', *Singapore Journal of Tropical Geography* 24(2): 169–83.

Chua, B.-H. (1995) 'Culture, Multiracialism and National Identity in Singapore', *Department of Sociology Working Papers* 125: 1–33.

England, K. (1994) 'Getting Personal: Reflexivity, Positionality, and Feminist Research', *Professional Geographer* 46(1): 80–9.

Henderson, J. (2002) 'Attractions and Tourism Development in Asia: A Comparative Study of Hong Kong and Singapore', *International Journal of Tourism Research* 4(5): 337–44.

Henderson, J. (2003) 'Ethnic Heritage as a Tourist Attraction: The Peranakans of Singapore', *International Journal of Heritage Studies* 9(1): 27–44.

Hill, M. and Fee, L.K. (1995) *The Politics of Nation Building and Citizenship in Singapore*. London: Routledge.

Kahn, J. (2006) *Other Malays – Nationalism and Cosmopolitanism in the Modern Malay World*. Singapore: Singapore University Press.

Katz, C. (1994) 'Playing the Field: Questions of Fieldwork in Geography', *Professional Geographer* 46(1): 67–2.

Lee, P. (2004) *Singapore, Tourism and Me*. Singapore: Pamelia Lee Pte.

Leong, L.W.-T. (1997) 'Commodifying Ethnicity: State and Ethnic Tourism in Singapore', in M. Picard and R. Wood (eds), *Tourism, Ethnicity, and the State in Asian and Pacific Societies*. Honolulu: University of Hawai'i Press.

Othman, M.R. (2002) 'Conflicting Political Loyalities of the Arabs in Malaya before World War II', in H. De Jonge and N. Kaptein (eds), *Transcending Borders: Arabs, politics, trade and Islam in Southeast Asia*. Leiden: KITVL Press.

Relph, E. (1976) *Place and Placelessness*. London: Pion.

Rose, G. (1997) 'Situating Knowledges: positionality, reflexivities and other tactics', *Progress in Human Geography* 21(3): 305–20.

Saunders, K.J. (2004) 'Creating and Recreating Heritage in Singapore', *Current Issues in Tourism* 7(4): 440–8.

Sim, L.L. (1996) 'Urban Conservation Policy and the Preservation of Historical and Cultural Heritage – the case of Singapore', *Cities* 13(6): 399–409.

Singapore Tourism Board (STB) (1996) *Tourism 21. Vision of a Tourism Capital*. Singapore: STB.

Tembo, F. (2003) 'Multiple Identities, Representations and Categorisations: Experiences in the Study of People's Life-worlds in Rural Malawi', *Singapore Journal of Tropical Geography* 24(2): 229–41.

Teo, P. and Yeoh, B. (1997) 'Remaking Local Heritage for Tourism', *Annals of Tourism Research* 24(1): 192–213.

Urban Redevelopment Authority (URA) (1991) *Conservation Guidelines for Kampong Glam Conservation Area*. Singapore: Urban Redevelopment Authority.

Woon, K.K., Wan-Ling, C.J.W. and Chia, K. (eds) (2000) *Rethinking Chinatown and Heritage Conservation in Singapore*. Singapore: Singapore Heritage Society.

Yeoh, B. and Huang, S. (1996) 'The Conservation–redevelopment Dilemma in Singapore – The case of the Kampong Glam historic district', *Cities* 13(6): 411–22.

Yeoh, B. and Kong, L. (1994) 'Reading Landscape Meanings: State Constructions and Lived Experiences in Singapore's Chinatown', *Habitat International* 18(4): 17–35.

Yeoh, B. and Kong, L. (eds) (1995) *Portraits of Places – History, Community and Identity in Singapore*. Singapore: Times Editions.

# 10 Cosmopolitan methodology

## Implications of the ethnographer's multiple and shifting relationships in studying ethnic tourism

*Malita Allan*

### Introduction

In its most characteristic form, the method of ethnography involves 'the ethnographer participating, overtly or covertly, in people's everyday lives for an extended period of time, watching what happens, listening to what is said [and] asking questions' (Hammersley and Atkinson 1995: 1), related to the issues that are the focus of the research. As such, personhood is one of the most important methodological 'tools' of anthropologists.

Understanding who one is as a person and what this entails in local categories, especially regarding one's kinship status, is not new; however, reporting style and representation has changed. In the 1960s and 1970s, feminist, culturalist, postmodernist and postcolonialist critiques posed ethical, political and methodological difficulties for the doing of anthropology as a scientific project. This led to a call for reflexivity in the sense that studies of others must also be studies of researchers in their relationships with those others (Davies 1999). Since then anthropologists have increasingly reflected on their particular social, cultural, gendered and political identities in the field and the implications this has for research. For example, issues are raised relating to being women (Golde 1986), tourists (Crick 1991), non-Western and non-native (Fadzillah 2004) and to insider/outsider identities of researchers in the field more generally (Hume and Mulcock 2004).

However, Kuper (1994) dismisses such critiques, particularly those advocating nativist anthropology, which he asserts threaten an end to the doing of anthropology. Instead he argues for a 'cosmopolitan project' of anthropologists to 'aspire to contribute a comparative dimension to the enlightenment project of a science of human variation in time and space . . . that cannot be bound in the service of any political program' (Kuper 1994: 551).

More recently, Kahn (2003) has challenged Kuper. Kahn uses Immanuel Kant to define the term 'cosmopolitan' with its origins in the philosophy of the Enlightenment and describes Kuper's argument as indicative of a return by some anthropologists to 'Kantian universalism' (Kahn 2003: 404). In contrast, Kahn argues that anthropologists, in the doing of 'anthropology as cosmopolitan practice', must seriously engage with critiques which suggest that universalising logics are Eurocentric and therefore racist, as well as sexist and classist. He believes that anthropologists seek to study 'a world not of discrete and isolable other cultures and societies, but a world of "intercultural" or "intercommunal" relationships' (2003: 406) in which they embed themselves (see also Beck and Sznaider 2006).

In this chapter I aim to make a contribution to the methodological dimensions of cosmopolitan anthropology as defined by Kahn. I reflect on the 'intercultural' relationships in which I was embedded whilst conducting ethnographic fieldwork for eight months in 2003–4 in two neighbouring ethnic Tai tourism villages in northern Vietnam. These relationships were structured by the different identities I had. I discuss how I negotiated multiple and shifting identities in this pluralistic setting: as a researcher (*nha nghien cuu*), tourist (*khach du lich*), Westerner (*Tay*), villager as a young female (*em/noong* or *chi/ay*) and household member as younger sister (*em/noong*), older sister (*chi/ay*), niece or granddaughter (*chau/lan*) (I provide the terms in Vietnamese and Tai here but for the rest of the chapter I use only the Vietnamese terms, as I mainly conversed with the villagers in Vietnamese), and an anthropologist and fellow traveller among tourists, and how in turn they influenced my research.

## Ethnographic research

Believed to have migrated from the southern China/northern Vietnam border in the fourteenth century, the Tai have since settled in these two villages cultivating wet rice in a breathtaking valley among the mountains in the northwest of Vietnam. The elderly villagers' lives have changed dramatically in their lifetime from French colonialism to Vietnamese socialism and nationalism, into which the villagers have become integrated and where the global market is playing an increasing importance in their lives today. Tourism began in one of the villages in the 1960s and in the neighbouring village in the 1990s. Today domestic and foreign tourists visit the villages throughout the year, where they can stay overnight in a homestay, watch a cultural performance, purchase handicrafts and walk or cycle to surrounding villages.

My research methods included common anthropological strategies such as participant observation and ongoing conversations with key informants as well as interviews and surveys. I stayed with a family in each village who shared their homes and lives with me. I always stayed with members of the same family in each village, that of *anh* and *chi* Ninh and *chu* and *co* Thay (pseudonyms are used). These host families became my key informants with whom I shared meals, conversations and other experiences, and participated in financial, gift and favour exchanges. This built our friendship and a sense of loyalty, helped to establish a rapport, and also created complex relations and awkward moments, as discussed below.

I began my research by conducting a household survey in order to meet the villagers. Many people were extremely welcoming and helpful, some were happy to talk about their lives and proud to discuss their culture, others were suspicious (see below). We chatted over cups of tea in their stilt houses or outside whilst they were attending to their handicraft stalls or sewing. I observed the villagers, tourists and others and their interactions. I partici-pated in village society when invited. I ate with many villagers. I attended parties, festivals, and rituals such as *Tet* (New Year celebrations), *Com Moi* (New Rice festival), funerals and weddings. Not only did I meet many people during these occasions but also my relations with my host families and their neighbours and relatives were strengthened by my being there with them and I was able to get more of an 'insider's' view of their lives. I kept a journal and took photos. I also carried out informal interviews with tourists and tour guides and more formal interviews with officials. Such research methods became easier over time as my language skills improved.

At times I was accompanied to the villages by *em* Sinh, a junior researcher in Hanoi. To say her role was to assist me by translating interviews and texts, which we initially negotiated, is too narrow. She ate, slept, observed and participated. Being of Tai ethnicity herself, she helped me to understand what I was learning by giving explanations, making comparisons with her life and learning experiences, and raising questions. I learnt some Tai and Vietnamese language from her as well as more about the Tai people in Vietnam from her perspective. Not only did she become a key informant, as we worked and lived in the villages experiencing highs and lows together, but she also became a good friend. Just as her positioning with me altered, so too did it with the villagers. During her stay her identity shifted among metropolitan, tourist, guest, young woman, friend and relative. Generally, villagers opened up much more as soon as they understood she was Tai. Despite her family being from a neighbouring province in Vietnam now living in Hanoi, to the villagers they were related to one another, they were Tai. They spoke a different Tai dialect so she mostly conversed in Vietnamese as she found this to be easier and I preferred it as I could understand more.

## Negotiating multiple identities

The above ethnographic methods took shape through the intercultural and intersubjective experiences related to my multiple identities. Villagers and tourists classified themselves, each other and me in various ways at various times during my stay: according to kinship status, gender, age, region, nation-ality, ethnicity, occupation, economic status and prestige. They 'rank' them-selves and others in a social hierarchy, which dictates status and also appropriate manners and language to be used in social interactions, therefore influencing interactions and conversations (Fadzillah 2004: 33). I will now discuss in more detail how I negotiated these identities and how they influenced my research, noting these identities are interwoven and overlap, creating complex levels of relationships and interactions.

## Researcher in rural Vietnam

Early in my stay, after the household members had retired to bed around 11.30 p.m., a group of officials and policemen visited. Their noisy cars and motorbikes disturbed the sleeping village. *Chi* Ninh scampered out of bed to greet the entourage. One had come all the way from the provincial town, two hours' drive away. *Chi* Ninh was reprimanded for not registering me. In an official manner they viewed my papers and told me that I was free to do research; their only concern was that I be registered. The atmosphere was tense. After about half an hour they said they did not wish to disturb us and left. We looked at one another, laughing and breathing sighs of relief as we returned to bed.

Later it was explained to me that particularly before *doi moi* (renovation) in 1986, foreigners could not do research without police involvement to ensure the government was not betrayed. During his fieldwork in a small Mekong Delta village in the early 1990s, Taylor (1999:20) gathered 'critical commentary' from locals which was 'incapable of publication' and, along with the feeling of being taken for an enemy and a spy, was led to abandon the rural field site. My experiences have embroiled me in various ethical questions, although not to the extreme of altering the rural field site due to my being situated in government-promoted 'cultural tourism villages' (*ban van hoa du lich*) and due to a relatively more open and less suspicious environment in Vietnam a decade later. Nevertheless, the above incident occurred, which, along with the feeling of being watched, I felt brought my hosts and me closer. Although it occurred at the beginning of my stay in the village, I could feel a division forming: 'us' (the villagers and myself) and 'them' (the officials). In her field research among ethnic Cham in southern Vietnam, Nakamura (1999: 78) mentions a similar divide between the authorities and herself and the Cham. She likened her frustrations of bureaucracy in the field to the experience of frustration of Cham living as minority people in Vietnam. Similar surveillance is experienced by Vietnamese researchers.

Such surveillance affected my research, particularly in the beginning, as many villagers repeated the 'official line' in response to my questions. On the one hand, I learnt that due to the integration of the villagers into the Vietnamese nation villagers believe in the 'official line'. On the other hand, villagers seemed conditioned not to talk about everyday practices that may run counter to given policies or social norms. When I conducted the household survey many people were willing to share their stories, in a politically neutral way. For example, one man said that he only discusses the positives of the government and that everything was good in the village. This meant I had to carefully select the language I used in my questioning. Like Lloyd and colleagues (2004: 15), I obtained information about ethnic relations by listening to people's life histories and experiences under different policies and historical periods. Rather than referring to 'problems' or 'conflicts', I would choose less controversial language by asking about their involvement in development programmes and their impact on their lives. In all situations I remained respectful of their decisions of what to share, which in time became greater as trust and closer relationships developed.

However, being a researcher in rural Vietnam is not just an experience of someone who is subject to state surveillance; it is more complex than this (Taylor 1999). It also involves a prestigious and powerful status, having respect as a literate person, and with the cooperation of the government. My relations with the state were more complex than a them/us division, just as they were between the locals and the state.

### Tourist/Westerner/outsider

Crick (1991) suggests that anthropologists, particularly those studying tourism, have identities which overlap with that of the tourist. At times during my fieldwork villagers treated me as they would a tourist, which had various implications for my research.

When I was discussing different types of tourists with one of my host families I discovered they differentiated between tourists and researchers when *chi* Ninh said to me, 'you are a researcher not a tourist'. However, before I introduced myself or if word had not spread to them, villagers assumed that I was a tourist and treated me as such. I used these experiences to inform my research and found the identity of 'tourist as researcher' to be useful as it provided insights on what it is like to be a tourist in these villages. Villagers were polite, hospitable and sometimes pushy, and our interactions were mainly based on economic exchanges. If I asked questions, for example, about a handicraft product, sometimes they lied about who made it and what it was made from, thinking I would buy it if they had made it from natural materials. Like Little's (2004: 30) experience with Maya vendors, villagers were interested in gaining some sort of economic benefit from me, such as through selling handicrafts to me. I could not afford, nor did I desire, to purchase items from all the villagers with whom I worked. I therefore waited and took friends and tourists wanting a souvenir or drink to their shop, so that we could mutually benefit from the exchange.

Of course, not all villagers' interactions with tourists are based on economics alone. They are also influenced by the historical context and behaviour of the tourist. The most common word I heard wherever I was in Vietnam was *Tay*. *Tay* literally means 'west', and also means 'western', 'occidental', 'French'. It is used to refer to people as Westerners and more generally as foreigners. The term immediately evokes the French colonial era and reveals assumptions and expectations about hierarchy. On the one hand, villagers have an image of Westerners as 'modern' (*hien dai*) and 'developed' (*phat trien*). For example, locals asked me for information and advice on things like the best farming and agricultural practices in Australia, which I have no experience of. On the other hand, *Tay* evokes memories of repression and mixed feelings of anger and sadness, hence the following comment from another villager: 'Visitors may come from America and I have a negative feeling about that. My brother died in the American war.'

Villagers were more comfortable talking about the behaviour of domestic tourists with me, being a *Tay*. One man complained, 'foreign tourists are more polite than the Vietnamese, for example, foreigners do not make noise and respect the hosts. Vietnamese students are noisy.' Furthermore, in general I witnessed villagers become quiet and formal in their interactions with domestic tourists. Nevertheless, the villagers as hosts are polite and hospitable with tourists, whom they treat as their guests. They are well known for their hospitality and their success is partly reflected in the following comment by a villager, 'If the local people here are polite with tourists then the tourists will be friendly with them.'

When tourism began in the 1960s, experts and government officials from other socialist republics in the world such as the former Soviet Union were escorted by Vietnamese authorities, who led them around the villages. The villagers were not allowed to have contact with the tourists, who did not pay for such visits but sometimes gave gifts of food. The tourists never stayed the night in the village. Today, with homestay there are opportunities for much more contact, particularly for expatriates with Vietnamese language skills. Tourists are not escorted, do not require a tour guide and can travel independently. 'They came here as friends, guests, not as tourists', a villager commented about a group of 'French and English' who worked in Hanoi but made regular visits to the village in the 1990s to play soccer. Not only do relations between tourists and villagers extend beyond economics, but the boundaries between tourists, guests and friends are blurred and their meanings overlap. This made my status more ambiguous.

### Villager/'young' female

At the beginning of my stay the most common words I heard as I walked around the villages were '*Tay*', 'allo, you buy?', '*mua guip*?' (help buy), which continued with some villagers I did not get to know during my stay. Over time, however, greetings changed as I took on roles as a family member and became a friend, neighbour and villager; '*chao em*' (hi younger sister), '*chao* Ma-li-ta' (hi Malita) or '*pay in no*' (Tai for 'go out', an acknowledgment equivalent to 'how are you?' where a response is not expected).

As I stayed longer in the villages I experienced a change in identity to 'honorary villager', and the more 'villager' I became over time, the more I was expected to conform to rules for women. Importance of hierarchy is illustrated in the villages by the seat positioning of people in their houses during important gatherings, such as parties and funerals, according to both gender and age. In general, men sat at the front of the house, women and children at the back, near the kitchen. Older men sat at the most important position in the house, in front of the altar. As an 'honorary villager' I was sometimes assigned a higher status, which put me in conflicting positions, such as when

I was asked to sit with the men to the front of the house. Although I felt uncomfortable, such positioning of me by the villagers enabled me to speak with men also. As a researcher I was also able to speak with a range of men through the household survey and with officials in the People's Committees, the majority of whom were male. As a female villager I generally spent more time with women.

I learnt quickly of the expectations of respect based on age. Younger people should listen to their elders without interrupting and without directly questioning what they have to say. Even though I found it hard to avoid, I learnt not to ask 'why' questions as they were too direct and disrespectful. In order not to offend anyone, I was quieter than usual.

Young people's status becomes higher once they marry. Although I was unmarried, I felt that once the villagers had met my partner, I was treated with more respect. The persistent jokes about my marrying a Tai or Vietnamese husband changed to questions on when we were marrying and conversations about good and bad years to do so. Just as I was observing the villagers, they were observing me; I was 'an object of curiosity and attention' (Golde 1986: 10). Their questioning and comments to me helped make me more real to them, thus reducing psychological distance. It also provided me with indirect insights about what they valued through their constant questions about my marriage status and family.

### Household member

Kinship is a long-standing and central subject to anthropology, particularly in relation to kin terms and classification. Speakers of Vietnamese and Tai, like speakers of other languages in Southeast Asia, use kinship terms rather than personal pronouns in systems of person reference (Benedict 1943; Luong 1990). This means that instead of referring to oneself as I/me/you, terms such as younger sibling (*em*) and uncle (*chu*) are used depending on whom one is talking with and about. This use of kinship terms highlights the enduring kinship roles of the referents in relation to one another and structures their interactions accordingly (Luong 1990: 38). Kinship terms are also used in numerous contexts among non-relatives. This is in order to structure 'hierarchical and solidary relations' (Luong 1990: 38) among the referents of the kinship terms. During my time in Vietnam I became used to using such kinship terms with the people I met. However, I learnt more about the complexity of the kinship terms, their meanings and subsequent interactions when living with the families in the villages. I developed various relations, became accustomed to certain roles and experienced occasional awkward moments in these households.

My familial positioning allowed me to 'fit in' with the families and determined some of my roles in the households. As I am younger than *chi* Ninh but older than her children, I referred to her as older sister (*chi*) and she called me younger sister (*em*). However, although I was her younger sister, at times

I felt like one of her daughters. Furthermore, although I was the eldest, I felt like the youngest child whilst I was given language lessons, instructions on tasks and explanations mainly by *chi* Ninh, but also by her children. So too in *co* Thay's household, where I was a niece (*chau*) and older sister (*chi*). Nevertheless, as I became more familiar with the lifestyle I was able to carry out everyday tasks such as helping to prepare meals, carrying the food table and sweeping the floor. I also helped in the rice paddies. Such tasks were related to my roles as sister, niece and daughter. At various times I was told to sit up straight, to grow my hair longer and to serve meals. However, sometimes when I offered to help more I was reminded that I was a guest/ researcher when they insisted that I relax or do my work instead.

Through shared living and other shared experiences such as supporting each other through grief and family feuds, venturing on trips and hosting tourists together, which created moments of both ease and awkwardness, a closeness nevertheless developed. I gained access to more personal issues that I will not write about on ethical grounds out of respect for the families.

### Fellow traveller/anthropologist

I also encountered research implications with the tourists in the villages. I unexpectedly experienced difficulty in gaining access to tourists for a number of reasons. Unfortunately, in 2004 part of the major highway forming the most direct route from Hanoi to the villages was under construction and was closed for six months. This affected the number of tourists visiting the villages. However, this situation enabled me to consider how villagers cope when tourism disappears and also highlighted that tourism is not stable and can disappear temporarily or permanently for different reasons. There were also fewer tourists in the villages due to SARS and bird flu.

The finding of suitable 'observation posts' seems to be a crucial element in the ethnographic study of tourists and tourism, especially as tourists themselves are such a mobile and transient group. On discussing his fieldwork on tourism in Sri Lanka, Crick (1992) talks about his relationship with 'Ali', a pavement hawker, and how the street corner where Ali sold his goods became an important observation post from where Crick could interact with and observe interactions with tourists. Similarly, Little (2004) sat with Maya handicraft vendors in Guatemala to observe their interactions with tourists. In the villages, tourists often remained within the confines of the houses they were staying in because of length of stay (usually one night), the type of tourism and the layout of the village. I found such a private sphere more difficult to penetrate and therefore had less access to tourists unless they were staying in the same house. I had greater access to tourists in the public sphere as they walked around the village, looking at and buying handicrafts.

Access to tourists also depended on their openness. Similar to Tucker's (2003) experience in conducting tourism research in a village in Turkey, my ability to meet foreign package group tourists in the villages was limited to a few chance encounters and observations. It was my experience that they were mostly insular and closed and therefore not so welcoming to 'outsiders'. By contrast, domestic tourists tended to travel in larger groups where the focus was on having fun through mixing with many people and were more inclusive and happy for others to join in. Also, for some, foreigners were as big an attraction as the villagers.

When Crick (1991) suggests that anthropologists have identities which overlap with those of the tourist, he does not really bring out the ethical difficulties of sitting between these two roles. How does one negotiate one's role between the local community and tourists, when one is trying to access and gain the trust of both? When I did have access to international tourists I straddled insider/outsider identities. International tourists, for example, would see me as one of them, but sometimes as a 'guide' with special 'insider' knowledge. Some treated me like a curiosity, that is, as an 'exotic' and real-life anthropologist in the twenty-first century. On the other hand, I was able to be more on the 'in'-side of villagers at times when they were talking and joking about tourists. I was fully aware that my presence at times affected the nature of tourists' experience and interaction. At times I acted as a translator for both foreign tourists and villagers in simple transactions such as when tourists wanted more information about accommodation or a handicraft product and when villagers wanted to know how long they were staying for and about dietary requirements. I also found myself in the role of culture broker, answering tourists' questions on the lives of villagers whilst answering villagers' questions on the lives of foreigners.

I felt torn between being insider/outsider when tourists who were staying with my host family commented that the prices they were being charged for their food and accommodation were too expensive. They asked my advice as they did not want to be 'ripped off'. I understood their position but knew they were being charged the standard price for foreign tourists in the village. They could have bargained the price down but I did not highlight this. I distanced myself from the situation as I felt a sense of loyalty to the household.

## Conclusion

During ethnographic fieldwork in neighbouring ethnic Tai tourism villages in Vietnam, I was embedded in a web of relationships. The multiple identities I experienced were often ambiguous, overlapping and shifted at different times with various people. Being an 'in-between' person had its benefits and challenges, reminding me that I could not take things for granted. My identities as researcher, tourist, *Tay*, friend, villager, family member, and as a fellow traveller (with tourists), all provided different and contradictory outcomes and enabled me to straddle both insider/outsider viewpoints. Such experiences were highlighted by doing an ethnography with a focus on tourism.

Cosmopolitan methodology in anthropology highlights that ethnographers are embedded in a web of 'intercultural relationships' (Kahn 2003) when conducting fieldwork so that studies of others must also be studies of ethnographers in their relationships with those others. No matter who the ethnographer, analysing aspects of their identities and interactions is as important as analysing the research subjects' identities and interactions, since both affect research outcomes (Fadzillah 2004: 33). Whilst I was embedded in a web of different relationships that were fraught with difficulties, they also multiplied the possibilities of gaining insights from different positions into the identities and relations of ethnic tourism in Vietnam.

## Acknowledgments

This research was made possible with financial support from the Faculty of Humanities and Social Sciences at La Trobe University and from an ARC Discovery – Projects (2003–2007) grant entitled 'Asia-Pacific Cosmopolitanisms: Managing Diversity and Identity Politics in a Changing Region'. I would like to thank Philip Taylor, Joel Kahn, Maribeth Erb, T.C. Chang, Wendy Mee and Alberto Gomes for their help and useful comments.

## References

Beck, U. and Sznaider, N. (2006) 'Unpacking Cosmopolitanism for the Social Sciences: A research Agenda', *British Journal of Sociology* 57(1): 1–23.

Benedict, P. (1943) 'Studies in Thai Kinship Terminology', *Journal of the American Oriental Society* 63(2): 168–75.

Crick, M. (1991) 'Tourists, Locals and Anthropologists: Quizzical Reflections on "Otherness" in Tourist Encounters and in Tourism Research', *Australian Cultural History* 10: 6–18.

Crick, M. (1992) 'Ali and me: An Essay in Street-corner Anthropology', in J. Okely and H. Callaway (eds), *Anthropology and Autobiography*. London: Routledge.

Davies, C. (1999) *Reflexive Ethnography: A Guide to Researching Selves and Others*. London, New York: Routledge.

Fadzillah, I. (2004) 'Going beyond "the West" and "the Rest": Conducting non-Western, Non-native Ethnography in Northern Thailand', in L. Hume and J. Mulcock (eds), *Anthropologists in the Field. Cases of Informant Observation*. New York: Columbia University Press.

Golde, P. (ed.) (1986) *Women in the Field*. Berkeley, Los Angeles: University of California Press.

Hammersley, M. and Atkinson, P. (1995) *Ethnography: Principles in Practice*. New York: Routledge.

Hume, L. and Mulcock, J. (eds) (2004) *Anthropologists in the Field. Cases of Informant Observation*. New York: Columbia University Press.

Kahn, J.S. (2003) 'Anthropology as Cosmopolitan Practice?' *Anthropological Theory* 3(4): 403–15.

Kuper, A. (1994) 'Culture, Identity and the Project of a Cosmopolitan Anthropology', *Man* 29(3): 537–54.

Little, W.E. (2004) *Mayas in the Marketplace. Tourism, Globalisation, and Cultural Identity*. Austin: University of Texas Press.

Lloyd, K., Miller F. and Scott, S. (2004) 'Changing research spaces: Doing Human Geography Fieldwork in Vietnam', paper presented at the 15th Biennial Conference of the Asian Studies Association of Australia, Canberra, 29 June–2 July. Online. Available HTTP: <http://coombs.anu.edu.au/ASAA/conference/proceedings/asaa-2004-proceedings.html> (accessed 2 June 2006).

Luong, Hy V. (1990) *Discursive Practices and Linguistic Meanings*. Amsterdam: John Benjamins.

Nakamura, R. (1999) 'Cham in Viet Nam. Dynamics of ethnicity', Unpublished PhD dissertation, University of Washington, Seattle.

Taylor, P. (1999) 'The Shifting Heart: Encountering the Modernities of Post-war Southern Vietnam', *Canberra Anthropology* 22(2): 15–25.

Tucker, H. (2003) *Living with Tourism: Negotiating Identities in a Turkish Village*. London: Routledge.

# 11 Allowing women's voices to be heard in tourism research

## Competing paradigms of method

*Jo Bensemann*

## Introduction

This chapter explores some of the philosophical and methodological foundations of fieldwork in tourism, using a study of copreneurship as a basis for discussion. Copreneurs are couples who share ownership, commitment and responsibility for a business together (Barnett and Barnett 1989), or as Marshack (1994) put it, copreneurship represents the dynamic interaction of the systems of love and work. The study explored the experiences of owners of rural tourism accommodation businesses in New Zealand within the framework of copreneurship. It examined roles within copreneurial rural tourism businesses and studied women's experiences of entrepreneurship within the copreneurial environment. To do this, the study used a mixed method approach (a survey and in-depth interviews) to elicit information about copreneurs operating rural tourism businesses, and about how women experience copreneurship within rural tourism.

The chapter begins with a brief overview of the wider philosophy of social science research and this leads to the acceptance of the interpretivist approach and discussion of its validity for this type of research. The importance of reflexivity is raised and the relevant significance of situating myself as researcher is presented because critical reflexivity or consideration of the researcher as a research instrument is an important principle of tourism fieldwork, which inevitably involves talking with real people. Contextualising the research within a feminist approach is also discussed, along with feminism providing a pathway to understanding the lived experiences of others. The second part of this chapter describes the research design of the copreneurship study and proposes that triangulating methods and data sources within an interpretive approach was essential for gaining a fuller understanding of the experiences of copreneurs in the context of rural tourism. The research design enabled the methodological importance of reflexivity where the researcher is an insider to the study to be stressed.

## Research paradigms and philosophy in social science research

Paradigms provide the framework within which research is carried out. They reflect fundamental beliefs or metaphysics and are concerned with the essential and underlying principles that shape and define perceptions of the world, its nature and the place of people within it. There are four major paradigms which structure research: positivist, post-positivist, critical and interpretive. Each provides flexible guidelines that connect theory and method and help to determine the structure and shape of any enquiry (Goodson and Phillimore, 2004). The suitability of these paradigms (in terms of research activity) can be assessed by exploring their ontological, epistemological and methodological positions (e.g. for further discussion see Denzin and Lincoln 1994; and Goodson and Phillimore [2004] for a tourism perspective).

Positivist researchers often claim the advantage of being more objective and value-free, producing 'hygienic' research in which the researcher is absent (Marsh *et al.* 1996). In refutation of this, Clark and colleagues (1999: 15) explain that scientific research in the positivist tradition is not objective, 'as any human observer of natural, as well as social phenomena, brings to their observation values and beliefs that impinge upon their interpretation of those phenomena'.

Many of the assumptions and characteristics of positivism are perhaps appropriate in a natural science; however, in social science they negate room for participants' experiences, and involvement by the researcher. Many social science fields, however (tourism included), still show a strong bias towards positivist approaches, advocating the rigid separation between researcher and subject.

## Crisis of representation and reflexivity

The fact that women often become the object rather than the subject of research is a major feminist critique of the positivist research paradigm. Postmodernism served as a corrective to these criticisms, stressing that researchers need to cite their authority and construct research that allows women's realities and voices (Lunn 1997). The inclusion of a feminine viewpoint to extend what is seen as the prevailing masculine ideology supporting research and theorisation has been recommended (Aitchison 2001). According to Ateljevic (2000: 371), 'the "crisis of representation" encapsulated many of the concerns encountered in the feminist critique of the all-pervasive hegemonic dominance of masculinist Western academic approaches'. The epistemological bases of mainstream science's claims to objectivity are the starting points for feminist critiques of objectivity (Lunn 1997). This is relevant for the copreneurship study being used here as an example because one of the aims of the study was to allow women's voices to describe their own experiences of copreneurship.

Issues raised by the crisis of representation in the social sciences have slowly emerged for consideration in tourism research. One issue highlighted as crucial is the investigator(s)-as-instrument, as only the human instrument can grasp the interactions in context, and the multiple realities known through implied understanding (see Patton 1982; Riley and Love 2000; Dana and Dana 2005). In response to the 'crisis of representation' new strategies have been developed in a bid to find a way which satisfies an individual researcher's desire to reconcile concepts of structure and agency, difference and multiplicity without excluding our ability to say something (Ateljevic 2000). Consideration needs to be given to the subject (in this case, the copreneur), to avoid assigning them a passive role in research concerned with the value of their experience.

One of the issues of representation is that of the *researcher* (though there are also issues of representation of the research itself, and of the researched (see Lunn 1997), and relates to practices of reflexivity on the part of the researcher. Reflexivity is a process whereby 'researchers place themselves and their practices under scrutiny, acknowledging the ethical dilemmas that permeate the research process and impinge on the creation of knowledge' (McGraw, Zvonkovic and Walker 2000: 68). Reflexivity calls for consideration of issues such as the role, bias and gaze of the investigator. In the tourism context, Goodson and Phillimore (2004: 36) assert that 'the critical roles of both values and context in knowledge production mean that these two aspects of the research process have to be explored in some depth'. This means undertaking research in a reflexive way, whereby ethical, political and epistemological dimensions of research are explored as an integral part of producing knowledge. From this perspective then, only through openly reflexive interpretation can validity be claimed for any research, regardless of whether it is quantitative or qualitative (Goodson and Phillimore 2004).

Critical reflexivity or consideration of the researcher as a research instrument is an important principle of feminist practice. Marsh and colleagues (1996) affirm that feminist practice calls for the researcher to be located in the same plane as the researched. They call for reflexivity, saying that researchers' beliefs, motives and social position must be scrutinised if it is accepted that they cannot be detached from the process but rather are a part of it. Clark and colleagues (1999) argue similarly that social researchers can never divorce themselves entirely from the subjectively constructed social contexts of which they are a part. As the researcher responds as a whole person, he or she serves as an instrument in the collection and interpretation of the data.

## The interpretive approach

The interpretive approach emerged as an encapsulating philosophy addressing concerns raised by the crisis of representation. Jamal and Hollinshead (2001) have argued that in order to move towards more interpretive, qualitative tourism research, it is necessary to depart from more static, quantitative and positivist knowledge bases to more dynamic, experiential and reflexive approaches. Here, there is recognition that social agents are central to the construction of knowledge and that the researcher's voice is one among many that influence the research process (2001: 67).

Tribe (2004) asserts that tourism knowledge is generated using a variety of research methods and offers 'deeper insight' using Habermas's (1978, cited in Tribe 2004: 55) theory of knowledge-constitutive interests, demonstrating that the pursuit of knowledge is never interest-free but rather that human enquiry is motivated by one of three interests. First, technical interest seeks control and management; second, practical interest seeks understanding; and third, emancipatory interest seeks freedom from falsehood and emancipation from oppression. Each of these interests is served by a different methodological paradigm. Scientific positivism serves the technical; interpretive methods seek understanding; and critical theory seeks emancipation (Tribe 2004).

Interpretive methods seek understanding by researchers entering a research setting with some pre-understanding and a general plan; the study is then allowed to unfold with the assistance of informants. Emphasis is placed on investigating phenomena in their naturally occurring states, requiring the researcher to get close to the data, acknowledging interaction between data and data collection methods (Connell and Lowe 1997). Cooperation between the researcher and the researched reduces researcher bias and encourages women's voices. The importance of getting close to the participants in research is noted by Patton (1982), when he states:

> The methodological mandate to be contextually sensitive, inductive, and naturalistic means that researchers must get close to the phenomenon under study. The institutional researcher who uses qualitative methods attempts to understand that setting under study through direct personal contact . . . through physical proximity for a period of time and through the development of closeness.
>
> (Patton 1982: 10)

According to Crotty (1998), the theoretical perspective of interpretivism emerged in contradiction to positivism in the attempt to understand and explain human and social reality. For the interpretivist, the primary goal of research is to understand. Emphasis is placed on meanings and understanding, rather than just facts and generalisations. However, researchers cannot achieve *the* understanding, but rather an understanding of a phenomenon at a point in time (Hudson and Ozanne 1988).

Interpretivists take a more holistic, particularistic approach to research; studying a specific phenomenon in a particular place and time. Geertz (1973) labelled this context-dependent form of explanation as thick description, a focus which enables the development of theory that makes sense out of a local situation. This is because the interpretive approach facilitates generalisation within the context or case. It is suited to studying women as feminists acknowledge that their perspective is not universal or unpremised, recognising that women's perspectives might in fact be different if the world were different (Sherwin 1988).

Quantitative data-gathering techniques are often aligned exclusively to a positivist approach and qualitative techniques to the interpretivist approach. Eyles and Smith (1988) argue that few researchers end their endeavours with revealing the meanings of those they observe, as often scientific constructs are used to give shape to the meanings observed from everyday experience. Lee (1991) advocates for both positivist and interpretive approaches in strengthening collaborative research efforts, instead of approaches that maintain a separate co-existence.

Related to this, Denzin and Lincoln (1998) argue that many researchers operate in the moment that best fits the researcher's needs in relation to the research problem and the research setting. Riley and Love's (2000) review of tourism journals from their launch in the 1970s to 1996 showed that some scholars dipped into and out of Denzin and Lincoln's different moments depending on the research task at hand, and Beeton (2004) argues that for a broad-ranging, psychologically complex field such as tourism, 'there is no singular pertinent research modality. In order to achieve the desired outcomes of tourism research, alternative methods must be considered and used conjointly' (2004: 37). Phillimore and Goodson (2004) argue that a selective approach to deciding to adopt a particular approach shown by established and experienced tourism researchers should be applauded, as it encourages experimentation and sets a precedent for less experienced academics. The hermeneutic, interpretive approach used, particularly in relation to the interview part of this research, is discussed below.

## Conceptual coordinates of a study into copreneurship

Discussion continues among tourism scholars concerning methodological issues, research orientations and the most appropriate approaches to tourism study (Phillimore and Goodson 2004; Tribe 2004). However, from their analysis of quantitative versus qualitative articles in the tourism field, Riley and Love (2000: 180) argue that the dominant paradigm remains positivism, which is 'not surprising when considered chronologically, as interpretive paradigms have lagged behind their positivist predecessor'.

Given that tourism is a relatively new area of study, there should be greater tolerance for eclectic and diverse approaches to investigation (Echtner and Jamal 1997). The interpretive approach places more reliance on the people being studied, as the researcher tries to 'get inside the minds of subjects and see the world from their point of view' (Veal 1997: 31). This model leads to a more flexible and inductive approach to data collection. While it primarily involves qualitative methods, it can also incorporate quantitative approaches.

Echtner and Jamal (1997) call for toleration of both qualitative and quantitative methodologies due to the high behavioural content and diverse nature of tourism. These methods can be used in union within an interpretive approach. As Veal (1997: 35) states: 'while the debate between protagonists of qualitative and quantitative research can become somewhat partisan, it is now widely accepted that the two approaches complement one another'. The strengths of each can result in greater understanding of a phenomenon. Bridging the divide to thwart such polarisation will be beneficial in tourism research.

Authors in tourism such as Oppermann (2000) and Decrop (1999) advocated for approaches like triangulation to bridge the divide between positivist and interpretivist tourism researchers. Decrop proposes triangulation as a way to make qualitative findings more robust, to gain increased acceptance of qualitative tourism studies. He cites support (e.g. Jick 1979; Webb *et al.* 1996) for the use of qualitative and quantitative methods as complementary, instead of rival camps. Combining data sources, methods, investigators and theories, triangulation opens the way for richer interpretations (Decrop 1999). Oppermann (2000: 141) explains that triangulation is used as 'a crossing bridge between the pre-eminent quantitative studies and the growth in number of qualitative studies'.

The choice of an appropriate research strategy should not depend on the qualitative/quantitative dichotomy, but rather on the study's goals and related research questions (Decrop 1999) and issues of access (Faulkner 2001). The copreneurship study discussed here used both quantitative and qualitative methods to achieve its goal of exploring experiences of copreneurship in rural tourism.

## *Women's voices*

Inclusion of the feminine perspective in research, as the researcher or the researched, is vital in tourism where women participate as employers, employees, business owners, researchers and/or consumers. Women differ in their personal experiences, and individual perceptions shaped by social influences. The use of a feminist perspective paradigm will challenge the dominant patriarchal hegemony that pervades tourism research. According to Jennings (2001: 47), until recently 'most studies have been androcentric in nature and have not taken into account the gender bias prevalent in most tourism research'.

In her audit of leisure and tourism journals, Aitchison (2001) found that little attention is given to the role of gender-power relations in the production, legitimation and reproduction of knowledge. She found the ratio of male to female authors of refereed articles is four to one. By quantifying the dominance of the male gaze and voice and research, she reveals the codification of knowledge in these fields 'as a product of both structural and cultural power' (Aitchison 2001: 1). This power contributes to a lack of feminist perspectives in tourism literature, especially through the voices of women and other marginalised groups. This chapter argues for voices of women business owners to contribute to a gendered perspective in tourism literature.

Details of the process undertaken to achieve this are in the following section of this chapter. This section has shown that the purpose of research, particularly its aims and objectives, dictates to a large extent the appropriate research approach. The study used as an example here was complex, requiring investigation of copreneurship within the rural tourism sector. According to Walle (1997), an eclectic approach of determining research methods is recommended because tourism researchers and practitioners deal with complex phenomena. In the context of this study the researcher came to know that she could not rigidly separate herself outside of the research due to roles as a management and tourism researcher and as a past and current business owner, specifically in a copreneurial role; an acknowledgment that became important in terms of reflexivity.

## An insider's view

As noted previously, accounts of any discipline and of research within that field of study are *situated*; that is, they depend on the point of view of the author, which in turn reflects how he or she is positioned intellectually, politically and socially (Barnes and Sheppard 2000). Hall proposes that 'In terms of why we research what we do, one cannot ignore the personal, yet this is almost completely ignored in discussions of tourism research' (Hall 2004: 148). The things we research flow from the personal, as 'the personal subjectivities of our experiences are vital to our choice of research paths, yet typically go unacknowledged' (Hall 2004: 149).

I consider myself an insider in the study being discussed here; with the ability to empathise with and get close to participants. My professional roles have required me to travel for business purposes and I enjoy travel for personal recreation. Travel for both work and pleasure, then, along with strong interest in rural tourism and small business ownership, provided one of the foundations of my personal leanings towards the particular study topic.

I consider my experiences, with the combination of methods and data sources, to be a strength of the research design of the copreneurship study discussed here. As Bates (1999: 17) states: 'We all have some form of built-in gender bias and that presents a Catch 22. Even though we may feel we are being objective and looking only at the facts, the very facts we see may be influenced . . .'.

This detail that the very facts we see may be influenced raises the notion and acknowledgment that we may not be objective at all. It is possible that researchers (including this one) may have preconceived notions of what the research will reveal. Built-in gender bias and my experiences as a woman are acknowledged and recognised as a potential disadvantage, as well as a strength.

Lunn (1997: 79) asserts: 'that research tends to reflect what is important to the researchers rather than the priorities of those being studied is hardly surprising if little is known of the realities of the lives of a group of people being studied'. Being an insider rather than a distant authority has advantages in understanding. Having the insider perspective into the meanings of women's experiences has helped in the identification of issues and interpretation of themes. As an 'insider', the 'researcher will acquire an in-depth knowledge of the tourism phenomena or experience that is grounded in the empirical world – a world where there are multiple realities rather than one "truth" to explain tourism phenomena' (Jennings 2001: 40).

There are, of course, positive and negative aspects to being an insider to the research. A few hours inside a woman's home talking about her business and role within the business and also in the family situation may mean that personal details about themselves and about others are revealed, for example. It is possible that personal involvement encouraged this revelation of details that might not otherwise have been shared. There is also implied professional danger as work may be devalued if objectivity, rationality and value-freedom, rather than involvement and subjectivity, are given academic status. It is possible that being an insider to the study and getting close to the phenomenon under study may be considered a bit self-indulgent and intellectually sloppy, but biographical narratives (revealed during the interview part of this research) are fascinating and many truths are revealed.

During my research I found myself analysing stories told to me in relation to my own experiences. The participants provided me with opportunities to empathise with them, as well as opening my eyes to new issues for consideration and representation. The research design enabled participants to reveal true stories and attitudes, and reflexivity calls for building trust. I can identify with many of the realities that copreneurs face and I have also had firsthand experience of many of the stressors that participants associate with rural tourism and copreneurship. The experiences of long days worked, blurring of the work/leisure dichotomy, competing demands of family and work, resulting in increased feelings of fatigue, are appreciated. The challenges of balancing personal and professional life with the need to consider one's own and also others' well-being are also something that I have encountered.

Benefits and tensions aside, an advantage of conducting research of this type is the further opportunity available to experience rural tourism firsthand. A study such as this requires trips to conduct interviews with copreneurs, and gaining further experience as an ethnographer and a tourist in the field is always enjoyable. Being in the research provided a heightened awareness of my own experiences and of the portrayals and realities of copreneurship within rural tourism in New Zealand.

## The role of feminism in this research

Each researcher has a unique understanding of and relationship to 'feminism' that has to do with our experiences, who we are and what social space(s) we occupy, or into which we are interpellated (Eriksen *et al.* 2007).

Eriksen and colleagues (2007) also note that there are material, cognitive and emotional consequences, both positive and negative, for engaging in 'feminist' scholarship and being labelled a (pro-)feminist.

Understanding the personal, subjective, narrative nature of this type of research (particularly the interviews) is perhaps more meaningful in understanding a position with respect to feminism and of feminism than to simply categorising within a particular feminist camp, because there are many 'feminist perspectives'. This research and the exploration of women's experiences of copreneurship may also serve to advance understanding of the researcher with respect to the topic of feminism, so that she can grapple with how she is part of the scholarship, not something separated from it. The world being researched is not separate from one's experience of that world.

Accordingly, whilst the implication of possessing certain epistemological and ontological assumptions has been addressed earlier in this chapter, it may be more relevant to focus on 'the complex, interactional and emergent nature of our social experience' (Cunliffe 2003: 984). In other words, a researcher is more complex than the ontological and epistemological assumptions, and these other parts are worthy of and essential to exploration and becoming a more critically reflexive scholar. Therefore, feminism, for this study, is not something that exists 'out there' separate from the researcher and the study, but rather it is an idea that is created and sustained through the research and all its interactions, and it affects understandings, processes and conclusions.

## What was actually done?

This study investigated experiences of copreneurship in rural tourism, and triangulation of various data sources enables study of the composite copreneurship experience. The design also limits personal and methodological biases (Decrop 1999). The next section of this chapter briefly describes the method of the copreneurship study and presents some reflections after the fact.

### *Informal interviews*

Informal interviews conducted before questionnaire development informed this research, and development of the questionnaire and interview questions throughout the research process. Informal interviews (conversations) took place with rural tourism operators and organisations. Conversations took place in a number of settings within the study area; for example, when the researcher was at leisure or partaking in a rural tourism experience or was attending a conference of rural tourism operators. Conversations also took place in a number of social settings as rural tourism business owners were encountered. Owners of these businesses were without exception keen to introduce their business and chat generally about running the businesses, the rewards and the challenges particularly.

*Questionnaires*

For this study, a questionnaire was used to elicit descriptive information from a larger number of rural tourism businesses. The information was not as 'rich' as the themes established in the subsequent interviews, but it did permit initial identification of which small business owners were in copreneurial relationships and would therefore be invited to participate in the interviews. Information collected from the questionnaires also enabled data to be gained on a broader spectrum of issues. This was important given the scarcity of scholarly research on copreneurship in tourism, in both the New Zealand and worldwide contexts. Questionnaire data were also comparable with other studies on farm tourism (e.g. Getz and Carlsen 2000; Hall and Rusher 2004).

The aim of the questionnaire was to help to gain an understanding of respondents' characteristics, opinions and their business's characteristics, not to collect representative data to make mass generalisations (Chia and Yeo 1999) about rural tourism or about copreneurs. The questionnaire was designed to be easily answered in the hope of eliciting a favourable response rate. The majority of the questions required either a tick-the-box answer, or a circle to be drawn on a seven-point Likert scale. The use of Likert-type scales is 'a common research method for eliciting opinions and attitudes in the social and business sciences' (Ryan and Garland 1999: 107). The remaining questions required responses to open-ended questions, for example, 'What, for you, has been the most rewarding thing about owning and operating an accommodation business?'

Owners of rural accommodation businesses were sought as questionnaire participants, within the survey region of the River Region (Manawatu, Tararua, Rangitikei, Wanganui and Ruapehu), Nature Coast (Horowhenua), Wairarapa and Hawkes Bay. The survey reason was chosen because the researcher had experience with researching within this area, meaning that relationships existed which helped with access to participants. The survey area also remains an under-researched part of New Zealand, with respect to tourism, and rural tourism particularly (Ryan 1997; Hall and Rusher 2002, 2004). The questionnaire and sampling method enabled farmstay and B&B owners/operators to participate. The instrument and method also provided participant convenience and anonymity when reporting results.

*Interviews*

In this research I was concerned with theorising experiences of copreneurship in tourism and, in doing so, endeavouring to get inside the heads of the copreneurs to ask the questions of most relevance. I believed that the research designed within the interpretive paradigm would enable me to do this effectively. I thus chose, after collecting data quantitatively through the questionnaire, to gather data using in-depth, face-to-face interviews in which

I encouraged copreneurs to tell me about their experiences within a semi-structured framework. In doing so, I explored topics that might not have been thought about when designing the research project, but which the copreneurs themselves identified as being significant. Thus, instead of imposing my preconceived notions of copreneurship on the participants, I used the semi-structured questions as a guide to stimulate discussion about their actual experiences while operating rural tourism businesses.

The interview part of the copreneurship study had three broad objectives. The first was to further explore women's experiences of copreneurship by eliciting narratives from the female copreneurs themselves. The second objective was to build on knowledge gained from the survey instrument, particularly information about copreneurship from a women's perspective. This extended the existing discussion of copreneurship and rural tourism by eliciting women's experiences of copreneurship. The third objective was to explore existing gendered roles within the copreneurial venture.

The hermeneutic interpretive approach was used throughout reporting of interview findings and this allowed exploration of the personalised meanings by which the copreneurs understood their experiences of starting and operating a rural tourism business and the ways in which these experiences were manifested in their roles and activities. By analysing an interview text's salient metaphors, common expressions and categorical distinctions in light of the background information from literature and from survey data, insights into the copreneurs' experiences could be gained. The research aimed to give voice to women's experiences of copreneurship within rural tourism, and the type of research reported here (using the hermeneutic interpretive approach) provided the opportunity for respondents to talk about themselves at length. It is by listening and learning from other people's experiences that the researcher can learn that the 'truth' is not the same for everybody. Like Stanley (1995) and Letherby (2000), I believe that my involvement in sharing the women's voices did not disempower me intellectually; I could still be critical and analytical, both about the women's stories and about my involvement, and this resulted in a fuller picture of the research area.

The women interviewed not only answered my biographical questions (for example, 'How did you come to be operating this business?') frankly, but they also often introduced biographical flashbacks spontaneously when telling their stories. Their biographical digressions were not only of systematic value for evaluation, but also showed that the biographical approach was an important form of everyday hermeneutics, too.

From a hermeneutic perspective, the stories that the copreneurs told about their experiences were a prime locus of discovery. The insights offered by this hermeneutic mode of interpretation was particularly useful in bridging the gap between the copreneurs' overt awareness and stories of their life circumstances and the less overtly stated factors that shape their experiences and decisions about their businesses. The hermeneutic caveat, however, is that the voice of the given subject will often express a nexus of personal meanings that are formed in a complex field of social and historical relationships. As such, a subject's self-perceptions can exhibit a considerable degree of situational variability depending on which personal meanings are salient in a given context (Thompson 1997; also see Belk 1975; Stayman and Deshpande 1989). This is particularly so in the case of exploring women's roles in their business and family situations. Hermeneutic scholars emphasise that the process of textual interpretation cannot be reduced to the application of a 'method' (Gadamer 1993; Thompson 1997). Rather, the techniques used to formulate an interpretation are embedded within a framework of core assumptions and investigations, informed in this case by literature and background research, and also by the data gathered in the survey part of this study.

The role of the researcher is again important in this interpretive approach because it is the researcher interpreting the textual data. Hermeneutic research emphasises that an understanding of a text always reflects a fusion of horizons between the interpreter's frame of reference and the texts being interpreted (Arnold and Fischer 1994; Thompson 1997). The acknowledged implication is that the researcher's interpretive orientation (i.e. background knowledge, underlying assumptions, and questions of interest) enabled her to become attuned to specific characteristics and patterns afforded by the textual data. Thus, again, the hermeneutic approach selected sought to be open to possibilities afforded by the texts of the interviews, rather than projecting a predetermined system of meanings onto the textual data.

The interviews, which became biographic in many cases, portrayed life stories in relation to the women's experiences of operating a rural tourism business. This biographic approach, which was largely unintended, served to 'work outwards from the domestic instead of from the public inwards' (Edwards and Ribbens 1991: 487). The result is that 'the woman and not existing theory is considered the expert on her experience' (Anderson and Jack 1998: 166). This revelation made this study one of a small general movement towards this approach in the studying of rural lives, in particular the lives of women (e.g. Inhetveen 1990). As noted by Letherby (2000), with specific reference to auto/biography, it is relevant to refer to Stanley (1995), who argues that by 'becoming academics' as women and as feminists, we position ourselves both as insiders and outsiders (see also previous discussion in this chapter). Writing biographically also brings the danger that the writer may be accused of being non-academic (Letherby 2000) and many feminist writers have written of how and why women's work is devalued and the ways in which women have been excluded from the making of knowledge and culture (e.g. Stanley and Wise 1993). The study discussed here aimed to give voice to women's experiences of copreneurship within rural tourism, and acknowledged the involvement of the researcher in this process.

The researcher noted her insider status and research perspectives (see earlier discussion in this chapter), and feminist writers have previously exposed the hollowness of claims to objectivity (also see earlier discussion above). The researcher has in this case, however, had access to details of the contextually related reasoning process (see Stanley 1995), which then gave rise to the research findings. Triangulation of data sources, through literature and the survey component of this research, helped to inform analysis of the women's stories. However, it is still acknowledged that as a feminist researcher studying aspects of these women's lives, I report their biographies, whilst recognising that the biographies that I am given are influenced by the research relationship. In other words, the respondents may have had their own view of what the researcher wanted to hear, and I used my own experiences to help to understand those of the respondents. Thus, their experiences are filtered through me in reporting these experiences (see also Letherby 2000).

## Conclusions: truth and realities

It has become clear through this copreneurship study, also, that the 'truth' is not the same for everyone and one objective truth does not exist. Different experiences of the research issue (copreneurship) exist and it was not always possible to categorise and fit the women's experiences into existing or new theory. The quantitative research presented an aggregate of 'truths' but the narratives reported in the interview part of the research expressed different experiences of copreneurship. There may be a systematic process which would allow certain experiences of reality to be certified as objectively accurate – tying narratives back to survey findings, for example – but in actuality there may be several 'truths', each of which appears to be different from and just as true as the others.

Experienced realities of the women interviewed are realities which have been perceived by the senses, filtered by interests and interpreted according to reconstructed criteria. Analysing the interviews, I found that the biological narratives of the women coincided in essence with the quantitative findings. This fact legitimised the narrative approach and rendered the various truths and experiences all useful. For some respondents in the interview part of the research, involvement in the research also provided an opportunity to 'put the record straight' and to consider their own involvement in their business. Rosabel (thirties), soon after her interview had taken place, sent a note to me: '. . . it was good for me to recall just how far I have come with it [the business] and I felt quite inspired after our talk, so thank you for that'.

Reflection on the women's stories, along with self-reflexivity about my position in the research, enabled me to be both critical and analytical about my involvement, as well as the themes identified in the research, which resulted in a 'fuller' picture of copreneurship in rural tourism and also resulted in a greater appreciation of a mixed method approach to collecting data. Research in copreneurship, to date, has been epitomised by stories published in the popular press about partnership and success strategies, and has been further characterised by small empirical studies, none of which has taken a tourism or a rural focus. The mixed method approach taken in the copreneurship study discussed here meant that insights were raised by a review of the relevant literature fields and these insights contributed to the study method and directions. There has been some question about whether current research approaches and methodologies have adequately incorporated the reality of women's entrepreneurship (de Bruin *et al.* 2007). The reality of the experience of women starting rural tourism businesses (with their partners) is not a reality which has been widely explored in the rural literature and, often, rural research appeared to choose to privilege particular conceptions of reality over others.

It has become clear, however, to this researcher that the claim that 'there is some doubt as to whether current research approaches adequately incorporate the "reality" of women's entrepreneurship' (de Bruin *et al.* 2007: 329) may even understate the case. It became clear during the research for the study discussed here, through the triangulation of literature and the use of both quantitative and qualitative techniques, that there are actually at least two 'realities' to capture:

1    The reality of *what it is* like – who does what? and
2    The reality of how women experience this.

The quantitative research reported in this study provided information about descriptions of the owners and the businesses, and what happens within the business (the reality of *who does what?*), but the qualitative part of this research offered insights into women's experiences of this – not *what* happens, but *how it is experienced*. The interview part of this research meant that the gendered nature of work in and on the business became real and expressed. Exploring both 'realities' of copreneurship within rural tourism ended up showing that any perception of copreneurship as a tool for enabling women to become freed from traditional gender roles may not equal the reality.

## References

Aitchison, C. (2001) 'Gender and Leisure Research: The "Codification of Knowledge",' *Leisure Sciences* 23: 1–19.

Anderson, K. and Jack, D. (1998) 'Learning to Listen: Interview Techniques and Analyses', in R. Perks and A. Thomson (eds), *The Oral History Reader*. London: Routledge.

Arnold, S., and Fischer, E. (1994) 'Hermeneutics and Consumer Research', *Journal of Consumer Research* 21: 55–70.

Ateljevic, I. (2000) 'Circuits of Tourism: Stepping Beyond the "Production/consumption" Dichotomy', *Tourism Geographies* 2(4): 369–88.

Barnes, T. J. and Sheppard, E. (2000) 'Introduction: The Art of Economic Geography', in E. Sheppard and T.J. Barnes (eds), *A Companion to Economic Geography*. Oxford: Blackwell.

Barnett, F. and Barnett, S. (1989) 'Entrepreneurial Couples', *The Futurist* 23(3): 50.

Bates, D. (1999) 'Moderator's Gender can Influence a Focus Group', *Marketing News* 33(5): 17–19.

Beeton, S. (2004) 'The Case Study in Tourism Research: A Multi-method Case Study Approach', in B.W. Ritchie, P. Burns and C. Palmer (eds), *Tourism Research Methods: Integrating Theory with Practice*. Cambridge: CABI Publishing.

Belk, R.W. (1975) 'Situational Variables and Consumer Behavior', *Journal of Consumer Research* 2(3): 157–64.

Chia, A. and Yeo, W.L. (1999) 'Factors Influencing Frequent Business Travellers' Stress, Family Acceptance of Travel and Intention to Continue', in *Work and Employment in a Globalized Era Conference*. Cardiff: Cardiff Business School.

Clark, M., Riley, M., Wilkie, E. and Wood, R.C. (1999) *Researching and Writing Dissertations in Hospitality and Tourism*. London: Thomson.

Connell, J. and Lowe, A. (1997) 'Generating Grounded Theory from Quality Data: The Application of Inductive Methods in Tourism and Hospitality Management Research', *Progress in Tourism and Hospitality Research* 3: 165–73.

Crotty, M. (1998) *The Foundations of Social Research: Meaning and Perspective in the Research Process*. Sydney, Australia: Allen and Unwin.

Cunliffe, A.L. (2003) 'Reflexive inquiry in organizational research: Questions and possibilities', *Human Relations* 56(8): 983–1003.

Dana, L.P. and Dana, T.E. (2005) 'Expanding the Scope of Methodologies used in Entrepreneurship Research', *International Journal of Entrepreneurship and Small Business* 2(1): 79–88.

de Bruin, A., Brush, C.G. and Welter, F.W. (2007) 'Advancing a Framework for Coherent Research on Women's Entrepreneurship', *Entrepreneurship Theory and Practice* 31(3): 323–39.

Decrop, A. (1999) 'Triangulation in Qualitative Tourism Research', *Tourism Management* 20(1): 157–61.

Denzin, N.K. and Lincoln, Y.S. (1994) *Handbook of Qualitative Research*. Thousand Oaks: Sage Publications.

Denzin, N.K. and Lincoln, Y.S. (1998) *The Landscape of Qualitative Research: Theories and Issues*. Thousand Oaks: Sage.

Echtner, C.M. and Jamal, T.B. (1997) 'The Disciplinary Dilemma of Tourism Studies', *Annals of Tourism Research* 24(4): 868–83.

Edwards, R. and Ribbens, J. (1991) 'Meanderings around "Strategy": A Research Note on the Strategic Discourses in the Lives of Women', *Strategy* 25(3): 477–89.

Eriksen, M., Hope, A., Chaves, W.V. and Dugal, S.S. (2007) 'Creating a Community of Critically Reflexive Feminist Scholars', *Tamara* 6(4): 222–41.

Eyles, J. and Smith, M.D. (1988) *Qualitative Methods in Human Geography*. Cambridge: Polity Press.

Faulkner, B. (2001) 'The "Researcher's Gaze" towards the New Millennium', in B. Faulkner, G. Moscardo and E. Laws (eds), *Tourism in the 21st Century: Reflections on Experience*. London: Continuum.

Gadamer, H.-G. (1993) *Truth and Method*, 2nd edn. New York: Continuum.

Geertz, C. (1973) *The Interpretation of Cultures: Selected Essays*. New York: Basic Books.

Getz, D. and Carlsen, J. (2000) 'Characteristics and Goals of Family and Owner-operated Businesses in the Rural Tourism and Hospitality Sectors', *Tourism Management* 21(6): 547–60.

Goodson, L. and Phillimore, J. (2004) 'The Inquiry Paradigm', in J. Phillimore and L. Goodson (eds), *Qualitative Research in Tourism: Ontologies, Epistemologies and Methodologies*. London: Routledge.

Hall, C.M. (2004) 'Reflexivity and Tourism Research: Situating Myself and/with Others', in J. Phillimore and L. Goodson (eds), *Qualitative Research in Tourism: Ontologies, Epistemologies and Methodologies*. London: Routledge.

Hall, C. M., and Rusher, K. (2002) 'A Risky business? Entrepreneurial and Lifestyle Dimensions of the Homestay and Bed and Breakfast Accommodation Sector in New Zealand', in E. Arola, J. Karkkainen and M.L. Siitari (eds), *Tourism and Well-being: The 2nd Tourism Industry and Education Symposium May 16–18*. Jyvaskyla, Finland: 16–18 May, 2002.

Hall, C.M. and Rusher, K. (2004) 'Risky Lifestyles? Entrepreneurial Characteristics of the New Zealand Bed and Breakfast Sector', in R. Thomas (ed.), *Small Firms in Tourism: International Perspectives*. Oxford: Elsevier.

Hudson, L.A. and Ozanne, J.L. (1988) 'Alternative Ways of Seeking Knowledge in Consumer Research', *Journal of Consumer Research* 14(4): 508–21.

Inhetveen, H. (1990) 'Biographical Approaches to Research on Women Farmers', *Sociologia Ruralis* 30(1): 100–14.

Jamal, T. and Hollinshead, K. (2001) 'Tourism and the Forbidden Zone: The Underserved Power of Qualitative Inquiry', *Tourism Management* 22(1): 63–82.

Jennings, G. (2001) *Tourism Research*. Milton, Queensland: John Wiley & Sons.

Jick, T. D. (1979) 'Mixing Qualitative and Quantitative Methods: Triangulation in Action', *Administrative Science Quarterly* 24(4): 602–11.

Lee, A. S. (1991) 'Integrating Positivist and Interpretive Approaches to Organizational Research', *Organization Science* 2(4): 342–65.

Letherby, G. (2000) 'Dangerous Liaisons: Auto/biography in Research and Research Writing', in G. Lee-Treweek and S. Linkogle (eds), *Danger in the Field: Ethics and Risk in Social Research*. London: Routledge.

Lunn, M. (1997) 'What am I . . . for her?': Feminism and Disability with/in the Postmodern'. Unpublished doctoral dissertation, Massey University, New Zealand.

McGraw, L., Zvonkovic, A. and Walker, A. (2000) 'Studying Postmodern Families: A Feminist Analysis of Ethical Tensions in Work and Family Research', *Journal of Marriage and the Family* 62(1): 68–78.

Marsh, I., Keating, M., Eyre, A., Campbell, R. and McKenzie, J. (1996) *Making Sense of Society: An Introduction to Sociology*. Essex, England: Addison Wesley Longman.

Marshack, K.J. (1994) 'Copreneurs and Dual-career Couples: Are they Different?' *Entrepreneurship: Theory and Practice* 19(1): 49–70.

Oppermann, M. (1997) 'Rural Tourism in Germany: Farm and Rural Tourism Operators', in S. Page and D. Getz (eds), *The Business of Rural Tourism: International Perspectives*. London: International Thomson Business Press.

Patton, M. (1982) 'Qualitative Methods and Approaches: What are they?' in E. Kuhns and S.V. Martorana (eds), *Qualitative Methods for Institutional Research*. San Francisco: Jossey-Bass.

Phillimore, J. and Goodson, L. (eds) (2004) *Qualitative Research in Tourism: Ontologies, Epistemologies and Methodologies*. London: Routledge.

Riley, R.W. and Love, L.L. (2000) 'The State of Qualitative Tourism Research', *Annals of Tourism Research* 27(1): 164–87.

Ryan, C. (1997) 'Rural tourism in New Zealand: Rafting in the Rangitikei at River Valley Ventures', in S. Page and D. Getz (eds), *The Business of Rural Tourism: International Perspectives*. London: International Thomson Business Press.

Ryan, C. and Garland, R. (1999) 'The Use of a Specific Non-response Option on Likert-type Scales', *Tourism Management* 20(1): 107–13.

Sherwin, S. (1988) 'Philosophical Methodology and Feminist Methodology: Are they Compatible?' in L. Code, S. Mullet, and C. Overall (eds), *Feminist Perspectives: Philosophical Essays on Method and Morals*. Toronto: University of Toronto Press.

Stanley, L. (1995) 'My Mother's Voice?: On Becoming a "Native" in Academia', in L. Morley and V. Walsh (eds), *Feminist Academics: Creative Agents for Change*. London: Taylor & Francis.

Stanley, L. and Wise, S. (1993) *Breaking out Again: Feminist Ontology and Epistemology*. London: Routledge.

Stayman, D., and Deshpande, R. (1989) 'Situational Ethnicity and Consumer Behaviour', *Journal of Consumer Research* 16(3): 361–71.

Thompson, C. (1997) 'Intepreting Consumers: A Hermeneutical Framework for Deriving Marketing Insights from the Texts of Consumers' consumption stories', *Journal of Marketing Research* 34(4): 438–55.

Tribe, J. (2004) 'Knowing about Tourism: Epistemological Issues', in J. Phillimore and L. Goodson (eds), *Qualitative Research in Tourism: Ontologies, Epistemologies and Methodologies*. London: Routledge.

Veal, A.J. (1997) *Research Methods for Leisure and Tourism: A Practical Guide*, 2nd edn. Harlow: Pearson Education.

Walle, A.H. (1997) 'Quantitative versus Qualitative Tourism Research', *Annals of Tourism Research* 24(3): 524–36.

Webb, E., Campbell, D.T., Schwartz, R.D. and Sechrest, L. (1996) *Unobtrusive Measures: Non-reactive Research in the Social Sciences*. Chicago: Rand McNally.

# Part III

# Methods and processes

This third section of the volume focuses on issues surrounding the methods utilised and the processes by which fieldwork is undertaken.

Chapter 12 by Salazar examines the role of multiple scales in tourism research by reference to the notion of glocal ethnography. According to Salazar, since tourism is a multi-layered phenomenon – marked by a plethora of politico-economic, socio-cultural, and other processes of production, consumption, representation, and regulation on local, national, regional, and global levels – many studies fail to understand and explain it adequately. Collaborative, mixed-methods, and multi-sited research have been proposed as possible ways to tackle and unpack tourism's complexity. However, these are demanding to engage with as a graduate student, often with limited time, experience, and resources. Using his dissertation fieldwork in Yogyakarta, Indonesia as an example, Salazar demonstrates how a 'glocal ethnography' approach helped him capture the details of the local tourism scene while at the same time paying attention to the way that local reality is firmly embedded in and continuously interacting with broader processes and power structures. In this chapter, he offers a tentative description of what glocal ethnography entails and illustrates the use of this methodology by drawing on his study of tour guiding.

Chapter 13 by Hoogendoorn and Visser examines some of the methodological challenges inherent in researching second home tourism in South Africa. The chapter makes three main observations. First, there is a difficulty in accessing appropriate statistical data for tourism research. In the case of second homes in South Africa this occurs because, in common with a number of other countries (Hall and Müller 2004), second homes are not a recorded census entity. Therefore, a range of creative ways of identifying their presence is required. Second, as with many chapters in this volume, researcher positionality is identified as fundamentally framing the different creative avenues that should be selected in gathering baseline data. Third, researcher positionality also plays a role in gathering information from second home owners and permanent residents once second homes have been identified. This latter point is also connected to the relations that exist within and between different communities in post-apartheid South Africa. As the authors observe, 'What makes the South African situation unique is its own configuration of many different cultures and races, which plays a dominant role in presenting obstacles to, and opportunities for, accessing information.' But there is a universal message for those undertaking fieldwork when they conclude, 'fieldworkers should attempt to understand why informants from different groups may react to them in different ways, and develop strategies for approaching them successfully'.

In Chapter 14 Gillen seeks to respond to the question of how researchers who see value in off-the-record discussions with respondents in the field proceed to categorise and use such knowledge and information. (See also Sin, Chapter 19.) In responding to this issue, which is a common experience in fieldwork, Gillen uses Rose's (2004) two-part deconstructive/reconstructive project and integrates this with his personal field experiences in Ho Chi Minh City, Vietnam. In the first part of the chapter Gillen offers the notion of 'deconstruction as method' in an attempt to broaden the debate on the use of information gained in the field and question how qualitative researchers come to categorize valid knowledge in the first place. He argues that the categories researchers design into their methodological toolkits are unstable and they must in turn be constructed with a critical examination of what counts as truth and untruth in specific field sites. The second part of the chapter implements the 'reconstruction' of informal data into value-laden categories. Gillen states that calling informal data points 'truths' disrupts objectivity and clarity in the scientific sense and suggests that – despite the recognition that methodologies are contextual and processual – there must be persistence of a clear science that is explainable and translatable to other scientists about who the researcher is in dialogue, or what Rose (2004) coins a 're-embrace of metaphysics'. His conclusion posits that the work of deconstruction and reconstruction in the generation of data categories is best translated as a biography, or a concurrent writing of researcher and respondent lives. Biographical experiences, aside from mirroring Rose's (2004) project, epitomise the twin punctuations of the field: the desire to categorize and clearly explain scientific knowledge on the one hand and to account for and validate the messiness of daily life on the other.

Chapter 15 by Chio also extends consideration of usable knowledge gained in fieldwork in her study of the use of visual media in tourism research. Chio's study on which the chapter is based sought to understand what happens when Chinese rural village residents see themselves in mass media while depending on 'being seen' for economic revenue from tourism? As she notes, the direction of the research was different from what she imagined when she first started:

> But just the first showings of footage set in motion certain expectations about what my future video work would entail. I found myself and my work relegated within certain local categories of understanding visual media and its usages, and in order to understand these categories and why they existed, I needed to work within them.

Chio's chapter therefore not only raises fundamental questions about relationships between researchers and 'subjects' in the field and how the nature of a study can change while being in the field, but also raises broader questions about the role of media and the visual in tourism fieldwork more generally. Referring to the work of Friedman (2006), Chio notes how video footage can be considered 'a medium through which viewers reflect on their own lives and relationships with salient others and define a place for themselves in a larger social universe' (Friedman 2006: 606), and emphasises the methodological efficacy of turning an ethnographic eye to the event of media consumption. This stands in stark contrast to Banta and Hinsley's (1986: 119) comments that 'Many fieldworkers choose not to use the camera because it can create additional distance between researcher and subject. Others are reluctant to employ photography because they want to be regarded in the field as scientists rather than tourists.' Leading Chio to conclude:

> Some twenty years later, I would argue it is quite useful and important in tourism research to acknowledge, and even embrace, the curious position of the tourism researcher as both a host and a guest in fieldwork situations. Tourism researchers are a host of immense knowledge, ideas, and experience which can be shared to interesting and significant ends with research participants; at the same time, we are guests and must act with the utmost, respectful awareness of the needs, curiosities, and desires of our host societies. Long-term fieldwork demands this delicate balance. We, as researchers studying tourism, are not alone in the field, and the research process needs to acknowledge that our very presence in research sites brings (and can bring) much potentially significant and revealing data to the whole of the study and to the lives of those involved. Tourism research, and long-term ethnographic research in particular, demands a participatory approach that can take full advantage of the researcher's presence and the researcher's productions, visual or otherwise. Using a video camera to create opportunities for reflexivity in my project was just one way to begin exploring the possibilities of putting the visual to work.

Issues of 'balance' in fieldwork also emerge in McMorran's chapter on participant observation in the study of labour relations/human resource management in tourism (Chapter 16). Similar to Chok (Chapter 4), McMorran utilises an understanding and awareness of power relations in the field as a way of contextualising the method that was adopted in the field. This chapter summarises his own methodological negotiations with power, and how these took him on an intellectual journey from his own awareness of his potentially negative influence in a tourist site to the realisation that the most effective way to conduct research and mitigate the influence of other powerful players on his research was to subject himself to the same power matrices as his study population. This meant taking a job in the very industry he was researching.

The chapter argues that the method of working in the study site as a form of participant observation helped remove the potentially deleterious effects of the author's relationship with tourist managers (the owners of capital) by creating camaraderie with the workers (labour). McMorran argues that this method levelled the playing field with informants who were previously intimidated and confused by his position, and provided him with invaluable insight into the daily interactions with power that the workers experienced. Perhaps in a manner that reflects many in the tourism industry's view of tourism education, but not for the same reasons, McMorran's chapter calls on researchers who wish to study workers in tourist destinations to put down their tape recorders and notebooks for a few hours and wash some dishes, as this will open lines of communication with informants and help mitigate the researcher's role in power-imbued relations.

Chapter 17 by Wall Reinius also deals with issues of communicating with informants but from a very different context. One of the great problems in undertaking tourism research in outdoor recreation settings such as national parks and nature reserves is in gaining access to respondents. Indeed, in the case of some locations, such as wilderness areas, their very nature means that there will be few people around. Wall Reinius discusses these issues with respect to her doctoral and other studies in northern Sweden. Indeed, as she notes, a common difficulty in research that focuses on tourist use of larger nature areas is the challenge of finding people, or at least, how to reach them in a systematic way. In Sweden, as in many countries, there is no tradition of undertaking systematic visitor surveys in protected areas and, as a result, the information about visitor numbers, patterns, and impacts is rather limited (Fredman 2004). Wall Reinius outlines the procedures that were utilised in her studies and details what did and did not work. Critical to the success of the research was not so much the method itself but the role of gatekeepers in ensuring that the visitor survey was performed in an appropriate manner. Therefore, good communication with those involved in the research acted as the lynchpin for success.

In Chapter 18 Finsterwalder and Kuppelwieser also examine issues associated with undertaking consumer studies in outdoor settings with reference to research on white water rafting in New Zealand. As the authors note, the literature on research in tourism or related fields, such as services and marketing, propose research methodologies and recommendations to follow specific processes in undertaking research. However, although planned thoroughly by the researcher, the actual data collection in the field led to unforeseen challenges that were not part of the processes discussed in research methods texts. Therefore, field conditions or incidents can confront researchers with situations where they have to alter or adapt their approach. In the case of the survey work undertaken by Finsterwalder and Kuppelwieser, this meant changing the data collection process on the spot to ensure they could later meet their targets of collecting enough valid information from the research participants for appropriate statistical analysis. Their contribution describes the intended research project and objectives defined by the researchers as well as the planned data collection process. It then follows the execution of the data compilation on site at a white water rafting provider, identifies pitfalls and provides an outlook of the key learning experience during the data collection phase.

The final chapter in the section, by Harng Luh Sin (Chapter 19), returns to the issue of what can and cannot be used from discussions in the field. The chapter addresses what Sin feels are the 'unfinished' parts of her research on volunteer tourism – the encounters in the field that she had not or could not formally include as part of her fieldwork. As with all research that use one-to-one interviews as a chief source of accessing respondents' perspectives and opinions, Sin encountered those who had refused to grant her interviews or to participate in her research. The chapter discusses the arrangement she had with the student leaders of one particular group of volunteer tourists who, from the onset, told her that they would not be comfortable with her basing her research on interviews with their members. However, as her then boyfriend (and now husband) was a member of the said team, she was able to join the team's activities in Phnom Penh and Siem Reap in Cambodia. In addition, she also interviewed the local non-government organisation that was hosting the team during the time of their volunteer stint. This arrangement meant that she was able to observe the team from a third-person perspective, even though she was not actually allowed to interview any team members for her research. Detailing her encounters with those who refused to grant her interviews, the chapter poses questions to other researchers: Can we include in research those who reject participation? Does the self-selective process in which potential respondents choose whether to participate or not to participate not affect the end result of research? And, specifically in terms of volunteer tourism, although this could be applied to research on almost every form of activity or special interest tourism, has research been too focused on capturing only the periods whereby tourists are engaged in a special interest or activity, at the expense of painting a more comprehensive picture if one was to also look at other tourism activities beyond times spent on the activity? Sin hopes that her personal reflections on what she had not included in her research could fundamentally question how we as researchers delineate what is or is not valid 'fieldwork'. Indeed, by only including those who say yes, are we already manipulating our research findings, or have we simply missed the point?

## Suggested further reading

Bailey, C. (2001) 'Geographers Doing Household Research: Intrusive Research and Moral Accountability', *Area* 33: 107–10.
Although primarily aimed at geographers, the paper is broadly applicable to those undertaking household research as well as reflection on ethical issues in the research process.

Bennett, K. and Shurmer-Smith, P. (2001) 'Writing Conversation', in M. Limb and C. Dwyer (eds), *Qualitative Methodologies for Geographers: Issues and Debates*. London: Arnold.
Very useful account of the tasks confronting researchers with respect to recording and writing data from conservations. The book as a whole is also extremely useful.

Elwood, S. and Martin, D. (2000) ' "Placing" Interviews: Location and Scales of power in qualitative research', *Professional Geographer* 52(4): 649–57.
Highlights the importance of location with respect to issues of power in undertaking qualitative research.

England, K. (1994) 'Getting Personal: Reflexivity, Positionality, and Feminist Research,' *Professional Geographer* 46(1): 80–9.
A widely cited paper on positionality and reflexivity that highlights many of the challenges involved in qualitative fieldwork and implications for methods.

Finn, M., Elliott-White, M. and Walton, M. (2000) *Tourism and Leisure Research Methods: Data Collection, Analysis, and Interpretation*. Harlow: Longman.
A useful introductory text to issues involved in research in tourism.

Hair, J.F., Lukas, B.A., Miller, K.E., Bush, R.P. and Ortinau, D.J. (2008) *Marketing Research*, 2nd edn. Boston, MA: McGraw-Hill.
A good standard text on marketing research that provides a useful introduction to the issues involved in undertaking research.

Hall, C.M. and Müller, D.K. (eds) (2004) *Tourism, Mobility and Second Homes: Between Elite Landscape and Common Ground*. Clevedon: Channel View.
Edited volume on a very specific area of tourism that is of interest because of issues of concept definition in different locations and settings.

Jackson, J. (2004) 'Ethnographic *film*flam: Giving Gifts, Doing Research, and Video-taping the native subject/object', *American Anthropologist* 106(1): 32–42.
Very useful account of some of the issues involved with the use of video in ethnography.

Kajala, L., Almik, A., Dahl, R., Diksaité, L., Erkkonen, J. and Fredman, P. (2007) *Visitor Monitoring in Nature Areas. A Manual Based on Experiences from the Nordic and Baltic countries*. Stockholm: The Swedish Environmental Protection Agency.
The manual provides managers with guidelines, methods and tools for measuring visitor use and behavior. Although it has a northern European managerial focus, it is extremely useful for researchers in outdoor recreation and natural tourism settings.

Laurier, E. (2003) 'Participant Observation', in N. Clifford and G. Valentine (eds), *Key Methods in Geography*. London: Sage.
A good introduction to participant observation, while the book as a whole is useful for understanding key methods in the social sciences.

Manning, R.E. (1999) *Studies in Outdoor Recreation: Search and Research for Satisfaction*, 2nd edn. Corvallis: Oregon State University Press.
Manning's book is a standard text on outdoor recreation and protected areas for both managers and scholars. It includes a wide range of studies on, for instance, motivation and benefits in recreation and recreation conflicts, and it discusses practical management implications.

Milner, H.R. (2007) 'Race, Culture, and Researcher Positionality: Working Through Dangers Seen, Unseen, and Unforeseen', *Education Researcher* 36: 388–401.
Extremely valuable account of race and culture as a factor in fieldwork and research.

Mullings, B. (1999) 'Insider or Outsider, Both or Neither: Some Dilemmas of Interviewing in a Cross-cultural Setting,' *Geoforum* 30(4): 337–50.
Highlights some of the issues involved in interviewing across cultures. Ideally should be read in conjunction with the Milner article above.

## References

Banta, M. and Hinsley, C. (1986) *From Site to Sight: Anthropology, Photography and the Power of Imagery*. Cambridge: Peabody Museum Press.
Fredman, P. (2004) 'National Park Designation – Visitor Flows and Tourism Impact', in T. Sievänen, J. Erkkonen, J. Jokimäki, J. Saarinen, S. Tuulentie and E. Virtanen (eds), *Proceedings of the Second International Conference on Monitoring and Management of Visitor Flows in Recreational and Protected Areas*. Rovaniemi, Finland: Finnish Forest Research Institute.
Friedman, S. (2006) 'Watching Twin Bracelets in China: The Role of Spectatorship and Identification in an Ethnographic Analysis of Film Reception', *Cultural Anthropology* 21(4): 603–32.
Hall, C.M. and Müller, D.K. (eds) (2004) *Tourism, Mobility and Second Homes: Between Elite Landscape and Common Ground*. Clevedon: Channel View.
Rose, M. (2004) 'Reembracing Metaphysics', *Environment and Planning A* 36: 461–8.

# 12 Studying local-to-global tourism dynamics through glocal ethnography

*Noel B. Salazar*

## Introduction: the global–local nexus in tourism

Tourism, the multifaceted global phenomenon of travel-for-leisure, offers many fascinating research topics across disciplines. Tourism-related ethnographic research has come a long way, from anthropologists ignoring tourists during their fieldwork and disregarding the seriousness of tourism research (Lévi-Strauss 1978 [1955]) to academics taking active roles in tourism planning and development (Wallace 2005). Tourism is now commonly seen as one of the exemplary manifestations of global flows that blur traditional territorial, social, and cultural boundaries, and create hybrid forms (Clifford 1997). Destinations worldwide are adapting themselves to rapidly changing global trends and markets while trying to maintain, or even increase, their local distinctiveness. This competitive struggle to obtain a piece of the tourism pie becomes a question of how 'the local' is (re)produced through the practices of touristified representations. On the one hand, global marketing companies and national as well as local authorities play a crucial role in manufacturing and selling images and imaginaries of destinations. On the other hand, tourism stimulates localization, a dynamic process characterized by the resurgence of competing localized, socio-culturally defined identities (Cawley *et al.* 2002).

In my own research, I explore the discourse, politics, and practices of tour guiding, by way of a multi-sited ethnography of local tour guides in Yogyakarta, Indonesia, and Arusha, Tanzania, some of whom are transnationally networked with one another (Salazar 2005; 2006). This chapter deals exclusively with the Asian part of my study, although I could make a similar analysis for the African part as well. I chose to focus on tour guides because they are key vehicles through which global and local processes and flows get articulated. Understanding how and why these cultural mediators create, negotiate, and transform the meaning(s) of natural and cultural heritage for tourists as well as local people in two different socio-cultural settings reveals new insights about how processes of worldwide interdependence, convergence, and local differentiation intersect, overlap, and conflict. In what follows, I describe a novel ethnographic methodology to capture the intricacies of the global–local nexus and I discuss how it is distinct from other approaches and why it is particularly useful when researching tourism. I then present the challenges I faced with this methodology during my own fieldwork in Yogyakarta. I end with a critical reflection on the use of glocal ethnography in the context of tourism studies and more generally.

## Glocal ethnography: what's in a name?

The holistic mixed-methods contribution of socio-cultural anthropology to tourism studies is widely acknowledged (Graburn 2002; Nash 2000; Palmer 2001; Sandiford and Ap 1998; Smith and Brent 2001; Wallace 2005). The interpretive approach characterizing this discipline is ethnography, a methodology that has been applied successfully to the study of tourism (e.g. Adams 2006; Adams 1996; Bruner 2005; Ness 2003; Strain 2003). In the strict etymological sense of the term, 'ethnography' refers to something that is written about a particular group of people. The basis for this descriptive writing is an extended period of fieldwork, which traditionally involves participant observation, but very often includes other methods like interviews, surveys, and questionnaires (Bernard 2002). More broadly, the term 'ethnography' is used to describe a kind of research methodology, whose characteristics include: sharing in the lives of those under study, gaining an emic understanding of things, a holistic approach, and the observation of everyday life. Because theory has tended to lag behind mere ethnographic description, academics now stress the need to link fieldwork with theoretical development (Snow *et al.* 2003).

Twenty years after the so-called crisis of representation, much of which was centred on the question of 'ethnographic authority' (Kaspin 1997), ethnography as a research methodology is facing a new challenge: What do detailed studies of the local tell us about the global and globalization – the complex process of growing worldwide interdependence and convergence? Critics have pointed out that much ethnographic writing invokes notions of the global or globalization, rather than empirically analysing them. The result is ethnography situated within an imagined, if not imaginary, global context or studies of globalized processes that lack ethnographic detail. Underpinning such criticisms is a perfectly understandable intellectual tension. On the one hand, there is the persistent question of whether ethnographic research of the global is possible. On the other hand, there is a clear recognition that this question does not make much sense since it is not feasible to fully separate the local from the global (Marcus 1998). Scholars still have a long way to go in understanding exactly how the local and the global are connected, disconnected, and reconnected. The fact that such linkages exist is indisputable; the major problem is how to operationalize them so that they can be studied and analysed.

Contemporary anthropological theorizing acknowledges that 'the local' refers not solely to a spatially limited locality (Gupta and Ferguson 1997);

it is, above all, a socio-cultural metaphor for a collectively imagined space inhabited by people who have a particular sense of place, a specific shared way of life, and a certain ethos and worldview. It is the site where global processes and flows fragment and are localized – transformed into something place-bound and peculiar (Wilson and Dissanayake 1996). 'The local' is constructed in contradictory ways and has always been, at least in part, the product of outside influences (Appadurai 1996: 178–99). The global and local need not, and should not, be treated as binary oppositions. The global–local dichotomy is artificial and arose as a heuristic necessity to meet the shortcomings of a model that tied group and socio-cultural characteristics to territory and simply saw the global as a metaphor for all that the model could not account for. Globalization theories too easily encourage the equation of an abstract global with capital and change versus a concrete local (or national) with labour and tradition (Prazniak and Dirlik 2001). In reality, processes of globalization and localization assume numerous forms connected by highly unequal power relations (Kearney 2004; Rees and Smart 2001). It is therefore more accurate to employ a relational understanding to globalization than a territorial one. Globalization always takes place in some locality, while the local is (re)produced in the global circulation of products, discourses, and imaginaries. In other words, 'the local' does not oppose but constitutes 'the global', and vice versa (Salazar 2005). The processes of all place making and force making are both local and global; that is, both socially and culturally particular and productive of widely circulating interactions.

Because globalizing processes operate across time and space, traditional ethnographic methods, which tend to be place-bound, must be supplemented with information linking the particular research moment to the broader historical context, and the research site(s) to the broader translocal forces, connections, and imaginations that constitute the global (Bamford and Robins 1997). Using the extended case study method, Burawoy (2000) described a set of strategies for combining abstract, theoretical insights about globalization with concrete, historically contextualized, geographically situated practices – an approach he and his team of researchers termed 'global ethnography'. Marcus (1998) suggested scholars should create 'multi-sited ethnographies' – works based on research conducted in several geographic locations – as a tool for capturing complex supra-local interdependencies. Such a research strategy maintains the local focus of ethnography while at the same time complicating the definition and construction of the larger system. Robertson (1995) developed the notion 'glocalization' to better grasp the many interconnections between 'the global' and 'the local'. He argued against the tendency to perceive globalization as involving only large-scale macro-sociological processes, neglecting the way in which globalization is always localized. In other words, the local contains much that is global, while the global is increasingly penetrated and reshaped by many locals. The term 'glocalization' captures the dynamic, contingent, and two-way dialectic of the two realms.

Building on Robertson's conceptual framework, I propose the neologism 'glocal ethnography' to describe my own research in Yogyakarta, Indonesia. I tentatively define glocal ethnography as a fieldwork methodology to describe and interpret the complex connections, disconnections, and reconnections between local and global phenomena and processes. This is achieved by firmly embedding and historically situating the in-depth study of a particular socio-cultural group, organization, or setting within a larger (and, ultimately, global) context. This happens figuratively by putting the 'g' of 'global' in front of the concept 'local': g-local. This implies that the stress is still on the local, but that local is now embedded in a larger (and, ultimately, global) context. Contrary to Burawoy's (2000) global ethnography approach, the stress is not on the global but on the intricate ways the local and the global are linked. In contrast with Marcus's (1998) multi-sited ethnography, glocal ethnography does not necessarily involve on-site research in more than one geographical location.

Tourism offers many possibilities for glocal ethnography, especially where international tourists meet local manufacturers, retailers, and service providers in the production, representation, and consumption of glocalized tourism goods and services (Yamashita 2003). As Bruner (2005: 17) elucidated, this 'touristic borderzone' is about the local, but what is performed there takes account of global crosscurrents. Most of these global–local connections in tourism are marked by inequalities and power struggles (Alneng, 2002). Without using the conceptual framework of glocalization, geographers studying tourism have repeatedly stressed the importance of the global–local nexus. T.C. Chang and colleagues, for example, argued that 'the global and the local should be enmeshed in any future theoretical frameworks that are developed to help understand the processes and outcomes of . . . tourism' (1996: 285). Similarly, Teo and Li stated that 'for tourism, the global and the local form a dyad acting as a *dialectical process*' (2003: 302, original emphasis). In what follows, I briefly sketch how I experimented with glocal ethnography to study tourism-related processes of globalization and localization in Yogyakarta, Indonesia.

## A glocal study of tourism in Jogja

Yogyakarta is the name of both a province on the island of Java and its capital, a city with a population reaching half a million. The region has been participating in international tourism for almost thirty years. Since the early stages, it was promoted by the Indonesian government as 'the cultural heart of Java' (or even Indonesia), and an ideal cultural heritage destination for both domestic and international markets. The most important attractions include the eighth-century Buddhist stupa of Borobudur and the ninth-century Hindu-Buddhist temple complex of Prambanan (both recognized in 1991 as UNESCO World Heritage Sites). The city, with its *Kraton* – the eighteenth-century walled palace where the Sultan resides – cherishes its

Javanese roots, attracting a large number of painters, dancers, and writers. Jogja, as the city is affectionately called by locals, is famous for crafts such as *batik* (textile design), silverware, pottery, clothing, woodcarving, and *wayang* (puppets). Although Jogja is a small provincial capital, its vibrant communities of artists and students ensure it is well connected nationally as well as internationally. Interestingly, the current tourism discourses about Jogja – as uttered by the government, by travel agencies, marketers, and by tour guides – focus on only the renowned heritage sites mentioned above and traditional arts and crafts performed or produced in the city itself or in its vicinity (Salazar 2005).

The core of my research centres on analysing the discourses and practices of local tour guides. More particularly, I want to understand how guides in Jogja rely on global networks and resources to better 'localize' their products – narratives of local cultural and natural heritage – for a wide array of international tourists. I started my year of fieldwork in December 2005. The fact that I had been in Jogja before on two different accounts seriously reduced the expected cultural shock. In the summer of 2000, I spent one month exploring the islands of Java and Bali as a tourist. I returned to Jogja for three months of preliminary research in 2003. Since my first visit, I have studied Indonesian informally and in an intensive language course at one of Jogja's private language schools. Due to my multicultural European background, I am also fluent in English, Dutch, German, French, Spanish, and Italian. Proficiency in these languages has proven to be of great value when observing the interactions between tourists and guides and when interviewing people. As is usual for ethnographic fieldwork, I spent considerable time interviewing guides (using various interview formats) and directly observing them while guiding. However, in order to capture how the guides are influenced by global crosscurrents of information and imaginaries promoted by the tourism industry, my research had to include many other facets as well.

*Collecting data*

Because tour guides are often the only local people with whom tourists interact for a considerable amount of time, it is in the interest of authorities to streamline their narratives and practices. In the case of Jogja, guiding is constricted by guidelines and regulations imposed by local (Yogyakarta Tourism Department), provincial (Yogyakarta Provincial Tourism Board), national (Ministry of Culture and Tourism, Indonesian Guide Association), and global (UNESCO, World Federation of Tourist Guide Associations) organizations and institutions. One of my first fieldwork tasks consisted of contacting these regulatory bodies, interviewing their employees, and obtaining copies of the various laws and directives. I also interviewed some of the local travel agency owners who employ the guides (most of whom work on a freelance basis). Although being Indonesia's second most important destination, Jogja's tourism growth is highly dependent on the development of tourism on the neighbouring island of Bali. This power hierarchy translates on many levels. For example, the current Minister of Culture and Tourism, Jero Wacik, is Balinese. A considerable number of Jogja's travel agencies are branch offices from Balinese tour operators. In other words, it is in Bali that tour packages for Jogja are constructed and sold. Obviously, these larger structural characteristics of tourism are beyond the control of the local guides in Jogja.

Two ways the narratives and practices of guides can be shaped and controlled are through education and by licensing. The second step in my research therefore involved investigating how guides are professionally trained. Since there are no specific guiding degree programmes in Jogja, I visited various tourism schools that offer elective courses on guiding. I interviewed teachers, gathered information about curricula and teaching materials, and observed some of the courses. One school spontaneously invited me on two of their practice excursions. Since many guides in Jogja are autodidacts who did not receive much formal training, I also sent around a questionnaire to find out which resources they rely upon to prepare their tours. Based on the usefulness of the information returned, I then contacted twenty-five respondents to conduct in-depth interviews about the same theme. The licensing of tour guides is in the hands of the Lembaga Sertifikasi Profesi Pariwisata (Institution of Certification for Tourism Professions), currently outsourced by the local government to the semi-private Jogja Tourism Training Centre (JTTC). The licensing process is controlled by Dinas Pariwisata (Yogyakarta Tourism Department) as well as Himpunan Pramuwisata Indonesia (Indonesian Guide Association, Yogyakarta Chapter) and the Association of the Indonesian Tour and Travel Agencies (ASITA). Untangling this web of interrelated organizations involved interviewing people working for each one of them.

In order to grasp the complexity of tour guiding in Jogja, it is necessary to place the contemporary local tourism scene in a wider historical, politico-economic, and socio-cultural context. Part of this was done through my three years of coursework at the University of Pennsylvania and in preparation for my oral examination. During my fieldwork, I undertook background literature research in the local libraries of the Centre for Tourism Studies at Gadjah Mada University, the Centre for Tourism Training and Development at Sanata Dharma University, and the Stuppa Indonesia Foundation for Tourism Research and Development. I frequently consulted secondary media sources like Indonesian newspapers (*Kedaulatan Rakyat, Kompas*, and *The Jakarta Post*), magazines (*Tempo* and *Kabare*), and websites. Regular discussions with Indonesian anthropologists, tourism scholars, and students in Jogja were useful to test some of my preliminary explanations and hypotheses. I also had the unique opportunity to discuss my research with various Indonesia experts during the Asia Pacific Week 2006 at the Australian National University and with tourism scholars during an international conference on tourism of Asian origin at the National University of Singapore.

## Flexible fieldwork

I had planned to spend most of the high season observing guide–guest inter-actions, and talking to both parties before and after the tours. However, a series of natural disasters – repeated volcanic eruptions, earthquakes, and a tsunami – seriously altered the course of my research. Many of the guides I was working with lost not only their houses or relatives, but also their income, because many tourists cancelled their trip to Jogja. One of the advantages of ethnography is its flexibility to adapt research agendas to such rapidly changing field conditions. Ironically, the calamities provided me with extra data on how closely the local and global scales are interconnected. I was invited to help as a volunteer with Java Tourism Care, an initiative of various local tourism stakeholders aimed at assisting in the relief, rehabilitation, and recovery of the region's tourism sector. I was present at various planning meetings and joined damage assessment teams at many of the province's attractions. I systematically gathered local as well as international news media reports about the disasters in order to compare these with the actual situation on the ground. Because there were so many disparities, I felt the need to start my own anthropological blog. This offered me an extra opportunity to reflect on the current situation and receive feedback from readers abroad. I also collected the travel warnings issued by the governments of Jogja's largest inbound Western markets (France, the Netherlands, and Germany). Finally, I was asked to be a consultant for the Jogja Tourism Information Centre, recently founded by Keluarga Public Relations (Yogyakarta Public Relations Association) in collaboration with Badan Pariwisata Daerah (Yogyakarta Provincial Tourism Board). While helping the local tourism sector, these new involvements gave me easier access to some of its key players.

The severe 27 May earthquake revealed many hitherto hidden facets of local tour guiding in Jogja. It stressed how for most people guiding is only a temporary job. After the golden years of tourism (1985–95), few people on Java are able to survive from guiding alone. Most freelance guides now have second jobs as teachers or owners of little businesses (often tourism-related). In the aftermath of the quake, many of them earned extra income by working as translators and scouts for international non-government organizations (NGOs), medical teams, and government delegations. The never-ending sequence of catastrophes also disclosed the politics and poetics of the local tourism industry. The global–local nexus and the low position that guides occupy in the hierarchy of tourism became particularly relevant in the case of the Prambanan temple complex. It took almost a month before international experts from UNESCO came to measure the damage to the World Heritage Site. During all that time the monument was closed to visitors. After the assessment, a newly built viewing platform (very similar to the ones erected after 9/11 around Ground Zero, New York) allowed tourists to see the temples from a safe distance, without being allowed to enter them. However,

PT Taman Wisata, the Indonesian government enterprise managing the park, decided not to lower the entrance fees (10 USD for foreigners). Anticipating tourist complaints, many local travel agencies decided to temporarily suspend tours to Prambanan. The few tourists who still visited the temple complex did not want the service of a local guide (approximately 5 USD) because they knew that they could not get near the temples anyway. This left the Prambanan guides in a very precarious situation.

This volatile situation shifted my original research design in the direction of an exploration of the extremely fragile position of guides within the glocal tourism context. Although most of them are well networked, they do not seem to be able to capitalize on their global connectedness, at least not for their work as guides. The local chapter of the Indonesian Guide Association is not in a bargaining position to give its members more job security. I ended my period of fieldwork with a long series of in-depth interviews with guides about their work, the current situation, tourism in general, tourists, and globalization. These meetings gave me an excellent opportunity to test my interpretations of the preliminary findings. I also talked to local travel agents, trying to find out how they value the service of local guides. The last part of my stay in Jogja was dedicated to filling holes in the data collection and a first synthesis of all the collected materials.

## Conclusion: understanding the 'glocal' side of tourism

Tourism research can, and does, cover the gamut from global systems to dyadic host–guest interactions. For those scholars wanting to conduct in-depth studies of tourism, glocal ethnography offers a valuable methodology. Yamashita stated, 'What cultural anthropology today should illuminate is the realm which lies between the global and the local' (2003: 148). In a similar vein, Tsing (2005) recently called for ethnographies with greater humility, listening skills, and attentiveness to local processes, with full analytical scrutiny of every complexity and connection. The potential of this methodology lies not in a reduction of complexity, not in the construction of models, but in what Geertz (1973) called 'thick description'. Ethnographies of 'the local' only gain in significance when placed in larger global and historic frameworks, in complex macro-processes, because combining understanding at the level of experience with the abstractions of impersonal processes is bound to reveal hitherto invisible processes and contingencies. At the same time, we have to pay attention to ensure that ethnographies sensitive to translocal dynamics do not resort to potentially misleading assumptions of ethereal global forces.

Ideally, a holistic approach like the one glocal ethnography proposes takes into account the global–local nexus. This attention to various scales should not imply a trade-off between depth and time. Unfortunately, structural limitations frequently force ethnographers to work in less than ideal circumstances. This is often the case with student ethnographers, who have limited time, resources, and experience. There is no methodological reason why ethnographic research should be carried out by only one individual. Ethnography gains in depth only by being a joint enterprise and allowing multivocality. However, degree programme requirements often prohibit this. Maybe the time has come for less ivory tower rigidity. We live in a complex world and understanding it (let alone trying to change it for the better) is a challenging task. Our research should not be determined by theoretical frameworks and methodologies but rather creatively combine theory and method to find answers to pressing questions.

As described above, my own experiments with glocal ethnography were not without challenges. While the methodology I propose might help to make case studies of 'the local' more relevant by increasing our understanding of the global–local nexus, it is not a magical tool that automatically answers all questions. As with other methodologies, much depends on the personal qualities and qualifications of the ethnographer. Take the ethics of the conducted study, for example. It is the personal responsibility of the researcher to resolve moral dilemmas encountered whilst in the field. The degree to which an ethnographer is accountable to the people he or she is working with depends largely on the researcher's subject position and the context of the study. Under all circumstances, it is important to remain honest and humble, and to ensure that the study does not harm or exploit those among whom the research is done. Ethnographers do not possess the truth and neither do the people under study. Ultimately, the receptiveness for multiple points of view gives ethnography a great advantage over other methodologies. Echoing Tsing (2005), I would therefore like to call for tourism ethnographies that are grounded (in the local), critical, analytical, and multivocal. Tourism scholars in Asia and beyond have a great opportunity to take the lead, thereby demystifying the common stereotype that all they are able to do is applied research.

## Acknowledgments

Permission to conduct research in Indonesia was granted by the Indonesian Institute of Sciences (LIPI) and kindly sponsored by the Tourism Studies Centre at Gadjah Mada University. A Doctoral Dissertation Research Improvement Grant from the National Science Foundation (Grant No. BCS-0514129) allowed me to carry out fieldwork in Yogyakarta between December 2005 and December 2006. My greatest debt is to the dozens of Indonesian people who welcomed me into their homes and lives.

## References

Adams, K.M. (2006) *Art as Politics: Re-Crafting Identities, Tourism, and Power in Tana Toraja, Indonesia*. Honolulu: University of Hawai'i Press.

Adams, V. (1996) *Tigers of Snow and Other Virtual Sherpas: An Ethnography of Himalayan Encounters*. Princeton, NJ: Princeton University Press.

Alneng, V. (2002) 'The Modern does not Cater for Natives: Travel Ethnography and the Conventions of Form', *Tourist Studies* 2(2): 119–42.

Appadurai, A. (1996) *Modernity at Large: Cultural Dimensions of Globalization*. Minneapolis: University of Minnesota Press.

Bamford, S. and Robins, J. (1997) 'Introduction. Special Issue. Fieldwork Revisited: Changing Contexts of Ethnographic Practice in the Era of Globalization', *Anthropology and Humanism* 22(1): 3–5.

Bernard, R. (2002) *Research Methods in Anthropology: Qualitative and Quantitative Methods*, 3rd edn. Walnut Creek: AltaMira Press.

Bruner, E.M. (2005) *Culture on Tour: Ethnographies of Travel*. Chicago: University of Chicago Press.

Burawoy, M. (ed.) (2000) *Global Ethnography: Forces, Connections, and Imaginations in a Postmodern World*. Berkeley: University of California Press.

Cawley, M., Gaffey, S. and Gillmor, D.A. (2002) 'Localization and Global Reach in Rural Tourism: Irish Evidence', *Tourist Studies* 2(1): 63–86.

Chang, T.C., Milne, S., Fallon, D. and Pohlmann, C. (1996) 'Urban Heritage Tourism: The Global–local Nexus', *Annals of Tourism Research* 23(2): 284–305.

Clifford, J. (1997) *Routes: Travel and Translation in the Late Twentieth Century*. Cambridge, MA: Harvard University Press.

Geertz, C. (1973) *The Interpretation of Cultures: Selected Essays*. New York: Basic Books.

Graburn, N.H.H. (2002) 'The Ethnographic Tourist', in G.M.S. Dann (ed.), *The Tourist as a Metaphor of the Social World*. Wallingford: CABI Publishing.

Gupta, A. and Ferguson, J. (eds) (1997) *Culture, Power, Place: Explorations in Critical Anthropology*. Durham, NC: Duke University Press.

Kaspin, D. (1997) 'On Ethnographic Authority and the Tourist Trade: Anthropology in the House of Mirrors', *Anthropological Quarterly* 70(2): 53–7.

Kearney, M. (2004) *Changing Fields of Anthropology: From Local to Global*. Lanham, MD: Rowman & Littlefield.

Lévi-Strauss, C. (1978 [1955]) *Tristes Tropiques* (trans. J. Weightman and D. Weightman). New York: Athenaeum.

Marcus, G.E. (1998) *Ethnography through Thick and Thin*. Princeton, NJ: Princeton University Press.

Nash, D. (2000) 'Ethnographic Windows on Tourism', *Tourism Recreation Research* 25(3): 29–35.

Ness, S.A. (2003) *Where Asia Smiles: An Ethnography of Philippine Tourism*. Philadelphia: University of Pennsylvania Press.

Palmer, C. (2001) 'Ethnography: A Research Method in Practice', *International Journal of Tourism Research* 3(4): 301–12.

Prazniak, R. and Dirlik, A. (eds) (2001) *Places and Politics in an Age of Globalization*. Lanham, MD: Rowman & Littlefield.

Rees, M.W. and Smart, J. (eds) (2001) *Plural Globalities in Multiple Localities: New World Borders*. Lanham, MD: University Press of America.

Robertson, R. (1995) 'Glocalization: Time–space and Homogeneity–heterogeneity', in M. Featherstone, S. Lash and R. Robertson (eds), *Global Modernities*. London: Sage Publications.

Salazar, N.B. (2005) ''Tourism and Glocalization: "Local" Tour Guiding', *Annals of Tourism Research* 32(3): 628–46.

Salazar, N.B. (2006) 'Touristifying Tanzania: Global Discourse, Local Guides', *Annals of Tourism Research* 33(3): 833–52.

Sandiford, P.J. and Ap, J. (1998) 'The Role of Ethnographic Techniques in Tourism Planning', *Journal of Travel Research* 37(1): 3–11.

Smith, V.L. and Brent, M.A. (eds) (2001) *Hosts and Guests Revisited: Tourism Issues of the 21st Century*. New York: Cognizant Communication Corporation.

Snow, D.A., Morrill, C. and Anderson, L. (2003) 'Elaborating Analytic Ethnography: Linking Fieldwork and Theory', *Ethnography* 4(2): 181–200.

Strain, E. (2003) *Public Places, Private Journeys: Ethnography, Entertainment, and the Tourist Gaze*. New Brunswick, Canada: Rutgers University Press.

Teo, P. and Li, L.H. (2003) 'Global and Local Interactions in Tourism', *Annals of Tourism Research* 30(2): 287–306.

Tsing, A.L. (2005) *Friction: An Ethnography of Global Connection*. Princeton, NJ: Princeton University Press.

Wallace, T. (ed.) (2005) *Tourism and Applied Anthropologists: Linking Theory and Practice*. Special issue, NAPA Bulletin 23.

Wilson, R. and Dissanayake, W. (eds) (1996) *Global/Local: Cultural Production and the Transnational Imaginary*. Durham, NC: Duke University Press.

Yamashita, S. (2003) *Bali and Beyond: Explorations in the Anthropology of Tourism* (trans. J.S. Eades). New York: Berghahn Books.

# 13 Researching second home tourism in South Africa

## Methodological challenges and innovations

*Gijsbert Hoogendoorn and Gustav Visser*

## Introduction

The past three decades have seen feminist, social, cultural, political and economic geographers re-examining the way in which we conduct research (Mullings 1999). Although 'fieldwork' is a familiar term to social scientists such as geographers, Driver notes:

> [I]t's striking how rarely we have reflected on the place of fieldwork in our collective disciplinary imagination. While the methodological and ethical dimensions of field research have preoccupied human geographers of late, reflecting broader concerns across the social sciences, surprisingly little attention has been paid to the specifically geographical dimensions of fieldwork.
>
> (Driver 2000: 267)

While progress is being made towards unpacking what it means to do fieldwork, many of the concerns reflected in this statement are not remarked on in any depth in the contemporary South African research environment.

Since the demise of apartheid, South Africa has experienced a number of fundamental changes in private and public institutions and structures, as well as fundamental changes in the ways different races, classes and genders relate to one another. South African researchers, as well as the international research community interested in its changing spatialities, have engaged productively with these changing dynamics. The intersection of institutional change and the process of field-based research, particularly with regard to research students, has, however, been neglected in research literature (see Visser 2001 for a rare exception). This chapter aims to comment on the changing South African research context in relation to research students and second home development in the country. In particular, the chapter positions the experiences of students of various types relative to a research programme focused on second homes, requiring access to institutional elites, businesses and organizations, as well as different types of property owners.

Although international systemic research into second homes has a long history of focused investigation beginning in the 1950s and 1960s (Hall and Müller 2004), the same cannot be said for the South African context. Here, second homes research has only very recently emerged as a field of interest and is in large part linked to a particular set of post-apartheid urban geographic debates. Since the end of apartheid, a range of new research themes has aimed to address its legacies. Local economic development (LED) has been a particularly well-researched area of investigation in South Africa (see Nel 2001; Rogerson 2006). Within the LED research field, seminal work has emerged in which there has been particularly animated discussion of tourism development as an LED strategy aimed at inducing economic upliftment, community development and poverty relief (see Binns and Nel 2002; Rogerson 2002). These investigations increasingly coalesced with research focused on the tourism system and its peripheries (Rogerson and Visser 2005; Donaldson 2007). It is within the growing recognition of tourism's role in a range of development endeavours that second homes research started to emerge as a field of investigation in South Africa. Since then, a slowly growing body of literature has developed, with the exploratory work of Visser (see 2003; 2004a; 2006) and his research students in a selection of South African urban places (Hoogendoorn and Visser 2004; Hoogendoorn, Mellet and Visser 2007) providing the main contours of second home development debates. In general, this research has focused on how the presence of second homes and second home owners, as well as their consequent tourism-induced expenditure patterns, assist (or hinder) employment creation and broader economic development (Hoogendoorn 2008). However, issues concerning the methodological and data mining challenges that have been encountered along the way in this research have not been remarked on.

It is the task of this chapter to report on experiences gained by a number of different master's and doctoral students while conducting fieldwork in a range of South African second home locations. Three key observations are made, providing the main structure of the chapter. First, as second homes are not a recorded census entity in South Africa, a range of creative ways of identifying their presence is required. Second, researcher positionality fundamentally frames the different creative avenues that should be selected in gathering baseline data to identify second homes. Third, researcher positionality plays a role in gathering information from second home owners and permanent residents once second homes have been identified.

## Obstacles to constructing second home databases in South Africa

Müller notes that 'in most Western countries second homes can be identified in census data' (2004: 388). However, he also notes that there is often a shortage of comparable data when investigating factors which second homes affect. This is, in part, because of diverging definitions. Ambiguities emerge when applying different research methods and definitions to different types of second homes when ownership, private rental income and the duration of occupancy are taken into account. In the case of South Africa and other countries of the developing world, these challenges are worsened by additional factors such as the presence of informal dwellings and traditional dwellings, which may or may not be included in definitions of first and second homes. Moreover, a large part of South Africa's population lead transient lifestyles and occupy rural homes seasonally, or over vacation periods, but not necessarily for recreational purposes (Hoogendoorn 2008). As a result, questions arise as to what constitutes not only a second home, but indeed the primary residence. Further methodological problems arise when attempting to identify possible second homes that are categorized as informal dwellings and as such could conceivably have no title deeds or services such as electricity and water connections. Moreover, although there is a category in South African census data specifically for recreational homes, its accuracy has been challenged. If one assumes that all second homes fall under the census category of 'recreational homes', then the census data show that there are only 12,407 second homes in South Africa. This count is, however, undoubtedly incorrect, as the Western Cape's Overstrand Local Municipality (which includes Hermanus, Pringle Bay and neighbouring towns) alone, for example, has been shown to have over 20,000 recreational second homes (Pienaar 2008).

Therefore, the quality of available data on the number of possible second homes is unhelpful and essentially unclear. As a result, second home researchers in South Africa have to employ innovative, pragmatic approaches where access to data and information determines the validity of a study. Because of the broad inconsistencies in national data, researchers have no option but to construct their own databases to investigate second home development. This situation is far from unproblematic.

## Overcoming the obstacles to constructing second home databases in South Africa

The initial second home research in South Africa analysed the rates-base data of local municipalities. In most cases two addresses per property can be identified from rates-base address listings. The first address indicates the street address of the property and the second where the rates and taxes bill is sent to. The second address on the listing can often indicate a second home property. The researcher has to assume that if a property is in, for example, Hermanus, which is a well-known holiday destination, and the second address is in another area, for example, Cape Town, the property in Hermanus is a second home and the owner's primary residence is in Cape Town. After obtaining this information, a questionnaire can be sent to the second home owner at the second address, or if telephone numbers are included in the database, a telephone call can be made to conduct an interview with the second home owner.

This approach is, however, not altogether unproblematic for a range of reasons. For example, on most rates-base address listings there is no indication of whether or not a property is an actual second home, or an empty stand. Therefore time and money may be wasted on contacting a range of potential informants who do not have a second home but rather a second property, which might become a second home or primary residence sometime in the future. Moreover, the registered owner of a property might be a legal entity such as a family trust or business trust, in which case the available second address or telephone number may be that of the representative attorneys and not the owner. Thus, if a questionnaire is sent to these addresses there is no guarantee that it will end up with the actual second home owner. In addition, the rates-base address listings do not tell one whether a property is a complex of timeshare units, an important subcategory of second homes. If a questionnaire is sent to the second address listed for a complex of timeshare units, again there is no way of knowing if it will end up at the timeshare owners, rather than a property manager. Indeed, on a recent fieldwork trip investigating the social and economic impacts of second homes on Dullstroom, Mpumalanga (see also Visser 2004b) it was found that a significant number of second homes in the town are connected to the region's recreational trout fishing industry in such a way that many second home owners are part of so-called trout syndicates. These trout syndicates are a specific type of timeshare which is run by syndicate managers, to whom rates and taxes bills are addressed. A similar observation was made in Cape Town's De Waterkant district, where most of the second home properties are used as tourist accommodation, and thus the second address on the rates-base address listing is most often that of a letting agent or property manager rather than the owner (Visser 2004a).

Undoubtedly, then, rates-base address listings do not make very specific reference to residential property use. Moreover, in many cases address listings are outdated: for example, some address listings observed in recent studies had last been revised in 2004.

An alternative is to visit the physical addresses of suspected second homes on an address listing in person and directly enquire whether or not a property is a first or second home. This could entail visits during either the high season for tourism, or the low season. Seasonal occupation hampers the possibility of conducting face-to-face interviews with second home owners or occupants. Numerous examples exist where second home owners occupy their second homes only over summer holiday periods, particularly around Christmas and New Year (Visser 2004b; Hoogendoorn *et al.* 2008). This is not necessarily the most comfortable time for second home owners to spend time being interviewed by fieldworkers. The alternative is to visit in low season, but this will not yield any responses from second home owners and so will still require postal questionnaires or telephone interviews.

To overcome this problem, fieldworkers have to turn to permanent residents who take care of second homes in the low season or know of their owners in some other way, to identify second home owners. A snowballing technique, here meaning 'allowing pre-existing networks of friendship, kinship and community to guide choice [of informants]' (Miles and Crush 1993: 87), can then be deployed as a means of obtaining a respectable response rate from second home owners via identification by permanent residents.

From the above it is evident that a variety of factors hamper the exact identification of second homes. The following provides some insights into steps that have been taken to overcome these limitations.

First, in recent research conducted on the coast of the Eastern Cape in a small second home village called Cannon Rocks, the valuation roll suggested that there were over 545 properties that belonged to owners who permanently reside outside of the village, out of a total of 754. After conducting a survey on foot it was established that only 270 actual houses existed in the village. Out of this total, only about 200 of these houses were found to belong to second home owners. What can be deduced from this is that a far more accurate result can be obtained through on-foot surveys than through using official address listings.

Secondly, in ongoing research in the Western Cape, some innovations have recently been made. Data collected on the water consumption recorded for properties in the Pringle Bay area were used to identify second homes based on average usage over the three months of highest water consumption in the year, compared to the average consumption for the remaining nine months. This method assumes that if consumption at a property is negligible over the lowest nine months, a property is a second home, and that peak times in usage indicate when owners frequent their second homes. It was found that in deploying this method, all the empty stands were discarded from the data by default because they showed little or no water consumption. According to Pienaar (2008), the reason for this is that the municipality in question does not allow an empty stand to have a water connection unless there is an approved building plan for the site. If rates-base address listings are used to identify possible second home owners and water consumption data are superimposed onto this, it could be argued that a more accurate database of the number of second homes in a specified area could be constructed. It is therefore essential for the researcher to triangulate by using a variety of procedures to identify the number of actual second homes in a particular locality. Unfortunately, though, this is only half the battle won. The next section will focus on personal challenges faced by fieldworkers when accessing data from local government, ratepayers' associations, second home owners, permanent residents and other key informants, whether in face-to-face interaction or by telephone interviews.

## Accessing baseline databases and second home owners: the challenge of researcher positionality

When conducting research, the positionality of the researcher vis-à-vis the researched can significantly influence access to informants and information.

The focus here is on researcher positionality in the context of interviewing members of elites. In fact, methods for elite research (beyond political science) have until fairly recently received relatively little attention. As Cormode and Hughes (1999: 299) note, 'Researching the powerful presents very different methodological and ethical challenges from studying "down". The characteristics of those studied, the power relations between them and the researchers and the politics of the research process differ considerably between elite and non-elite research.'

In addition, as Milner (2007) observes, more general researcher characteristics such as social class, as well as racial and cultural positionality in the research environment, can affect the relationship between researcher and researched. The combinations of these issues generate what many researchers have referred to as different 'insiders' and 'outsiders'. There have been a number of debates focusing on how researchers gain access to elite viewpoints and information (Herod 1999). The consensus currently suggests that the notion of an insider/outsider binary opposition creates the impression that positionalities are frozen in place: being an 'insider' or 'outsider' is a fixed attribute. On the contrary, as Mullings (1999) suggests, the insider/outsider binary is in reality a boundary that is highly unstable, subject to dynamism of positionalities in time and through space (also see Ward and Jones 1999). This observation appears to be very relevant to research students working in the context of South African private and public institutions as well as individuals. The examples drawn on in the remainder of this section illustrate this point.

Irrespective of the methodology used to identify second homes, building a second homes database usually requires access to municipal rates-base data at its beginning point. Therefore, a cooperative relationship between the researcher and informants in local government institutions is a prerequisite for the investigation to get started. In the South African context, despite gains made in inter-racial reconciliation since the end of apartheid, race can play a particularly critical role in gaining cooperation and access to the relevant datasets.

For example, in research undertaken in Dullstroom, a white Afrikaans-speaking man merely went to the local municipality's offices in the neighbouring town of Belfast, asked to speak with the senior accounts manager and explained his situation, and the accounts manager said that the fieldworker should return in an hour and he would have the information ready. When the fieldworker returned, the listing was duly provided. Another white Afrikaans man requiring rates-base data for the Overstrand Municipality was equally fortunate. In these cases the attitude of the officials was highly professional and they were highly competent. These well-educated groups of officials/informants immediately understood the relevance of the investigation to them and their work. However, the fact that both researchers and the informants were predominantly white and Afrikaans-speaking appeared to have aided access to the relevant information. In addition, a network of white male informants developed through referrals aided the subsequent gathering of data and analysis.

However, the very same personal characteristics created many difficulties when dealing with the predominantly black, Sesotho-speaking staff of the Dihlabeng Municipality in the eastern Free State. The white, Afrikaans-speaking fieldworker spent a total of eight hours trying to get address listings in an endeavour which was ultimately fruitless. The fieldworker was sent from one office to another. He experienced that most municipal officials did not know what he wanted and did not know what kind of procedures to follow to give him access to it. The concept of a vacation home/second home/holiday home or weekend home had to be explained repeatedly to officials. This is despite the fact that second homes are a developing phenomenon in that municipal area and undoubtedly contribute significantly to local government revenue and economic stimulation in an otherwise economically depressed area. After being sent from one office to another, the fieldworker ended up speaking to the municipal manager.

After the fieldworker displayed his identification and staff cards, the municipal manager asked outright if he was from the Scorpions, an infamous and soon-to-be-disbanded anti-corruption directorate. After a day of unsuccessful information gathering and frustration, another strategy was formulated whereby a female, black Sesotho- and Setswana-speaking postgraduate student who also studies second homes went to the municipality and underwent similar procedures but also failed. This is an unfortunate situation, especially since Section 32 (1) of the Constitution of the Republic of South Africa, Act 108 of 1996 provides that everyone has the right of access to records and/or information held by the State, and the Promotion of Access to Information Act 2 of 2000 was promulgated to protect this right (Kollapen 2007).

Positionality issues concerning the gender and race of the fieldworker also come into play when collecting data from second home owners and permanent residents. For example, a female Indian fieldworker experienced particular difficulty when speaking face-to-face with second home owners and permanent residents who were nearly exclusively white and male. In her experience, very uncomfortable situations arose when she enquired about personal income and expenditure patterns. Moreover, permanent residents expressed their discontent with her asking 'nosy' questions about the occupancy habits of second home owners. However, she found it much easier to obtain email addresses of second home owners via property agents who managed their properties and to correspond with the owners via email (Naidoo 2008). Thus, the use of indirect methods to interview second home owners was more successful. A creative method had to be found to obtain the information needed: in this case, minimizing face-to-face contact with second home owners and permanent residents.

Second home owners in general (or rather those who have been contacted and analysed thus far in research) are in large part a homogenous group (white, wealthy and male), with fairly similar opinions about their contribution to the local community. However, the challenge in determining their impact on the local context lies in accessing the views and opinions of impoverished majorities who live in villages and towns that are dominated by second homes. These views might be at variance with those of the key second home role players in these settlements. In our opinion it is fruitful to understand the opinions of those people who spend their whole lives (not only their leisure time) in a locality where the majority of formal housing belongs to people who spend minimal time occupying these dwellings. Personal in-depth interviews with key stakeholders do not always present the true feeling of the community as a whole.

In research conducted in Clarens, Free State in 2004 (see Hoogendoorn and Visser 2004) it emerged that the town's economic development from a tourism perspective was dominated by an individual who had seen the tourism potential of the town and developed it from there. The unfortunate reality of the town's subsequent economic expansion was that a significant number of permanent residents were to an extent forced from Clarens because of drastic changes in living costs. Therefore, when interviewing that particular individual developer, researchers received a very positive view of a town that had dragged itself out of a very dire situation. But when they branched out and spoke to different sectors of the population, they developed a different understanding. They realized that the changes were not necessarily perceived positively by all, but rather were seen by many as consequences of the domination of an individual who had not necessarily taken into account the needs of the broader population of permanent residents. Thus the challenge lies in obtaining a more representative response to second home development, and the only way of getting this is to speak with as many permanent residents as possible.

Again, however, the issue of researcher positionality comes to the fore. A white, middle-class researcher would find it easier to access data from the second home owners because they, like the researcher, are predominantly white, middle-class or upper-class individuals and tend to have an understanding of why research might be conducted into second home impacts. The same cannot be said for informants who are poor and black, speak a different home language to the researcher and are not well educated and hence do not always see the value of participating in second home research.

It has been argued that white men could be perceived as having a disadvantage when doing research in the context of present-day South Africa (Visser 2001). In especially remote rural areas it has proven to be difficult for white male fieldworkers to interview black female informants, who often presented these fieldworkers with direct yes/no responses to questions and a reluctance to elaborate or motivate an answer. This may be because these informants experienced white male fieldworkers as intimidating as a result of historical socialization. Conversely, when white Afrikaans-speaking men conduct interviews, especially with other white Afrikaans men or women, these are perceived to be more successful because there is a smaller likelihood of prejudice interfering in the data collection.

Informants are more often than not very helpful to fieldworkers when attempting to access data. It could be argued that bridging the racial and gender gap between researchers and affluent home owners or key role players in communities is a matter of innovation and that means exist to access the information needed.

For example, to try to decrease distances in positionalities between researcher and researched, a white male Afrikaans researcher has exploited his dual identity as a student at the University of the Free State, a traditionally Afrikaans-language, conservative university, and a staff member at Rhodes University, an English-language, liberal university. He alternately introduced himself to informants as being from either one university or the other, depending on the socio-political context he perceived himself to be in. The intention of this was to set informants at ease and thereby access information in a more comfortable context. This has proven to be a successful method of accessing information for this researcher.

A second way to minimize the impact of positionality in the research process is for different types of researcher to choose different areas of research concerning second homes, involving different types of informants. For example, a young black Setswana- and Sesotho-speaking woman researcher tailored a project deliberately around a set of second home environmental impacts because she felt that it was highly unlikely that she would get cooperation from predominantly white second home owners owing to her race and gender. She decided to look instead at issues that would require access to the mainly black-staffed provincial government, as she perceived that she would have far fewer problems accessing information from it than from second home owners. A white, middle-aged woman, on the other hand, decided to focus on the social impacts of second homes in the same research area because she felt that she would have easier access to the many white owners of second homes than either the black female researcher or the white male researchers would. She did not need to access information from the provincial government as individuals felt more comfortable sharing information with someone who had a similar demographic profile to them.

## Conclusion

The development and impact of second homes in South Africa is a new research niche. Initial research has identified a variety of obstacles and opportunities. It has been argued that the fieldworker researching second home development in the current socio-cultural and political disposition of South Africa has to be resourceful and creative. It is vital in data collection methods to overcome numerous obstacles that may hamper interaction with various levels of government, second home owners and permanent residents. The unfortunate situation in South Africa is that one's race, gender and general connections within the socio-cultural make-up of the country will determine a large part of one's success during data collection and fieldwork. What makes the South African situation unique is its own configuration of many different cultures and races, which plays a dominant role in presenting obstacles to, and opportunities for, accessing information. More particularly, fieldworkers should attempt to understand why informants from different groups may react to them in different ways, and develop strategies for approaching them successfully. In addition to this, a variety of methods should be followed to identify and clarify the number, distribution and impact of second homes in a locality.

Continued research on the visible, yet largely unknown occurrence of second homes is important in understanding their economic, social and environmental impacts. Moreover, this continued research should aim to highlight the point that official data are of utmost importance in understanding the impact of this form of tourism, in the case of South Africa and, for that matter, the developed world as well. Until such official data are available, creativity and non-standard research techniques should be employed to expose and fulfil our need to understand second homes.

## References

Binns, T. and Nel, E. (2002) 'Tourism as a Local Development Strategy in South Africa', *Geographical Journal* 168(3): 235–47.

Cormode, L. and Hughes, A. (1999) 'The Economic Geographer as a Situated Researcher of Elites', *Geoforum* 30: 299–300.

Donaldson, R. (2007) 'Tourism in Small Town South Africa', in C.M. Rogerson and G. Visser (eds), *Urban Tourism in the Developing World: The South African Experience*. Edison: Transaction.

Driver, F. (2000) 'Editorial: Field-work in Geography', *Transactions of the Institute of British Geographers* 25: 267–8.

Hall, C.M. and Müller, D.K. (eds) (2004) *Tourism, Mobility and Second Homes: Between Elite Landscape and Common Ground*. Clevedon: Channel View.

Herod, A. (1999) 'Reflections on Interviewing Foreign Elites: Praxis, Positionality, Validity and the Cult of the Insider', *Geoforum* 30(4): 313–27.

Hoogendoorn, G. (2008) 'A Changing Village: Second Homeownership in Rhodes, South Africa', paper presented at ENHR Homeownership Conference, Delft, November 2008.

Hoogendoorn, G. and Visser, G. (2004) 'Second Homes and Small-town (Re)development: The case of Clarens', *Journal of Family Ecology and Consumer Sciences* 32: 105–15.

Hoogendoorn, G., Mellett, R. and Visser, G. (2007) 'Second Homes Tourism in Africa: Reflections on the South African Experience', in C.M. Rogerson and G. Visser (eds), *Urban Tourism in the Developing World: The South African Experience*. Edison: Transaction.

Kollapen, N.J. (2007) *The Guide on How to Use the Promotion of Access to Information Act – Act 2 of 2000*. Pretoria, Republic of South Africa.

Miles, M. and Crush, J. (1993) 'Personal Narratives as Interactive Texts: Collecting and Interpreting Migrant Life-histories', *Professional Geographer* 45: 84–94.

Milner, H.R. (2007) 'Race, Culture, and Researcher Positionality: Working through Dangers Seen, Unseen, and Unforeseen', *Education Researcher* 36: 388–401.

Müller, D.K. (2004) 'Mobility, Tourism, and Second Homes', in A.A. Lew, C.M. Hall and A.M. Williams (eds), *A Companion to Tourism*. Oxford: Blackwell.

Mullings, B. (1999) 'Insider and Outsider, Both or Neither: Some Dilemmas of Interviewing in a Cross-cultural Setting', *Geoforum* 30(4): 337–50.

Naidoo, M. (2008) 'An Investigation into the Socio-economic Impacts of Second Homes in Cannon Rocks, Eastern Cape', unpublished report, Rhodes University.

Nel, E. (2001) 'Local Economic Development: A Review and Assessment of its Current Status in South Africa', *Urban Studies* 38(7): 1003–24.

Pienaar, J.J. (2008) 'The Implications of Second Homes for Planning in South Africa: Some Guidelines for Smaller Towns – a case study of the Overstrand Local Municipality', unpublished report, University of the Free State.

Rogerson, C.M. (2002) 'Tourism and Local Economic Development: The Case of the Highlands Meander', *Development Southern Africa* 19(1): 14367.

Rogerson, C.M. (2006) 'Pro-poor Local Economic Development in South Africa: The Role of Pro-poor Tourism', *Local Environment* 11: 37–60.

Rogerson, C.M. and Visser, G. (2005) 'Tourism in Urban Africa: The South African Experience', *Urban Forum* 16(2–3): 63–87.

Visser, G. (2001) 'On the Politics of Time and Place in a Transforming South African Research Environment: New Challenges for Research Students', *South African Geographical Journal* 83(1): 233–9.

Visser, G. (2003) 'Visible, yet Unknown: Reflections on Second-home Development in South Africa', *Urban Forum* 14(4): 379–407.

Visser, G. (2004a) 'Second Homes and Local Development: Issues Arising from Cape Town's De Waterkant', *GeoJournal* 60(3): 25971.

Visser, G. (2004b) 'Second Homes: Reflections on an Unexplored Phenomenon in South Africa', in C.M. Hall and D.K. Müller (eds), *Tourism, Mobility and Second Homes: Between Elite Landscape and Common Ground*. Clevedon: Channel View.

Visser, G. (2006) 'South Africa has Second Homes Too! An Exploration of the Unexplored', *Current Issues in Tourism* 9(4/5): 351–83.

Ward, G.W. and Jones, M. (1999) 'Researching Local Elites: Reflexivity, "Situatedness" and Political-temporal Contingency', *Geoforum* 30(4): 301–12.

# 14 Off the record

## Segmenting informal discussions into viable methodological categories

*Jamie Gillen*

## Introduction

Eager, young, and naïve researchers are pervasive in the social sciences. I was certainly no exception, and although I still may be considered naïve, I am probably not as eager as I once was. I think back to the first years I worked in Vietnam. My approach to interviews with officials, employees, tour guides, and executives in the Ho Chi Minh City (HCMC) tourism industry was the antithesis of elegance. I would send a generic email to hundreds of people in the industry in the days before I arrived in HCMC stating that I would be there from this day to that one, write a (short) biography and research agenda (in horrifically esoteric language), include some questions to discuss, and list times and dates when I was available; all in English, not Vietnamese. I am surprised I received any feedback at all! Those who did respond were invariably employees in foreign-owned tourism companies who have a glint of contextual understanding about the nature of the 'Western business interview'. The majority, however, responded in a more appropriate (and for me, frustrating) way: with silence. Over the course of years spent conducting research in Vietnam, I have come to learn that scholarly eagerness is best left behind in the US. The most fulfilling feedback I have received on Vietnam's *doi moi* (open door) policies, ideas of Vietnamese culture, and entrepreneurialism through the lens of the HCMC tourism industry has come from informal gatherings, usually at a home or a restaurant. Asian scholars with methodological leanings toward the qualitative are doubtless familiar with the importance of time spent in the home, at restaurants, and in the early mornings and late evenings in order to facilitate answers to their research questions. I too have conducted some of my work in these places and under these conditions, and there would not be anything called scholarly 'progress' without them.

This chapter is not necessarily about how to facilitate those times, nor why they are 'culturally' contextual, nor whether they are a requirement of fieldwork, but rather how they should be treated epistemologically. What do we call these data? Are we able to categorize them? How? Provided we can, how do we validate these categories to our advisors who oversee our dissertations? How do we validate them with our friends/respondents? For answers to these questions I primarily rely on a short piece written in 2004 by Mitch Rose entitled 'Reembracing Metaphysics'. In it he describes – following Derrida (1976; 1982) and Dixon and Jones III's discussions of post-structuralist thought (1996; 1998) – something he calls 'deconstruction as method' which 'conceptualizes deconstruction as a tool that can be used to illustrate the arbitrary nature of certain "taken-for-granted" truths' (Rose 2004: 462) and therefore also to enlighten certain 'undiscovered truths' such as the value of informalities in qualitative research. Although the academic landscape in geography (and to a greater extent, the social sciences) has shifted in the past thirty or so years (this is a vague statement; I am thinking primarily of the shift in emphasis in geography away from spatial science and toward behavioral and feminist approaches to geography that incorporate what human beings say about their worlds, and how they describe themselves within those worlds), to recognize the importance of interviews and participant observation in a researcher's methodological toolkit and thus has established these methods as 'truth', it is debatable whether or not 'hanging out' in informal circumstances has. I argue that informality and off-the-record interaction is a key component of research and knowledge attainment in a place like Vietnam, where hierarchies, formal appointments, and 'official documentation' are met with wariness and provide certain doom if principally employed by a researcher. Informal exchanges are the 'stuff' of truth in HCMC. I argue, following Rose, that illustrating what resides as scholarly 'truth' and 'untruth' is arbitrary, and that informalities can count as 'truth' in an academic setting where Vietnam is at the center of one's research interests. No less than deconstructing the often preordained/stable epistemological and methodological categories of qualitative research is at stake under this line of thinking. This goes about the justification for including these casual arrangements under the gaze of a dissertation committee's suspicious eye and leads to a tentative conclusion to this segment, that (again following Rose) 'deconstruction as method' dissects what researchers have decided are categories of valid knowledge and what – like informal  discussion – remains on the fringe of qualitative methods.

But, and in answer to the question – How do we go about segmenting informal discussions into coherent categories? – researchers must reconstruct what has been broken with respect to this ostensibly laid-back approach and to the partiality of methodological categories more generally. Including informalities and calling these points 'truths' destabilizes the epistemological categories of objectivity and explanation in the scientific sense. Scientists, whether their ways of looking at the world are indeed constructed, partial, and indeterminate, are also called upon to offer something that is precise, clear, and knowable. This is so because the 'deconstruction as method' position a researcher takes with regard to interaction with his or her respondents is still a privileged one, and still one that attempts to make the world knowable to others through the act of translation. Rose explains thus: 'In making the world "make sense" we open certain pathways, close down others, and defend our constructs against their inevitable deconstruction. We present the world as something knowable, explainable, and representable' (Rose 2004: 464). For Rose, this reconstructive project should be embraced as 'metaphysics': 'a recognition of a search for a philosophical architecture which can account for and explain the essential features governing everyday reality (that trajectory of thought which philosophy has traditionally termed "metaphysics")' (Rose 2004: 461). One of the central tenets of my research is the off-the-record dialogue because these informal quips, narratives, and anecdotes govern everyday livelihoods in HCMC. Indeed I could not present a completed research program without their (truthful) existences. So the science of placing off-the-record truth into categories and giving them a shape can be a path to explicate and justify how we go about knowing during fieldwork and also conceptually bounds that which has long been considered the deep secret of a Vietnam researcher's fieldwork experience. Conceptual boundaries are the primary way researchers delineate all knowledge, and off-the-record dialogues should be afforded no special privilege in this endeavor.

My conclusion argues that this process of deconstructive and reconstructive scientific methodology is best translated as a *biography*. I use the term 'biography' rather than 'autobiography' here on purpose. Biography suggests the writing of living organisms, while autobiography is the writing of the self. An autobiography posits the world, first and foremost, from one's own standpoint. For researchers who utilize off-the-record discussions in their analysis this arrangement is far too simplistic because we are writing other people's worlds concurrently with our own. Researchers will always be representing something or someone, whether it be themselves, a respondent's ideas, a numerical equation, and/or a cadastral map. A biographical rendering presents the world of the researcher and of his or her subjects through active, dialogic translation, bearing in mind one's own positionality vis-à-vis his or her respondents but with the simultaneous understanding that the respondent's experiences are being presented as well. Writing in this way, as I will show in the conclusion, also validates science as truthful because it is important to rehash these discussions with respondents before they are translated into science through biography.

The truths in everyday reality that Rose, Derrida, and others theoretically espouse lend themselves to translations of biographical experiences on the part of the researcher. Biographical experiences in the field epitomize the twin punctuations of the field: the desire to categorize and clearly explain scientific knowledge on the one hand and to account for and validate the messiness of daily life on the other. The best writing that employs qualitative methods – including off-the-record discussions – should be read as both a record of science *and* of a researcher's field life. The argument has been successfully made that claims of reflexivity are and should be a component of science (see Clifford 1986; Becker 1996; Mohammad 2001). Shifting the broader discussion in qualitative methods from the need for a reflexive kind of fieldwork to the importance of biographical writing that emerges out of fieldwork is a step toward more precise writing because it takes into account the deconstructive/ reconstructive actions of the scientific production of a knowable, yet untidy world.

## Truths in HCMC, Vietnam

I can remember when I first recognized that on the one hand, fashioned, orderly interviews with Vietnamese employees in the HCMC tourism industry were not giving me much in the way of valuable results and, on the other, that there were other routes to take in order to attain truth claims regarding the questions I was asking. I had arranged for a meeting with an HCMC tour guide named Bac (this name is a pseudonym), someone I had met on a tour to the Mekong Delta I had attended, and he had tentatively said, 'Yes.' We were to meet at 2.00 p.m. one Sunday afternoon at a coffee shop near his house. I dutifully brought my tape recorder, notebook, and dressed well. At around 2.10 p.m. Bac called and in a stammer explained that he had had something come up and asked if we could reschedule. Realizing his hesitancy in meeting with me, I defaulted to asking him if he wanted to come to my room one night to watch a football match (although I know nothing about soccer, I had remembered his voice rising when he discussed Vietnam's team on the tour). His voice eased. 'Of course!' he said. We decided to meet that night and I gave him the address. I opened my door to Bac without any preordained methods for extracting knowledge, or for positioning myself within that knowledge. We were going to watch the game, chat, and that was the extent of our 'contract'.

It was during the game that I came to recognize the importance that these communications could afford my research project. We touched on *doi moi* policies, his livelihood as a tour guide, the tenets of Vietnamese culture, and what he does to make money when the local tourism industry enters its low season between May and August. All of his narratives were stories and vignettes drawn out over the course of two and a half hours, and my sense then (and even more so now) is that our conversation held much more meaning for both of us than anything we could have said in his office or under the stuffy conditions of a coffee shop. Midway through our time I slipped in a question I had held since he walked through the door: 'Can I write some of this down?' Feeling comfortably disarmed he replied: 'Yes.' I wrote as feverishly as I could with the prescient feeling that asking to include an audiotape recorder at that juncture would be catastrophic to any future socializations (he later informed me that had I asked to tape-record our conversation it would have been the end of any future meetings between the two of us). I followed up with him a week later and Bac has been not only a respondent during my fieldwork time but also a valued and trusted friend. (Not all of my experiments with loose interaction congeal as easily, or as quickly, as this one did. But it is a good example of how valid knowledge can come out of informal contact.)

In Vietnam, one (research) could not have come without the other (friendship). I am struck with the stakes that have emerged from my research; not only are my research subjects and my research itself hanging in the balance of our interactions but also the friendships that we have nurtured through these exchanges. If my project was developing in such a way as to only include non-Vietnamese (specifically Westerners) as research subjects, then there may be no reason for me to negotiate this entanglement. But my questions have been and continue to be concerned with how local Vietnamese understand Vietnamese culture in the tourism industry. Does this count as truth? Resoundingly yes. How can Vietnamese understandings of their culture best be apprehended by a researcher? Through casual conversation, time spent without a tape recorder in hand, and always with a nod to the importance of patience. Deconstructing what is commonly agreed upon as ethical and pertinent research methods is a task with one general underlying assumption: that research happens, that it does not simply exist 'out there' to be parsed with certain aspects taken and some left behind. Even as social scientists today have embraced the untidiness of data collection, it is still tacitly understood that this disarray can be sifted through – whether during or right after a fieldwork session, and the best parts can be embellished as truth while the residual matter can drift away into the backpages of one's journal. In Vietnam, however, the residual matter is often a more interesting truth than respondent window dressing that occurs in formalized settings. This point reflects the processual nature of doing ethnographic research in Vietnam and probably in other parts of the world as well.

Doing research under these auspices is an emergent, *happening* process and not the means to an end, with the ostensible end being a dissertation, book, article, or book chapter and the means being scientific, precise, detachment from a unitary object. If I were to employ this style of ethnography I would have to reinvent the wheel every time I desired to return to Vietnam to conduct research. Additionally, due to the informal networks that exist and produce new networks among and between human entities in HCMC, my name would probably not be known as a trustworthy one. In sum, I would be doing poor-quality research should I rely on traditional methods of science (even of a qualitative nature). However, the categories we supplant and rewrite if we choose to take my considerations are legion (see Dixon and Jones III 2004 for a list of epistemologies that could be rendered unstable under this line of thinking). We are in positions to 'change (the) terrain in a discontinuous and irruptive fashion' (Derrida 1982: 135), and with this charge comes the invariable onslaught of questioning from knowledgeable advisors, committee members, and other scholars: How is it possible to determine, verify, and replicate 'truth' if there is no audio recording of your conversations (more on this question in the conclusion)? Are all of your 'data' just memory recall? This seems rather self-involved and easy, does it not? How can one make sure that – as a human subject – the importance of these conversations for one's research is understood fully beforehand? Is this what science/scholarship/our discipline/

graduate work has come to? (Discussing these answers explicitly is beyond the scope and word limit of the chapter, save the question about verification.)

In retort we can say that the process of assembling categories in the social sciences has been a synchronized project of stylization and institutionalization – progressing toward that which is 'natural' – and we can point to the historical evolution and current ubiquity of the interview and 'active' participant observation in qualitative methods today as cases in point. We can argue passionately and accurately that the prearranged categories contrasted by our advisors are always-already forms that are in need of deconstruction, and that in 'exposing fixed power relations as socially derived rather than naturally derived, "deconstruction as method" illustrates how the "taken for granted" is always vulnerable to the undermining process of deconstruction' (Rose 2004: 463).

And that will probably only take us so far. But I think it should be central to one's research trajectory that traditional means of data and knowledge accumulation do not work 'on the ground' in every context, and this conclusion has consequences not simply for the future of methodological approaches in geography and the social sciences but also the broader epistemological foundations that ground these methodologies and allow them to reproduce apace in the scientific community today.

This brief colloquy is meant to illustrate and celebrate the value of Rose's 'deconstruction as method' in a place like HCMC, Vietnam, where traditional qualitative methodological approaches can only take one's work so far. Informal discussions with Vietnamese colleagues and friends are valid knowledges because it is the truth of everyday life in Vietnam. Convincing advisors and the larger social scientific scholarly community of this is best accomplished by deconstructing what constitutes valid methodological knowledge and pointing out the arbitrary, ill-conceived nature of the methods many researchers use to accumulate data. How best to reaffirm our privileged place as hunters of knowledge, haulers and creators of epistemologies, and to turn our advisors' argument back around is the other side of Rose's argument.

## *(Re)Assemblages*

Rose argues that after a researcher goes about conducting the project of 'revealing the uncertain nature of social life' (2004: 463) through the method of deconstruction; 'reembracing metaphysics' reorients deconstruction toward science. For Rose (2004: 465), 'reembracing metaphysics means an acknowledgment that, in spite of deconstruction, we as researchers have an idea of a world that does not deconstruct'. Scholars search, consistently, for truths which can stabilize our worldview(s) and that reinforce preconceived notions about social relationships. We then believe these things enough to want to speak and write about them clearly. Stability and clarity reflect the central characteristics of the scientific method, or the process by which scientists venture to construct an accurate, objective, non-random representation of the world. 'Reembracing metaphysics' is a route that bridges our abilities to deconstruct social categories while recognizing that we ourselves are the ones with tendencies to build and rely on objectivity in our own academic lives. Rose's position is Derrida's (1976):

> Reembracing metaphysics is a desire to recognise not only the movement of deconstruction but also the movement of what Derrida calls our *dreams of presence*: our dreams of being a subject, our dreams of living in a world of consistency and transparency, our dreams of predictable expectations and outcomes, our dreams of being immune to the forces that continually shift our desires.
>
> (Rose 2004: 465; emphasis in original)

Our desire, Rose continues, is for an 'undeconstructed' (Rose 2004: 468) world, and therefore we can delimit boundaries around off-the-record discussions under the same conditions with which we construct other categories that ease our abilities to explain and comprehend our worlds, and jointly work to make those worlds clearer for our audiences.

In HCMC, a qualitative method toolkit is lacking without at least the acknowledgment of informal discussion's import as a category used to build knowledge. Making sense of my research requires actors in the HCMC tourism industry to explain how they interpret the rules that they are required to abide by in the 'socialist free market' that defines the new Vietnam under the country's *doi moi* policies. However, due to the various and deeply im-bedded surveillance techniques that surround every business in the country, the vestiges of Vietnam's informal marketplace, which continue to dictate how business deals are very truthfully accomplished, are minimized in a pro-fessional atmosphere. Constructing a clear, explainable HCMC business world through qualitative research would leave these significant exchanges out if Vietnam researchers continued to stand by methods such as interviews, focus groups, participant observation, and content analyses of documents. All of these approaches generally leave out the power of informalities in data collection.

I concede the conclusion – relativism – that may come out of the accept-ance of off-the-record discussions as a scientific category. Criticism that 'informal dialogue as science' breeds includes: How far is too far? Where do we stop vis-à-vis what is an acceptable method? Are payments, gifts, and so on acceptable avenues to access subjects? What about sexual relations? What are the effects on science, and (maybe) more importantly, on funding ethno-graphic research? Good questions all. And so my response to these questions parallels Rose's, who states rather perfunctorily, 'The world falls apart. Whether we are there or not, whether we like it or not, deconstruction con-tinually occurs. The world simply does not stop. There is no theory, no repre-sentation, and certainly no power that can stand against the excess of life' (Rose 2004: 465). This final point seems to me to support the inclusion of informal discussions with respondents/friends/colleagues outside of pre-ordained temporal and spatial domains as a viable qualitative method in the context of HCMC. After all, the excesses of life – and the truths that these excesses engender – continue long after the tape recorder has been turned off.

## Biographies

Writing a biography out of the deconstructive/reconstructive methodology I have just described accomplishes two goals, which mirror the twin acts of deconstructing methodological categories and reconstructing knowable science in the face of this deconstruction. The first goal involves validating discussions with respondents in order to use these conversations as data in a researcher's work. A biographical writing of a researcher's informal discussions with respondents allows the researcher to confirm these valuable conversations with respondents. In so writing a biography of this nature, the researcher reinforces the messiness of what qualitative researchers do when we engage with other people's words and actions and supports the idea that researchers are not the sole authors of the research they conduct because they are not in sole control of the valuable excesses that something like off-the-record discussions offer the research project.

A brief example of the practice of validation supports my argument. Approximately one month after Bac and I first met for a soccer match, I came back to him with a document in Vietnamese that I believed reflected our conversation. The work involved was lengthy. My first act of translation was to write up the notes of our conversation in English. This served as a segment of my written biography in HCMC. I included in these notes my personal reflections on our conversation, pointed out perceived awkward moments, silences, stumbles, and wrote out long segments of dialogue. Surely there was fact in these pages, and there was much fiction in it as well. As Strathern (1987) states, a researcher must submit that all ethnography is fiction in the sense that it is the product of the author or authors (quoted in Bennett and Shurmer-Smith 2001: 261). The next act of biographical translation was to write up these notes in some coherent fashion back into Vietnamese in order to coordinate them with Bac. My thinking in presenting the account back to Bac was to align our biographies into something we both believe is truth. My package of notes and documents in hand, Bac and I went back over these quotes, seemingly endlessly editing, arguing, and laughing over our introductory meeting together. Indeed our biography was at stake in these writings! Once we settled on what counted as truth in our biography, we found ourselves more clearly understanding each other, our separate and collective goals for the relationship, and the documents themselves served as our currency for a more fruitful, clear, and knowable relationship.

The settlement Bac and I agreed on serves as a grounded way to conceptually reconstruct categories of knowledge, the second goal of the biographical-writing agenda. Truth in our case is certainly processual. In fact it is a dirty business in the sense that we had lively disagreements about what we said, what our actions meant, and how they were to be translated on paper. These disclaimers aside, our meeting did have boundaries based on a compromise of our disparate ideologies and perspectives of what counts as valid knowledge. Our work as qualitative methodologists must involve our respondents, whose lives we write in coordination with them, not because of them. Under this line of thinking we as researchers are not necessarily doing research any differently, but we are shifting the emphasis from a purely reflexive, unresolvable field experience to one that recognizes the need, indeed the desire, for there to exist a knowable world that can be explained to others.

Windows into worlds we inhabit can close when we begin our work solely from a reflexive position, because we very often use reflexivity to implicitly suggest that meanings are unalterable beyond those which we, only by ourselves, decide are meaningful. Lest I stray too far from the broader point, researcher actions upon research and its meanings are important. But so are our respondents' meanings. Writing qualitative work as biography serves the twin goals of validating data points with respondents in order to call them truthful and concurrently draws conceptual boundaries around epistemological categories. There are many ways to write a biography besides the example I put forth involving Bac and me. It is exciting to think that the excesses of qualitative work may certainly include off-the-record discussions, and an attempt to harness and hold on to those excesses as knowledge is a step toward a more precise type of science.

## Acknowledgments

I thank Tim Winter for organizing a stimulating graduate workshop on research methodologies in Singapore in September 2006, where this paper was first presented. Many thanks are also due to T.C. Chang, whose comments on this manuscript were most welcome and needed.

## References

Becker, H. (1996) 'The Epistemology of Qualitative Research', in R. Jessor, A. Colby and R. Schweder (eds), *Essays on Ethnography and Human Development*. Chicago: University of Chicago Press.

Bennett, K. and Shurmer-Smith, P. (2001) 'Writing Conversation', in M. Limb and C. Dwyer (eds), *Qualitative Methodologies for Geographers: Issues and Debates*. London: Arnold.

Clifford, J. (1986) 'Introduction: Partial truths', in J. Clifford and G. Marcus (eds), *Writing Culture: The Poetics and Politics of Ethnography*. Berkeley: University of California Press.

Derrida, J. (1976) *Of Grammatology*. Baltimore: Johns Hopkins University Press.

Derrida, J. (1982) *Margins of Philosophy*. Chicago: University of Chicago Press.

Dixon, D. and Jones, J.P. III. (1996) 'For a Supercalifragilisticexpialidocious Scientific Geography', *Annals of the Association of American Geographers* 86: 76779.

Dixon, D. and Jones, J.P. III. (1998) 'My Dinner with Derrida, or Spatial Analysis and Poststructuralism do Lunch', *Environment and Planning A* 30: 24760.

Dixon, D. and Jones, J.P. III. (2004) 'What Next?', *Environment and Planning A* 36: 38190.

Mohammad, R. (2001) 'Insiders' and/or 'Outsiders: Positionality, Theory and Praxis', in M. Limb and C. Dwyer (eds), *Qualitative Methodologies for Geographers: Issues and Debates*. London: Sage.

Rose, M. (2004) 'Reembracing Metaphysics', *Environment and Planning A* 36: 4618.

Strathern, M. (1987) 'Out of Context: The persuasive fictions of anthropology', *Current Anthropology* 28: 1–24.

# 15 Know yourself

## Making the visual work in tourism research

*Jenny Chio*

## Introduction

Tourism can begin anywhere, at any time, and in any place. Research by Graburn (1977), Bruner (2005), and especially Harrison (2003) on tourists pre- and post-tour, their motivations, and their ways of being tourists, shows how tourism can be deeply significant to everyday lives in the form of stories, anticipation, and future expectations. But, of course, tourism is not just about the tourist. Recent works on the impact of tourism in host communities provide critical perspectives on the experience of living in tourism and of depending upon tourism for everyday economic survival (e.g. Abram, Walden and Macleod 1997; Oakes 1998; Walsh 2001).

Both aspects of tourism research are important. Nevertheless, if tourism research continues to be perceived as a two-sided endeavour, concerned with *either* the host *or* the guest, our understanding of tourism as a total phenomenon may stagnate into a false dualism that neither reflects nor explores the mobile reality of the world today. Tourism is shaped by images, influences, and ideas drawn from national and global media networks (television and film especially, e.g. Ruoff 2006), international projects and their agencies (e.g. UNESCO, the World Bank), and memories recounted by those who return from travels. Hosts can be guests, and sometimes guests are hosts – the line between the tourist and the toured is increasingly blurred and indistinct.

My research explored how tourism is experienced by residents of rural tourist villages in contemporary China. The sites of my research included two rural villages in Guizhou Province and the Guangxi Zhuang Autonomous Region, both of which are signed and marked as tourist destinations by provincial tourism boards, national travel guidebooks, and international promotions. I collected and analysed stories of travel from rural villagers, many of whom have travelled as migrant workers or as tourists (and for some, I learned, leaving the village as a migrant was also motivated by a touristic desire to 'see the world').

An additional component of my research was a study of the Chinese mediascape (Appadurai 1996) in which migration, tourism, and travel are represented as significant aspects of contemporary Chinese life experience in television programmes, advertisements, and print publications. The key research problem I sought to understand was: What happens when village residents see themselves in the mass media while depending on 'being seen' for economic revenue from tourism? I was interested in how media representations of tourism influenced and shaped tourist village residents' opinions and ideas about tourism development. At the beginning of field research, I expected to seek answers to this question through discussions with residents about television travel programmes. I also planned to use a mini-digital video camera to shoot footage for a documentary film on the experience of being a tourism destination in rural China. Little did I know that my camera, and my footage, would become more than just tools for documenting my research.

## (1)

Seeing is not just believing; in tourism, seeing is understanding and knowing, as exemplified in the Chinese phrase 体验 (*tiyan*), which means 'to learn through personal experience'. The first step in *tiyan* is to see it for oneself, and while the importance of sightseeing in tourism has been well established (e.g. van den Abbeele 1980; Adler 1989; MacCannell 1990), more often than not the first place where a potential tourist sees a tourist experience is in the mass media, whether in television travel shows, in films, or in magazines and newspapers. Previous studies of the relationship between media and travel narratives demonstrate the efficacy of television and films to both stimulate and saturate audiences with a perceived desire to be somewhere else (Ruoff 2002; see also Ruoff 2006).

Prior to field research, I studied critical approaches to media studies and the privileging of the visible prevalent in touristic discourses. The concept of the tourist gaze (Urry 2002) seemed useful, but we should not forget that often-times the spectacle of observation may become the spectacle itself (Foucault 1994: 13–14). I wanted to build an ethnographic account of competing interpretations and meanings of tourism as postulated by those whose image it is (tourist village residents) and those who produce the images (media workers). Advertisements for tourism to each of my field sites capitalize on the ethnic minority cultural traditions of the residents – who belong to China's state-recognized Zhuang and Miao minority groups – and emphasize features of the visible, built environment of each village. Research on audiences (e.g. Ang 1991; Abu-Lughod 2005; Friedman 2006) demonstrates that consumers produce wide-ranging interpretations of media products that may coincide with or contradict the producer's intents.

A fundamental premise of this research is that tourism and the visual economy of tourism are intricately linked phenomena which should be studied together in order to determine what tourism means to those whose lives are wound up in it. From Poole (1997: 10), I take visual economy to mean the cultural systems of technologies, manufacture and circulation 'through which graphic images are appraised, interpreted and assigned historical, scientific and aesthetic worth'. The close study of the relationship between visual images and tourism in China sheds new light on how identity categories such as 'ethnic minority' and 'rural' are woven into the fabric of the contemporary Chinese nation through the promotion and representation of tourism.

The visual economy of tourism circulates not only amongst potential tourists but also those who work in tourism. My methodological intervention, initially conceived of as interviews and joint viewing of television travel shows, developed into an interactive process of thinking through tourism and travel by using video-production and the consumption of visual footage as ways to talk about these topics. Because I frequently was seen by villagers while filming things of interest to myself, many began expressing interest in viewing what I recorded. Their interest suggested to me a direction for research I had not yet considered – asking for residents' opinions on my own footage, and not just that from the media. I bore in mind Jackson's (2004) notion of 'visualizing the anthropologist' through video-recording which suggests that, with a camera in hand, the anthropologist can render her- or himself even more visible and create a situation to openly discuss the anthropologist–informant relationship. Furthermore, Jackson points out the theoretical, ethical and methodological imperatives of giving video materials as gifts to informants, which reinscribes the 'use-value' of the videos with a deeply symbolic 'exchange-value' between the anthropologist and the informant.

In this way, sharing my video *did* more than using mass media images. The visual was being put to work. While watching my footage, residents became not only consumers of images but also potential producers as they offered me suggestions and ideas. Through their responses, I began to unravel how tourism is made meaningful to the village residents and how they situated the growth of tourism industries in their home villages within narratives of personal life experiences.

## (2)

My research took place in two villages – Ping'an village in the Guangxi Zhuang Autonomous Region and Upper Jidao village in Guizhou province. I was interested in building a comparative study of tourism development conditions in each of these places.

A brief description of circumstances in each village can help situate the project and research conditions. Ping'an village in Guangxi is about 90 kilometres north of the city of Guilin, a famous tourist destination in China. Ping'an is one of thirteen villages within a designated tourism scenic area called the Longji Terraces Scenic Region, which currently is managed and operated by a private company under contract to the local county government, based in the nearby town of Longsheng. Ping'an has just under 200 households with a total population of around 800. The steeply terraced fields surrounding Ping'an are the most heavily advertised and well-known tourist feature in the entire scenic area.

Tourism to Ping'an began before the entry of the local county government and the management company; villagers told me that the earliest 'tourists' arrived in the mid- to late 1970s (some say as early as the late 1960s). Villagers said that it was the photographs taken by early tourists, which won international competitions across Asia and the world, that initially attracted more and more visitors to the village. The first villager-run guesthouse opened in 1991, and the village government organized the sale of entry tickets to tourists starting in 1992. The number of homestay guesthouses exploded in the 1990s up to today, with the introduction of large hotels in 2003/4 (following data from Wen 2002). During my research stay in 2006–7, I found that most of the villagers' daily activities and livelihoods revolved around tourism in the form of running guesthouses, restaurants and small-scale souvenir shops, and guiding.

In Guizhou province, I conducted research in Upper Jidao village, which was selected to be part of a provincial-level tourism development for a poverty alleviation program begun in 2002, funded in large part by the World Bank. Upper Jidao village is separated from Lower Jidao by a few hundred metres of road, but tourism plans have focused on Upper Jidao (although administratively Upper Jidao and Lower share the same village government). I only conducted fieldwork in Upper Jidao, which has about 100 households and an official population of about 424, though villagers told me there were usually about 250–300 people actually living in the village – many residents migrated to cities for employment.

In Upper Jidao, their efforts at creating a viable tourism industry for the village have proceeded in fits and starts. 2007 and 2008 were hopeful years for the village, with a surge in tourist arrivals. Village residents performed Miao songs and dances for groups on request, and funds from prefectural and provincial government bureaus were used to construct a larger performance space and a cultural centre. The built environment of the village was promoted as an architecturally and traditionally Miao ethnic minority village, by naming and signing the village's paths, houses, trees, and barns as '100-year-old'. However, even as recently as 2010, there were no souvenir stalls, plans to build a village hotel were still uncertain, and tourist arrivals had slowed dramatically due to a massive road construction project, restricting the amount and type of vehicles that could access the village.

My research in Upper Jidao was motivated by the study of tourism as anticipation and expectation – Upper Jidao is located near two established Miao tourism villages, Nanhua and Langde, which are well known and generally considered successful (Chio 2009). Because tourism to Upper Jidao was in its early stages of planning and growth through government efforts from above (unlike tourism in Ping'an, which began more locally), I was interested in how villagers of Upper Jidao prepared themselves and their homes for tourism as a part of a larger programme.

**(3)**

The video work in my research method took up the question of how tourism develops senses of oneself through the seeing/being seen that is a part of the tourism experience for guests and hosts. The concurrent history of photography and tourism to Ping'an arguably changed local perceptions of nature and the built landscape, leading many residents to acknowledge that the terraces are 'beautiful' and not merely functional (see Xu 2005). For Upper Jidao, an ethnic Miao village, visual images of the Miao are widely circulated in Guizhou and nationally, and I found residents were well aware of how 'the Miao' are supposed to look to tourists. Both villages also promote the 'ruralness' of each place as a desirable aspect of visiting. Thus, tourism to Ping'an and to Upper Jidao is very much about looking – as a physical and psychological act. My video work tried to turn looking into a way for villagers to share and discuss their own opinions about tourism.

The process of this visual research method was as follows. During field research stays in each village, I shot video footage of what I considered to be the most interesting or simply 'good-looking' aspects of tourism (or potential tourism) in both Ping'an and Upper Jidao. When I returned to my computer in between field stays, I edited the footage into short segments on each village – the first video compilation I created had about 15 minutes of footage from Ping'an and about 12 minutes from Upper Jidao. I made multiple copies of the edited footage onto video compact discs (VCD, the most common type of video playback machine in both villages). When I returned to the villages, I asked residents if they were willing to watch and respond to the footage. I made a point of seeking out those residents who featured in the VCD. During showings, I video-recorded reactions to the footage as well as our discussions. After each showing, I left a copy of the VCD with the household, and later I also gave copies of any previous showings (featuring our conversations).

The latter recordings of our viewing sessions provided an additional layer of visual material to consider, thickening the reflexive potential of my research. Over multiple showings, conversations with villagers changed to not only revolve around the footage of the villages, but also turned to past comments made and differences of opinion. This created a dynamic atmosphere for conversations, in that we were all able to 'change our minds' and rethink our perspectives in light of external circumstances (whether it be encounters with tourists, news reports, or developments in village affairs). Additionally, because I am not conversant in Miao or Zhuang minority languages, which are spoken widely in Upper Jidao and Ping'an respectively, I had to ask for help with translations of certain conversations. This made video-recording our viewings of my footage even more important for the later translation work.

Because I was following the visual side of tourism development and living in tourism, showing and sharing my own video recordings had the effect of creating a useful distance for reflecting upon one's own situation and for thinking about concurrent circumstances in other parts of China. The project grew in complexity and reflexivity – from the first disc, which was entirely my own footage and edited by my own choosing, to later discs, which were informed by villager comments on what they wanted to see and what they thought looked good. Some villagers would offer to let me film them when they did an activity that they thought was worth being recorded, such as embroidery, harvesting rice, or shucking corn, and I complied. This constant process of thinking about, and thinking through, the visual in turn influenced my conversations and interviews with village residents on tourism, its development, and its role in their futures.

## (4)

Before going into the methodological issues that emerged through the process of sharing videos, a short summary of some of the reactions and responses to my footage will help frame the circumstances in which this visual material was received.

In Ping'an, most residents assumed I wanted to produce a promotional video aimed at publicizing the merits of visiting the village, and many people offered me advice about what to include, when the terraces are best looking, and how to structure the voice-over. One man suggested I purchase a VCD produced by the local government tourism board in order to get ideas about how such a video ought to look. Others suggested I include some songs and footage of 'special' events in the village, such as dance performances (usually only performed for tourists now) and interior shots of hotels. The latter, one man said, was important so that people would realize that in Ping'an the accommodation facilities are large enough for tour groups.

Reactions by Ping'an villagers to footage of Upper Jidao were varied. With one family, I talked about language differences and how difficult it would be for the villagers to participate in tourism industries if they did not speak standard Mandarin more fluently. Many Ping'an residents were intrigued by how poor Upper Jidao appeared – they likened the look of the wooden houses to how Ping'an used to be, before tourism became such big business. Opinions about this 'look' varied – for one couple, the wife said that the village ought to preserve the wooden houses, whereas her husband said decisively that Upper Jidao looked *luan* (乱) – chaotic, disorderly, and undesirable.

In Upper Jidao, I showed footage to a range of residents, from village leaders to those individuals more involved in tourism plans (through participation in the Upper Jidao Tourism Association, which is locally organized), and families who have expressed an interest in being a part of the tourism industry, either through serving meals or fixing up rooms for guests. Teacher Pan, a retired secondary school teacher who is the main contact person in the village for tourism-related events, often watched footage with others. This gave the viewings an added depth because Teacher Pan could explain the

Ping'an footage based upon his own experience visiting there during a 'study tour' organized in 2004 through a training programme funded by the New Zealand International Aid and Development Agency.

Many Upper Jidao residents were interested in how Ping'an *does* tourism – what do they sell? How did they run the guesthouses and restaurants (types of food served, levels of services)? They talked about how modern the village looked with some restaurants having glass doors and neon signs, and whether or not Upper Jidao should attempt this. Because most residents of Upper Jidao had gone to Langde and Nanhua villages before, they had a sense of what tourism is like in those places and some Upper Jidao residents have been tourists themselves in a few of China's more popular destinations, such as tropical Hainan Island in the South China Sea.

I learned early into my fieldwork that in my absence, the VCDs I made were being watched multiple times and shown to other families. On the one hand, this was unsurprising: most people enjoy seeing themselves or their friends and family, and because I left copies of my footage with different families, people played the discs for their relatives. More importantly, I was told during a second field research trip to Upper Jidao that the villagers had decided that they wanted to produce a promotional video. As in Ping'an, my visual materials were seen as potentially useful work that could play a role in the future of their villages – and, as in Ping'an, in Upper Jidao we discussed what sorts of shots of the village would be the best looking and what other content to include in a promotional video. They mentioned certain parts of the village which were more or less attractive (the oldest buildings being preferred over newer ones) and certain activities to film (namely *lusheng* – bamboo reed flute – playing, dancing, and singing).

The villagers in Upper Jidao were aware of their visual attractiveness as Miao, and over the years there has been much media attention poured on this region, from local, private sector videographers to national central television programming. These programmes usually feature Miao songs, clothing, and dance. Residents would often tell me I should record them in their festival clothes and not so much in their everyday work clothes, so as to match the typical images in mass media. My video work, therefore, seemed to slip seamlessly into local understandings of how and why they, the Miao of Guizhou, are supposed to be imaged. The more I was seen filming, the more frequently villagers would offer up their suggestions of where, what, and when I ought to record for the purposes of attracting tourists.

## (5)

Unsurprisingly, in retrospect, I imagined this research quite differently before I actually started. My original intent was to watch television travel shows with some village residents and video-record interviews with individuals in each village, and then perhaps use these taped interviews for discussions with larger groups. But just the first showings of footage set in motion certain expectations about what my future video work would entail. I found myself and my work relegated within certain local categories of understanding visual media and its usages, and in order to understand these categories and why they existed, I needed to work within them. Processing which aspects of each village best suited its tourism promotion was the first step in exploring what work the visual could do for residents of rural tourism villages in southwest China.

I was interested in the residents' knowledge of their villages as tourism destinations, their concerns, and how they 'saw' media production as a potentially useful activity. By taking up the villagers' initial suggestions for a promotional video, I tapped into the connections between tourism, visual aesthetics, and media that are so crucial for tourism to be successful in these two rural villages. Every year in Ping'an, around May or early June, photographers descend upon the village to photograph the flooding of the terraces, and villagers are often hired as guides and/or porters to lead them around the area. The continued success of tourism in Ping'an relies upon the dissemination and attractiveness of these photographs in national and international media outlets. In Upper Jidao, residents similarly watched my footage with the intent of discovering or deciding for themselves just how the village ought to look in order to best attract tourists. In 2008 I was asked to tape one of their song and dance performances so that they could use the video as a study aid for improving their show. Moreover, when Upper Jidao residents watched footage from Ping'an, they saw how tourism looked in other parts of China.

Following Friedman's study of spectatorship and audience receptions of the feature film *Twin Bracelets* (1990), I believe that video footage also can be considered 'a medium through which viewers reflect on their own lives and relationships with salient others and define a place for themselves in a larger social universe' (Friedman 2006: 606). She points to the methodological efficacy of turning an ethnographic eye to the event of media consumption. As she explains, while first intending to tape-record discussions after showing the film at her research sites, she realized that audiences talked continuously throughout the film. Therefore, she writes (Friedman 2006: 607), 'I decided to tape the entire film screening. My tapes reveal an intriguing palimpsest of viewers' comments and interjections overlaid with film dialogue and background music as well as the sounds of children crying, household members talking on the telephone, and the passing roar of diesel engines.'

Similarly, my video-recordings of audiences in Upper Jidao and Ping'an watching my footage revealed the ways in which residents interacted with the material spontaneously, and how their viewing of the material prompted them to discuss issues with me, as both a producer and a consumer of the footage. Sharing my video footage and sharing in the viewing of the footage added ideas and thoughts to our conversations about tourism development, and I found it gave residents and me a foundation on which to discuss issues and concerns involved in tourism.

Media production and consumption have a significant influence on social life throughout China. What is important to understand is how the media, its circulation, and the knowledges it claims to provide offer ways of understanding and looking at oneself and one's place in the world. To be sure, the footage that the residents of Ping'an and Upper Jidao watched was all produced and edited by myself – by no means could I ever claim that the footage showed 'their' (the villagers') views as opposed to 'mine'. This simple fact, however, is what made the research process more dynamic.

That the footage was mine and I presented it as mere footage and not as a finished product became the most important aspect of this method. The critical edge in my visual methodology was my overt presence in the production, consumption, and reproduction of video footage. Not only did residents watch my footage, but my attendance at showings also provided an immediate forum for feedback and questions; furthermore, my long-term residence in the villages allowed residents to offer up suggestions for what to record next, thus influencing my production of further visual recordings. Again, as in Friedman's study, the significance of my presence and role in the showings tied together the methodological and analytical processes of conducting field research; she writes (2006: 604): 'My analysis [built] not only on my viewing of the film but, more importantly, on my participation in their viewing experiences and on comparing those experiences with other ethnographic encounters I have had in the community.' In this way, methodology and analysis are brought to bear upon each other – my method of collecting data (shared viewings of footage) also played a role in how I began to analyse the data collected (as a process of producing ideas about what tourism looks like).

Arguments and debates about the role of the anthropologist as an image-maker have sometimes led to the disavowal of visual materials as a legitimate source of ethnographic enquiry and data. This has created amongst some filmmakers, anthropologists, and others engaged in creating representations of real social lives a desire to 'give the camera back', with the belief that this handover could resolve certain issues of power and politics inherent in the endeavour. In the exhibition catalogue for a 1986 exhibition, 'From site to sight: Anthropology, photography, and the power of imagery' at the Peabody Museum at Harvard University, curator Melissa Banta wrote (Banta and Hinsley 1986: 119): 'Many fieldworkers choose not to use the camera because it can create additional distance between researcher and subject. Others are reluctant to employ photography because they want to be regarded in the field as scientists rather than tourists.'

Twenty-five years later, I would argue it is quite useful and important in tourism research to acknowledge, and even embrace, the curious position of the tourism researcher as both a host and a guest in fieldwork situations. Tourism researchers are a host of immense knowledge, ideas, and experience which can be shared to interesting and significant ends with research participants; at the same time, we are guests and must act with respectful awareness of the needs, curiosities and desires of our host societies. Long-term field-work demands this delicate balance. We, as researchers studying tourism, are not alone in the field, and the research process needs to acknowledge that our very presence in research sites brings (and can bring) much potentially signifi-cant and revealing data to the whole of the study and to the lives of those involved. Tourism research, and long-term ethnographic research in particular, demands a participatory approach that can take full advantage of the researcher's presence and the researcher's productions, visual or otherwise. Using a video camera to create opportunities for reflexivity in my project was just one way to begin exploring the possibilities of putting the visual to work.

I am not giving the camera back; I am sitting in the room with the camera and talking and asking questions and watching. To write myself out of the process was impossible – in fact, by sharing footage of one village with resi-dents of the other, I made my project more transparent to my informants. They literally could see where I was when I was not in their village and get a sense of what I was doing. Nevertheless, this was not a navel-gazing video project about me either. Rather than just showing images, we talked about how to produce images and why and what for. Not only did this model the 'sightseeing' experi-ence for my research participants, but it also spurred new ways of thinking about how tourism utilizes and deploys certain socio-cultural expectations about what rural, ethnic minority China ideally ought to look like. In this way, I tried to integrate video-production into the ethnographic flesh of my project, by using video's portability and its visibility as a means of creating data about living in, through, and beyond tourism development in China.

## References

Abram, S., Waldren, J. and Macleod, D. (eds) (1997) *Tourists and Tourism: Identifying with People and Places*. Oxford: Berg.

Abu-Lughod, L. (2005) *Dreams of Nationhood: The Politics of Television in Egypt*. Chicago: University of Chicago Press.

Adler, J. (1989) 'Origins of sightseeing', *Annals of Tourism Research* 16(1): 7–29.

Ang, I. (1991) *Desperately Seeking the Audience*. New York: Routledge.

Appadurai, A. (1996) *Modernity at Large: Cultural Dimensions of Globalization*. Minneapolis: University of Minnesota Press.

Banta, M. and Hinsley, C. (1986) 'From Site to Sight: Anthropology, Photography and the Power of Imagery', exhibition catalogue. Cambridge: Peabody Museum Press.

Bruner, E. (2005) *Cultures on Tour: Ethnographies of Travel*. Chicago: University of Chicago Press.

Chio, J. (2009) 'The Internal Expansion of China: Tourism and the Production of Distance', in T. Winter, P. Teo, and T.C. Chang (eds), *Asia on Tour: Exploring the Rise of Asian Tourism*. London: Routledge.

Foucault, M. (1994) 'Las Meninas', in M. Foucault, *The Order of Things: An Archae-ology of the Human Sciences*. New York: Vintage Books.

Friedman, S. (2006) 'Watching Twin Bracelets in China: The role of spectatorship and identification in an ethnographic analysis of film reception', *Cultural Anthropology* 21(4): 603–32.

Graburn, N. (1977) 'Tourism: The Sacred Journey', in V. Smith (ed.), *Hosts and Guests: The Anthropology of Tourism*. Philadelphia: University of Pennsylvania Press.

Harrison, J. (2003) *Being a Tourist: Finding Meaning in Pleasure Travel*. Vancouver: University of British Columbia Press.

Jackson, J. (2004) 'Ethnographic *film*flam: Giving Gifts, Doing Research, and Video-taping the Native Subject/object', *American Anthropologist*. 106(1): 32–42.

MacCannell, D. (1999) *The Tourist: A New Theory of the Leisure Class*. Berkeley: University of California Press.

Oakes, T. (1998) *Tourism and Modernity in China*. London: Routledge.

Poole, D. (1997) *Vision, Race, and Modernity: A Visual Economy of the Andean Image World*. Princeton, NJ: Princeton University Press.

Ruoff, J. (2002) 'Around the World in Eighty Minutes: The Travel Lecture Film', *Visual Anthropology* 15: 91–114.

Ruoff, J. (ed) (2006) *Virtual Voyages: Cinema and Travel*. Durham, NC: Duke University Press.

Urry, J. (2002) *The Tourist Gaze*. London: Sage.

Van Den Abbeele, G. (1980) 'Sightseers: The Tourist as Theorist', *Diacritics* 10(4): 2–14.

Walsh, E. (2001) 'Living with the Myth of Matriarchy: The Mosuo and Tourism', in T. Chee-Beng, S. Cheung and H. Yang (eds), *Tourism, Anthropology and China*. Bangkok: White Lotus Press.

Wen, T. (2002) 'On Developing Family Inn Industry: A Case Study of Dragon Ridge Terrace Scenic Spot', *Tourism Tribune* 17(1): 26–30.

Xu, G.L. (2005) 'The Exploration and Evaluation of the Folklore Tourism in Longji, Guangxi Province', *Guangxi Minzu Yanjiu* 2: 195–201.

# 16 Work it out

## Using work as participant observation to study tourism

*Chris McMorran*

All tourism students have experienced that moment – at a dinner party, or the first day of a course – when we announce that we study tourism, only to have others smirk and make comments like, 'Why didn't I think of that?' The implication is that studying tourism is easy. My research in Japanese hot springs villages (*onsen*) brings even more misunderstanding. 'Wow, that must be really rough!' Friends joke about me soaking in baths, towel wrapped around my head and a scuba diver's pen in hand, interviewing whoever happens to be nearby. There is a sense of decadence to such research, and especially for colleagues who study the Greenland ice sheets or villages in the Andean highlands, there is envy of the field site's accessibility.

Research in a tourist destination presents far fewer initial roadblocks than research in, say, a prison, a diamond mine, or even an executive office, which may be difficult to reach or require special permission to enter (Thomas 1995; Mullings 1999). Tourist sites are usually very accessible and actively encourage visitors. However, the qualities that make tourism attractive and seemingly easy to research can also create the greatest obstacles. Tourist destinations are structured specifically to welcome money-spending visitors. Even the planned display of backstage areas is done for tourists, *not* researchers (MacCannell 1999). Thus, the researcher must constantly justify his or her presence in tourist space. Also, the complex power relations that shape tourist destinations, stemming primarily from land ownership and labour control, are hidden from view in order to preserve an overall harmonious effect. Labour unions are rare, and the friendly smiles of workers help conceal dissatisfactions. Therefore, research into the human relations found in a tourist destination requires a delicate negotiation of one's position with regard to workers and the powerful local elites who recruit and manage labour.

My interests in political economy and feminist perspectives led to research questions and methodologies that promised to be more emotionally taxing than conducting interviews while bathing. After visits to several hot springs villages in Kumamoto Prefecture, located on the island of Kyushu, I became interested in the gendered work relations found in a particular style of accommodation called *ryokan*. The term *ryokan* is composed of the characters for 'travel', *ryo*, and 'residence', *kan*, which combine to mean 'inn'. The most common translation is 'Japanese style inn', which is intended to differentiate the *ryokan* from a Western-style hotel. While most small *ryokan* are staffed by the owner-family, larger *ryokan* demand more labour to serve guests, clean rooms, prepare meals, scrub baths, and answer phones. In a pilot study I learned that, while even larger *ryokan* felt homelike, the labour pool consisted mostly of domestic migrant workers. Many of these workers were older women who had left their own homes for jobs in *ryokan*, meaning that a highly mobile workforce was employed to create a feeling of home for guests. This became the conundrum at the heart of my research plan.

I decided to accept the ethnographical challenge proposed by Clifford: 'Why not focus on any culture's farthest range of travel while *also* looking at its centers, its villages, its intensive fieldsites?' (1997: 25). Studying a *ryokan* would allow me to do both, since the field site was a tourist destination that also promoted itself as a cohesive village. Although the *ryokan* is not the *farthest* range of Japanese travel, the proposed research site was located in a remote mountainous location, hours from the nearest city and built to represent a potentially vanishing, traditional, and rural Other standing opposed to modern urban society. This made the *ryokan* distant from its guests in both time and space (Ivy 1995; McMorran 2008). In general, I wanted to talk to both *ryokan* owners and workers to learn how workers were recruited and trained for their positions, the reasons that workers chose this line of work, and the relations that developed between management and labour. Did the *ryokan* become a surrogate home for migrant workers? Did the workers and management share a family spirit, as some owners previously told me? And what attracted so many migrant workers to work in *ryokan* in the first place?

Research methodology courses typically emphasize the importance of choosing the method that best suits one's research questions. In the following I describe the evolution of my methods to fit my questions, given an ever-growing awareness of the special characteristics of my field site. I chart the methodological obstacles I faced in the field, most of which involved negotiating my presence within several matrices of power. These included: (1) negotiating past a strict host–guest relationship that prevented backstage access to the site; (2) both requesting and limiting the assistance (and potential interference) of *ryokan* owners; and (3) subjecting myself to some of the same unequal power relationships experienced by *ryokan* workers. In the end, I used participant observation as an employee in a *ryokan* to investigate my research questions. As a result, I advocate using work to actively engage the processes being studied in tourist destinations. I call on students of tourism, especially those with an interest in labour relations, to put down their tape recorders and notebooks for a few hours and wash some dishes. This will open lines of communication with informants and help mitigate the researcher's role in power-imbued relations.

## Negotiating powerful spaces, or getting past the lobby

The first obstacle to my research was the physical separation of the tourist setting into front- and backstage settings (MacCannell 1999). In other words, I had trouble getting past the lobby to meet potential research subjects. The *ryokan* is organized spatially like a Japanese home. The *genkan* (entrance) is considered a liminal space that is part public, part private, while the rooms beyond become increasingly private and off-limits. In many homes, a visitor can step right into the *genkan* after saying a perfunctory *shitsureishimasu* (excuse me). Most interaction with salespeople and other non-guests is handled in this liminal space. Only houseguests are invited to remove their shoes and actually enter the home, although guests often are restricted from entering some rooms, like the kitchen and bedrooms. The *ryokan* lobby resembles a home's *genkan*. Because the door to the *ryokan* usually remains open, all visitors can freely enter the lobby, but non-guests likely will not be able to proceed past the entrance.

My first method for investigating labour relations in *ryokan* involved simply walking in off the street and starting a conversation with the front staff. I hoped to make a good first impression and arrange a meeting afterwards with this person, in which a longer interview could take place. I also longed for a short tour of the inn, during which I could meet other workers and schedule interviews with them as well. When I first walked into a *ryokan* for my pilot study, a young man in a simple dark blue uniform warmly greeted me, '*Irasshaimase*', I stepped into the lobby and momentarily lost myself in the reassuring position of a guest in a country renowned for its customer service. The lobby's highly polished wooden floor glowed a deep, dark brown, and the flower arrangement by the door had a rustic simplicity quite different from those I had seen in the large hotels of Osaka and Tokyo. The clerk's friendly demeanour immediately set me at ease, and I hoped that this would translate into open reception of my research. Joining him at the counter, I offered my name card, indicating my affiliation with a prestigious Japanese university, and began to explain my purpose.

However, it soon became clear that since I was neither an overnight guest nor a day visitor for the bath, the clerk did not know how to react. My introduction was interrupted with various 'huh?'s and 'ehh . . .'s, as he was faced with a situation for which he had received no training. Not only did I struggle to justify my unexpected presence in that space, but I soon became a nuisance, as the telephone started ringing, followed by a deliveryman picking up the day's laundry. I wanted to ask this young man about his working experience and his relationship with the owners, but the space was not designed to permit this tangential use (see also Adler and Adler 2004). He expected to play the role of front desk clerk to my role of guest. Because I did not fulfil my role, he could not fulfil his. I wanted to meet the dozens of other workers in the building. However, I could feel him pulling away, sealing off access both to himself and the others. In meetings with clerks at other *ryokan*,

I again interfered with their jobs. In rare cases when a clerk was not too busy to talk, the answers felt forced. The clerk's role as a polite, welcoming individual required him or her to assist me, even if this contradicted his or her real desires. And all of this talk with front desk clerks still did not get me past the lobby.

These initial forays into studying labour in a *ryokan* brought a great deal of guilt and self-doubt. How could I move beyond the lobby, and more importantly, how could I physically be in a *ryokan* without being considered a guest? Being treated like a guest meant being placed in a position of respect, which would then create an imbalance of power in which the worker felt compelled to answer questions. This felt unethical, as it did not ensure the voluntary cooperation of research subjects. Plus, it was unreasonable to spend endless days sitting in *ryokan* lobbies, disturbing workers or watching them from across the room. The spatial organization of the *ryokan* and the roles expected to be performed conflicted with my research goals. Clearly, I needed another method and a different venue to meet informants.

## Positionality and power: gatekeepers and vulnerable subjects

Part of the problem with striking up a conversation with a *ryokan* worker is that, despite the public feel of the entrance, the *ryokan* is private property. Thus, I was ethically required to obtain permission from the inn's owners before talking to any workers. I was aware of the importance of personal introductions to gaining access to information and people in Japan; however, when it came to accessing workers for interviews, I was wary of using the owners as my intermediary. A trusted local contact suggested the owners could *convince* their workers to cooperate with my study, but this suggested coercion and would prevent investigation of my research questions. I wanted to avoid the experience of Mullings in her study of global economic restructuring and information processing firms in Jamaica, in which one manager told employees, 'Go and answer the questions that the lady outside want[s] to know' (1999: 342). Needless to say, the workers were reluctant to participate, and those who did often feared that Mullings would reveal their responses to either the government or management.

As both a social scientist and a human being, I wanted to ensure the voluntary participation of my research subjects and assure participants that I would protect their anonymity. Therefore, I was eager to avoid using the subtle or overt pressure of bosses to meet informants. The demographics of the *ryokan* labour force added further concern to the problem of voluntary participation. The bulk of the labour demand at *ryokan* is for *nakai*, the person (almost exclusively a woman) who serves the evening and morning meals and cleans guestrooms after checkout. A typical inn will have one *nakai* for every two to three rooms, so a medium-sized inn with 20 rooms will employ around 10 *nakai*. The *ryokan* is well known for providing a favourable employment option for women aged 40 to 65 who are divorced, widowed, or otherwise separated from the relative economic security of marriage. In addition to income, workers receive accommodation in dormitories, uniforms, three meals a day, and a job that requires no technical skills. Larger *ryokan* often offer childcare, which is especially attractive to young mothers with small children who may be going through divorce or leaving an abusive relationship. Far from individuals freely selling their labour as equal participants in a relationship with the owners of capital, women who migrate to work in *ryokan* tend to be especially vulnerable to the influence of their employers. How could I speak with these workers without becoming intertwined in a complex web of power relations in which the workers potentially felt at risk of losing much more than just a job? How could I receive approval from their bosses, yet avoid the coerced participation of workers? Finally, how could I convince these vulnerable workers to open up to a foreign male researcher?

One idea was to bypass permission of the *ryokan* owners and contact workers when they were not at the *ryokan*. This would help balance our relationship by removing the host–guest association and the possibility of coercion from the owner. We would just be two people having a conversation, with our relationship defined neither by tourism nor a powerful gatekeeper. But how would I identify someone as a *ryokan* worker? Would I wait outside the employee entrance of inns and hand out business cards? This felt like stalking. Could I ask my local contact to arrange individual meetings with workers and hope for a snowball effect? This seemed to give too much power to yet another intermediary gatekeeper (Oakes 2005). And would workers even talk about their work relations without the permission of their bosses? While I knew that I should request permission from *ryokan* owners to conduct research on the *ryokan* premises, my local contact made it seem that I would need the owners' permission to interview workers *outside* the workplace as well, even if I avoided questions about their specific *ryokan*. I was beginning to feel that I was running out of suitable options.

While thinking about these problems, a more difficult and practical question struck me: *when* would I meet workers? My images of long evening talks at informants' dinner tables quickly evaporated as I learned of their demanding work schedules. Like labour in all tourist destinations, *ryokan* workers must adapt to the needs of guests. Work at a *ryokan* involves preparing and feeding guests both dinner and breakfast, as well as cleaning their rooms after checkout. Thus, a *ryokan* requires labour at staggered times of the day. Most employees (except the front desk clerk) work from 7.30 a.m. to 12.00 p.m., then again from 3.00 p.m. to the end of the day, usually 9.00 or 10.00 p.m., leaving only three hours in the middle of the day during which I feasibly could conduct interviews. However, I soon discovered that these hours were cherished for running errands, taking walks, watching television, or napping, a common habit amid the 10- to 11-hour workday. And most workers have only five or six days off per month, during which they catch up on laundry, visit relatives, or escape elsewhere to shop and relax. In most cases, I could not bring myself to ask workers to sacrifice this precious time for me.

Clearly, my research questions and the specific characteristics of the field-work site meant that there was no single, perfect methodological solution. I had to balance constraints of space and time, the practical 'where and when' of fieldwork, with more conceptual, yet no less critical, worries about negotiating my presence within and around various matrices of power. As a relatively young, non-Japanese male proposing to investigate mostly older Japanese women, I had to conceive of a way to mitigate the power differential that could arise from our vast differences. I did not want to be seen as an outside expert or a spy working for the *ryokan* owner. I did not want to trivialize or romanticize their work as quaintly 'cultural' or 'traditional', especially while working within a political economy and feminist-inspired perspective. And, although I would have ultimate control over the collection and interpretation of the data, as well as the final published product, I wanted to conduct the fieldwork in a way that attempted to minimize my power in the moment.

## Working it out: participant observation as an employee

A local professor finally suggested a solution to my methodological quan-dary: work in a *ryokan*. In hindsight this choice seems obvious, but at the time I could not imagine how the plan would work. Who would hire a foreigner to work in such a purposefully Japanese place, and what job could I do? Fortunately, the informal nature of the *ryokan* industry meant that some obstacles, like a work visa and job contract, were never mentioned. I am still unsure of the legality of the arrangement, but it served the interests of both the inn and the research to ignore such matters. I was simply a friend of a friend offering to help a short-handed family business. A *ryokan* owner gladly accepted me as a researcher who wanted to experience work in a *ryokan* and talk to co-workers about their own experiences.

As a worker, I immediately entered into a locally significant *sempai–kohai* (senior–junior) relationship with the others. I was the humble junior relying on my seniors for advice and instruction. For women who believe that their poor educational background means that they have no knowledge worth sharing, I was able to turn any potential education-based power imbalance on its head. My advanced degrees were useless in this context. England (1994: 82) refers to this position as 'researcher-as-supplicant', which 'is predi-cated upon an unequivocal acceptance that the knowledge of the person being researched (at least regarding the particular questions being asked) is greater than that of the researcher'. While researchers interviewing powerful elites may need to exaggerate their intelligence or importance to gain respect (Schoenberger 1991; Mullings 1999), I found that the less I knew about the job but was eager to learn, the more willing the *nakai* were to both teach me and subsequently open up to me. Although the *nakai* often told me that their job required no skills – 'It's not difficult, anyone can do it'; 'This is just what I did as a housewife for 20 years' – my initial ignorance of the proper way to fold a futon or the importance of turning around a guest's slippers in a doorway, showed the *nakai* that their knowledge trumped institutional learning.

Two final aspects essential to understanding my relationship with *nakai* was my foreignness and maleness. Because my study centred on the particularly Japanese economic and cultural space of the *ryokan*, my initial ignorance of the work necessary to reproduce it and my desire to learn what workers called the 'Japanese way' (*nihon no yarikata*) minimized any possible power imbalance based on being a foreigner. I had no designs for imposing Western management practices on a Japanese business, and I had no illusions of instructing women in their fifties and sixties how to do domestic tasks that they had performed over their entire adult lives. Finally, as a male in a predominantly women's world, my eagerness to learn tasks considered 'women's work' helped diminish any possible power difference due to sex. I was reminded daily of my differences, but by purposefully placing myself in a position subordinate to the workers I was able to gain their trust and observe their interactions (England 1994).

Accepting a position as a worker meant sacrificing some of the freedoms enjoyed by other researchers in the field. I was not able to spend hours each day exploring the area, walking down random alleyways and chatting with passers-by. The particularities of my field site required a different approach. Plus, I found that the mobility afforded a researcher in the field stood in great contrast to the often-restrictive embeddedness of the people with whom I wanted to talk (see Kondo 1990). Therefore, I willingly gave up some freedom in order to gain a clearer understanding of the impacts of work on people's lives, which better fit my research goals.

Importantly, this method placed me in a relation to capital similar to that of workers. Because my dissertation research absolutely depended on this experience, like the workers I was largely unable to resist the demands of the *ryokan* owners. I, too, desperately needed the position and sacrificed my time and energy for the *ryokan* owner's profit. Thus, instead of simply observing a workplace, I allowed myself to be manipulated by it, which went far toward mitigating class differences and building solidarity and trust with workers. Selling my labour to the *ryokan* meant obeying a regular schedule, arriving at 7.30 a.m. and working 10 or more hours a day, five to six days a week. It also meant working mandatory unpaid overtime without prior notice, providing a taxi service for the owner's family members, having my work schedule changed at short notice, and cleaning up after guests, no matter how repulsive the mess. Being on the receiving end of blatant violations of Japanese labour laws and seeing the liberties taken with labour by *ryokan* owners enabled me to immediately speak with workers about the harsh realities of working in a *ryokan*, as well as the joys of meeting new guests every day and building relationships with co-workers.

I could have asked to simply shadow workers and speak with them as they worked. However, the constant movement required of *nakai*, especially when cleaning rooms or delivering food, meant that the *nakai* would be literally tripping over me as they worked. Plus, as anyone who has ever moved house or washed dishes in front of an idle spectator knows, it can be difficult to resist asking such a person the frustratingly obvious question/suggestion: 'Why don't you make yourself useful?' Prompting such a reaction would not put me in good stead with the workers and would highlight my privileged position as someone who, in the eyes of workers, was *not* working (Kurotani 2005). Kurotani discusses her participant observation with the wives of men who have been transferred to work in Japanese corporations in the United States. Since her research often involved chatting with groups of Japanese women during their informal afternoon meetings at each other's homes, Kurotani was often considered an *asobimono*, or one who always plays. She could not explain that her work, research, was being conducted precisely during the time that the other women considered their break time.

## Benefits and drawbacks

Before working at a *ryokan*, I had difficulty accessing workers and arranging time to meet them. The most important benefit of using work as a methodology was that it allowed hours of unpressured time with workers, where conversations about their work histories and relations with guests and management could be removed from the weighted idea of an 'interview', and instead be seen as chitchat that helped speed the work day along. My co-workers imagined interviews to be somewhat confrontational interactions that were only appropriate for people in powerful positions. They preferred the informality of chatting while working, with its stops and starts and its tendency towards gossip and complaints. This provided opportunities to ask all of the questions that I could not have asked even over the course of dozens of interviews. Like most *nakai*, one woman with whom I worked refused an interview from day one. However, she often invited me along for walks during our afternoon breaks. For around an hour we two would hunt for chestnuts or the latest flowers in bloom. She also spoke candidly about single-handedly raising two children, earning a meagre living as a seamstress, then, once her children had grown and moved away, accepting a job as a *nakai*. She detailed her ambivalent relations with the company and other employees and shared more than I could have ever hoped for with a simple interview. Near the end of my stay I jokingly asked her again for an interview, to which she laughingly replied, 'No. Anyway, I already told you everything.' She was willing to answer all of my questions and more, but not under the auspices of an official, power-charged 'interview'.

Working alongside informants also solved the age-old predicament of *where* to conduct interviews (Elwood and Martin 2000). This may be an afterthought in research involving politicians, academics, business managers, or others who have offices; however, there are few locations in which to have a long, uninterrupted conversation with a *nakai*. Since most *ryokan* owners forbid members of the opposite sex from entering worker dormitories, and most *nakai* find visits inappropriate or inconvenient, interviews in the rooms of *nakai* were out of the question. As workers who are in the semi-public eye for most of the day, *nakai* tend not to want to be seen in public during their breaks, which also made interviews in cafés or restaurants problematic. However, while working, short interviews could take place in such unofficial locations as the pantry next to the dining room, where dinner trays were prepared, or in guestrooms while cleaning or putting away futons.

Quite possibly my best 'interview' took place in the dining room when a *nakai* requested my help with a one-day-only job of filling lotion bottles. This task required little concentration and allowed us to talk freely for two undisturbed hours. With little persuasion, she proudly described her first job over 40 years ago, working as the only woman at a company that treated her as an equal and respected her for her accounting skills. She was trained to operate the company's first calculator, which she used to calculate the staff's wages. However, her career ended upon marriage, since she quit her job like so many other new brides do. Unfortunately, her marriage ended several years later in divorce. She has regretted her choice to quit her job ever since, because her lack of continuous skill development has given her little choice but to accept a lifetime of unskilled jobs. Another major reason for her lack of career choices is due to the fact that she quit her position in mid-career. Especially for women, and less so for men, one's initial job following education is critical. Since nearly all labour recruitment is done directly out of university, trade schools or high school, it is very difficult to enter the workforce as a full-time employee after a certain age or after one has already ended a career elsewhere. Now in her mid-sixties and without a home, she works to stay youthful and active, and to save some money before (hopefully) moving into her daughter's home after retirement. These and other examples of impromptu discussion show how the continuity of the methodology of work ensured an endless array of opportunities to witness and directly speak with workers about their relations with one another and with the owners of capital outside the stuffy confines of a traditional 'interview'.

The main drawback of this method is that it required the permission of a *ryokan* owner, again placing me in the position of relying on a powerful individual for access to workers. This presented a methodological issue that remains unresolved in my mind to this day. My position as a worker forced others to work with me. Even those who might not want to participate in any ethnographic research suddenly found themselves washing dishes and laying out futons with a geographer. Was it ethical of me to write about these experiences and snippets of conversation? Was it fair for me to consider their actions and comments 'on the record'? On day one, I introduced myself, described the purpose of my study, and assured all that I would use my observations solely for academic purposes and maintain their individual anonymity. I passed out copies of my release form, and all glanced at it and verbally agreed to it. But did they really have a choice in the matter? To not agree would have been difficult in front of their peers and in front of me, who at that point was still considered a guest. And because the inn was incredibly busy, many of them did not care about the research part; they were just happy to have an extra helping hand.

I conducted participant observation in the spirit of voluntary participation by the subjects. Therefore, I always let others ask the first questions. If they expressed interest in my private life, I felt that I could ask similar questions. (I only asked private questions when no other workers were nearby. I vowed to not ask any questions of workers who did not initiate their own questions about me. However, by the end of the second or third day, every worker had asked me very personal questions about my family, my income, my student status, and my home life.) By the first few days, everyone knew most of my life history, either through direct discussion or through the grapevine. As a researcher hoping to ask personal questions of the informants, I had to first open myself to their questions. This further allowed me to balance the power inherent in a typical researcher–informant relationship. By showing my vulnerability and sharing my secrets, the workers could feel that I was not just digging for bits of information from a safe distance. I had to be an open book in order to justify my writing of my co-workers' lives.

## Conclusions

A year before I began work in a *ryokan* I had the experience of shadowing workers one morning as they cleaned rooms. I followed *nakai* with a note-book as they replaced toothbrushes, washed teapots, placed clean towels in closets and vacuumed floors. They were willing to talk, but I constantly felt in the way (because, as I later found out, I was). Simply put, the difference between watching work and wiping off a table completely changed the rela-tionship between researcher and researched. As solely observer, I was difficult for them to fathom. One worker later said of that first visit: 'I thought, "Who is this strange *gaijin* [foreigner] following me around asking all of these questions?"' However, as a worker my presence in the *ryokan* made sense. I was able to move past the entrance and past the powerful role of guest. Because tourist space is specifically constructed for guests and the people who serve them, tourism researchers must strive to meet the challenge of not perfectly fitting into either of these categories. I found this was best achieved by using work as a form of participant observation.

Another crucial benefit from working in the *ryokan* was that it allowed me to negate any possibility that I would be seen as an agent of the inn owner. One of my biggest fears from the beginning of the research was that workers would suspect that I was spying on them for the owners, which several work-ers later told me had been the case. However, over time, their fears subsided as they complained ever more loudly about their lack of pay rises or bonuses, their long hours, the constant shortage of employees, and the tightfisted and inefficient practices of management. I firmly believe that these are neither the kinds of comments that I would ever have heard from a front desk clerk while standing in the lobby as a guest, nor the comments that anyone would write on a survey administered by an anonymous scholar. I was able to mitigate the powerful influences of the owners of capital by not aligning myself with them and instead subjecting myself to the same matrices of power experienced by the workers. Therefore, I was able to share the workers' experience and understand their complaints, as well as their powerlessness to ask for better conditions. Also, I was able to mitigate any possible imbalances of power based on class, educational attainment, nationality or sex through my acceptance of the role of learner of the *nakai* knowledge.

Finally, using work as a form of observation provided a level of ongoing contact with the location and study population that would have been impossible with any other method. One of the frustrations of an interview is that it ends. On the other hand, working in a *ryokan* was like a year-long interview with a group of people who normally feel that their life stories and opinions are of little import and not worthy of academic study. Every day provided a rich new source of situations that could be mined by talking with the numerous other employees all around. And while there may be no ideal place to interview a *nakai*, the physical layout of the *ryokan* enabled hundreds of impromptu micro-interviews that, when pieced together, reveal a colourful mosaic of the everyday working life of a tourist destination. Using the method of working as participant observation can serve tourism researchers anxious to mitigate (but not erase) the relations of power inherent in tourist destinations.

## References

Adler, P.A. and Adler, P. (2004) *Paradise Laborers: Hotel Work in the Global Economy*. Ithaca: ILR Press.

Clifford, J. (1997) *Routes: Travel and Translation in the Late Twentieth Century*. Cambridge, MA/London: Harvard University Press.

Elwood, S. and Martin, D. (2000) ' "Placing" Interviews: Location and Scales of Power in Qualitative Research', *Professional Geographer* 52(4): 649–57.

England, K. (1994) 'Getting Personal: Reflexivity, Positionality, and Feminist Research', *Professional Geographer* 46(1): 80–9.

Ivy, M. (1995) *Discourses of the Vanishing: Modernity, Phantasm, Japan*. Chicago: University of Chicago Press.

Kondo, D. (1990) *Crafting Selves: Power, Gender, and Discourses of Identity in a Japanese Workplace*. Chicago: University of Chicago Press.

Kurotani, S. (2005) *Home Away from Home: Japanese Corporate Wives in the United States*. Durham, NC: Duke University Press.

MacCannell, D. (1999) *The Tourist: A New Theory of the Leisure Class*. Berkeley and Los Angeles: University of California Press.

McMorran, C. (2008) 'Understanding the "Heritage" in Heritage Tourism: Ideological

Tool or Economic Tool for a Japanese Hot Springs Resort?', *Tourism Geographies* 10(3): 334–54.

Mullings, B. (1999) 'Insider or Outsider, Both or Neither: Some Dilemmas of Interviewing in a Cross-cultural Setting', *Geoforum* 30(4): 337–50.

Oakes, T. (2005) 'The Story of Secretary Wang: Hero, Savior, Liar, Scoundrel', *University of California International and Area Studies: Global Field Notes.* Paper 5 (1 December 2005).

Schoenberger, E. (1991) 'The Corporate Interview as a Research Method in Economic Geography', *Professional Geographer* 43(2): 180–9.

Thomas, R. (1995) 'Interviewing Important People in Big Companies', in H. Hertz and J. Imber (eds), *Studying Elites Using Qualitative Methods.* Thousand Oaks: Sage.

# 17 Researching tourists in the outdoors

## Challenges and experiences from protected areas in Sweden

*Sandra Wall Reinius*

### Introduction

In the Nordic countries, nature is an important tourist attraction and is one of the strongest brands in tourism promotion (Hall *et al.* 2009). Nature tourism is encouraged and supported in rural areas, and in protected areas, due to positive economic potentials leading to regional development (e.g. Eagles and Bushell 2007). Information on tourists is important at different levels and for different purposes in society. In spite of that, information on tourist use of nature, including national parks and other protected areas, is often very limited, particularly in countries and regions where there are no standardized measurements or reporting of tourist use (Watson *et al.* 2000; Kajala *et al.* 2007). A common difficulty in research that focuses on tourist use of larger nature areas is the challenge of finding people or, at least, reaching them in a systematic way. In Sweden, there is no tradition of undertaking systematic visitor surveys in protected areas and, as a result, the knowledge of visitor numbers, patterns and impacts are rather limited (Fredman 2004).

Researching actual visits or tourists on site include fieldwork. In this chapter, I draw on experiences from my doctoral research and fieldwork during the summers of 2003, 2004 and 2005 in the northwestern part of the Swedish mountain region (the Norrbotten Mountains). This region includes several protected areas that many would consider pristine nature or wilderness; however, the same area has a long history of Sami (the indigenous people) presence, including contemporary reindeer herding. In the region, touristic infrastructure has developed since the end of the nineteenth century. The research questions of the thesis dealt with how tourists perceive, conceptualize and practise the landscape. The main focus was on tourist behaviour and motives as well as on landscape values and interpretations of wilderness. A combination of quantitative and qualitative techniques was employed. The aim of this chapter is to describe and reflect on my experiences of fieldwork, data collection and cooperation with gatekeepers in a 'wilderness' area. The methodological challenges during my doctoral research were primarily connected to the specific geographical dimensions of the study area and how to find tourists with an outspread activity pattern. Only data which come from on-site registration cards, postal structured questionnaires and on-site interviews are taken into account in this chapter (for more information on my doctoral research, see Wall Reinius 2009).

## The study area

The Norrbotten Mountains are located north of the polar circle and feature a sub-Arctic environment. They consist of a mixture of high alpine peaks, high plateaus, valleys, glaciers, rivers and lakes. There are five national parks within the study area and they cover 5,335 square kilometres (they count for nearly 95 per cent of the total area dedicated to national parks in Sweden). The local economy is mainly based on tourism and Sami reindeer herding. The area is covered by a network of marked hiking trails, and mountain cabins are located every 15 kilometres on average. Back-country hiking and cross-country skiing are the main recreational activities; other activities are offered around tourist establishments along main roads. The Laponia World Heritage Site is also included in the study area. Laponia was inscribed in the World Heritage list in 1996 with regard to its natural and cultural qualities. The Laponian site is relatively difficult to access, although there are roads reaching close to the Laponian borders. The overnight statistics in the Laponian site show that the area has about 20,000 guest nights per year (Wall 2004). Two organizations (Swedish Tourist Association and Bádjelanta Laponia Tourism Association) are responsible for the overnight cabins. It is very hard to determine the number of visitors; counting equipment has been used in the past. The best estimates are made by looking at overnight statistics – a stable trend can be seen in the Norrbotten Mountains (including national parks and non-protected areas between the national parks) from the middle of the 1970s until 2003, with the area receiving around 200,000 guest nights per year (Wall 2004).

## Visitor surveys

Many techniques can be used to investigate visitors in large nature areas and the choice of methods depends on what kind of questions you want to answer, but also on the terrain, the location of the area and the number of visitors (Hornback and Eagles 1999; Watson *et al.* 2000; Vuorio 2003; Kajala *et al.* 2007). However, in research on tourists in nature areas – as in many other areas of tourism research – there has been a domination of the positivist paradigm relying on structured surveys and quantification (e.g. Mehmetoglu 2008). Questionnaires are widely used for collecting data on tourists in nature areas. How to reach the tourists and how to distribute the questionnaires can be challenging. A common way of finding potential respondents in the outdoors and in protected areas in North America as well as in Australia and Scotland is to distribute self-administered questionnaires on site at main access points (e.g. Walker *et al.* 1998; Tylor and MacGregor

1999; Flemming and Cook 2008). In research carried out on visitors to nature areas in Nordic and Baltic countries the on-site guided survey and the postal survey function best (Kajala *et al.* 2007). One way of getting in contact with visitors for a postal questionnaire is to use self-registration cards as a primary source of information on visitors. Self-registration cards that are placed with boxes at main access points or along marked hiking trails have been used in studies in the Nordic countries (e.g. Vistad 1995; Vuorio 2003; Fredman *et al.* 2005). The use of boxes can be problematic in areas where it is difficult to identify where the actual entrance points are. However, in those areas it may be better to cooperate with organizations or managers whose staff members/ personnel can hand out the registration cards (e.g. Ankre 2007). This is also the data collection procedure used in my doctoral research. Problems with the use of self-registration cards as a data collection technique are analysed further in Ankre and Wall Reinius (2009) and in Fredman and colleagues (2009).

## Assistance by tourist organizations and quantitative data on visitors

When I started my research project I contacted the organizations responsible for overnight cabins in the area for their assistance in collecting data. Also, the county administrative board, which is responsible for the management of protected areas, was contacted for cooperation. These stakeholders, or 'gatekeepers', from whom I got access to people working in the field, were positive about being a part of the research project. I informed them about the project, and about the procedure with handing out registration cards to visitors. My main 'partners' then in turn informed their personnel (staff members at mountain cabins) about the work with registration cards. The gatekeepers were also involved in the formulation of questions on the registration card. The cooperation with the gatekeepers also meant that they gave feedback to questions in the follow-up questionnaire, and some of them even formulated questions themselves for the questionnaire, which also contributed to their engagement in the research project.

The selection of cabins for the distribution of registration cards was based on their location along hiking trails or at entry/terminal points. The selection was also based on previous knowledge regarding hikers' movements and the number of visitors at each cabin (Bäck and Bäck 1986). Thirteen cabins were selected and registration cards were distributed every second week from late June until the beginning of September in 2003. In each cabin a wall chart in three languages (Swedish, English and German) presented the research project to the visitors. I had also made some information sheets with instructions to the personnel about when and to whom they were going to hand out the cards (e.g. to visitors older than 15 years). Except for asking about the respondent's name, year of birth, sex and address for a follow-up survey, the cards also contained questions concerning starting point and terminal point, date of arrival and planned departure, and the number of nights spent in cabins and in a tent, respectively. The card was written in Swedish, English and German. The personnel at the cabins handed out the cards at the same time as the visitors paid their overnight/service fee. In total, 2,422 cards were collected and, of those, 87 cards could not be used because of incomplete names or addresses, or because some visitors filled in the card twice (double registration). Follow-up questionnaires were sent to all Swedish and German addresses from the registration card ($n = 1991$) and the final response rate was 76 per cent. The follow-up questionnaire contained different sections dealing with general questions about the visit (e.g. travel reasons, accommodation and activities), detailed questions about hiking, experiences of reindeer, and of the World Heritage Site, as well as questions about expenditures, wilderness purism and socio-demographic background.

During fieldwork in the Laponian World Heritage Site, I visited three of the cabins which handed out registration cards and I talked to the personnel about the study. I also hiked on trails to observe hikers and to talk informally to them to get a deeper idea about hiking and how to understand the landscape and its use. I also contacted some of the other cabins included in the study by telephone to make sure that the data collection was proceeding.

## Lessons from the survey procedure

Under the right circumstances the use of registration cards gives a large respondent group and pre-contact yields a high response rate in the follow-up survey. Nevertheless, the disadvantages are connected to bias such as representativeness, and the study would have benefited from a more thorough analysis of non-compliance. Only visitors at the 13 mountain cabins were included in the survey; visitors that were omitted were people who spent time in other cabins, and hiked off-trail or slept in a tent without paying the service fee to the cabin. This could mean that this research study missed a tourist segment often defined as purists (Stankey 1973). I may therefore have underrepresented visitors, particularly in one of the national parks (Sarek NP) since there are no cabins there. However, it is likely that they stayed at one of the overnight cabins, for example, to use the service or to stay for one night before leaving the area, and were thus included in the study anyway. In this type of procedure, when the visitor voluntarily fills in the card, at least to some extent you will likely get a biased sample of the population.

At one of the mountain cabins, the personnel did not collect the registration cards, because of misunderstandings of the collection procedure. The cards never reached me; consequently that cabin was not included in the study. If possible, a personal contact in an early stage of the study with all establishments involved would reveal how they have handled their obligations with the cards so far. A contact would also have given an opportunity to ask how many cards they had collected. Furthermore, in the larger cabins, where various staff members work at different times of the day and during different times of the season, it is likely that some of them did not get hold of the necessary information, since it was the head of personnel who had primary information. In these cases, a contact means an opportunity to explain the research project and its use of registration cards.

## On-site interviews with visitors

Based on research aims and questions of my thesis, I decided to carry out interviews with back-country hikers and I had to find interviewees where they tended to concentrate, which was around overnight cabins. The interviews served to gain more thorough understanding of landscape perceptions and reasons behind their visits.

On-site semi-structured interviews were carried out with 26 individuals (17 different interview situations) over a period of two weeks in the summer of 2005. The interviewees were hikers in the Laponian World Heritage Site who stayed at one of the four cabins selected because of their geographical and strategic location in terms of popular hiking trails. These places were also accessible within a one-day hike from the road and it was therefore possible for me to carry out the interviews within the fieldwork period of two weeks. In the two smaller mountain cabins, all visitors present were approached and requested to participate in the survey. In the two larger cabins, tourists who were not obviously occupied with something (cooking, putting up the tent, on their way to the sauna, etc.) were requested to participate. One person refused to be interviewed due to a lack of time; each interview took about one hour. Because of the semi-structured nature of the interviews, it was possible to follow up questions, and to use visual aids (such as maps and information sheets) if needed.

The interviewees were Swedish and German men and women between 17 and 64 years of age. Depending on whether the persons were hiking in company or alone, the interviews were carried out as individual or group interviews. Six interview situations were carried out with two or more persons at the same time, while 11 persons were interviewed alone (10 of those were also hiking alone). Questions addressed travel motives, experiences of hiking, Sami culture and reindeer herding, landscape perceptions and conceptualization of wilderness. All interviews, except for one, were recorded with a micro-cassette and field notes were taken. Afterwards, the interviews were transcribed and analysed in relation to the different themes.

## Lessons from the interviews

There are some difficulties associated with interviewing hikers in the field. Among the complicated factors that I had to deal with were accessibility and the visiting patterns in relation to time, location and dispersed flow of visitors. This is a back-country area with a rather low number of visitors (the number of visitors varies in the area; at the larger mountain stations and at more accessible hotels there are a significant number of guests). Furthermore, these relatively time-consuming interviews could take place at the tourist accommodation only during late afternoons or evenings when the hikers arrived for the evening. This meant that the data collection was rather ineffective, since no interviews could be carried out during daytime and I did not know if anyone was coming to the cabin or how many people were going to be there for the evening. One problem related to interviewing tourists in the most accessible cabins close to the starting point for the hike was that some of them had just begun their several-days' hike and, as a result, it was difficult for them to answer questions about experiences. However, several positive aspects are related to the utilization of interviews. In my thesis, the interview results have been treated as complementary information to the questionnaire regarding, for instance, travel motives and landscape perceptions. The interviews gave a deeper understanding of attitudes and views of nature and wilderness. My experience is that the hikers were very positive and willing to talk about their stay.

## Concluding remarks

Generally, many people participate in different phases of a quantitative visitor study; therefore it is essential that everyone (gatekeepers, personnel, assistants) knows why and how the visitor survey is being performed. The degree of gatekeepers and personnel involvement was an important aspect of the procedure with registration cards and it is concluded that detailed information and continuous contact with the tourist cabins is necessary. When cooperating with gatekeepers, one problem can be related to whether he or she agrees to be part of the study but forgets to inform the personnel about this. A reason for visitors not filling in the cards may be related to the missing link between the gatekeeper and the personnel, and also the cards are perceived as 'extra work' (see also Ankre and Wall Reinius 2009).

Qualitative methods seem not to be generally well applied in research focusing on *the tourists* in nature, but more common in research addressing, for example, tourism impacts, and trail assessment (e.g. interviewing managers), or attitudes among local people and tourist entrepreneurs. Qualitative research on tourists in wilderness areas is time-consuming, which above all is connected to where and when to find potential interviewees. The conclusion is that fieldwork in nature-based tourism research (including interviews, observations, field notes, participation in activities and spending time in overnight cabins) gives valuable information on tourist behaviour and tourist use of nature as well as important insights into experiences, attitudes and perceptions through visitors' spontaneous conversations with each other. If possible, future research on tourists in the outdoors should apply a mixed-methods approach – for example, a combination of registration cards (followed by a web survey) and interviews on site with tourists selected from the ones who directly complete a registration card (cf. method triangulation) (Decrop 2004).

Nevertheless, such a procedure in a large nature area has limitations, since, above all, it can imply the need of assistance and fieldworkers to a higher extent.

## References

Ankre, R. (2007) 'Understanding the Visitor: A Prerequisite For Coastal Zone Planning'. Licentiate thesis 2007:09. Karlskrona: Blekinge Institute of Technology.

Ankre, R. and Wall Reinius, S. (2010) 'Methodological perspectives: The Application of Self-registration Cards in the Swedish Coasts and Mountains', *Scandinavian Journal of Hospitality and Tourism*, forthcoming.

Bäck, L. and Bäck, E. (1986) *Effekterna av ett Vägbygge – Väg 98 Mellan Kiruna och Riksgränsen. En Studie av Friluftslivet i Norrbottenfjällen 1979–1985*. Uppsala: Acta Universitatis Upsaliensis, No. C 52.

Decrop, A. (2004) 'Trustworthiness in Qualitative Tourism Research', in J. Phillimore and L. Goodson (eds), *Qualitative Research in Tourism: Ontologies, Epistemologies and Methodologies*. London: Routledge.

Eagles, P.J. and Bushell, R. (eds) (2007) *Tourism and Protected Areas: Benefits beyond Boundaries*. Willingford: CABI Publishing.

Flemming, C. and Cook, A. (2008) 'The Recreational Value of Lake McKenzie, Fraser Island: An Application of the Travel Cost Method', *Tourism Management* 29: 1197–205.

Fredman, P. (2004) 'National Park Designation: Visitor Flows and Tourism Impact', in T. Sievänen, J. Erkkonen, J. Jokimäki, J. Saarinen, S. Tuulentie and E. Virtanen (eds), *Proceedings of the Second International Conference on Monitoring and Management of Visitor Flows in Recreational and Protected areas*. Rovaniemi, Finland: Finnish Forest Research Institute.

Fredman, P., Hörnsten Friberg, L. and Emmelin, L. (2005) *Friluftsliv och Turism i Fulufjället. Före – efter Nationalparksbildningen*. Stockholm: Naturvårdsverket, rapport 5467, Dokumentation av de svenska nationalparkerna, nr 18.

Fredman, P., Romild, R., Emmelin, E. and Yuan, M. (2009) 'Non-compliance with On-site Data Collection in Outdoor Recreation Monitoring', *Visitor Studies* 12(2): 164–81.

Hall, C.M., Müller, D.K. and Saarinen, J. (eds) (2009) *Nordic Tourism: Issues and Cases*. Bristol: Channel View Publications.

Hornback, K.E. and Eagles, P.F.J. (1999) *Guidelines for Public Use Measurement and Reporting at Parks and Protected Areas*. Gland: International Union for Conservation of Nature.

Kajala, L., Almik, A., Dahl, R., Diksaité, L., Erkkonen, J. and Fredman, P. (2007) *Visitor Monitoring in Nature Areas. A Manual Based on Experiences from the Nordic and Baltic Countries*. Stockholm: The Swedish Environmental Protection Agency.

Mehmetoglu, M. (2007) *Naturbasert turisme*. Bergen: Fagbokforl.

Stankey, G.H. (1973) *Visitor Perception of Wilderness Recreation Carrying Capacity*. USDA, Forest Service, Research Paper INT-142.

Tylor, J. and MacGregor, C. (1999) *Cairngorms Mountain Recreation Survey 1997–98*. Scottish Natural Heritage Research, Survey and Monitoring Report No. 162. Perth: Scottish Natural Heritage.

Vistad, O.I. (1995) 'I Skogen og i Skolten – Ein Analyse av Friluftsliv, Miljøoppleving, Påverknad og Forvaltning i Femundsmarka, med Jamføringar til Rogen og Långfjället'. Doctoral thesis in Human Geography. Trondheim: Trondheim University.

Vuorio, T. (2003) 'Information on Recreation and Tourism in Spatial Planning in the Swedish Mountains – Methods and Need for Knowledge'. Licentiate thesis 2003:03. Department of Spatial Planning. Östersund: Blekinge Institute of Technology and ETOUR Mid Sweden University.

Walker, G., Hull, B. and Ruggenbuck, J. (1998) 'On-site Optimal Experiences and their Relationship to Off-site Benefits', *Journal of Leisure Research* 30(4): 453–71.

Wall, S. (2004) *Vandringsturism i Laponia – Besökare, upplevelser och attityder till världsarvet*. Working Paper, Östersund: European Tourism Research Institute.

Wall Reinius, S. (2009) 'Protected Attractions: Tourism and Wilderness in the Swedish Mountain Region'. Doctoral thesis. Department of Human Geography. Meddelande 140. Stockholm: Stockholm University.

Watson, A.E., Cole, D.N., Turner, D.L. and Reynolds, P.S. (2000) *Wilderness Recreation Use Estimation: A handbook of methods and systems*. USDA Forest Service Rocky Mountain Research Station, General Technical Report RMRS-GTR-56.

# 18 Challenges in fieldwork

Researching group service
experiences at a white water
rafting provider in New Zealand

*Jörg Finsterwalder and Volker G. Kuppelwieser*

## Introduction: our study

Surveying research participants seems to be a straightforward task: think about what you want to do (definition of research problem and scope) and sketch up a questionnaire (selection of appropriate research method). Then ask people to fill it out, enter the data in a suitable statistical program (collection and preparation of data), crunch the numbers to find out what you want to know (analysis of data) . . . hopefully this matches your initial thinking . . . and then publish the results (transformation of analysis into information; see Hair *et al.* 2006; 2008). We believe that most researchers are used to this or a similar process and have experienced it themselves. If you are not familiar with it (any more), you can consult various sources which discuss the appropriate methods (e.g. Walle 1997), will help you follow the right steps (e.g. Finn *et al.* 2000; Hair *et al.* 2006, 2008) and even provide you with practical guidance (e.g. Veal 1992). Following the standard approach we planned our research project, designed our questionnaire and tried to collect data.

The background of our study was a new topic identified as a potential research project that emerged from the experiences of one of the researchers with a group service. First, a theoretical approach was taken to identify the relevant literature, conceptually exploring the topic and research gaps, identifying its potential facets and discovering potential research arenas (see Finsterwalder and Tuzovic 2010) before an empirical study was planned. During this process we realised that not much research had been conducted on customer groups. We found that researchers were of varying opinions as to what constitutes a group (Lewin 1948; Forsyth 1999), and some seemingly avoided defining it (e.g. Dholakia *et al.* 2004) or offered different avenues for capturing what a group is (Ohl and Cates 2006). To simplify this process, we formulated a working definition of group as an assemblage of two or more people who share common interests or goals, perceive or may develop some form of cohesiveness and who interact with one another on a social and/or task-oriented level (Finsterwalder and Tuzovic 2010). We found the service provision to customer groups and the related aspects of co-creation (e.g.

Prahalad and Ramaswamy 2004), and also its relation to quality perceptions, of interest (e.g. Parasuraman *et al.* 1985). This was based on the conceptual paper and on the different publications identified in group psychology (e.g. Lewin 1948) as well as in the field of services and tourism (e.g. Arnould and Price 1993). Additionally, we wanted to focus on leadership within groups of customers, such as is discussed in Wickham and Walther (2007). In trying to select potential service providers for our project, we identified certain tourism and leisure operators as suitable with an ideal constellation of customer groups including potential informal leaders within the group as well as formal leaders provided by the service firm. Following this preparation, the research team decided to 'embark on a journey' to investigate group service experiences of tourists going on a white water rafting trip.

In this chapter we reflect on our experiences surveying these customer groups by distributing questionnaires in the field. We describe the process of data collection preparation and execution and we then revisit this process in the light of our experiences in the field and stress what we would do differently now.

## How we got ready: designing and testing the questionnaire and preparation of data collection in the field

After we made the decision to do our empirical work using a quantitative approach, we were faced with the task of designing a suitable questionnaire which would capture the different facets of group interactions. Our research objectives were threefold. We aimed at researching aspects of co-creation among customer group members, including the service provider's staff members, as well as analysing related quality perceptions and embedding this in a context of leadership. We realised that this meant the questionnaire would have to have interlinked sections and would require a more complex structure than other questionnaires we knew of. This view was based on our literature research on co-creation, quality and leadership as follows.

The concept of co-creation relates to the customer's role as a part of the production and delivery process of the service. Research suggests that customers as external factors have to contribute to a varying degree in order to be able to produce and consume the service (Kelley *et al.* 1990) either by personally getting involved or providing some objects or information to the co-creation process, effectively co-creating value (Berry and Lampo 2000; Grönroos 2008; Payne *et al.* 2008). The 'joint creation of value by the company and the customer' (Prahalad and Ramaswamy 2004: 8) requires the willingness, motivation and the capability of the customer to become part of the service operation and the co-creation process. Literature seems to mostly discuss co-creation aspects without the contextual factor of other customers involved in co-creation but in fact, as Prahalad (2004: 23) states: 'Customers are not isolated. The firm–customer relationship is not bilateral.

Customers, customer communities, and firms interact. Customer communities can be an integral part of the value-creation process . . .' We realised that on the one hand we had to focus on the individual customer in our research because co-creation 'depends highly on individuals. Each person's uniqueness affects the co-creation process as well as the co-creation experience' (Prahalad and Ramaswamy 2004: 14). On the other hand we also had to keep the group aspect in mind, as evident in the following quote from Gouthier and Schmid (2003: 123): 'activities carried out by the customer have to be combined with activities carried out by the service firm and by third actors (for instance by other customers)'. Therefore, sections of the questionnaire had to be designed to look at the way participants in the service experience perceived their own performance and that of other group members when co-creating the service encounter. In addition, questions had to be included which referred to the performance of the service provider helping to facilitate the white water rafting trip.

The approach taken with our questionnaire design was reinforced by the lack of literature on quality models in services (e.g. Parasuraman *et al.* 1985) which relate to quality aspects of customers interacting with one another. The latter appeared to us to be a crucial yet neglected aspect. By reviewing the roles of a service customer this became evident. Büttgen (2008) lists several functions (see also, e.g., Lengnick-Hall 1996; Normann 1991; Gouthier and Schmid 2003). Two of them were particularly interesting with regard to service quality and group services. One is the customer's role as a contributor to quality (Normann 1991). The customer can function as a control mechanism feeding back potential flaws in the service so that it can be improved. The second one is the customer's role as an aid for other customers in co-creating the service (Büttgen 2008). These suggestions had to be taken into account in the design of the survey by asking customers questions where they had to evaluate their own contribution to the group experience and also the contribution of selected other group members.

Our third pillar for the questionnaire was leadership, distinguishing formal and informal leaders (Kickul and Neuman 2000). Researchers have different views on informal leadership, how it emerges and what it influences (Harris *et al.* 2007; Jacques *et al.* 2008; Neubert and Taggar 2004; Pescosolido 2001, 2002; Wheelan and Johnston 1996). This supports the need to define different roles within the group; specifically the roles of team-member, formal leader and informal leader. As a result, we needed to cover all these roles in the questionnaire, especially if we wanted to explore the interactions among the three roles taken by participants and providers. Therefore, we had to find a way to identify each role after the surveys were completed by the participants. Bearing anonymity of the participants in mind, we covered these issues by planning to assign a number of alias names to everyone in the team and asking people to refer to this number/alias in their questionnaire. The distribution of the number/alias was done randomly and anonymously. To allow participants to evaluate each other, self-adhesive tags bearing the numbers/aliases and the group identification were prepared for data collection.

The final questionnaire covered identical underlying constructs in view of the different roles in service co-creation as well as the quality aspects. Based on our identification of the service industry in focus for our study, we decided to ask people directly rather than asking them days after their service experience due to their fresh impression of the group encounter. This also influenced our choice to use a paper-based version. In the end we designed a questionnaire with multiple pages covering all aspects as described above, using a mix of even-numbered and uneven-numbered rating scales derived from literature of the three research arenas we wanted to link. We pre-tested the questionnaire with participants of a group experience in an educational setting by using bachelor students who had completed a group project in a marketing course. After refining the questionnaire based on the students' comments, we prepared for our fieldwork with the white water rafting provider.

Based on a research plan which included information relevant for the acquisition of tourism providers for the study, members of the research team contacted potential service providers offering white water rafting in New Zealand. Appropriate operators were identified. In the meantime approval for the research project from the Human Ethics Committee at the university of one of the leading researchers was sought. After approval was granted, information sheets and consent forms were ready to be distributed to the service provider and participating customers. A data collection sheet was also designed which was to help the research team keep track of the name of the researcher(s) in the field, the name of the service provider, date and time of data collection, group alias name or number to identify members of the same group, the number of returned surveys, alias name or number of the formal leader and space for other comments.

## How we got it done: working in the field collecting data at the service provider's premises

When members of the research team departed to the chosen white water rafting provider, which was located in relative proximity to the largest city in the South Island of New Zealand, the following facts were already known to the research team due to information received from the provider or acquired from the website. Each rafting boat would be boarded by approximately five to seven people, with an additional rafting guide provided by the operator. Boat crews (tourists) may or may not know each other before the rafting trip. Due to the nature of the tourist experience, teams were most likely to be more perishable than in other service experiences, such as indoor soccer experiences where players can repeatedly meet to play again under the supervision of a referee. We also had information about the logistics of the white water rafting trip. Usually, participants were shuttled from the city to the white water rafting site with the option to overnight in a lodge on site if desired.

Staff members would greet them on arrival with all necessary equipment and instruction. Following the rafting trip, tourists were offered a barbecue before being shuttled back to the city. These pieces of information allowed us to identify the most logical moment for data collection. The barbecue immediately after the boat trip and the bus trip back were deemed the most suitable times to distribute the questionnaires to each member of the groups.

A decision was made to integrate the researcher into the whole group trip, except for the boat trip itself. Equally, having a researcher present to interact with the group enabled us to explain or reinterpret any questions for the participants in the survey, as well as provide us with a better perception of the experience firsthand. In some cases, the researcher could decide whether or not to stay the night to continue data collection the next day(s) if booking numbers were high enough to justify a continuation of the data collection. We strived for numbers of around 30 participants per rafting trip, i.e. around four to six groups to be surveyed at once.

In regard to managing the different participants in the survey, i.e. the groups of customers on the rafting trip equalling team-members and consisting of potential informal leaders and the white water rafting guides as formal leaders, for the informal leaders we decided to hand out random numbers for 'identification' within the group during data collection. Our view was that people would then be able to identify and rate other team-members anonymously when filling out the questionnaire. We were also aware of the fact that some team-members might resent having to rate their peers or not agree with the idea of an informal leader within the group. Additionally, we assumed that participants would get confused with the roles of formal and informal leader. Therefore, the researchers on site were briefed and ready to answer questions relating to this distinction.

In managing the individual surveys, we had to distribute the questionnaires to several groups at once at the same time whilst having their barbecue. This meant the on-site researcher had to ensure each group of individuals understood what was expected of them in a timeframe of 45 minutes to an hour. Our advantage was that groups and their formal leaders stayed together for the barbecue so that we had reasonable opportunities to complete as many surveys as possible before the barbecue finished. At times, given the numbers and limited timeframe, the researcher in the field could manage to survey only a certain number of groups and had to continue data collection with the remaining teams on their trip back to the city on the bus.

When collecting data, we also had to bear the formal team leaders in mind, e.g. the rafting guides, and whether or not to ask them to fill out the survey for each team guided. During our planning process we had realised that the latter would mean missing the opportunity to capture the views of the formal guide. Including the formal leaders, on the other hand, would mean having to ask the guide repeatedly for each new group. We decided to include the formal leader in every group surveyed, as each group and every constellation of people differed, but we asked the formal leader to fill out only the group-specific parts of the questionnaire every time a new group had been guided. In our quest to keep the level of motivation up while surveying staff and customers, we gave away incentive gifts after the completion of the surveys and also brought some presents for the participating rafting guides and owner to thank them for their participation.

## What we struggled with: problems during data collection in the field

In order to get a reliable and valid sample size, we aimed for 200 to 250 questionnaires with a group size of five (to seven) tourists (plus guide), equalling approximately 40 (29) to 50 (36) groups needed. Depending on the weather and their personal travel schedules, tourists tended to book rafting trips at short notice. Hence, our research team was not able to make plans for data collection far in advance. We started with a day trip to join the groups booked for white water rafting but found that on the following day, numbers of groups and participants were not large enough to do efficient surveying. Therefore, the field researchers of the team had to be available ad hoc, i.e. when booking numbers were large enough to justify a trip.

Another issue to arise when participants filled out the questionnaires was that some participants took 45 minutes or longer to fill out the survey which when pre-tested with students had only taken 20 minutes to fill out. In other words, it took some tourists the whole barbecue to complete the question-naire. This was mostly due to the length of the rafting trip on the water (approximately three hours), which had exhausted participants. Participants simply were not able to fill out a questionnaire with multiple pages after the trip. We then tried to use the bus tour back to the city as a fall-back option. This was not very successful as people were so tired that they fell asleep on the way back to town.

It also seemed that some participants had the feeling that they had paid for a service experience going on a white water rafting trip but not to fill out questionnaires. Rafting trips are usually not a cheap service to consume, so participants were focused on the rafting experience and the barbecue as an offering rather than spending their time during the barbecue on going through a survey. Hence, their motivation to be involved in our survey was relatively low.

The service provider itself was also not experienced with having researchers on site, even though we were given permission to survey the customers. As such, and despite the fact that we offered to share the findings with the provider, the motivation to assist in data collection was comparably low. In addition, we experienced a dropping number of white water rafting guides willing to fill out the questionnaires several times. As the number of rafting guides was limited, we could not circumvent this problem other than trying to motivate but not force them to repeatedly fill out the respective parts of the survey.

One of the most critical issues in terms of the length of the timeframe for data collection was the weather. Our approach of surveying customer groups at a white water rafting provider was heavily dependent on the weather. While rafting trips can take place every day of the week, strings of bad weather either lowered the number of participants or made the river unsafe to raft, which led to cancellations of entire trips. This is a potential issue in any outdoors adventure-type activity.

Our suspicion the survey was too long and daunting was also confirmed due to the interlinked sections. Some participants were therefore unwilling to fill it out completely or correctly.

The last issue we encountered was related to the type of people surveyed. Tourism operators in New Zealand provide their services to a large number of international visitors. Respondents from abroad filling out our questionnaire were at times faced with language problems understanding the questions, or social/cultural issues led to the unwillingness to rate others within the group, give honest feedback or fill out questionnaires from a stranger.

## What we would do differently: lessons learned from data collection in the field

There are several measures we would take to combat the issues which arose during data collection. One is to focus on building good relationships with key individuals to allow for easier surveying. During our fieldwork we had multiple contacts with people from the service provider. This involved the bus driver who already helped us and explained to tourists that they were going to be interviewed while boarding the bus. He also allowed for data collection to occur on the trip back. The other individuals are the rafting guides who were important in this process. They were in charge of individual groups and acted as formal leaders of the groups. Due to their role they should be asked to persuade their group to fill out the questionnaires.

Although we put a lot of time into the development of the questionnaire and were conscious of its length, in light of tourists going through the tiresome physical activity of white water rafting before filling out questionnaires, we would now try to reduce the number of questions. It seems that a lengthy and partially difficult questionnaire does not fit the circumstances of a long-lasting and exhausting white water rafting trip. Therefore we would propose asking the rafting guides for possible breaks and use these for asking participants to fill out the questionnaire, because at these times in the trip the groups would not be as exhausted as they would be at the end.

Finally, although it might be difficult, we would try to find a better incentive (gift) for the groups to fill out the questionnaires. While the rafting operators were trying to give their best in performing the service, it was difficult to find an appropriate gift for the participants as the complete tour package already included transport, rafting and barbecue. For that reason, additional benefits were difficult to fit in. Our original idea to offer discount vouchers for the next trip did not seem to be suitable due to the fact that a rafting trip is usually a one-off experience which tourists hardly ever repeat.

## What we can summarise: conclusions from doing fieldwork at a white water rafting provider

Data collection at the white water rafting provider has been an interesting experience, in particular with regard to the unexpected challenges in surveying the participants. This has shown us again that, despite the recommendations in scholarly papers, research guidelines and books, what really counts is the experience in the field with the process of data collection. This experience seems to be the best 'takeaway' for us in hindsight. Despite the fact that fieldwork activity is different and each service provider or tourism operator varies not only by the services offered but also in regard to the logistical factors such as the site of the service experience and other factors, learning from each fieldwork process is a valuable asset for any future research projects.

## References

Arnould, E.J. and Price, L.L. (1993) 'River Magic: Extraordinary Experience and the Extended Service Encounter', *Journal of Consumer Research* 20(1): 24–45.

Berry, L.L. and Lampo, S.K. (2000) 'Teaching an Old Service New Tricks', *Journal of Service Research* 2(3): 265–75.

Büttgen, M. (2008) 'Formen und Ansätze der Kundenintegration' ['Types and Approaches of Customer Integration'], in U. Fueglistaller (ed.), *Dienstleistungskompetenz. Strategische Differenzierung durch konsequente Kundenorientierung* [*Service Competence. Strategic Differentiation through Consistent Service Orientation*]. Zurich: Versus.

Dholakia, U.M., Bagozzi, R.P. and Klein Pearo, L. (2004) 'A Social Influence Model of Consumer Participation in Network- and Small-group-based Virtual Communities', *International Journal of Research in Marketing* 21(3): 241–63.

Finn, M., Elliott-White, M. and Walton, M. (2000) *Tourism and Leisure Research Methods: Data Collection, Analysis, and Interpretation*. Harlow: Longman.

Finsterwalder, Jörg and Tuzovic, Sven (2010) 'Quality in Group Service Encounters: A Theoretical Exploration of the Concept of a Simultaneous Multi-customer Co-creation Process', *Managing Service Quality – An International Journal* 20(2) 109–22.

Forsyth, D. (1999) *Group Dynamics*, 3rd edn. Belmont: Wadsworth Publishing Co.

Gouthier, M. and Schmid, S. (2003) 'Customers and Customer Relationships in Service Firms: The Perspective of the Resource-based View', *Marketing Theory* 3(1): 119–43.

Grönroos, C. (2008) 'Service Logic Revisited: Who Creates Value? And Who Co-creates?', *European Business Review* 20(4): 298–314.

Hair, J.F., Bush, R.P. and Ortinau, D.J. (2006) *Marketing Research: Within a Changing Information Environment*, 3rd edn. Boston, MA: McGraw-Hill.

Hair, J.F., Lukas, B.A., Miller, K.E., Bush, R.P. and Ortinau, D.J. (2008) *Marketing Research*, 2nd edn. Boston, MA: McGraw-Hill.

Harris, A., Leithwood, K., Day, C., Sammons, P. and Hopkins, D. (2007) 'Distributed Leadership and Organizational Change: Reviewing the Evidence', *Journal of Educational Change* 8(4): 337–47.

Jacques, P.H., Garger, J. and Thomas, M. (2008) 'Assessing Leader Behaviors in Project Managers', *Management Research News* 31(1): 4–11.

Kelley, S.W., Donnelly, J.H. and Skinner, S.J. (1990) 'Customer Participation in Service Production and Delivery', *Journal of Retailing* 66(3): 315–35.

Kickul, J. and Neuman, G. (2000) 'Emergent Leadership Behaviors: The Function of Personality and Cognitive Ability in Determining Teamwork Performance and KSAs', *Journal of Business and Psychology* 15(1): 27–51.

Lengnick-Hall, C.A. (1996) 'Customer Contributions to Quality: A Different View of the Customer-orientated Firm', *Academy of Management Review* 21(3): 791–824.

Lewin, K. (1948) *Resolving Social Conflicts: Selected Papers on Group Dynamics*. New York: Harper.

Neubert, M.J. and Taggar, S. (2004) 'Pathways to Informal Leadership: The Moderating Role of Gender on the Relationship of Individual Differences and Team Member Network Centrality to Informal Leadership Emergence', *Leadership Quarterly* 15(2): 175–94.

Normann, R. (1991) *Service Management – Strategy and Leadership in Service Business*, 2nd edn. Chichester: John Wiley & Sons.

Ohl, T. and Cates, W. (2006) 'The Nature of Groups: Implications for Learning Design', *Journal of Interactive Learning Research* 17(1): 71–89.

Parasuraman, A., Zeithaml, V.A. and Berry, L.L. (1985) 'A Conceptual Model of Service Quality and its Implications for Future Research', *Journal of Marketing* 49(4): 41–50.

Payne, A.F., Storbacka, K. and Frow, P. (2008) 'Managing the Co-creation of Value', *Journal of the Academy of Marketing Science* 36(1): 83–96.

Pescosolido, A.T. (2001) 'Informal Leaders and the Development of Group Efficacy', *Small Group Research* 32(1): 74–93.

Pescosolido, A.T. (2002) 'Emergent Leaders as Managers of Group Emotion', *Leadership Quarterly* 13(5): 583–99.

Prahalad, C.K. (2004) 'The co-creation of value – Invited Commentaries on "Evolving to a New Dominant Logic for Marketing",' *Journal of Marketing* 68(1): 18–27.

Prahalad, C.K. and Ramaswamy, V. (2004) 'Co-creation Experiences: The Next Practice in Value Creation', *Journal of Interactive Marketing* 18(3): 5–14.

Veal, A.J. (1992) *Research Methods for Leisure and Tourism: A Practical Guide*. Harlow: Longman.

Walle, A.H. (1997) 'Quantitative versus Qualitative Tourism Research', *Annals of Tourism Research* 24(3): 524–36.

Wheelan, S.A. and Johnston, F. (1996) 'The Role of Informal Member Leaders in a System Containing Formal Leaders', *Small Group Research* 27(1): 33–55.

Wickham, K.R. and Walther, J.B. (2007) 'Perceived Behaviors of Emergent and Assigned Leaders in Virtual Groups', *International Journal of e-Collaboration* 3(1): 1–17.

# 19 Facing rejection

## Volunteer tourists whom I could not interview

*Harng Luh Sin*

## Introduction

My time with W's team has been immensely enlightening [W is the pseudonym I have given for my husband, who was my boyfriend at the time of research]. Perhaps because the dynamics of the team was rather different than the group of volunteer tourists I had based my research on in South Africa, or perhaps 'cause of the outsider perspective I had, many things I might have otherwise taken for granted appeared to be very significant to me. Despite not being able to interview anyone in the team, I realized that in the short time I spent with them, I had made many very interesting observations and notes in my field journal. But then despite this, I don't think I can include these observations in my research can I? The leaders of the team have very explicitly said they would prefer it if I didn't interview any of their team members. Does this also mean that I am not allowed to document participant observation? . . . So is this form of covert observation ethical? Can I include these sorts of covert observation in my research? There seems to be so many interesting strands of thought I could develop simply from reading my field journals of the past few days. But when they have already said no upfront to interviewing, I suppose it's also a general no to being included in research at all isn't it? I suppose I should just leave these parts out then. I'd feel guilty to include them in, yet I almost feel guilty too – like I'm manipulating my data and intentionally including bits and excluding bits. Everything I've read about the power of the researcher in controlling what is represented or not – what a difficult position to be in.

(author's field journal entry, June 2005)

In recognition that 'research is a *process* [and] not just a product' (England 1994: 82; emphasis in original), this chapter aims to elucidate some of the methodological concerns the author encountered in the course of her research on volunteer tourism. As alluded to in the quotation from the author's field journal quoted above, of key concern here in this chapter is the author's desire to re-present the process of research – where the researcher actively constructs what is to be included or not included in research, and how we as researchers might be able to include 'rejections' in our writing. As with any other research using in-depth interviews as a key methodology, the author encountered a number of potential respondents who had declined to be interviewed. And responding in similar ways that most other researchers do, I had put aside such 'rejections' and nowhere in my dissertation did I once mention such encounters of rejection. It was as if I had voluntarily suffered partial amnesia and that such encounters with rejection were wiped off my memories.

Indeed, a cursory glance at existing research papers in the field of social sciences in general and tourism in particular would reveal that few researchers discuss the element of rejection in their writings. This neglect in discussing rejections has prevailed despite the recognition that 'knowledge does not arise in a vacuum' (Proctor 1999: 9), and the call for increased reflexivity and introspection on the part of the researcher to question one's positionalities and subjectivities in research (see Madge 1993; Rose 1997; Cloke *et al.* 2004). Feminist and postcolonial critiques over the past two decades have criticized the 'positivist understandings of objective, impartial, value free knowledge', where the researcher presents him- or herself as an 'omnipotent expert extracting information from the passive subject' (Valentine 2002: 116). In response, recognition is now increasingly given to researchers' unique positionalities, and that 'different researchers will approach the same research situation differently, and thereby construct different data from it' (Cloke *et al.* 2004: 368). In line with this, it is now advocated that researchers should not make an unrealistic attempt to qualify their research as entirely objective but to 'recognize and take account of . . . [the researcher's] position, as well as that of . . . [his or her] research participants, and *write this into* . . . [the] *research practice*' (McDowell 1992: 409; emphasis in original). However, the call for reflexivity, I argue here, goes beyond the recognition of one's multiple positionalities in research and in relation to research respondents. Instead, it is also important to be reflexive also of research as a process of decision-making – who we decide to approach as research respondents, who we do manage to interview and, especially lacking in current-day research writing, who we do not manage to interview.

Indeed, what we as researchers are often aware of, yet seldom write about, is the fact that in all research dependent predominantly on in-depth interviews for field data, it is never easy to persuade respondents to allow us interviews, and rejections on interview requests often abound. This reflects the self-selection on the part of whoever or whatever makes up the end-product of research, where who we as researchers are able to re-present is often a result of who allows us interviews in the first place. Elaborating on the rejections faced in research, then, could possibly highlight hidden or tacit sides of the story which were not re-presented simply because respondents were unwilling to be interviewed. This can be especially interesting in research, as it is very possible that some respondents may have chosen to reject interview requests because they do not trust the researcher; do not wish to be represented; or simply have no time to 'entertain' the researchers' requests.

There are very obvious challenges in including rejections in research writing, however – most immediately, is it even ethical to talk about those who have explicitly stated their desire not to participate in your research? What this chapter aims to provide, then, is an account of some of the deliberations I had as a researcher on how one can or should include rejections in research writing, using an anecdote with a group of volunteer tourists that I was not allowed to interview, but had the opportunity to spend some days with during my fieldwork on volunteer tourism in Cambodia.

## Researching on volunteer tourism in Cambodia

I had conducted research in Cambodia with recipients of volunteer tourism over a period of five weeks in May to June 2005. My research respondents were coordinators of non-government organizations (NGOs) and local aid-recipients that have previously received volunteer tourists from Singapore. Discussions and informal interviews were used as the primary means of research, and these were taped and later transcribed with the consent of all respondents. My research in Cambodia had focused solely on the perspectives of hosts or recipients of volunteer tourism, while a separate trip to South Africa as a full member of a team of volunteer tourists formed the basis of analysis for a section on perspectives of volunteer tourists in my Master's dissertation. I had found that this separation of fieldwork into two distinct parts had the advantage of allowing me to position myself appropriately to my respondents (the volunteer tourists in South Africa, and the recipients of volunteer tourism in Cambodia), and was helpful in enabling me to discuss sensitive opinions that at times could be critical of the other party involved (for example, recipients interviewed in Cambodia could feel free to criticize behaviours of volunteer tourists without feeling that these comments will be offensive to the researcher).

However, advantages and justifications aside, the truth is – I did intend to, and had made attempts to, arrange for interviews with volunteer tourists in Cambodia as well. These attempts, however, as earlier revealed, were fraught with rejections, and I had to instead abandon idea(l)s of interviewing both volunteer tourists and recipients within the Cambodian context. Prior to embarking on fieldwork in Cambodia, I had contacted both the Youth Expedition Project (YEP) and a team planning to volunteer in Cambodia (under the YEP programme) to ask if it was possible for me to interview some of their volunteer tourists. YEP is a programme under Singapore's National Youth Council (a statutory board) that has been broadly responsible for encouraging international volunteerism in Singapore since its inception in 2000. YEP also provides funding support to approved international volunteering projects, subject to these proposed projects meeting its funding criteria (Youth Expedition Project 2007).

YEP informed me that it was difficult for them to direct me to specific teams, and I accepted this as well, as I thought that the top-down approach would affect the dynamics of how potential respondents could possibly see my connections with their volunteer tourism project's funding body. I decided instead to use a bottom-up approach and contacted teams where I had personal connections. Incidentally, W, my then boyfriend (and now husband) got to know of a student-led team (that was to be funded by YEP) and had decided to join this team for volunteering in Cambodia. Based on this very personal connection, I spoke informally to his team's leaders, and asked for them to consider allowing me the opportunity to interview their members for my research. I met, however, with rejection – the team's leaders told me (via W) that they were 'not comfortable with me interviewing any of their team members during the time they were in Cambodia' (personal communication, January 2005). After they told me this, and after facing several other rejections of possibly interviewing volunteer tourists during their stint in Cambodia, I decided to focus instead on interviewing only NGOs and local aid-recipients during my fieldwork period in Cambodia. However, W's team, who did not grant me interviews, were very helpful in other ways – I had to travel to a rural part of Cambodia where they were volunteering to interview some NGOs, and when they realized this (through W, I presume), they told me that I could tag along on their team's vehicle as it was difficult to arrange for transport to that part of Cambodia, especially since I did not speak Khmer well. As such, I arranged my schedule to coincide with theirs and ended up joining their team for three days. I therefore joined the team for their edu-recreational activities in Phnom Penh (including a visit to Toul Sleng Genocide Museum), their trip back to the village where they were volunteering and stayed overnight at their accommodation in the village, before heading off to visit the NGOs I had arranged to meet. I also briefly met the team again at the end of their trip as they went to Siem Reap to see the Angkor monuments, while I was there to interview other NGOs. Although my encounters with W's team were constantly recorded in my field journals that I had written at the end of every day, these were deliberately omitted in my Master's dissertation, as I had supposed that their team leaders' refusal from the start meant I could not or should not document any part of my experiences with the team at all. It is only now, several years after these encounters, that I finally discuss these encounters in any formal writing. And, while original deliberations which stopped me from including these encounters in my research writings do and still exist, I am now writing about them in hope of bringing to light some of these dilemmas and uneasy decisions made in research, without (I hope) infringing on any ethical boundaries in research. However, the more I consider them, the more I realize that ethical boundaries in research are indeed fraught with uncertainties and ambiguities, some of which I will discuss in further detail here.

## On facing rejections: how do we include them in research?

It is now recognized that the 'multiple, interweaving and intersecting ways in which our various positionalities and identities are revealed, negotiated and managed in research encounters are crucial to the conduct of ethical research' (Hopkins 2007: 388). Many works have since extolled the virtue of reflexivity (see Rose 1997) and the importance of presenting the researcher's positionalities (Jackson 1993) and the 'politics of position' (Smith 1993: 305) in our research. Such considerations of the researchers' multiple positionalities may include 'aspects of identity – race, class, gender, age, sexuality, disability' (Hopkins 2007: 390), and much of it has centred around constructions of gender and sexuality (see, for example, Valentine 2002; Vanderback 2005), and race and ethnicity in research (see, for example, Mohammad 2001; Archer 2003). Our positionalities and 'selves' as *researchers*, however, have received surprisingly little attention in academic literature. Indeed, before our potential respondents can associate or dissociate with us as men/women, white/ Asian/African (and so forth), or young/old (categories which are in themselves very fluid and very worthy of discussion), in the onset of approaching potential respondents, the first and foremost identity and positionality we bring across is likely to be that of an academic researcher. And it is also this position of the academic researcher that often determines whether an interview is granted or not. Thus, my call for including rejections in research is very much also a call for understanding our own positionalities as researchers and how this is projected onto potential respondents that we approach.

Most importantly, as researchers are increasingly called to become an 'interpreter speaking for and with the host community and its environment' (Bauman 1987, cited in Humberstone 2004: 128), it is crucial to realize that it is very possible that significant factions of what constitutes the 'host community' may not even be interested in speaking through the researcher. Taking their disinterest in being represented in research into account could possibly reveal tangents previously unconsidered. For example, I have always personally suspected that those who rejected my requests for interviews had done so either because of their general distrust towards researchers (some potential respondents did cite bad experiences with previous researchers as a reason for being uninterested) or a belief that academic research was of little importance and made little difference to the 'real world' (none of those potential respondents I approached ever said this to me, but personal friends working in the private sectors do often question my research in such a critical manner!). Dwelling on the reasons for rejections – who rejects us and why they do so – could therefore possibly bring out an array of considerations previously little discussed. Indeed, perhaps we could stop seeing rejections as our failures as researchers that need to be swept under the carpet in our writings, but to acknowledge them and carefully explore what such rejections might say about our research findings.

For example, in my research on volunteer tourism in Cambodia, I always suspected that part of the reason why I was denied interviews with W's team was due to the fact that I could have appeared to be a 'Miss-know-it-all' to the team leaders, as I have previously led two volunteer tourism trips and was then conducting research that was obviously somewhat critical of volunteer tourism. I suppose the leaders of the team could have been wary of what I might say about their team and how this could undermine their volunteer work and possibly team morale, and that these were disturbances they could do without in an already intense experience of leading a team to volunteer overseas (author's field journal entries, January 2005). However, these were purely suspicions on my part and I was unable to verify their validity at all with the leaders without being overbearing as a researcher! And indeed herein lies the greatest challenge of including rejections in research – how can we possibly infer from rejections, since potential respondents hardly give reasons for why they refuse an interview request in the first place? Any speculations on who rejects us and why they do so remain only as such: speculations. The challenge I pose to all researchers, then, is to develop a means of talking about rejections, a means of being honest about rejections as a reflexive process, without speculating excessively on encounters which we do not have many concrete data on.

Indeed, at least I was 'fortunate' enough to spend quite some time with the team that rejected me, and had the opportunity to base my speculations on actual participant observations. And even so, was it ethical for me as a researcher to document participant observations with a team who have explicitly stated their unwillingness to be interviewed? An underlying component of almost all established research ethics review or protocol involves the notion of 'informed consent' (see Royal Geographical Society with IBG 2006). Specifically, the *Statement of Professional Ethics* used by the Association of American Geographers clearly states that

> Informants and local researchers should be asked whether they prefer anonymity or recognition, and the project should be implemented and its results should be presented in keeping with these individuals' preference. Prior to participation, informants and local collaborators have a basic right to know the purpose of the project and the end uses of the information.
>
> (2009)

Indeed, the journal entry in the opening points towards such dilemmas I personally had – research ethics protocol tells me that, to relay power to the respondent, I had to ensure that all those referred to in my research were aware of this, and that they had a 'basic right to know the purpose of the project and the end uses of the information'. This notion of informed consent, however, seems to be inherently in conflict with the methodologies of participant observation, especially when this is done covertly. Yet, elsewhere, in instructions on how to do participant observation, it was also mentioned that 'there are sensitive settings where you will want to keep your status as a researcher more low key. In such an event you may end up scribbling notes in the toilet or in the bus afterwards, or some other hidden place, and there are plenty of amusing stories from experienced geographers about doing so' (Laurier 2003: 138).

Amusement aside, are such covert observations always ethical? For example, in Routledge's (2002) article detailing his experiences of assuming the 'undercover identity' of Walter Kurtz, a false identity he had conjured up with his partner organizations to collect evidence of illegal activities by hotel developers in Goa, India (2002), Routledge continuously called for 'reciprocity between researcher and researched' (Bailey 2001, cited in Routledge 2002: 491). What he did not acknowledge responsibility for or seek to obtain informed consent from were the hotel developers he spoke to, who can in some ways be also considered as his 'researched'. The problem with writing about rejections, then, is that once interviews are denied, the often sole means of assessing such potential respondents falls into areas of observation (which sometimes need to be covert), and these could very likely breach established notions of ethical research practices. Again, there is no perfect solution in the negotiation of such ethical pitfalls in writing about rejections – however, if one were to seriously consider including rejections in research writings, it is important to deliberate over these considerations and reflect them in writing.

## The embodied and unreflexive selves in volunteer tourists

Coincidentally or not, my encounters with this team of volunteer tourists who rejected my requests for interviews also brought about interesting tangents that I did not previously discuss in any of my research writings. Indeed, it was the observations I made during the team's edu-recreational activities that revealed such 'embodied unreflexive selves' (Edensor 2000) of the volunteer tourists, selves which reflect embodied values of who they are and where they come from, unfiltered by what they desire to perform as their 'selves'. Despite having done prior fieldwork with a group of volunteer tourists to South Africa, and having joined the said group's activities wholeheartedly as a member, what I gathered from fieldwork in South Africa said little in terms of volunteer tourists' behaviours outside of the volunteering stint. Possibly because I had by then become a highly integrated member of the team to South Africa, or possibly because the volunteer tourists to South Africa were constantly aware of my status as a researcher amongst them, what was eventually observed was inevitably filtered through their desires to re-present a 'self' that they deemed to be a 'responsible' volunteer tourist (see Sin 2006). In contrast, the team I encountered in Cambodia was mostly unaware of my status as a researcher – amongst its 30 or more members, I believe most ranged between being only vaguely aware of my existence to those who knew who I was but thought I was simply joining the team on the few occasions because W, my then boyfriend, was part of the team. As such, my researcher identity was somewhat covert, and I explained my purpose and research to only the few members who asked. Even so, those who asked mostly only did so because they were closer friends of W. I was also never formally introduced to the team – I had just joined them as they entered Toul Sleng Genocide Museum and only those members who were more observant or were good friends of W noticed my joining the team then. Indeed, I suppose my position in relation to the team was more that of a 'visiting girlfriend' of one of the members, and quite a few members of the team had come up to me to ask me about why I was even in Cambodia on my own after seeing me hang around with the team for the day. When asked, I of course honestly answered that I was in Cambodia for fieldwork for my Master's dissertation, and to those who remained interested I explained what my research on volunteer tourism was all about.

While I questioned the ethical issues in covert participant observation earlier, I must admit that 'lying low' as a researcher does have its advantages. Being entirely unconscious of me as a researcher, most team members behaved in a seemingly natural state, and while I was aware that I was not going to include these as fieldwork for my Master's dissertation, I did record instances of such 'embodied unreflexive selves', that seemed to contradict notions of responsible behaviour or heightened awareness towards local contexts amongst volunteer tourists. For example, during the visit to Toul Sleng Genocide Museum, I made the following observation:

> [the movie on genocide during the Khmer Rouge regime in Cambodia] in my most honest opinion a little too long and slow and what made it worse was that it's shown in an entirely dark and enclosed room that was supposedly air-conditioned but is actually very hot and humid. Hot and sticky conditions do not make much for encouraging empathy amongst the team members I think. I realized that by midway through the almost one-hour-long film, half the team had fallen asleep and the other half were kept awake probably by the mosquitoes in the dark room.
>
> (author's field journal entry, June 2005)

Indeed, here conditions in the room where the movie was screened, coupled with the volunteer tourists' exhaustion from having travelled all morning to arrive at Phnom Penh, meant that most of the team members were in no condition to appreciate the film or to engage intellectually with what was being presented in the film. I had not watched the film with other tourists and am therefore unable to comment on whether this behaviour was typical of tourists in general. However, what did occur to me was perhaps that volunteer tourists can choose to shut off entirely from local contexts, despite their stated desire to engage in a form of tourism that is meant to bring about good to locals. This was followed with another observation made during a discussion session held by one of the team's leaders the day after the visit to the genocide museum:

Peter (pseudonym) began by asking what everyone thought of the visit to Phnom Penh in general and to Toul Sleng genocide museum in particular. At first nobody responded and everyone seemed really quiet ... Then Pamela (pseudonym) started with saying that she thought Toul Sleng was a very sad place, that a lot of people died and it seemed very cruel that people could torture and kill people like that. Most of the other members responded in agreement with her, saying it's very depressing and sad. Another team member that I can't remember his name however said that he didn't think it was particularly bad. He said that people are cruel by nature and that torture and war is a very evident part of all cultures and human history. He also said that he saw no difference between the tortures in Toul Sleng, versus what the Japanese had done to our forefathers during the Japanese Occupation of Singapore and Malaya in World War II.

(author's field journal entry, June 2005)

What surprised me at this point was that nobody pointed out to this particular member that genocide in Cambodia was different in the sense that it involved the systematic prosecution of anyone related to the colonial rulers, and that this meant that children could be told to monitor and at times report on their parents, and that victims could very possibly be tortured and executed by schoolmates or neighbours. Unable to put aside my unreflexive selves as an academic tutor and as a previous leader of other volunteer tourism teams, I voiced out these opinions and these were met with a rather uncomfortable silence from the team. These instances recorded in my field journals made me wonder if volunteer tourists were at all more sensitive to local contexts, and if they were unaware of violent histories that were so recent in Cambodia, could they also possibly be insensitive in their encounters with the locals in their volunteer sites? Indeed, perhaps it was in such covert participant observation where such embodied selves could best be detected, and perhaps it was also the fear of such observations the researcher could make that led to the team leaders rejecting my requests for interviews in the first place.

## Conclusion

Despite these thoughts, however, I had time and again chosen not to include in my formal research any recordings of rejections encountered in fieldwork. In this chapter, I reveal bits and pieces of these 'unofficial' field journal entries only to showcase how my research could have followed very different trajectories had I seriously considered including those who rejected my requests for interviews. Indeed, talking about rejections could possibly tell a fuller and more complete picture in research, even if one is unable to say much about those who rejected interviews beyond stating the difficulties encountered in recruiting potential respondents. The call for including rejections in research writing is thus also a call to consider how one can extrapolate data from rejections without risking unethical research behaviours. Covert participant observation as done in this case could be a possibility, but this is not without ethical concerns, since covert observation also necessarily means that informed consent cannot be obtained from respondents. It is hoped, though, that this chapter has brought to light some of the deliberations I had as a researcher, and strikes a chord with other researchers who I am sure have encountered rejections at some point in their own research, and will in turn encourage further academic thought on how we as researchers should and can write about rejections we face.

## References

Archer, L. (2003) *Race, Masculinity and Schooling: Muslim Boys and Education.* Maidenhead: Open University Press.

Association of American Geographers (1998) *Statement on Professional Ethics.* Endorsed by the Council of the Association of American Geographers, 18 October 1998. Updated 5 April 2005. Revised 1 November 2009. Online. Available HTTP: <http://www.aag.org//info/ethics.htm> (accessed 10 December 2008).

Bailey, C. (2001) 'Geographers Doing Household Research: Intrusive Research and Moral Accountability', *Area* 33: 107–10.

Bauman, Z. (1987) *Legislators and Interpreters: On Modernity, Post-modernity and Intellectuals.* Cambridge: Polity Press.

Cloke, P., Cook, I., Crang, P., Goodwin, M., Painter, J. and Philo, C. (2004) *Practising Human Geography.* London: Sage.

Edensor, T. (2000) 'Staging Tourism: Tourists as Performers', *Annals of Tourism Research* 27: 322–44.

England, K. (1994) 'Getting personal: Reflexivity, Positionality and Feminist Research', *Professional Geographer* 46: 80–9.

Hopkins, P.E. (2007) 'Positionalities and Knowledge: Negotiating Ethics in Practice', *ACME: An International e-Journal for Critical Geographies* 6: 386–94.

Humberstone, B. (2004) 'Standpoint Research: Multiple Versions of Reality in Tourism Theorizing and Research', in J. Phillimore and L. Goodson (eds), *Qualitative Research in Tourism: Ontologies, Epistemologies and Methodologies.* London: Routledge.

Jackson, P. (1993) 'Changing Ourselves: A Geography of Position', in R.J. Johnston (ed.), *The Challenge for Geography, A Changing World: A Changing Discipline.* Oxford: Blackwell Publishers.

Laurier, E. (2003) 'Participant Observation', in N. Clifford and G. Valentine (eds), *Key Methods in Geography.* London: Sage.

Madge, C. (1993) 'Boundary disputes: Comments on Sidaway (1992)', *Area* 25: 294–9.

McDowell, L. (1992) 'Doing Gender: Feminism, Feminists and Research Methods in Human Geography', *Transactions, Institute of British Geographers* 17: 399–441.

Mohammad, R. (2001) '"Insiders" and/or "Outsiders": Positionality, Theory and Praxis', in M. Limb and C. Dwyer (eds), *Qualitative Methodologies for Geographers: Issues and Debates.* London: Arnold.

Proctor, J. (1999) 'Introduction: Overlapping terrains', in J. Proctor and D. Smith (eds), *Geography and Ethics: Journeys in a Moral Terrain.* London: Routledge.

Rose, G. (1997) 'Situating Knowledges: Positionality, Reflexivities and Other Tactics', *Progress in Human Geography* 21: 305–20.

Routledge, P. (2002) 'Travelling East as Walter Kurtz: Identity, Performance and Collaboration on Goa, India', *Environment and Planning D: Society and Space* 20: 477–98.

Royal Geographical Society with IBG (2006) *Research Ethics and a Code of Practice.* Online. Available HTTP: <http://www.rgs.org/NR/rdonlyres/CBD85FFC-9B56-4C2F-A615-7B41DD02C6B8/0/NewResearchEthicsandaCodeofPractice.pdf> (accessed 10 December 2008).

Sin, H.L. (2006) ' "Involve Me and I Will Learn": A Study of Volunteer Tourism Originating from Singapore'. Unpublished Master's thesis, Department of Geography. Singapore: National University of Singapore.

Smith, S.J. (1993) 'Bounding the Borders: Claiming Space and Making Place in Rural Scotland', *Transactions of the Institute of British Geographers* 18: 291–308.

Valentine, G. (2002) 'People like us: Negotiating Sameness and Difference in the Research Process', in P. Moss (ed.), *Feminist Geography in Practice: Research and Methods.* Oxford: Blackwell Publishers.

Vanderback, R. (2005) 'Masculinities and Fieldwork: Widening the Discussion', *Gender, Place and Culture* 12: 387–402.

Youth Expedition Project (2007) 'YEP project grant'. Online. Available HTTP: <http://www.yep.sg/funding/yep_project_grant.html> (accessed 12 November 2008).

# Part IV

# Future directions and new environments

This final collection of chapters examines a number of issues that are emerging with respect to fieldwork in tourism and the way the subject responds to social, technological and environmental change.

In Chapter 20 Hall discusses the issues surrounding the conduct of ethnography and fieldwork in virtual space. The chapter highlights the way in which technology, and computer-mediated communication (CMC) in particular, is changing understanding of what constitutes fieldwork and the accompanying methodological and ethical issues that emerge as a result. Special attention is given to the concept of netnography (Kozinets 2002; 2010), although, as the chapter points out, this approach is but one dimension of virtual ethnography and fieldwork.

Although social science research has placed substantial focus on the ethical and methodological issues arising from undertaking fieldwork in other cultures in other countries (Gibbs 2001), the concerns raised by research on indigenous communities in developed countries are arguably more recent (Kievit 2003; Tuhiwai-Smith 2005; Gearhead and Shirley 2007). Moreover, such research is often related to access to 'natural areas' and the undertaking of environmentally related research rather than social scientific research. As is becoming increasingly apparent, the conduct of natural scientific fieldwork cannot ignore the socio-cultural and political issues and protocols that surround access to and ownership of knowledge, ways of decision-making and communication, access to land and natural resources, and sampling methods.

In Chapter 21, through a series of reflexive and critical narratives, Lemelin and colleagues discuss how they have implemented and conducted action research with indigenous communities in northern Canada. The chapter addresses the discourses provided by indigenous scholars and local stakeholders in advocating the implementation of new research approaches with communities, and the increasing 'tension' between knowledge holders and knowledge dissemination in indigenous communities and non-local and/ or non-indigenous community researchers. The authors argue that a balance can be achieved between the conceptual and the applied, and conclude that praxis can be achieved in community research with indigenous communities.

Issues of communication and personal relationships and the responsibilities this may have for researchers when conducting fieldwork are also discussed in Chapter 22 by Duval. The chapter provides an appropriate conclusion to the volume as it poses questions as to what happens to the social and personal relationships that were developed while undertaking fieldwork once it and the research project are finished. Duval reflects on his own experiences in the Caribbean and the issues that he faced. The chapter therefore reinforces one of the key concepts that have arisen in the various contributions to the volume, which is the need in fieldwork to understand not just the subjects of one's research but also 'self'. Perhaps more than any other form of research the successful conduct of fieldwork reinforces that it is just as important to hold a mirror up to those who are undertaking research as it is to understand the subject of one's studies.

## Suggested further reading

*Anthropology Matters*, <http://www.anthropologymatters.com>.
This is a graduate-oriented open-access journal that has excellent commentary on fieldwork and its trials, tribulations and successes.

*Forum Qualitative Social Research* (2007), Special Issue on Virtual Ethnography, 8(3). Special issue of a very good open-access journal featuring nine papers on virtual ethnography.

Hall, C.M. and Valentin, A. (2005) 'Content Analysis', in B. Ritchie, P. Burns and C. Palmer (eds), *Tourism Research Methods*. Wallingford: CAB International.
Provides an overview of content analysis and its application in tourism studies with an example of its application with respect to the aftermath of 9/11 and the role of media in influencing policy making.

Johnson, J.T., Cant, G., Howitt, R. and Peters, E. (2007) 'Creating Anti-colonial Geographies: Embracing Indigenous Peoples' Knowledges and Rights', *Geographical Research* 45(2): 117–20.
This is the editorial from a special themed issue of the journal on indigenous peoples' knowledges and rights. The editorial provides an excellent outline of the issues faced by researchers when considering working with indigenous peoples and in their environment, but the issue as a whole is worth examination.

Kozinets, R. (2010) *Netnography: Doing Ethnographic Research Online*. London: Sage.
This book brings together much of Kozinets' previous work on netnography and updates it to create a number of revised frameworks for understanding consumption in virtual communities.

Mead, M. (1969) 'Research with Human Beings: A Model Derived from Anthropological Field Research', *Daedalus* 98: 361–86.
Although rather dated, this influential article provides a good start to charting and questioning the way in which the human subjects of ethnography should be approached and treated by fieldworkers. It can be usefully compared and contrasted with more recent writing on research methods in ethnography and anthropology, such as the influential work of Agar (1980).

O'Hara, K. and Shadbolt, N. (2008) *The Spy in the Coffee Machine: The End of Privacy As We Know It*. Oxford: Oneworld.
Provides an interesting and provocative perspective on concepts of public and private and their implications for ethics, policy and research.

Robinson, L. and Schulz, J. (2009) 'New Avenues for Sociological Inquiry: Evolving Forms of Ethnographic Practice', *Sociology* 43(4): 685–98.
Provides a good overview on the way that ethnographic practice is developing from sociological perspectives.

Spradley, J.P. (1979) *The Ethnographic Interview*. New York: Holt, Rinehart and Winston.
A classic and highly influential work with respect to the conduct of ethnographic interviews and understanding the relationship between the researcher and the researched.

Williams, M. (2007) 'Avatar Watching: Participant Observation in Graphical Online Environments', *Qualitative Research* 7(1): 5–24.
An interesting application of ethnographic method to virtual environments. The ongoing development of avatars and virtual worlds also starts to herald new challenges to online ethnography as the result of transitions from text to visual and oral communication.

## References

Agar, M.H. (1980) *The Professional Stranger: An Informal Introduction to Ethnography*. New York: Academic Press.
Gearheard, S. and Shirley, J. (2007) 'Challenges in Community-research Relationships: Learning from Natural Science in Nunavut', *Arctic* 60(1): 62–74.
Gibbs, M. (2001) 'Toward a Strategy for Undertaking Cross-cultural Collaborative Research', *Society and Natural Resources* 14(8): 673–87.
Kievit, J.A. (2003) 'A Discussion of Scholarly Responsibilities to Indigenous Communities', *American Indian Quarterly* 27: 3–45.
Kozinets, R. (2002) 'The Field behind the Screen: Using Netnography for Marketing Research in Online Communities', *Journal of Marketing Research* 34(1): 61–72.
Kozinets, R. (2010) *Netnography: Doing Ethnographic Research Online*. London: Sage.
Tuhiwai-Smith, L. (2005) 'On Tricky Grounds: Researching the Native in the Age of Uncertainty', in N.K. Denzin and Y.S. Lincoln (eds), *The Handbook of Qualitative Research*. Thousand Oaks: Sage.

# 20 In cyberspace can anybody hear you scream?

## Issues in the conduct of online fieldwork

*C. Michael Hall*

### Introduction: the Internet/virtual communities

It is now widely acknowledged that changes in technology have transformed the organisation and experience of leisure activities including those associated with tourism (e.g. Bryce 2001) and the concept of where fieldwork occurs (see Hall, Chapter 1, this volume). Communications, computer technology and the Internet have emerged as important locations of contemporary leisure activity, creating new spaces for leisure and travel participation as well as new business opportunities for booking, promotions, experience and relationship development (Morgan and Watson 2009). The Internet integrates personal and mass media, creating a new mode of communication, enabling participants to take part in two-way mass communication as part of the development of new social worlds (Sade-Beck 2004).

Holge-Hazelton (2002) argues that grounding of the Internet in computer-mediated communications means that its culture is different from conventional understandings of both oral and written culture. For Lévy (2001: xvi) cyberculture is 'the set of technologies (material and intellectual), practices, attitudes, modes of thought, and values that developed along with the growth of cyberspace'. The Internet, e-mail, multi-user dimensions (MUDs), and newsgroups have led to the formation of thousands of social group developments discussing a range of topics, playing games and entertaining each other (Smith and Kollock 1999), and where consumers are using the Internet to build communities and communicate with fellow consumers, who are seen as a more objective source of information (Kozinets 2002). Virtual communities allow users to satisfy their own needs and to share purpose such as an interest, need, information exchange, or service that provides a reason for the community (Baglieri and Consoli 2009). However, online communication not only structures relations, but it is also the structure within which the relations occur that includes altered experiences of time and space as well as both synchronous (as in MUDs) and asynchronous (as in newsgroups) interactions (Bryce 2001). 'In this respect virtual communities and virtual worlds are some of the concepts used to describe the new forms of social life that exist and the new arenas where they take place' (Croon Fors and

Jakobsson 2002: 2). However, they also represent a new spatial location for fieldwork which challenges traditional concepts of the geographic context of fieldwork and replaces them with more complex and nuanced notions of both 'the field' and 'fieldwork' (Heckman 2000; Miller and Slater 2000; Beaulieu 2004).

Although online communities are often referred to as 'virtual communities', the term 'virtual' implies that they are less 'real' than physical communities (Kozinets 2002). But these communities have a real existence for participants with associated affects on many aspects of their behaviour. Virtual communities were defined by Rheingold (1993: 5) as 'social aggregations that emerge from the net when enough people carry on . . . public discussions long enough, with sufficient human feeling, to form webs of personal relationships in cyberspace'. As Rheingold (1993) notes, people in online communities 'exchange pleasantries and argue, engage in intellectual discourse, conduct commerce, exchange knowledge, share emotional support, make plans, brainstorm, gossip, feud, fall in love, find friends and lose them, play games, flirt, create a little high art and a lot of idle talk' (1993: 3).

Online multiplayer games have also become complex social worlds; which to play requires more than simply accomplishing the games' objectives: they also involve socialisation into a community of gamers (Ducheneaut and Moore 2004). Bishop (2009: 5) argues that

> To fully understand the role of the actor in web-based communities the virtual environment must be treated on par with the physical environment. Virtual environments contain other actors, structures and artefacts, such as mediating artefacts . . . Both virtual and physical environments can provide stimuli that create impetuses in actors, and actors will be driven to participate in both environments as a result of experiencing them.

Although there is a large body of literature on the Internet and computer-mediated communication (CMC) as well as on e-tourism, only some of this research is qualitative, and of this, an even smaller portion is ethnographic. It is also suggested that most virtual fieldwork has been conducted by social scientists with a marketing and consumer focus rather than a non-commercial interest (Kozinets 2010). Most ethnographic fieldwork is still conducted in the 'offline' social world, rather than in virtual worlds or, perhaps more cogently given the changed nature of communication and social communities, in the two worlds combined. This is a major deficiency given that, as Garcia and colleagues (2009) recognise, in order to adequately understand social, economic and political life in contemporary society,

> To continue to effectively explore some of the main and enduring concerns of ethnographic research (such as the nature of specific social worlds and subcultures; the construction of identity; the beliefs, values,

and world views underlying human action and social life; and the experience of everyday life) ethnographers must incorporate the Internet and CMC into their research.

Given the growth in CMC and the blending of online and offline social and economic worlds there is a clear demand on students of tourism to modify their research techniques and practices so as to accommodate these changes and gain a better understanding of the consumption and production of tourism. Indeed, given the role of CMC as part of co-creative and co-productive processes it can be argued that the tourism phenomenon over the different stages of travel cannot be fully comprehended unless both virtual and real-world research is undertaken. Yet, as Garcia and colleagues (2009) observe, there are at least three main ways in which the current blending of offline and online worlds challenge fieldwork and ethnographic methods with respect to the incorporation of CMC in their study design and the procedures for approaching and interacting with research subjects.

1. *Co-presence*. Because online fieldworkers are not physically co-present with their research subjects, they require a different set of interpersonal skills in order to access and interpret the social and economic worlds they are studying. With current technology, online fieldwork necessitates a strong set of skills in the analysis of textual and visual data, and in the interactional organisation of text-based CMC. Although the development of voice interaction is increasing, and is often combined with text and visual data, even new technological advances will not change the lack absence of co-presence and the fieldworker being able to employ the same set of 'cues' with respect to developing and understanding interpersonal relationships that occur in the physical world.

2. *Access*. The process of gaining access to the research setting and subjects is different in online fieldwork because of the lack of physical presence and the resulting anonymity provided by the medium. In many cases, such as in online multiplayer role-playing games, subjects will use an alias for their virtual world character. Researchers 'must therefore learn how to manage their identity and presentation of self in visual and textual media and to do impression management via CMC modalities such as e-mail, chat, and instant messaging' (Garcia *et al.* 2009: 53).

3. *Ethics*. The potential anonymity of the medium and the blurring of public and private communication in the online world raises substantial ethical issues around methodological approaches, access to data and techniques for the protection of privacy and confidentiality. Indeed, the Internet and CMC are changing the very ways in which privacy is being understood, given that the rise of social networking increasingly blurs the line between public and private. This situation has been well acknowledged by O'Hara and Shadbolt (2008: 16–17):

Digital information lasts a long time, effectively forever if it is periodically copied, backed up and stored using up-to-date formats. Copying is simple and accurate, and transfer from one person to another trivial. Searching through digital information is fast; discovering a tiny number of references to a person in a large database, virtually impossible to spot with the human eye, is a simple matter with a computer. Information that is harmless on its own can be placed in significant new contexts. While from the subject's point of view, it is hard to know when privacy has been breached, harder still to determine who is responsible, and there is no central authority from which to obtain redress.

The issue of privacy was also addressed by Facebook founder Mark Zuckerberg, who claimed at the beginning of 2010 that the rise of social networking online means that people no longer have an expectation of privacy and that privacy was no longer a 'social norm . . . People have really gotten comfortable not only sharing more information and different kinds, but more openly and with more people . . . That social norm is just something that has evolved over time' (quoted in Johnson 2010). However, in contrast, Danah Boyd, a social networking researcher for Microsoft, takes a different tangent with respect to privacy issues:

> Kids have always cared about privacy, it's just that their notions of privacy look very different than adult notions . . . Kids don't have the kind of privacy that we assume they do. As adults, by and large, we think of the home as a very private space – it's private because we have control over it. The thing is, for young people it's not a private space – they have no control. They have no control over who comes in and out of their room, or who comes in and out of their house. As a result the online world feels more private because it feels like it has more control.
>
> (quoted in Johnson 2009)

On the Internet a case-to-case (i.e. from message board to message board, from webpage to webpage, from list to list, from dungeon to dungeon) approach has to be utilised when deciding researchers are dealing with private, (semi-)private communication or public communication. Beckmann and Langer (2005) suggest that if access is restricted, by password or other means, then communications should be considered (semi-)private, which would necessitate the researcher apply standard guidelines and procedures for such communication. However, if access is not restricted, i.e. anybody can participate without restrictions, then this can be defined as a public communication. An additional issue here, which has not been adequately addressed in much of the online fieldwork literature, is the extent to which text-based communication on the Internet is subject to copyright and is therefore able to be used by researchers in their publications without permission of the copyright holder. When considering any online media source the golden rule should be to 'check the small print' so as to see whether there is any information provided with respect to copyright and fair use provisions.

Beckmann and Langer (2005) also argue that in CMC covert research may be an appropriate methodology, especially when studying sensitive research topics. With reference to Lee (1993), who distinguishes between absolutist, pragmatic and sceptical positions in relation to ethics in covert research, Beckmann and Langer (2005) suggest the need for pragmatism in undertaking virtual fieldwork. The pragmatic response recognises the potential difficulties associated with covert research and acknowledges the rights of research participants, but accepts covert studies if there is no other means to obtain the necessary data. Regardless of the approach used, those undertaking research in cyberspace 'must learn how to apply standard principles of human subject protection to a research environment which differs in fundamental ways from the face-to-face research contexts for which they were conceived and designed' (Garcia *et al.* 2008: 53). To which could perhaps be added, so should university and other institutional ethics committees.

This chapter is designed to discuss some of the ethical and methodological issues that arise out of undertaking fieldwork in cyberspace and is divided into two main sections. The first examines the conduct of qualitative research, while the second discusses netography. The chapter concludes by noting the business and social aspects of research in virtual space and some of the profound ethical questions it raises.

## Qualitative research in cyberspace

There is a substantial range of qualitative data available in cyberspace that is increasingly being accessed by tourism researchers. Much research has focused on the e-commerce dimensions although there is also growing non-commercial research interest in topics such as consumer behaviour, travel decision making, destination perception and service satisfaction (Morgan and Watson 2009).

Dholakia and Zhang (2004) identify a number of characteristics of Internet-derived qualitative data which will, in turn, also influence the selection of methodologies that will be used to access and process such data. These include:

1   *Text-based.* CMC is primarily text based, relatively informal, but is also open to people being able to be more selective in what they communicate, i.e. they are able to edit before they press 'send'. This characteristic obviously also provides significant opportunities for data recording and textual analysis.
2   *Publicly available.* There is a large amount of data that are either publicly or semi-publicly available. There are opportunities for non-obtrusive participant and non-participant observation that may reduce the potential of the distortion of data and the behaviour of subjects as a result of the presence of the researcher.

3   *Anonymous*. Anonymity can provide for access to the real thoughts of informants as well as unobtrusive participant observation. Studies investigating interpersonal communications in virtual communities have found that the relative or absolute anonymity of online communications enables users to express their emotions freely and reach a high level of self-disclosure (Sade-Beck 2004). However, it also raises issues with respect to the identity of informants and as to effects of whether informants are who they say they are.

4   *No material incentive*. There are usually no material incentives offered to informants in online settings.

5   *Unsolicited*. Virtual communities are usually characterised by the provision of unsolicited data.

6   *Temporal flexibility*. Much fieldwork can be grounded in asynchronous communication. This can be advantageous for the conduct of longitudinal studies, although it should be noted that MUDs and virtual worlds are synchronous with respect to communication.

7   *Spatial flexibility*. Online fieldwork is highly flexible in terms of its locations and is bounded more by the constraints of language and regulation of access to sites in particular national jurisdictions.

The characteristics of online data can also be further broken down by whether they are (a) data that are directly copied from the computer-mediated communications of online community members; (b) data that are generated through capture and recording of online community events and interactions; and (c) data that the researcher inscribes (Kozinets 2010: 19). Building on the criteria of Dholakia and Zhang (2004) Table 20.1 provides an assessment of different types of qualitative data that are generated in different online settings or genres (Dillon and Gushrowski 2000; Bishop 2009). The table is organised to indicate the increasingly dynamic and interactive nature of online data sources starting at the relative static server log and website through to the extremely dynamic chatrooms and virtual worlds, the latter being the most amenable to more traditional qualitative fieldwork approaches though communication still remains primarily text-based despite the potential to use real-time voice communication, e.g. Second Life. Interestingly, Dholakia and Zhang (2004) observe that the more online data types are controlled and directed by a central authority, the more quantitative data are usually available. For a discussion on the potential implications of the use of the semantic web (the name given to a conception of a web of linked data, underpinned by a series of technologies and standards developed under the auspices of the World Wide Web Consortium since the late 1990s), see O'Hara and colleagues (2010).

Using the criteria of Dholakia and Zhang (2004), it is possible to compare the general data characteristics of online data collection and analysis methods. Four methods are examined, of which online ethnography (Wittel 2000) or 'netnography' (Kozinets 2002; 2010) and content analysis are the

*Table 20.1* Characteristics of qualitative online data

| Online source | Characteristics | Text-based? | Publicly available? | Anonymous | Material incentive | Unsolicited? | Temporal aspects | Spatial aspects |
|---|---|---|---|---|---|---|---|---|
| Server log | A server log file is automatically generated by website serves which records the IP address for each visitor, length of view, location of access and potentially other user data | Mostly no | Generally no | Partly yes | Mostly no | Mostly yes | Variable | Creator defined |
| Website | A location on the World Wide Web that is usually a collection of linked hypertext webpages, images, videos or other digital assets that are addressed with a common domain name. Includes a beginning file called a homepage. May allow opportunity for feedback | Mostly yes, although use of images is common | Variable. Home page is usually public but further access may be restricted | Partly yes | Mostly no | Partly yes | Mostly long-term archive | Creator defined although tending to jointly defined |
| Blog | An online diary in which one or more individuals record observations for others to read. May allow opportunity for reader comment | Mostly yes, although travel blogs will often feature many images | Yes | Mostly no | No | Mostly no | Long-term archive | Creator defined |
| Bulletin boards | A medium that displays all messages that have been placed on it and their replies | Yes | Yes | Yes | No | Yes | Long-term archive | Jointly defined |
| Newsgroup | Based on interests they function to distribute all messages posted on its topic area to all users that have requested to receive them | Yes | Yes | Yes | No | Yes | Long-term archive | Jointly defined |
| Chatroom | An Internet site in which two or more users are signed on at the same time and where communication can occur in real time | Yes | Yes | Yes | No | Yes | Synchronous. Short-term archive | User defined |

*(Continued overleaf)*

Table 20.1 Continued

| Online source | Characteristics | Text-based? | Publicly available? | Anonymous | Material incentive | Unsolicited? | Temporal aspects | Spatial aspects |
|---|---|---|---|---|---|---|---|---|
| Virtual worlds | A term synonymous with interactive three-dimensional environments where users usually take the form of avatars. A type of online community that usually takes the form of a computer-based simulated persistent online environment. Some entities in this environment act under the direct control of individual users | Mostly text-based communication but the virtual environment also provides opportunities for image analysis. Use of real-time voice communication may also be possible | Yes but require hardware and software that not all computer users may have | Yes | Mostly no | Yes | Synchronous. Short-term archive | User defined |

*Table 20.2* Online data characteristics and research methods

| Online source | Text-based? | Publicly available? | Anonymous | Material incentive | Unsolicited? | Temporal aspects | Spatial aspects |
|---|---|---|---|---|---|---|---|
| Interviews | Yes | Generally no | Depends on research design. Generally no | Depends on research design. Often yes | Mostly no | Variable. Private archive of data, short-term or long-term | Researcher defined but greater tendency to subject defined in ethnographic interviews |
| Focus groups | Yes | Generally no | Depends on research design. Generally no | Depends on research design. Often yes | No | Variable. Private archive of data, short-term or long-term | Researcher defined although tending to jointly defined |
| Online ethnography / netnography | Mostly yes. Although virtual environments offer possibilities of examination of other forms of communication and interaction between subjects and subjects and their environment | Yes | Mostly yes | No | Mostly yes | Variable. Usually public archive of data for some genres such as news groups, chat rooms and bulletin boards | User defined. Potential to create researcher defined and jointly defined online ethnographic fields |
| Content analysis | Text and image | Yes | Mostly no | No | Yes | Variable depending on data source. Usually public archive of data for some genres such as news groups, chat-rooms and bulletin boards | User defined |

least intrusive (see Table 20.2). Content analysis has been widely used in tourism and leisure research to study a range of different online genres, although substantial emphasis has been given to website evaluation and other commercially oriented research with respect to customer use and service satisfaction (Hall and Valentin 2005; Bai *et al.* 2006; Gan *et al.* 2006). In addition, the method is better suited to the examination of static data, especially text, or at least for comparing different states of data over time. Nevertheless, online ethnography has become a subject of substantial interest to social scientists, although there is substantial debate about the approach and the extent to which online ethnography differs from ethnography in the offline world. These issues are dealt with in more detail in the next section.

## Virtual ethnography/netnography

'Ethnography' is a term used for a qualitative method of research, grounded in cultural anthropology that refers to both fieldwork, the study of the distinctive meanings, practices and artefacts of social groups and to the representations based on the study (Kozinets 2002). Although traditional ethnographies have tended to be based on ideas of locality, the development of the concepts of virtual ethnography (e.g. Hine 2000), virtual fieldwork (e.g. Wittel 2000), Internet ethnography (e.g. Sade-Beck 2004), Internet fieldwork (e.g. Robinson and Schulz 2009), online ethnography (e.g. Catterall and Maclaran 2001), online fieldwork (e.g. Heath *et al.* 1999), cyber ethnography (e.g. Ward 1999), cyber fieldwork (e.g. Gerber 2000) and netnography (e.g. Kozinets 1998) questions this concept at a theoretical level (Wittel 2000) and requires a revision of our understandings of ethnographic ideas, practices and spaces (e.g. Sade-Beck 2004). For example, Garcia and colleagues (2009) argue that ethnographers must alter their research techniques in order to research the online world. They suggest that ethnographers must develop skills in the analysis of textual and visual data and interactions based in CMC; learn how to manage their identity and presentation in virtual media; and learn how to apply standard principles of human subject protection online.

The range of terms used to describe online ethnography and fieldwork and their occurrence in academic research is indicated in Table 20.3, which indicates the results of a Google Scholar search conducted in January 2010. The table indicates that 'virtual ethnography' and 'fieldwork' are the most commonly used terms to describe online ethnography. The term 'netnography' has assumed a significant rate of usage by those involved with marketing and corporate ethnography (Kozinets 2010), although its uniqueness is clearly debatable.

The emphasis of marketing applications of ethnography has been on how consumers behave in their everyday lives and on the subjective dimensions of consumption (Catterall and Maclaran 2001). Consumer and marketing-related ethnography, like any ethnographic practice, requires considerable skill and a substantial investment of researcher resources. However, given its

*Table 20.3* Occurrence of online ethnographic and fieldwork terms in Google Scholar, January 2010

| Ethnographic term | Number of occurrences (hits) | Fieldwork term | Number of occurrences (hits) |
| --- | --- | --- | --- |
| Cyber ethnography | 142 | Cyber fieldwork | 12 |
| Internet ethnography | 170 | Internet fieldwork | 15 |
| Online ethnography | 330 | Online fieldwork | 49 |
| Virtual ethnography | 1,670 | Virtual fieldwork | 172 |
| Netnography | 751 | Netnographic fieldwork | 2 |

*Source:* Search undertaken 10 January 2010.

consumer and commercial emphasis, market-oriented ethnography is arguably also an unavoidably intrusive technique that precludes unobtrusive
observation of naturally occurring consumer behaviour (Kozinets 2002).

Netnography is an interpretive method designed to investigate the consumer
behaviour of cultures and communities present on the Internet (Beckmann
and Langer 2005). Netnography adapts the open-ended practice of ethnography to the online environment and, as a consumer and marketing
research technique, netnography uses information that is publicly available on
the Internet to identify and understand the needs and decision influences of
relevant online groups (Kozinets 2002; 2006). According to Kozinets (2010: 2):

> Netnography has been developed in the area of marketing and consumer
> research, an applied, interdisciplinary field that is open to the rapid
> development and adoption of new techniques. Marketing and consumer
> research incorporate insights from a range of fields, such as anthropol-
> ogy, sociology, and cultural studies, selectively applying their basic theor-
> ies and methods in a way analogous to the way pharmaceutical researchers
> might apply basic chemistry.

The concept of netnography has also been incorporated into a number of
tourism studies including topics such as online destination image (e.g. Dwivedi
*et al.* 2009), management of tour operator virtual communities (Baglieri
and Consoli 2009), environmental dialogue in online travel communities
(Rokka and Moisander 2009), hospitality industry migrant labour (Janta and
Ladkin 2009), travel citizenship (Duval 2008) and the mediation of tourist
experiences via online multimedia (e.g. Tussyadiah and Fesenmaier 2009).

De Valeck, van Bruggen and Wierenga (2009: 197) define netnography as
a 'written account resulting from fieldwork studying the culture and communities that emerge from online, computer-mediated, or Internet based
communications'. They go on to state that both the fieldwork and the textual
account are influenced by the qualitative methods utilised in consumer
research, cultural anthropology and cultural studies. Kozinets (1997; 2002),

with whom the term is usually associated, defined Internet-based ethnography or netnography in terms of both the product and the process of cyber ethnography. As a product, a netnography is 'a written account of on-line cyberculture, informed by the methods of cultural anthropology' (Kozinets 1997: 470). As a process or research method, netnography is a 'new qualitative research methodology that adapts ethnographic research techniques to study the cultures and communities that are emerging through computer-mediated communications' (Kozinets 2002: 62). Kozinets (2010: 5) has argued that there is a need for ethnography that is conducted online given that 'online social experiences are significantly different from face-to-face social experiences, and the experience of ethnographically studying them is meaningfully different', and claims that there are at least three differences in ethnographic approach. First, the manner of entering the online culture or community is distinct and diverges from face-to-face entrée in terms of accessibility, approach and the span of potential inclusion. He also suggests that both 'participation' and 'observation' can mean something different in person than online. Second, there are specific challenges and issues in gathering cultural data on the Internet and analysing them. Kozinets suggests that the idea of 'inscription' of 'fieldnotes' as well as the potential amount of data are radically different from offline ethnography. In particular, 'The ability to apply particular analytic tools and techniques changes when the data is already in digital form. The way the data need to be treated can be different' Kozinets (2010: 5). Finally, Kozinets argues that 'there are few, if any, ethical procedures for in-person fieldwork that translate easily to the online medium. The abstract guidelines of informed consent are open to wide degrees of interpretation' (2010: 5).

Of course the counter-argument with respect to Kozinets' (2010) claims as to the uniqueness of netnography are that ethnography and qualitative research are already flexible and adaptable and are inclusive of a range of philosophical and methodological practices depending on the researcher's focus. In response Kozinets argues that 'the pragmatic and applied approach to ethnography followed by corporate anthropologists is significantly different from the approach of academic anthropologists and thus merits its own guidelines and perhaps the coining of its own distinct name' (2010: 6). Perhaps so, and undoubtedly the debate will continue for many years to come, especially given that many scholars who conduct qualitative fieldwork on the Internet are not necessarily doing so from a corporate standpoint. In addition, it should be noted that, as discussed above, the interpretation of the ethical issues of online fieldwork will likely remain diverse regardless of the adoption of names of online research methods (see Table 20.3). This is because ethical perspectives will depend substantially on the cultural, institutional and legal base in which the researcher is grounded. For example, notions of privacy and private data change radically from jurisdiction to jurisdiction. And the legal capacity of a researcher to appropriate data and then publish from them will also depend on the location of the researcher as well as the source. Nevertheless, despite these issues, the value of conducting online ethnographic enquiry is clear. Therefore, the remainder of this section discusses some of the advantages and disadvantages of netnography as well as the development of specific netnographic guidelines.

Kozinets (2006) states that the most important standards of quality for ethnography must also be achieved in netnography: immersive depth, prolonged engagement, researcher identification and persistent conversations. The limitations of netnography include that it is largely text-based, anonymous, poses ethical issues, is often overwhelming and requires considerable researcher acuity (Kozinets 2006; see also Table 20.4). According to Kozinets (2002) netnography does not provide a firm basis for making comparisons or offering conclusions that are generalisable. Online information is only able to give part of the consumption story, as consumers' reality is multifaceted and the more facets investigated, the richer and more useful the portrayal proffered (Kozinets 2002). Arguably, this restriction is one faced by all ethnography with respect to the capacity to convey a truth. Richardson (2000) provided five criteria that could be used to evaluate ethnographies:

1   *Substantive Contribution*: Does the ethnography contribute to our understanding of social life?
2   *Aesthetic Merit*: Does the ethnography succeed aesthetically?
3   *Reflexivity*: How did the author come to write this text? Is there adequate self-awareness and self-exposure for the reader to make judgements about the point of view?
4   *Impact*: Does this affect me? Emotionally? Intellectually? Does it move me?
5   *Expresses a Reality*: Does the ethnography seem 'true'? Is it a credible account of a cultural, social, individual or communal sense of reality?

Moreover, the increasing extent to which many people, at least in the developed world, have both an online and offline presence in social networks and communities necessitates that both offline and online social practices need to be explored in order to understand how they are mutually constituted and influence practices such as consumption. Further value can also be added to netnography-based research when combined with qualitative research techniques such as in-depth interviewing (Simpson 2006).

One of the great advantages of netnography is the relative ease of data collection (Table 20.4). According to Kozinets (2010: 4), 'Doing netnography, you will find, is dramatically easier to begin than doing ethnography', although this also raises issues of managing the large amount of text that is often available as well as providing clear boundaries for any study. Both netnographic and ethnographic research in and on a network requires consideration about what areas of the network to include. By drawing research boundaries the netnographer consciously participates in the construction of spaces, which Wittel (2000) argues not only pre-structures the findings and

*Table 20.4* Advantages and disadvantages of netnography

| Advantages | Disadvantages/limitations |
|---|---|
| *Understanding subcultures*: Given the perspective that there has been social fragmentation into a myriad of cultures, subcultures and communities, understanding the particular language and customs of a group may be the most effective way to communicate with them (e.g. Kozinets 2006) | *Focus on online communities*: Its relatively limited focus on online communities and the lack of informant identifiers present in the online context that lead to difficulties in generalising results to groups outside the online community (e.g. Kozinets 2002) |
| *Ease of data collection*: Online data can be easily and economically downloaded. Because they can be examined from a researcher's desk, they are less costly and timelier (e.g. de Valeck *et al.* 2009) | *Text-based/Information overload*: Currently primarily text-based because of nature of the Internet. However, the sheer amount of data can mean that researchers face information overload. Due to the abundance of information available on the Internet, the time a researcher will be able to spend with one single site may decrease or otherwise only follow certain conversation threads or themes, negatively affecting the search for deep layers of meaning (e.g. Wittel 2000; Catterall and Maclaran 2001; de Valeck *et al.* 2009) |
| *Trustworthiness of online communicators*: From behind-screen identities respondents are more apt to talk freely about issues that could create inhibitions in a face-to-face communication (e.g. Dholakia and Zhang 2004) | *Lack of visual cues*: The lack of visual interactions in netnography results in a loss in layers of information, such as tone of speech and body language, making it harder for the researcher to be sure of the real meaning and intentions of an online informant. However, the lack of these cues may also mean that researcher interpretations are grounded in content rather than stylistic elements (e.g. Dholakia and Zhang 2004) |
| *Unelicited/naturalistic*: As it is unelicited, it is more naturalistic and unobtrusive than other qualitative research methods. Social interactions can be observed in a context that is not created or directed by researcher because the online researcher can remain hidden, using observations and downloads without the dangers of distorting data and behaviour through their presence (e.g. Kozinets 2002, 2006; de Valeck *et al.* 2009) | *Researcher acuity*: It may take an experienced and adept ethnographer to become a good netnographer. In order for the research to have the appropriate impact and reliability to inform decision making, the researcher needs to have a detailed cultural knowledge (e.g. Kozinets 2006) |
| *Status equalisation*: Participants are more likely to be involved in democratic conversation (e.g. Dholakia and Zhang 2004) | *Authority*: Due to the egalitarian nature of Internet communications, the researcher faces difficulties in defining their own status as the professional authority (e.g. Sade-Beck 2004) |

Sources: Wittel 2000; Catterall and Maclaran 2001; Kozinets 2002, 2006; Dholakia and Zhang 2004; Sade-Beck 2004; de Valeck *et al.* 2009.

conclusions of the enquiry but becomes a political practice as such framing. However, such boundary-fixing is obviously an issue with any form of qualitative research, with it also being a requirement in ensuring that studies are manageable. Again, in a similar fashion to ethnographies conducted in the offline world, Wittel (2000) also highlights the importance of gatekeepers in online communities, suggesting that a net ethnography usually cannot be conducted with the support of just one single gatekeeper, and that many gatekeepers will be required to gain access to various online communities.

The anonymity and status equalisation provided by the Internet tends to be regarded as a positive aspect of netnography. In more traditional forms of qualitative research the subjects or phenomena being studied are modified by the very act of observation, and problems can arise because of the presence of a researcher (Dholakia and Zhang 2004). Kozinets (2002) argues that in netnography the online researcher can remain hidden, using observations and downloads without the dangers of distorting data and behaviour through the presence of the researcher. However, as noted above, this raises considerable questions of research ethics. Because of the status-equalisation effects of the Internet, Catterall and Maclaran (2001) suggest that online researchers may want to create a website of their credentials that can be displayed alongside the details of the research project as part of ensuring appropriate research practice in virtual communities, including member checking of research.

Kozinets (1998) suggested that netnography is useful for three types of studies: first as a methodology to study virtual communities that do not exist offline; second as a methodological tool to study 'derived' virtual communities; and third, as an exploratory tool to study general topics. However, this has since expanded to include more general investigations of identity and the construction of a 'digital self', social relations, learning and creativity (Kozinets 2010).

## Stages/process of netnography

### *Planning and entrée*

Kozinets (2002) suggests that there are two initial steps involved in netnography: first, defining the specific marketing research questions and identifying particular online communities appropriate to investigate these questions and, second, learning as much as possible about the groups and individuals involved in the online communities. Over time online communities tend to share common value systems, norms, rules and a sense of association and identity (Catterall and Maclaran 2001). The cultural entrée involves non-participant observation, referred to as *lurking. Lurking* is vital to learn the norms and rules of the community; online communities can exhibit an idiosyncratic style which, unless the researcher searches for it, can be missed (Catterall and Maclaran 2001). Virtual communities include:

- Bulletin boards
- Rings, thematically linked webpages
- Newsgroups/lists
- Virtual worlds/dungeons, themed virtual locations, structured through role-playing rules
- Chatrooms.

Kozinets (2002) suggests evaluating the chosen online communities against the following criteria; preferred online communities should have:

- a focused and research question, a relevant topic
- higher traffic of postings
- larger numbers of discrete message posters
- detailed of rich information
- plenty of member-to-member interactions.

### Data collection and analysis (fieldnotes and other data)

The Internet offers a multitude of information that can be downloaded; these data may be gathered in a variety of forms. There are two elements to consider when the researcher is collecting data: data that are directly copied from CMC of online community members, and data that the researcher records from their observations of the members' communications, interactions and their meanings. Fieldnotes are still necessary to ensure researcher reflexivity and to map the data collection process (Catterall and Maclaran 2001).

Kozinets (1998) suggested that the contributors of online communities can be categorised by their level of involvement and consumption activity. He described four categories:

1   *Tourists*: lack deep interest and have weak social ties to the group
2   *Minglers*: have strong social ties but lack interest in the consumption activity
3   *Devotees*: have strong consumption interests but lack social ties
4   *Insiders*: have both strong social ties and consumption interest, often are frequent contributors and long-time members.

Devotees and insiders are regarded by Kozinets (2002) as the most valuable sources of information for market research as they are devoted, enthusiastic and sophisticated users, although he also noted that in marketing research it may be useful to track the development of users from minglers and tourists to devotees and insiders and the process of socialisation involved. Beckmann and Langer (2005) argue that devotees and insiders are not necessarily the most important data source and that tourists and minglers are also valuable for consumer research as they feel free to discuss topics without being forced to reveal their identities. Interestingly, Kozinets has more recently commented on the importance of 'alternatives to the rather essentializing clustering of all members of online communities into a single category of membership or non-membership' (2010: 32) and has replaced the tourist category in his 1999 paper with that of 'newbies'. He also goes on to describe four additional categories of the 'types' of relationship and interrelationship within a given online community. These are

1 *Lurkers*: are active observers who learn about a site through initially watching and reading
2 *Makers*: are active builders of online communities and their related social spaces
3 *Interactors*: reach into a given online community from other communities that arc highly cngagcd with thc spccific consumption activity
4 *Networkers*: reach into a specific online community in order to build social ties and interact with the members of that other community.

Kozinets (2002) suggests classifying postings as to whether they are primarily social or informational, and primarily on or off topic. Once messages that are directly related to the research questions are identified, a data analysis or similar approach can be conducted.

### *Providing trustworthy interpretation (identification/anonymity)*

As with any ethnography or fieldwork, researchers need to build trust and rapport within the online community. But cyberspace may present particular difficulties with respect to the identities of subjects.

It is important to be aware that identities in the virtual world are created, developed and discarded; participants in virtual worlds may have more than one online identity. Such a situation highlights the difficulties of monitoring and defining users in online communities, as people have the ability to change or modify their identities from site to site (Sade-Beck 2004). Indeed, Wittel (2000) states that the reason why the Internet is popular is due to its ability to allow users to modify their identity. Lysloff (2003: 255), for example, argues:

> When we go online, the computer extends our identity into a virtual world of disembodied presence, and at the same time, it also incites us to take on other identities. We lurk in, or engage with, on-line lists and usenet groups that enable different versions of ourselves to emerge dialogically. The computer, in this way, allows for a new kind of performativity, an actualization of multiple and perhaps idealized selves through text and image.

Of course, some would argue (including the present author) that this observation, although related to a particular medium, is no different from Goffman's (1959) perspectives on the presentation of self in everyday life and the relationship between performance and stage. In the early twenty-first century the Internet and the various forms of online environments can be understood as new stages on which to perform and portray particular aspects of identity. Indeed, Dholakia and Zhang (2004) note that the way in which we authenticate the identity of informants in the 'real world' is based primarily on the social context, and suggest that the same can be applied to online informants.

Kozinets (2002) also argues that direct misrepresentation of identity is discouraged in most online communities via community etiquette and social group pressure. Nevertheless, when human beings are translated into digital communications information is lost. Anonymity prevents the researcher from having confidence that they understand the discloser. There are currently no reliable means of knowing a participant's demographic details (Kozinets 2006).

Issues of authentication of identity and anonymity are not merely subjects of academic debate but raise fundamental issues as to whether results gained from online informants can be used to answer research questions based in the offline world. Of course, the division between online and offline contexts suggests there is a clear distinction between the two. However, as noted above, as participants bring their particular backgrounds, understandings and identities of their interpretations of life online there is no clear line of separation between the online and offline contexts (Kendall 1999, 2002; Jonsson 2007). The distinction between online and offline worlds is also becoming less useful as behaviour in these realms becomes merged and the two spaces interact and transform each other, with virtual reality not being 'a separate reality from other aspects of human action and experience, but rather a part of it' (Garcia *et al.* 2009: 54). Although this is no doubt true, it does nevertheless hold that for some types of online community activities that may be held as deviant some users will seek to disguise their observed identity in order to remain anonymous. Arguably the real need in ethnography is to seek to combine online and offline observations so as to gain a much more rounded appreciation of the extent to which online and offline consumption, behaviours, representation and performities inform and influence each other.

### Ethics

As noted earlier in the chapter, ethics is a major issue in online fieldwork. 'Ethical concerns over netnography turn on contentious concerns about whether online forums are to be considered a private or a public site, what constitutes informed consent, and what level of disclosure of research participants is appropriate' (Kozinets 2010: 19). Garcia and colleagues (2009) argue that ethnographers must learn how to apply standard principles of human subject protection to the online research environment. Alsmadi (2008) suggests that in relation to consumer and market research, which from Kozinets' (2010) perspective would include netnography, a respondent's right to 'informed consent' is dependent on whether the respondent is knowledgable enough about the nature of investigation and the implication of their involvement in the research. The notion of informed consent implies the participant is aware, from the beginning, of the research process itself. The respondent also has the right to privacy, which means that an individual has the right to choose whether or not to participate in the research. Alsmadi (2008) also notes that maximum care must be taken when subjects are children and, due to the lack of demographic data available online, this is clearly an ethical issue for netnographers to consider. Yet such considerations would appear to substantially challenge Kozinet's (2002; 2010) assertions as to the ease of undertaking netnography, at least if the full range of ethical considerations that may be played out in real-world consumer research are utilised in online ethnography. Indeed, as noted earlier in the chapter, Kozinets (2010) suggests that ethical procedures for in-person fieldwork do not translate easily to the online medium, with offline guidelines of informed consent being open to wide degrees of interpretation.

Kozinets (2002) recommends four ethical research procedures for marketing researchers utilising netnography. Researchers should:

1   fully disclose their presence and purpose to online community members during the research process
2   ensure confidentialiy and anonymity to all informants
3   seek and incorporate feedback from members of the online community
4   take a cautious approach to the private/public medium debate, requiring that they need to contact members and obtain their permission to use and postings that will be directly quoted.

Reflexivity has been considered as a central element in ethnographic research (Lin 2006); a trained ethnographer is encouraged to reflect upon their work, be self-aware and self-critical. With respect to the extension of reflexivity to virtual ethnography Lin argues for a new notion of 'mutuality', the notion that ethnographic data collected from virtual environments should be completed through collective efforts of the researcher and respondents that can help ethnographers decode technical activities and languages. Lin suggests that creating and enhancing mutuality between researchers and respondents can highlight the presence of the researcher and minimise the uneasiness of respondents being studied as they participate in the research. Lin (2006: 1) states that it is of 'great concern whether participants in a virtual field are informed of the existence of ethnographers and aware they are being watched'.

One response to the ethical dimensions of netnography is to provide what Kozinets (2002) refers to as a member check. This is where some, or all, of the final research document is presented to the community and the participants of the study in order to gain their comments and feedback. Kozinets (2002) suggests this for three reasons:

1   they enable the researcher to gain further, more specific insights into meanings and correct errors made by the researcher; deepen understandings based on observational online information;
2   they help smooth ethical concerns;
3   they can also establish and encourage a further exchange of information between the consumer group and the marketer.

Another advantage of this approach is that due to the low costs of CMC it is possible to supply online community members with the research text easily and in a timely manner.

### Exit

Cultural exit is as much of an issue in Internet ethnography as it is in the offline world (see Duval, Chapter 22, this volume). For many marketing applications of netnography, as well as the potential development of longitudinal studies, continued monitoring of the evolution of a particular online community is advantageous (Catterall and Maclaran 2001). However, where researchers have gone beyond observation or have openly participated in an online community in a research capacity, then there is a clear need for reflection on the extent to which links and relationships to an online community will be maintained or be allowed to lapse. Again, there is no easy answer to this question as it will depend on the researcher's personal ethics and, in reality, the strength of the personal relationships that have been built up.

### Conclusions

This chapter has discussed some of the issues arising from the conduct of online fieldwork, and online ethnography/netnography in particular. Fieldwork practices and processes have, and continue to be, substantially challenged by CMC and the development of virtual spaces. These challenges go hand-in-hand with a new appreciation, if not a complete redefinition, of community, identity and representation as a result of online social and economic worlds and the interconnectivity between being offline and online. In addition, these challenges are also to be found in the development of new online environments. For example, the presence of tourism and hospitality companies in the virtual world of Second Life, as well as virtual tourism in Second Life, reinforces the need for the development of online methods that are both responsive and adaptive in order to elicit reliable and valid data from rapidly changing online environments (Williams 2007) that also affect tourism-related consumption and production overall. Indeed, tourism studies itself reflects a broader imbalance in the social sciences 'between the tendency to theorise the Internet at a general level and not enough close-to-the-ground ethnographic study of the new social spaces the Internet makes possible' (Lysloff 2003: 233).

The chapter has suggested that online or virtual fieldwork also challenges conceptualisations of location in the field. It therefore agrees with VKS Ethnography (2009) that, 'In particular, ethnographic approaches must loosen their grip on co-location as a necessary requirement for "being in the field", if they are to consider important issues about knowledge production that arise in fields, such as those in the humanities or e-research.' As noted at the beginning of the chapter, co-presence rather than co-location should be regarded as a starting point to conceptualise and articulate fieldwork, whether virtual or otherwise. Indeed, the perspective from sociology that 'just as ethnographic practice continues to benefit from its encounter with mediated communication, so will other forms of sociological practice be enriched from engagement with new media' (Robinson and Schulz 2009: 685), applies equally to the study of tourism.

The consumption and production of tourism can be understood only via an integrated and nuanced understanding of both online and offline worlds. Undoubtedly this will provide substantial challenges for fieldwork and ethnographic and participant observation practices in particular, not least of which will be the need for a strong ethical reflexivity. Yet, Alsmadi's notion that ethical integrity in marketing (and other social science) research 'emphasizes the need to establish a universal model for regulatory requirements and well institutionalized practice of ethical research' (2008: 153) appears extremely unlikely, not least because, as noted in the chapter, different researchers operate under different institutional and legal jurisdictions which are in turn related to different research cultures and understandings of, for example, what constitutes public and private communicative space. Yet it would be true to say that the ethics committees of many universities and research institutions are lagging behind in their own understandings and the inadequacy of transferring protocols developed for co-located researchers and subjects to spaces of co-presence of online identities. Is it realistic for a customised avatar with an invented name to sign a disclosure and release form to participate in an online study in Second Life as may be required by a university ethics committee? In cyberspace people can hear or, more likely, read you screaming. Unfortunately, in the physical world many institutions remain deaf. As noted above, there is a need for pragmatism – along with reflexivity and sensitivity – in undertaking virtual fieldwork. And these are, arguably, the very same capacities that are required to successfully undertake and complete fieldwork in the real world.

## Acknowledgments

The assistance of Nicola van Tiel and Sandra Wilson is gratefully acknowledged in the development of this chapter, as are comments from David Duval on the final draft.

## References

Alsmadi, S. (2008) 'Marketing Research Ethics: Researcher's Obligations toward Human Subjects', *Journal of Academic Ethics* 6(1): 53–160.

Baglieri, D. and Consoli, R. (2009) 'Collaborative Innovation in Tourism: Managing Virtual Communities', *TQM Journal* 21(4): 353–64.

Bai, B., Hu, C. and Jang, S.S. (2006) 'Examining e-relationship marketing features on hotel websites', *Journal of Travel and Tourism Marketing* 21(2/3): 33–48.

Beckmann, S and Langer, R. (2005) 'Netnography: Rich Insights from Online Research', *Publiceret som tillaeg til Insights* 14(6). Online. Available HTTP: <http://frontpage.cbs.dk/insights/670005.shtml>.

Beaulieu, A. (2004) 'Mediating Ethnography: Objectivity and the Making of Ethnographies of the Internet', *Social Epistemology* 18(2–3): 139–64.

Bryce, J. (2001) 'The Technological Transformation of Leisure', *Social Science Computer Review* 19(1): 7–16.

Catterall, M. and Maclaran, P. (2001) 'Researching Consumers in Virtual Worlds: A Cyberspace Odyssey', *Journal of Consumer Behaviour* 1(3): 228–87.

Croon Fors, A. and Jakobsson, M. (2002) 'Beyond Use and Design: The Dialects of Being in Virtual Worlds', *Digital Creativity* 13(1): 1–14.

de Valeck, K., van Bruggen, G. and Wierenga, B. (2009) 'Virtual Communities: A Marketing Perspective', *Decision Support Systems* 47(3): 185–203.

Dholakia, N. and Zhang, D. (2004) 'Online Qualitative Research in the Age of E-commerce: Data Sources and Approaches', *Forum: Qualitative Sozialforschung/ Qualitative Social Research* 5(2). Online. Available HTTP: <http://nbn-resolving.de/urn:nbn:de:0114-fqs0402299> (accessed 11 December 2009).

Dillon, A. and Gushrowski, B.A. (2000) 'Genres and the Web: Is the Personal Home Page the First Uniquely Digital Genre?', *Journal of the American Society for Information Science* 51(2): 202–6.

Ducheneaut, N. and Moore, R.J. (2004) 'Gaining More than Experience Points: Learning Social Behavior in Multiplayer Computer Games', CHI 2004 Workshop on Social Learning Through Gaming, 19 April. Vienna, Austria.

Duval, D. (2008) ' "Claim you are from Canada, eh": Travelling Citizenship within Global Space', in P. Burns and M. Novelli (eds), *Tourism and Mobilities: Local–Global Connections*. Wallingford: CABI.

Dwivedi, M., Yadav, A. and Patel, V.R. (2009) 'The Online Destination Image of Goa', *Worldwide Hospitality and Tourism Themes* 1(1): 25–39.

Gan, L., Sim, C.J., Tan, H.L. and Janice, T. (2006) 'Online Relationship Marketing by Singapore Hotel Websites', *Journal of Travel and Tourism Marketing* 20(3/4): 1–19.

Garcia, A., Standlee, S., Bechkoff, J. and Cui, Y. (2009) 'Ethnographic Approaches to the Internet and Computer-mediated Communication', *Journal of Contemporary Ethnography* 38(1): 52–84.

Gerber, R. (2000) 'The Contribution of Fieldwork to Life-long Learning', in R. Gerber and G.K. Chuan (eds), *Fieldwork in Geography: Reflections, Perspectives and Actions*. Dordrecht: Kluwer.

Goffmann, E. (1959) *The Presentation of Self in Everyday Life*. New York: Anchor Books.

Hall, C.M. and Valentin, A. (2005) 'Content Analysis', in B. Ritchie, P. Burns and C. Palmer (eds), *Tourism Research Methods*. Wallingford: CAB International.

Heath, D., Koch, E., Ley, B. and Montoya, M. (1999) 'Nodes and Queries: Linking Locations in Networked Fields of Inquiry', *American Behavioral Scientist* 43(3): 450–63.

Heckman, J. (2000) 'Turning the focus online', *Marketing News*, 34(5): 15.

Hine, C. (2000) *Virtual Ethnography*. London: Sage.

Holge-Hazelton, B. (2002) 'The Internet: A New Field for Qualitative Inquiry?', *Forum: Qualitative Soziaforschung/Qualitative Social Research* 3(2). Online. Available HTTP: <http://www.qualitative-research.net/index.php/fqs/article/view/854> (accessed 8 January 2010).

Janta, H. and Ladkin, A. (2009) 'Polish Migrant Labor in the Hospitality Workforce: Implications for Recruitment and Retention,' *Tourism Culture Communication* 9(1–2): 5–15.

Johnson, B. (2009) 'Danah Boyd: "People looked at me like I was an alien". Microsoft researcher Danah Boyd talks about social networking, young people and how the web is more private than your home', *Guardian*, 9 December 2009. Online. Available HTTP: <http://www.guardian.co.uk/technology/2009/dec/09/interview-microsoft-researcher-danah-boyd> (accessed 10 December 2009).

Johnson, B. (2010) 'CES 2010: Privacy No Longer a Social Norm, says Facebook Founder', *Guardian*, 11 January 2010. Online. Available HTTP: <http://www.guardian.co.uk/technology/2010/jan/11/facebook-privacy> (accessed 11 January 2010).

Jonsson, F. (2007) 'Performing the Self in Cyberspace: A Study of Young Players' Styles of Self-presentation and Identity Performances in the Online Game World TIBIA'. Stockholm: Department of Computer and System Science, IT-university, Stockholm University/KTH Sweden. Online. Available HTTP: <webappo.sh.se> (accessed 11 December 2009).

Kendall, L. (1999) 'Recontextualising "Cyberspace" Methodological Considerations for Online Research', in S. Jones (ed.), *Doing Internet Research: Critical Issues and Methods for Examining the Net*. London: Sage.

Kendall, L. (2002) *Hanging Out in the Virtual Pub: Masculinities and Relationships Online*. California: University of California Press.

Kozinets, R.V. (1997) ' "I want to believe": A Netnography of the X-philes' Subculture of Consumption', *Advances in Consumer Research* 24: 470–5.

Kozinets, R.V. (1998) 'On Netnography: Initial Reflections on Consumer Investigations of Cyberculture', *Advances in Consumer Research* 25: 366–71.

Kozinets, R. (2002) 'The Field behind the Screen: Using Netnography for Marketing Research in Online Communities', *Journal of Marketing Research* 34(1): 61–72.

Kozinets, R. (2006) 'Click to Connect: Netnography and Tribal Advertising', *Journal of Advertising Research* 46(3): 279–88.

Kozinets, R. (2010) *Netnography: Doing Ethnographic Research Online*. London: Sage.

Lee, R.M. (1993) *Doing Research on Sensitive Topics*. London: Sage.

Lévy, P. (2001) *Cyberculture (Electronic Meditations)*, trans. Robert Bononno. Minneapolis: University of Minnesota Press.

Lin, Y. (2006) 'Mutuality between Researchers and Respondents in Virtual Ethnography', paper presented to the Virtual Ethnography Workshop, September 27–29, Amsterdam. Online. Available HTTP: <virtualknowledgestudio.nl> (accessed 11 December 2009).

Lysloff, R.T.A. (2003) 'Musical Community on the Internet: An On-line Ethnography', *Cultural Anthropology* 18(2): 233–63.

Miller, D. and Slater, D. (2000) *The Internet: An Ethnographic Approach*. Oxford: Berg.

Morgan, M. and Watson, P. (2009) 'Unlocking the Shared Experiences: Challenges of Consumer Experience Research', in M. Kozak and A. Decrop (eds), *Handbook of Tourist Behavior: Theory and Practice*. New York: Routledge.

O'Hara, K., Berners-Lee, T., Hall, W. and Shadbolt, N. (2010) 'Use of the Semantic Web in e-research', in W.H. Dutton and P.W. Jeffreys (eds), *World Wide Research: Reshaping the Sciences and Humanities*. Cambridge, MA: MIT Press.

O'Hara, K. and Shadbolt, N. (2008) *The Spy in the Coffee Machine: The End of Privacy As We Know It*. Oxford: Oneworld.

Rheingold, H. (1993). *The Virtual Community: Homesteading on the Electronic Frontier*. Reading: Addison-Wesley.

Richardson, L. (2000) 'Evaluating Ethnography', *Qualitative Inquiry* 6(2): 253–5.

Robinson, L. and Schulz, J. (2009) 'New Avenues for Sociological Inquiry: Evolving Forms of Ethnographic Practice', *Sociology* 43(4): 685–98.

Rokka, J. and Moisander, J. (2009) 'Environmental Dialogue in Online Communities: Negotiating Ecological Citizenship among Global Travellers', *International Journal of Consumer Studies* 33(2): 199–205.

Sade-Beck, L. (2004) 'Internet Ethnography: Online and Offline', *International Journal of Qualitative Methods* 3(2). Online. Available HTTP: <http://www.ualberta.ca/~iiqm/backissues/3_2/pdf/sadebeck.pdf> (accessed 11 December 2009).

Simpson, L. (2006) 'The Value in Combining Netnography with Traditional Research Techniques', in D. Grewal, M. Levy and R. Krishnan (eds), *2006 AMA Educators' Proceedings, Enhancing Knowledge Development in Marketing*, 17. Chicago: American Marketing Association.

Smith, M.A. and Kollock, P. (eds) (1999) *Communities in Cyberspace*. London: Routledge.

Tussyadiah, I.P. and Fesenmaier, D. (2008) 'Mediating Tourist Experiences: Access to Places via Shared Videos', *Annals of Tourism Research* 36(1): 24–40.

VKS Ethnography (2009) 'Co-presence as Ethnographic Approach', Sunday 6 December. Online. Available HTTP: <http://vksethno.wordpress.com/2009/12/06/ co-presence-as-ethnographic-approach> (accessed 10 January 2010).

Ward, K.J. (1999) 'Cyber-ethnography and the Emergence of the Virtually New Community', *Journal of Information Technology* 14(1): 95–105.

Williams, M. (2007) 'Avatar Watching: Participant Observation in Graphical Online Environments', *Qualitative Research* 7(1): 5–24.

Wittel, A. (2000) 'Ethnography on the Move: From Field to Net to Internet', *Forum: Qualitative Sozialforschung/Qualitative Social Research* 1(1). Online. Available HTTP: <http://nbn-resolving.de/urn:nbn:de:0114-fqs-0001213> (accessed 11 December 2009).

# 21 Integrating researchers and indigenous communities

## Reflections from Northern Canada

*R. H. Lemelin, E. C. Wiersma and E. J. Stewart*

## Introduction

This chapter is a discussion on the current state of community-based research with indigenous communities and, more specifically in a tourism context, by non-indigenous researchers. Particular attention will be paid to disentangling the various definitions and approaches to community-based research including action research, participatory action research, and community research, and linking these to larger issues of praxis. The increase in community and participatory research conducted in indigenous communities by non-indigenous researchers has generated a great deal of discussion (Huntington 2006; Louis 2007; Caine *et al.* 2009). We would like to continue and expand these discussions by presenting our own experiences in working with northern indigenous communities on tourism issues. These experiences include conducting research on the human dimensions of polar bear management in Manitoba (Lemelin 2006a, 2006b, 2007; Lemelin and Smale 2006, 2007; Lemelin and Wiersma 2007a, 2007b) and northern Ontario (Lemelin *et al.* 2010), examining the role of traditional ecological knowledge systems in tourism (Lemelin 2006a; 2006b), exploring resident attitudes toward tourism in the Canadian Arctic using collaborative research methods (Stewart and Draper 2006a; 2007), focusing on environmental dimensions of cruise tourism in Arctic Canada (Stewart and Draper 2006b; Stewart *et al.* 2007, 2008), examining wildlife management and tourism (Lemelin and Dyck 2007), and examining protected areas and tourism (Lemelin and Johnston 2008). Along with familiarity with the tourism industry in Churchill, Manitoba by all three authors, Lemelin and Wiersma have collaborated on previous research projects and publications, while Stewart and Lemelin are currently collaborating on three publications pertaining to tourism in Northern Canada.

In this chapter we use our various field study experiences and personal narratives to form the basis of a discussion on fieldwork. Inspired by Caine *et al.* (2009), we see this as praxis, where our work is guided by the discourse provided by tourism, protected areas scholars (Dyer, Aberdeen and Schuler 2003; McAvoy, McDonald and Carlson 2003; Mowforth and Munt 2003; Ateljevic, Pritchard and Morgan 2007) and indigenous scholars (Cole

2005; Butler and Hinch 2007), all who collectively have advocated the implementation of new research approaches in indigenous communities. Narratives will be used throughout the chapter to introduce topics and build discussion around themes such as tensions in the field, action (or lack thereof), community involvement throughout the research process (from developing initial aims through to publishing), and dissemination of research findings. The balance between the conceptual and the applied, and how praxis can be achieved in community research with indigenous communities, is discussed. A series of 'recommendations' for those new to community-based research and/or research in non-indigenous communities are provided in the conclusion.

## The themes: people, processes and outcomes

Based on our fieldwork and through an exploration of our own experiences as 'reflective practitioners' (Schön 1983; Denzin 2008), each of us has written what we call a 'reflexive narrative'. As in all research, critical reflection on the research process is an important element of learning about 'how to do better research', but this exercise is especially poignant in domains of action research. In these research domains, there is a need for open and honest reflection on the 'unique challenges and obstacles that community members and researchers confront . . . . and the lessons learned from such interactions' (Taylor *et al.* 2004: 6). The analysis of our written narratives involved a search for key themes and emerging patterns (Lofland and Lofland 1984). The result of this process was the further distillation of key questions to frame our discussion. In the analysis of our critical narratives, we found that our experiences prompted the following themes and questions:

1  *People*: What is it about us as individuals that drew us toward participatory research? Who/what influenced us – other researchers, context, and/ or theory? What did we think we could achieve at the outset? How did our own 'reality' impact the development of research relationships (perceived or real)?
2  *Process*: How did we involve community members in the research design/ overall process? How did we go about defining goals for the research, and what role did the community play in the data collection and analysis?
3  *Outcome*: How was 'successful' community research defined: by 'action', knowledge dissemination, by the development of trust, or by something else? However, action research does not always produce positive outcomes, work according to plan, or necessarily enact action. How researchers anticipate and deal with these issues is also part of the process of learning, both for communities and researchers.

The following discussion explores these questions and, wherever possible, we use extracts from our reflexive narratives to illustrate our points. Before we begin this discussion, however, we review and determine what we mean by action research.

## Types of action research

Action research (AR) can take many different forms. These different forms of research often depend on the purpose of the research. Reason (1994) describes three different types of action research: (a) cooperative inquiry; (b) participatory action research; and (c) action science or action inquiry:

a   *Cooperative inquiry* focuses on working together in a group with open authentic communication, which can help people choose how to live their lives free from restrictive social custom. Co-researchers and co-subjects are integrated in this process whereby their ideas, thoughts, and decisions contribute to all stages of the research. There is full reciprocity among co-researchers.
b   *Participatory Action Research* (PAR) emphasizes the political aspects of knowledge production, and starts with concerns about power, power-lessness, and knowledge. PAR emphasizes the shared ownership of the research project, community involvement and action; and is often associated with social transformation. Action research has two aims – to produce knowledge and action locally, and to empower people through the construction and use of their own knowledge. Genuine collaboration and commitment from all involved is also important.
c   *Action science and action inquiry* focus on organizations and communities and the development of effective action for greater effectiveness and justice (Reason and Bradbury 2006). Action science aims to bridge the gap between theory and practice, and sees the study of practice as a source of new understandings.

The cyclic process of action research in general involves planning, acting, observing, and reflecting, and then further planning, acting, observing, and reflecting (Pedlar 1995). First, the researcher must have some background and construct a preliminary picture of the organization and/or community and the issue under examination (Stringer 1999). These organizations or gatekeepers are contacted or visited. From these visits and discussions, the research focus is defined by all participants (Heron and Reason 2001). The team, ideally composed of researchers and community/organizational members, then decides on the most appropriate course of action after examining possibilities and alternatives. The research is then carried out by all. After the research is completed, all participants reflect and debrief on the process. From there, further planning is decided upon, and the research process starts anew. Action research, then, is a cyclical process of reflection, learning, and the development of critical consciousness (Gaventa and Cornwall 2001).

**People and concepts: coming to terms with both**

Behind the process of action research 'stands the personal biography of the researcher who speaks from a particular class, gender, racial, cultural and ethnic community perspective' (Denzin and Lincoln 2003: 29). For each of us, we brought different identities to the field meaning that we 'speak from within a distinct interpretive community that configures, in its special way, the multi-cultural, gendered components of the research act' (Denzin and Lincoln 2003: 30). As Lemelin reflects: 'we actually emphasized my status as a non-local, French-Canadian male in conducting interviews with various community members' (Lemelin, reflexive narrative). For example, this approach was necessary because the Mohawk nation at Akwesasne had recently undergone a period of high civil unrest and what was required was someone who could talk to all political and cultural components in the community, someone who had nearby connections, yet was not part of the community. Stewart reflects on how research relationships in her case study communities were catalysed by the presence of her infant son:

> My own reality of being a mother seemed to accelerate my acceptance into the case study communities, and enhance the development of research relationships. Between the ages of 9–22 months my son accompanied me . . . I decided to bring him along (because it was easier and cheaper to do so, rather than leave him at home), but it quickly became obvious that my son acted as a social 'catalyst' . . . I think this has to do with the child-centred nature of these communities, but also because I was seen as just another mother juggling her responsibilities. Since we had something in common, I was seen as accessible and approachable; a 'person' not just another researcher. In effect my son 'broke the ice' and he gave me a unique identity in the field. This seemed to have had the effect of breaking down several of the barriers some researchers face when entering communities for the first time, and perhaps gave me access to people that may have not been possible without him.
>
> (Stewart, reflexive narrative)

Researchers bring their own uniqueness to the field and, as we have illustrated, these personal characteristics can sometimes be helpful in developing research relationships; however, the personal values, beliefs and culture of researchers can also hinder the research process. A divergence in cultural beliefs between researcher and participant can sometimes be awkward and uncomfortable. As Lemelin reflects, 'I had to be careful about my perspectives on the current leadership, I learned very quickly in another unrelated project, that being free with one's opinions on politics can quickly end your research. Especially if your key informant just happens to be the cousin or the sister-in-law of the chief' (Lemelin, reflexive narrative). Regardless of whether developing research relationships are healthy or otherwise, boundaries still exist and need to be 'constantly negotiated through creative tensions' as the research process and individual relationships deepen (Lemelin, reflexive narrative). This is particularly the case when research relationships extend into the social network of the participants.

The relationship between the chief, gatekeepers, the funding agency, and the co-PIs had a significant impact on the process and outcome of one particular research project. I felt like I had to constantly negotiate the boundaries between the four partners. I found myself struggling with one of the representatives from the funding agency and his incessant demands for action.

> 'Why aren't tourism operators being created from this project?', he would ask us. That's not the way tourism is done in small community, you don't just convert a miner into a tourism operator overnight; you need to develop trust, and implement capacity, then when they are ready or feel capable they will initiate the process of becoming a tourism operator. Then, just when you think you have the agency understanding or least backing off, a gatekeeper becomes outraged at your request for further details on certain travail details and decides to cancel the presentation with three days left before the conference! What do you do? Can't tell her off, she's the chief's sister-in-law, and even if you decided to leave the project, you will most certainly see her at the next meeting for the regional environmental group. So you cool off, and clear the air, and re-open discussions. Hopefully, you didn't do too much damage to the project.
>
> (Lemelin, reflexive narrative)

The dynamics of these wider contextual relationships can impact research in significant ways both positively and negatively. Similarly, constant negotiation of research relationships was something Stewart did not anticipate in her research. For example, stakeholders interviewed at the start of the research had long moved on by the end of her research process, meaning that there was a lack of continuity. As Shaffir (1996: 56–7) notes, research is a partial process: 'it is not fixed at the outset but evolves over time in that it is negotiated and renegotiated with new casts of people; and may be mediated and shaped by contingencies beyond the researcher's control.' What is key throughout these projects is the understanding of the different viewpoints and perspectives that each actor brings to the research, and the temporal dynamics, meaning that gatekeepers and key informants may have several responsibilities, and your project is simply one of many which may, or may not have, any relevance to them.

There are many different human-to-human relationships to navigate in action research; not only the relationships between researcher and participant but a whole host of other human relationships which need to be developed and nurtured. Building research relationships often starts before research starts in earnest. Developing research contacts to enable access to certain populations or communities can be crucial to the long-term success of action research. But securing these initial contacts can be a long and frustrating process. As Stewart advises: 'the key was to stay active and eventually a couple of important openings presented themselves. For example, by chance, at a conference one lunch time I sat next to a sister-duo who were eager for me to visit their community to see if my study might work there' (Stewart, reflexive narrative). As decisions are made about where and what to study, other relationships need to be developed. In our reflexive narratives we all identify the importance of 'gatekeepers' (Burgess 1991: 47), prominent individuals who provide useful background information, suggestions of people to contact, and hints on how to develop a research project in their community (Patton 1990). These initial contacts in the community are regarded as important to the success of other important relationships which need to be developed. 'My gatekeepers facilitated access to key stakeholders in the community, with whom I could begin to build a research relationship' (Stewart, reflexive narrative).

Gatekeepers, key informants, and stakeholders are crucial at all stages of the research, but especially in the beginning phases. 'The action research process started with my initial contact with the organization and involvement in team meetings to become familiar with the organization and its goals' (Wiersma, reflexive narrative). Lemelin provides gatekeepers

> with information (usually the cover letter and consent form, although the questionnaire has also been requested at times). This process also provides an opportunity for the researcher to explain his/her rationale and outline the desired goals and outcomes (i.e., articles, conference proceedings), and some of the community members are also provided with an opportunity to ask questions, establish safeguards for accountability (i.e., gatekeepers, key informants, advisory boards), and determine outcomes.
>
> (Lemelin, reflexive narrative)

## Processes: non-indigenous researchers in indigenous communities, learning from creative-tensions

The research relationships developed prior to entering the field, as well as during the field research itself, are central to the success of all variants of action research. However, even when every effort has been made to create meaningful research relationships, it does not guarantee that the research process will be a success or will end in some form of capacity-building where empowerment and change are implemented. Indeed, as Lickers (Lickers *et al.* 1995) explains, researchers often place too much emphasis on the research and the end research product (i.e. the thesis, the publications), when what is more often important is the journey, the friendships, and the other contributions arising from the research. What researchers need to remember, according to Cole (2005), Deloria (1995), and Lickers (1994), are the concerns that often arise from community research. As Gegeo and Watson-Gegeo (2001: 58) explain:

Accounts of other people's cultures are not Indigenous accounts of those cultures, even though they may be based on interviews with and observations of indigenous communities, individuals, and societies. All of the foregoing activities, while they draw on Indigenous cultural knowledge, are imagined, conceptualized, and carried out within the theoretical and methodological frameworks of Anglo-European forms of research, reasoning, and interpreting.

In a playful way, one person in Cambridge Bay, where Stewart ended up conducting a large portion of her research, told her there was an analogy between snow geese and researchers. Snow geese arrive in the summer, make a lot of noise and a lot of mess, then leave at the end of the summer, only to return again the following year to repeat the process. In other parts of the Canadian Arctic, for similar reasons researchers have been referred to as 'siksiks' (ground squirrels in Inuktitut). As Gearheard and Shirley (2007: 63) point out, this analogy sometimes is used in a joking manner, but sometimes 'the nickname expresses negative feelings toward researchers; a mistrust that stems from a history of non-communication, miscommunication, and misunderstanding'. 'I did not want to conduct my research project in this manner and from this point forward I was resolved to do things in a different way' (Stewart, reflective narrative).

Some of these critiques are warranted for, as Deloria (1991: 457) states, research conducted by outsiders has often contributed to the perception that 'researchers derive all the benefits and bear no responsibility for the ways in which their research is used'. This can become problematic when research into indigenous communities does not work for the benefit of indigenous people, thereby reinforcing negative stereotypes associated with researchers in some Northern communities. However, the research by Stewart and Lemelin illustrates that there are potential advantages of being an outsider, that is, provided that the outsider is reflexive and reflective. Indeed, Louis (2007: 136) explains that he 'would much rather see non-indigenous researchers working with indigenous communities possessing the tools they need to ensure that their research agendas are sympathetic, respectful, and ethical from an indigenous perspective'. Thankfully there is some encouraging literature to this effect (e.g. Crazy Bull 1997; Rundstrom and Deur 1999; Kievit 2003; de Ishtar 2005; Hodge and Lester 2006).

In an attempt to bridge the various ontological, epistemological, and methodological gaps, Lickers and colleagues (1995) and Lemelin and Lickers (2004) suggested that indigenous methodologies should be based on a research approach known as CREE (capacity-building, respect, equity, and empowerment). These concepts help to promote research accountability and transparency, while also attempting to minimize and regulate researchers and their findings in communities (Lickers *et al.* 1995). CREE, much like action research, seeks to engage community members and researchers. It initiates a research approach where participants become actors in the process rather than just objects, and by giving them some control over the process, it potentially creates the kind of knowledge that will be more useful to communities. Capacity-building is defined as a process requiring an understanding of the impacts of different historical perspectives and socio-cultural beliefs. In order to accommodate these distinct perspectives, partners may need to develop new skills (i.e. openness and tolerance). Respect and sensitivity are essential to eliminate past stereotypes. Respect is activated when partners are willing to incorporate indigenous systems of lore and follow local protocols (Lickers *et al.* 1995). Establishing protocols is an important aspect of developing trust, as Lemelin explains:

> Throughout the past fifteen years, I have used the following two protocols, the lighting a fire at the wood's edge ceremony and the offering of tobacco, which were developed during my master's research. From a traditional Haudenosaunee perspective, lighting a fire at the wood's edge (note that the fire is symbolic here; emails, letters, faxes and phone calls can also be used) is a diplomatic request for a parlée. Here at the edge of the woods, the researcher awaits until a 'delegation' invites the researcher into the community. In this informal meeting, I always, when possible, presented tobacco, introduced myself and briefly informed them of the research. These informal meetings are required in order to answer and alleviate any preliminary concerns that the participant or community may have regarding the research. The gatekeepers are provided with information (usually the cover letter and consent form, although the questionnaire has also been requested at times). This process also provides an opportunity for the researcher to explain his/her rational and outlined what the desired goals and outcomes (i.e., articles, conference proceedings), and some of the community members are also provided with an opportunity to ask questions, establish safeguards for accountability (i.e., gatekeepers, key informants, advisory boards), and determine outcomes.
>
> (Lemelin, reflexive narrative)

Respectful representation according to Absolon and Willet (2004: 15) requires the researcher to 'consider how you represent yourself, your research and the people, events, phenomena you are researching'. Respect is not just about saying 'please' or 'thank you', it's about 'listening intently to others' ideas and not insisting that your ideas prevail (Steinhauer 2002: 73). Respect is also demonstrating humility, and developing patience with the process and 'accepting decisions of the indigenous people in regard to the treatment of any knowledge shared. This is because not all knowledge shared is meant for a general audience' (Louis 2007: 133).

Equity is often related to financial resources. However, equity in action research can be best defined as a 'back and brain approach' where the researcher can utilize 'the brain' dimensions of the research to assist the communities with tasks such as literature and document reviews, co-presentations, and co-publications. The 'back approach' can incorporate reclamation and landscape modification projects, tree planting, and community clean-ups. Empowerment in action research supports human rights and dignity; it seeks to inform as well as transform; it strives to decrease dependence by engaging the community in issues that are of relevance to them (Lickers *et al.* 1995). Empowerment in action research is achieved when communities control and direct the research. Accountability, appropriation, and the acknowledgment of one's rights and responsibilities, as Louis (2007) explains, are fundamental components of empowerment. These are discussed next.

a   Relational accountability is the interdependence of all beings, best illustrated through the web of life. In research, it implies that the researcher is not just responsible for nurturing and maintaining relationship with the community, but he or she is also accountable to give voice to 'all your relations'.
b   Reciprocal appropriation recognizes that all research, including action research, is in some way or another a form of appropriation. The best that researchers and community members can do is to recognize this reality and implement adequate benefits for all.
c   Rights and responsibilities refers to research that is driven by indigenous protocols, contains explicitly outlined goals, and considers the impacts of the proposed research (Smith 1999). This, according to Louis (2007: 133), is:

> meant to ensure that the research process is non-extractive and recognizes indigenous peoples' intellectual property rights to 'own' the knowledge they share with the researcher and to maintain control over all publication and reporting of that knowledge. It demands that the entire research process be a collaboration and any publication or announcement of 'findings' must be written in understandable language and shared with and receive the endorsement of the Indigenous community.

The implementation of CREE in research can help to create what Lickers and colleagues (1995) and Louis (2007) call academic allies. These non-indigenous academic allies are necessary, for 'if indigenous scholarship is to succeed, you are essential, especially if your department does not have any indigenous faculty. It is because of people like yourselves that indigenous scholars have come as far as they have . . . and a necessary next step is to provide room for indigenous faculty to take this cause even further' (Louis 2007: 136). Providing a perspective that is rarely discussed in indigenous research, Louis (2007: 136) explains that:

> the only way in which indigenous faculty members could attain the positions they have today is because there already were non-Indigenous faculty who not only believed in them, but who continue to create space for

different ways of knowing within the university setting. We need allies such as department heads and other university administrators who play crucial roles in the recruitment, retention, mentoring, and support of existing indigenous faculty and colleagues who review research for publication, grants, and tenure. As more and more indigenous students enter graduate programmes, where research is a central component for graduation, the need for more indigenous faculty to supervise, sit on committees, write letters of reference, and generally support these students, as well as those non-indigenous students wanting to do research on indigenous topics, is becoming pressing and urgent. We need help . . . we need allies.

We believe that action research along with key academic and community supports have provided us with the essential tools in becoming academic allies. The creation of academic allies is without a doubt an essential outcome of action research, but other tangible outcomes associated with our work are discussed next.

## Outcomes: going beyond the required

Community-research is much like a polar bear walking on newly formed sea ice. It usually takes a daring (some would say fool-hardy) individual to brave the ice, for there is always the chance that you are going to break through and get soaked, and even if the ice supports you, you never really know where the journey will take you, for like the sea ice, action research is dynamic and forever shifting.

(Lemelin, reflexive narrative)

Action research in indigenous communities is based on two premises: (1) that research produces some type of change in the lives and practice of co-researchers (or research participants); and (2) that individuals and communities are engaged in the change process. It combines the nature of research with social action to address social problems (Schwandt 2001). Action research is more concerned about producing change in practice than it is about generating knowledge (McNiff, Lomax and Whitehead 1996), although generating knowledge is also important (Pedlar 1995). One of the ways in which change is produced in practice is through engaging individuals and communities as co-researchers. Thus, although action research does not focus on methodological integrity as positivist quantitative research does (Guba and Lincoln 1989), there are characteristics that need to be evident in order for the research to be considered participatory action research. The most important characteristic is the engagement of participants.

The issue or problem is defined by the participants, the change intervention is decided upon by the participants, and the evaluation and reflection is also done by the participants. Regardless of the involvement levels of the participants, '[a]ction research requires (and fosters) a working environment which encourages collaboration and reflection, evaluation and exploration – and a culture which is innovative because it is supportive'.

(Winter and Munn-Giddings 2001: 26)

In many epistemological and methodological discussions on action and tourism, there is a focus on how the participants and/or communities are engaged in these projects (Belsky 2004; Jobbins 2004; Westwood 2006). Inherent in these discussions is often an assumption that if the researcher simply follows appropriate protocol for engaging participants and communities, then 'action' will be produced and the research will be successful. The number of writings on how to engage participants and communities gives credence to the focus on appropriate engagement and protocol as a prerequisite for a successful research project (e.g. Lykes and Maya Ixil Women 2006; Davidson-Hunt and O'Flaherty 2007). These discussions often imply a dependence on methodological rigour that is reminiscent of a positivistic approach to research. The question then becomes, 'Can the research fail (or not produce action) even if the researcher does everything right?' Participatory action research that has not produced results is often not discussed in the literature and thus we know little about research that has not produced action. However, three of our projects did not end up producing 'research' as traditionally defined. Stewart's attempts to approach the community of Churchill, Manitoba illustrates how using appropriate protocol to approach communities does not always guarantee entrance into that community, nor does it guarantee community support of the research or community involvement in the research process. While Stewart was able to finally access the community, this may have been due to her own persistence rather than proper or appropriate protocol. It is indeed conceivable that using proper and appropriate protocol can still leave a researcher with limited access or with access but difficulty in conducting the research.

Change and awareness as an outcome of the research is also known as catalytic validity (Guba and Lincoln 1989). Much of the literature documenting action research has focused on successes rather than what might be considered lack of success or lack of action. Yet, what happens with action research when there is no action? For researchers, this can be especially problematic, for we need to be transparent, clear, and open about projects that did not work or at least did not work according to how we anticipated they would. One of the characteristics of action research is that goals are determined by the individuals and/or community who are involved with the project. While this is a key step that emphasizes the fundamental philosophical differences between action research and 'traditional' research, having the co-researchers determine the goals or action of the project and the dissemination strategies does not always guarantee success. Actually executing the plan of action as outlined in the various scenarios was very difficult, and we discovered along the way that there is an intricate web of supports and enablers that need to be in place in order to achieve goals, regardless of intent and desire at the outset. The enablers and key informants are not simply external constraints but can also include psychosocial dimensions. Wiersma, in an unrelated action research project, reflected on her experiences with a project that may have been deemed 'unsuccessful'.

> What does a researcher do when there is no action? I have puzzled over this for three years now since this project was conducted. I have analyzed the factors that contributed to the 'lack of action', but yet, I still continue to wonder about my own role in this, about the role of relationships and how they impact the process, and the process itself. I have come to the conclusion that perhaps it is all of these factors together. But one thing is for sure, action research that doesn't produce 'action' isn't usually published . . . am I the only one that hasn't succeeded?
>
> (Wiersma, reflexive narrative)

Research that is not successful provides a unique opportunity for all of us to learn more about action research and the ways that it can be successful. As the saying goes, 'Learn from your mistakes'. Perhaps we should also be learning from each other's mistakes and lack of successes. Understanding how action research can be successful provides one more way for change to happen in a world that needs it. Unsuccessful action research should be published and written about to pave the way for other researchers to come along and be successful.

As stated above, indigenous scholars (Deloria 1995, 2003; Louis 2007) now advocate co-authorship in presentations and peer-reviewed papers. This is especially crucial when discussing the role of traditional knowledge in wildlife management or mapping sites of deep socio-cultural significance for future protected areas. Lemelin has co-published a number of papers (Fidler, Lemelin, Peerla and Walmark 2008; Lemelin, Peerla and Walmark 2008) and has facilitated and participated in co-presentations at conferences, e.g. Canadian Parks for Tomorrow: 40th Anniversary Conference. Reporting back and information dissemination are key components of action research, for, as Stewart explains,

> Dissemination of the research findings, an integral part of the research process, was intended to give residents the opportunity to view and comment on the emerging raw data. I chose a variety of mechanisms to report back initial research results to the communities (such as poster displays, weblogs, newspaper articles and radio interviews). Through this process of reporting, stakeholders in each of the case study sites identified a variety of possible applications of the research, including its

use in education and training programmes, local tourism development plans, and changes to territorial law relating to tourism. None of these suggestions for application of the research (I believe) would have been forthcoming if I had not engaged in disseminating research findings, confirming in my mind the importance of reporting activities. By behaving in this way, I hope researchers can see that there are other ways to conduct research in northern communities and ultimately avoid the label of being a 'snow goose'.

(Stewart, reflexive narrative)

New expectations by some territorial agencies and communities in Northern Canada are now promoting full co-authorship and research ownership, which means full access to the data, the codes, and analysis throughout all phases of the research. If certain community authorities like band councils or elder groups claim the ownership of the data as part of the research agreement, they should then be prepared to share responsibility for protecting the confidentiality of those who contribute to them.

## Discussion and recommendations

Practical suggestions promoting 'better' or more 'equitable' action research include the importance of preliminary research, on-site research, and follow-up visits. Information accessibility and dissemination is crucial throughout these phases and, as Stewart has indicated, can include a number of approaches and technologies. One of the challenges we noted is often associated with the sensitivity of certain topic areas, and the emergence of unforeseen topics. In business and politics, such factors are often mitigated or presented at the onset of projects through impact and benefits agreements (IBAs). In this fashion, partners and stakeholders are made aware of the potential impacts and possible benefits from development projects or the creation of protected areas. While IBAs have worked relatively well for some development projects, these agreements lack a research philosophy and standardized templates. One approach which provides both of these is Community Service Learning (CSL). CSL is an educational approach integrating service in the community with intentional learning activities by all participants (Reardon 1998). Within effective CSL efforts, members of research communities, educational establishments, and community organizations work together toward outcomes that are mutually beneficial (Canadian Alliance for Community Service Learning). CSL seeks to:

- Promote learning through active participation
- Create partnerships that are engaging as well as transformative
- Create research projects 'with' and 'for' the partners instead of 'on'
- Institute respect and responsibility in research
- Foster civic responsibility.

CSL is often equated with volunteering activities. However, CSL is not an episodic volunteer programme or community hours for students; CLS, much like action research, seeks to create capacity, generate equity (more often than not in the form of 'sweat equity'), and, when possible, foster empowerment. CSL also provides standardized templates highlighting goals and objectives, timelines, responsibilities, and sections requiring the signature of key actors. These contracts, which can be modified to any context, ensure that everyone is aware of and agreeable to the research. While similar to memorandums of understanding and IBAs, the CSL contract extends beyond the mere legalities, since it is supported by a research philosophy and approach. The CSL approach has been recently implemented in a tourism study being conducted by Lemelin and Koster and the Red Rock First Nation at Lake Helen.

Positive synergies and symbiosis can be created when combining action research, CREE, and CSL (Reardon 1998), with action research providing the ontological, epistemological, and theoretical framework, CREE providing the philosophical basis, and CSL providing the documentation, essential in the successful undertaking of community research (Figure 21.1).

Proponents of action research and indigenous scholars assume that if the appropriate techniques and protocols are employed, then indigenous community research will indeed produce action. However, as we have demonstrated, 'action' is not always the result of action research; therefore it is essential that we discuss this topic and present strategies and recommendations on what should be done when this occurs. How researchers anticipate

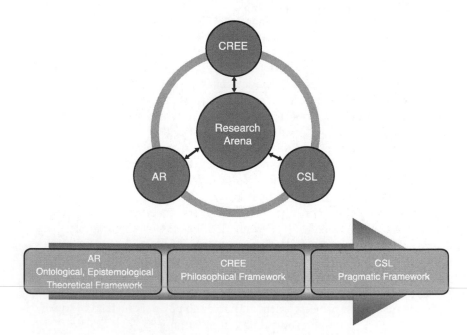

*Figure 21.1* The generative cycle of action research

and deal with these issues is also part of the process of learning, both for communities and researchers. One recommendation that was provided by Lickers to Lemelin early on in his Master's research was to bootstrap your research, that is, combine your research projects with something that the community really wants you to do, such as planting trees, finding out about polar bear management, or translating articles. The other recommendation, which is often quite difficult at the beginning of one's career, is to say no and walk away.

## Conclusion

Tourism is often perceived as atheoretical and apolitical, the fact that it is interpreted by many as a field perhaps indicates that material can be borrowed from many disciplines. Yet the subjects of traditional environmental know-ledge (TEK), climate change, revenues, empowerment, sustainability, which are often bandied about in tourism literature, are fundamental and delicate components, and researchers must employ caution when examining these issues. We believe that action research can be conducted in indigenous com-munities, especially if CREE and CSL are implemented at the onset of research projects. But this belief comes with a warning: action research is sometimes discouraged by supervisors, community members, and funding partners because funding, timelines, and deliverables are still structured around traditional guidelines (with research projects usually not exceeding three years), with limited funding opportunities for pre- and post-visits to communities. These limitations perpetuate the 'twin dilemmas of access and time which shape and limit research activities' (Smith 2001: 226) in indigenous communities. From an optimistic perspective or using the analogy of a gen-erative spiral, action research – whether it achieves action or not, if it is conducted properly through the help of CREE and CSL – can provide an essential learning opportunity for researchers and community members.

## References

Absolon, K. and Willett, C. (2004) 'Aboriginal Research: Berry Picking and Hunting in the 21st century', *First Peoples Child and Family Review* 1: 5–17.

Ateljevic, I., Pritchard, A. and Morgan, N. (eds) (2007) *The Critical Turn in Tourism Studies: Innovative Research Methodologies*. New York: Elsevier.

Belsky, J. (2004) 'Contributions of Qualitative Research to Understanding the Politics of Community Ecotourism', in J. Phillimore and L. Goodson (eds), *Qualitative Research in Tourism: Ontologies, epistemologies and methodologies*. London: Routledge.

Butler, R.W. and Hinch, T. (eds) (2007) *Tourism and Indigenous Peoples: Issues and Implications*. Oxford: Butterworth-Heinemann.

Burgess, R.G. (1991) 'Sponsors, Gatekeepers, Members and Friends: Access in Edu-cational Settings', in W.B. Shaffir and R.A. Stebbins (eds), *Experiencing Fieldwork: An Inside View of Qualitative Research*. London: Sage.

Caine, K.J., Davison, C.M. and Stewart, E.J. (2009) 'Preliminary Field-work: Method-ological Reflections from Northern Canadian Research', *Qualitative Research* 9(4): 489–513.

Cole, P. (2005) *Coyote and Raven Go Canoeing: Coming Home to the Village*. Montreal: McGill-Queen's University Press.

Crazy Bull, C. (1997) 'Advice for the Non-Native Researcher', *Tribal College: Journal of American Indian Higher Education* 9: 24.

Davidson-Hunt, I.J. and O'Flaherty, R.M. (2007) 'Researchers, Indigenous Peoples and Placed-based Learning Communities', *Society and Natural Resources* 20: 291–305.

de Ishtar, Z. (2005) 'Striving for a Common Language: A White Feminist Parallel to Indigenous Ways of Knowing and Researching', *Women's Studies International Forum* 28: 357–68.

Deloria, V. (1995) *Red Earth, White Lies: Native Americans and the Myth of Scientific Fact*. New York: Scribner.

Deloria, V. (2003) 'Custer Died for your Sins: An Indian Manifesto', in D.L. Fixico (ed.), *The American Indian Mind in a Linear World: American Indian Studies and Traditional Knowledge*. New York: Routledge.

Denzin, N.K. (2008) *Searching for Yellowstone: Race, Gender, Family, and Memory in the Postmodern West*. Walnut Creek, CA: Left Coast Press.

Denzin, N. and Lincoln, Y. (2003) 'The Discipline and Practice of Qualitative Research', in N. Denzin and Y. Lincoln (eds), *Strategies of Qualitative Inquiry*, 2nd edn. London: Sage.

Dyer, P., Aberdeen, L. and Schuler, S. (2003) 'Tourism Impacts on an Australian Indigenous Community: A Djabugay case study', *Tourism Management* 24(1): 83–95.

Fidler, A., Lemelin, R.H., Peerla, D. and Walmark, B. (2008) 'Hearing the voices of all parties', *WWF Arctic Bulletin* 1.08: 16–17.

Gaventa, J. and Cornwall, A. (2001) 'Power and Knowledge', in P. Reason and H. Bradbury (eds), *Handbook of Action Research: Participative Inquiry and Practice*. Thousand Oaks: Sage.

Gearheard, S. and Shirley, J. (2007) 'Challenges in Community-research Relation-ships: Learning from Natural Science in Nunavut', *Arctic* 60(1): 62–74.

Gegeo, D.W. and Watson-Gegeo, K.A. (2001) ' "How we Know": Kwara'ae Rural Villagers Doing Indigenous Epistemology', *Contemporary Pacific* 13: 55–88.

Guba, E.G. and Lincoln, Y.S. (1989) *Fourth Generation Evaluation*. Newbury Park: Sage.

Heron, J. and Reason, P. (2001) 'The Practice of Co-operative Inquiry: Research "with" Rather than "on" People', in P. Reason and H. Bradbury (eds), *Handbook of Action Research: Participative Inquiry and Practice*. Thousand Oaks: Sage.

Hodge, P. and Lester, J. (2006) 'Indigenous Research: Whose Priority? Journeys and Possibilities of Cross-cultural Research in Geography', *Geographical Research* 44: 41–51.

Huntington, H.P. (2006) 'Who are the "Authors" when Traditional Knowledge is Documented', *Arctic* 59(3): iii–iv.

Jobbins, G. (2004) 'Translators, Trust and Truth: Cross-cultural Issues in Sustain-ability Tourism Research', in J. Phillimore and L. Goodson (eds), *Qualitative Research in Tourism: Ontologies, Epistemologies and Methodologies*. London: Routledge.

Kievit, J.A. (2003) 'A Discussion of Scholarly Responsibilities to Indigenous Communities', *American Indian Quarterly* 27: 3–45.

Lemelin, R.H. (2007) 'Local Dimensions of Polar Bear Tourism in Churchill, Manitoba', in J. Higham and M. Lück (eds), *Marine Wildlife and Tourism Management*. Oxford: CABI Publishing.

Lemelin, R.H. and Dyck, M. (2007) 'New Frontiers in Marine Wildlife Tourism II: An International Overview of Polar Bear Tourism', in J. Higham and M. Lück (eds), *Marine Wildlife and Tourism Management*. Oxford: CABI Publishing.

Lemelin, R.H. and Johnston, M. (2008) 'Northern Protected Areas and Parks', in P. Dearden and R. Rollins (eds), *Parks and Protected Areas in Canada: Planning and Management*, 3rd edn. New York: Oxford University Press.

Lemelin, R.H. and Lickers, F.H. (2004) 'Implementing Capacity-building, Respect, Equity, and Empowerment (CREE) in the social sciences', in C. Rehbein, J.G. Nelson, T.J. Beechey and R.J. Paine (eds), *Proceedings of the Annual General Meeting from the Parks and Research Forum of Ontario: Parks and Protected Areas Research in Ontario 2004: Planning Northern Parks and Protected Areas*. Waterloo, Canada: Parks Research Forum of Ontario (PRFO).

Lemelin, R.H. and Smale, B.J.A. (2006) 'Effects of Environmental Context on the Experience of Polar Bear Viewers in Churchill, Manitoba', *Journal of Ecotourism* 5(3): 176–91.

Lemelin, R.H. and Smale, B.J.A. (2007) 'Wildlife Viewer Archetypes: Are Polar Bear Viewers in Churchill, Manitoba ecotourists?' *Tourism in Marine Environments* 4(2): 1–15.

Lemelin, R.H. and Wiersma, E.C. (2007a) 'Perceptions of Polar Bear Tourists: A Qualitative Analysis', *Human Dimensions of Wildlife Management* 12(1): 45–52.

Lemelin, R.H. and Wiersma, E.C. (2007b) 'Gazing upon Nanuk, the Polar Bear: The Wildlife Tourist Gaze and Ocular Consumption in Churchill, Manitoba', *Polar Geography* 30(1–2): 37–53.

Lemelin, R.H., Peerla, D., and Walmark, B. (2008) 'Voices from the Margins: The Muskekowuck Athinuwick/Cree People of Northern Ontario and the Management of Wabusk/polar bear', *Arctic* 61(1): 113–15.

Lemelin, R.H., McIntyre, N., Koster, R. and Johnston, M. (2010) 'Polar Bear Management in Polar Bear Provincial Park and the Washeo and Weenusk First Nations', in C.M. Hall and J. Saarinen (eds), *Tourism and Change in Polar Regions: Climate, Environments and Experiences*. London: Routledge.

Lickers, F.H. (1994) *First Nations: Environmental Knowledge and Approaches to Natural Resources: Methodological Approach*. Ottawa: IREE.

Lickers, H.F., Haas, G., Winslow, D., Doyle, D., Beram, L. and Associates (1995) *Building Respect: Native People and Environmental Assessment*. Ministry of Environment and Energy Ontario, and The Institute for Research on Environment and Economy, Ottawa.

Lofland, J. and Lofland, L. H. (eds) (1984) *Analyzing Social Settings: A Guide to Qualitative Observation and Analysis*. Belmont: Wadsworth Publishing.

Louis, R.P. (2007) 'Can you hear us now? Voices from the Margin: Using Indigenous Methodologies in Geographic Research', *Geographical Research* 45: 130–9.

Lykes, M.B. and Maya Ixil Women (2006) 'Creative Arts and Photography in Participatory Action Research in Guatemala', in P. Reason and H. Bradbury (eds), *Handbook of Action Research*. Thousand Oaks: Sage.

McAvoy, L., McDonald, D. and Carlson, M. (2003) 'American Indian/First Nation

Place Attachment to Park Lands: The Case of the Nuu-chah-nulth of British Columbia', *Journal of Park and Recreation Administration* 21(2): 84–104.

McNiff, J., Lomax, P. and Whitehead, J. (1996) *You and Your Action Research Project*. New York: Routledge.

Mowforth, M. and Munt. I. (2003) *Tourism and Sustainability: Development and New Tourism in the Third World*, 2nd edn. London: Routledge.

Patton, M.Q. (1990) *Qualitative Evaluation and Research Methods*. London: Sage.

Pedlar, A. (1995) 'Relevance and Action Research in Leisure', *Leisure Sciences* 17: 133–40.

Reardon, K.M. (1998) 'Participatory Action Research as Service Learning', *New Directions for Teaching and Learning* 73: 57–64.

Reason, P. (1994) 'Three Approaches to Participative Inquiry', in N.K. Denzin and Y.S. Lincoln (eds), *Handbook of Qualitative Research*. Thousand Oaks: Sage.

Reason, P. and Bradbury, H. (eds) (2006) *Handbook of Action Research*. Thousand Oaks: Sage.

Rundstrom, R.A. and Deur, D. (1999) 'Reciprocal Appropriation: Toward an Ethics of Cross-cultural Research', in J.D. Proctor and D.M. Smith (eds), *Geography and Ethics*. London: Routledge.

Schön, D.A. (1983) *The Reflective Practitioner: How Professionals Think in Action*. New York: Basic Books.

Schwandt, T.A. (2001) *Dictionary of Qualitative Inquiry*, 2nd edn. Thousand Oaks: Sage.

Shaffir, W.B. (1996) 'Doing Ethnographic Research in Jewish Orthodox Communities: The Neglected Role of Sociability', in S. Grills (ed.), *Doing Ethnographic Fieldwork: Fieldwork Settings*. Thousand Oaks: Sage.

Smith, L.T. (1999) *Decolonizing Methodologies: Research and Indigenous Peoples*. London: Zed Books.

Steinhauer, E. (2002) 'Thoughts on an Indigenous Research Methodology', *Canadian Journal of Native Education* 26: 69–81.

Stewart, E.J. and Draper, D. (2006a) 'Community Responses to Tourism in the Canadian North', in R. Riewe and J. Oakes (eds), *Climate Change: Linking Traditional and Scientific Knowledge*. Winnipeg: Aboriginal Issues Press University of Manitoba.

Stewart, E.J. and Draper, D. (2006b) 'Sustainable Cruise Tourism in Arctic Canada: An Integrated Coastal Management Approach', *Tourism in Marine Environments* 3(2): 77–88.

Stewart, E.J. and Draper, D. (2007) 'A Collaborative Approach to Understanding Local Stakeholder Perceptions of Tourism in Churchill, Manitoba (Canada)', *Polar Geography* 30(1–2): 7–35.

Stewart, E.J., Howell, S.E.L., Draper, D., Yackel, J. and Tivy, A. (2007) 'Sea ice in Canada's Arctic: Implications for Cruise Tourism', *Arctic* 60(4): 370–80.

Stewart, E.J., Howell, S., Draper, D., Yackel, J., and Tivy, A. (2008) 'Cruise Tourism in a Warming Arctic: Implications for Northern National Parks'. Paper presented at the Parks for Tomorrow conference, 8–13 May, University of Calgary, Canada.

Stringer, E.T. (1999) *Action Research*, 2nd edn. Thousand Oaks: Sage.

Taylor, R.R., Jason, L.A., Keys, C.B., Suarez-Balcazar, Y., Davis, M.I., Durlak, J.A. and Holtz Isenberg, D. (2004) 'Capturing theory and methodology in participatory research', in L.A. Jason, C.B. Keys, Y. Suarez-Balcazar, R.R. Taylor and

M.I. Davis (eds), *Participatory Community Research: Theories and Methods in Action*. Washington, DC: American Psychological Association.

Tuhiwai-Smith, L. (2005) 'On Tricky Grounds: Researching the Native in the Age of Uncertainty', in N.K. Denzin and Y.S. Lincoln (eds), *The Handbook of Qualitative Research*. Thousand Oaks: Sage.

Westwood, S. (2006) 'What Lies Beneath? Using Creative, Projective and Participatory Techniques in Qualitative Tourism Inquiry', in I. Ateljevic, A. Pritchard and N. Morgan (eds), *The Critical Turn in Tourism Studies: Innovative Research Methodologies*. San Francisco: Elsevier.

Winter, R. and Munn-Giddings, C. (2001) *A Handbook for Action Research in Health and Social Care*. New York: Routledge.

# 22 Managing post-fieldwork interpersonal relationships
## Mea (maxima?) culpa

*David Timothy Duval*

## Introduction

Managing the fieldwork process as a whole has always been the source of consternation for many graduate students in the social sciences. It generally fits in with other hallmark activities around the beginning of one's graduate career: commencing the development of their research, establishing a firm base of knowledge from within the existing literature, selecting a wider theoretical/philosophical orientation within which their research will (hopefully) fit, and balancing life needs (read: financial hardships). It probably should be noted at this point that much of this angst is inevitably repeatable once full-time academic work (not always the intended career path of PhD candidates, of course) is secured. Without question, however, the logistics surrounding fieldwork planning and execution can be daunting for a neophyte researcher. Critical within this, and perhaps overlooked more often than not in academic literature of the ethnographic fieldwork process or graduate seminars, is the subtle art of managing interpersonal relationships after the fieldwork has been completed.

My intent with this brief chapter is to invite readers on somewhat of a reflective journey on personal fieldwork undertaken for my PhD over ten years ago in a major Canadian city. It is not a chapter where ontological and/or phenomenological crafts (to borrow from Hollinshead 2004) are married to individualistic tendencies of 'being' or 'knowing', nor does it make any attempt to situate this reflexive *mea culpa* within a postmodern framework of 'self' or 'selfless' as framed by/within multiple social sciences (Becker 1996). Rather, my intent is more grounded in the practical 'how to' as opposed to the epistemologically grounded 'how come' or 'why'. I offer my own personal story on balancing life, employment and research, with some sombre, sobering and personal reflections on 'what went right' and 'what went wrong' during my own ethnographic fieldwork stint conducted nearly a decade ago.

## Precursor to fieldwork

My PhD was, at the time, perhaps not hugely typical in its structure and format. The programme to which I was attached was reasonably popular and total demand for entry far outstripped the logistical supply of full-time academic staff. Once 'inside', the range of students and interests was incredibly vast. This, in the end, turned out to be both beneficial and problematic to my own progress: beneficial in the sense that the richness of alternative ideas (most of which were completely outside any theoretical or methodological orientation my own research was taking) but problematic in that this richness in diversity of my PhD colleagues meant little chance of cross-fertilisation of ideas or experiences.

My own background is in anthropology, although I was trained as an archaeologist and worked in the Eastern Caribbean in the early 1990s on excavations and site surveys. Importantly, and unbeknownst to me at the time, the time I spent on various islands in the Eastern Caribbean ultimately set the stage for the nature of interactions with West Indian migrants living in Canada seven years later when I was struggling to make some headway with getting myself integrated within selected networks of West Indian migrants in a major Canadian city.

During my archaeological work in the Eastern Caribbean, doing anthropological fieldwork (of the ethnographic variety) was foreign to me, nor was it a salient interest. I did have some experiences that one might consider part and parcel of standard ethnographic fieldwork experiences, even though at the time I was not actually conducting research. For example, the heat of the Caribbean sun prevented productive archaeological work after about 2.00 p.m. on most days, so late afternoons were often spent exploring bits of the island or visiting friends that I had come to know. Part of ethnographic work is being visible (Coffey 1999), and I attained some degree of visibility amongst a few small networks or within a few smaller villages where various friends lived. This was beneficial in that it afforded a young graduate student experience in interacting with foreign nationals for extended periods of time in their own country. In other words, when it came time to figure out how I would work with West Indian migrants for the purpose of my PhD research some seven years later, establishing a meaningful rapport was hugely assisted by the tacit knowledge (and relatively recent information and knowledge at that) I held of their country or region of origin.

## Planning fieldwork

The topic I eventually chose for my PhD, which I began in 1997, was the broad notion of migrant experiences and the role of 'home' in assisting with their own integration within a new country. I was particularly interested in migrants' social and familial connections to 'home', but specifically why and how those ties were forged. I based my interest in a tourism context by suggesting that my research could expand current understandings of VFR (Visiting Friends and Relatives) tourism. I used transnationalism (then an almost brand-new social phenomenon, e.g. Basch *et al.* 1994) as a conceptual framework to understand the 'why' of what I was proposing to (hopefully) discover.

In order to address the research question I had formulated, it was clear that a qualitative approach, under an ethnographic methodological framework, was desirable in order to acquire rich and 'thick' data (to borrow from Clifford Geertz). That said, I remember thinking that Becker (1996) was probably correct when he stated that fieldwork, particularly of the qualitative variety, does really not allow the researcher to be fully removed from the data. I was acutely aware that data are generated (and perhaps even analysed 'on the fly') and consumed by the researcher almost simultaneously in the fieldwork setting. Once I had settled broadly on an ethnographic approach, made all the easier after enrolling in a PhD-level ethnographic methods seminar at my university, the next step was determining how to actually begin the process of actively generating (and creating) data. A problem became immediately apparent: how to engage with West Indian migrants to the point where I could conduct meaningful interviews or hold informal sessions in order to, hopefully, glean enough data that could be used to address the research question that framed my research.

Fieldwork, by its very nature, both is and takes place within a dynamic social space (Hastrup 2005), with the key word being 'social'. As an undergraduate and graduate student, I had read enough academic ethnographic work to know that rapport and socialisation are critical elements in the ethnographic fieldwork process (e.g. Agar 1996). Still, I wrestled with the question of access. I recall thinking that, while rapport was critical, how do I obtain access? What are the politics involved in securing access? To whom am I committed? From whom should I expect commitment? Perhaps the biggest practical question I had at the time was: How do I do it?

The simple fact was that I could not walk up to a person on the street, introduce myself and start asking questions. Such a 'shotgun' approach would have been seen as rude by potential respondents, and I knew this because I had a rough idea of social norms and degrees of acceptability in social interactions as a direct result of the time spent previously in the Eastern Caribbean. (As an aside, as senior undergraduates we used to frequently joke about Evans-Pritchard's [e.g., 1937; 1940] fieldwork tactics by adopting the stance of someone holding a shotgun, pointing it at a hypothetical research subject, and yelling: 'Who's your mother?' It was an inaccurate and woefully immature joke, but it went some way to helping us understand the politics of fieldwork and access.) During the planning of my fieldwork, I came to realise that the only way I was going to be able to access those whom I felt would be beneficial to my research (recognising the selfish undertone of that statement, both now and at the time) was to spend some amount of time integrating myself within the West Indian community.

Spatially, the West Indian 'community' in the large Canadian city where I conducted my fieldwork was concentrated in various residential pockets. While accessible and thus somewhat tempting in one respect, I felt uncomfortable with the idea of initiating a programme of 'hanging around' coffee shops in the hopes that someone (either myself or a migrant) would strike up a conversation. This also had the potential to be incredibly time-consuming, which was not financially feasible given that I was working full-time as a market research consultant at the time. (In addition to funding and access, existing employment commitments completes the triad of fieldwork nuisances.) By chance, I was introduced to a relatively recent (if memory serves) migrant through a mutual friend. This person was instrumental in introducing me to various migrants over the course of several months. Going back to my fieldwork diary at the time, this entry captures the level of integration I felt I was achieving:

> 15 August – Today is when I am truly able to say that I have made significant inroads into a small circle of people. One wanted desperately for me to come to some event, which I could go to. As a result, she wanted me to come on 3 September to a Dominican BBQ. She said I would have great fun and meet lots of interesting people, many of whom she has already spoken to about me.

I remember clearly at this point that my research actually became 'real' because I was interacting with real people. No longer were they objectified in the pages of a rather anaemic PhD proposal: they were sitting across from me and we were interacting. Of course, full integration within a 'community' in a fieldwork setting is, in my opinion, not possible. As a researcher, I could never have known exactly when full integration was achieved within a community or group as I was never sure of the parameters of that 'community'. Community is a fluid concept, one that is at once convenient yet frustratingly without true definition. I could, however, suggest that I had come to know some members of 'a' community, or what I referred to at the time as members of networks within a community.

I began to make contact with more West Indian migrants, largely through snowballing (Bernard 2006). Some contacts were strong, while others were more transient. Perhaps it is a function of a failing memory (or poor fieldnotes), but when looking back nearly ten years later I feel that my level of integration was neither immense nor intense. The time that I did spend talking to people, however, was highly productive and enjoyable. The data that I did glean were quite thick and highly informative. To my tacit knowledge of the Eastern Caribbean I was able to add important knowledge and understanding, over time, of the life of a West Indian migrant in a large Canadian city.

Although I conducted only very few formal interviews, on balance both the interviews I did conduct and fieldwork in general were productive and positive. Interestingly, as good as my contacts and key informants were, and my over-success at integration and rapport, I am now convinced that it was my direct experience in the Caribbean that afforded me what is perhaps the most critical element in fieldwork: credibility. I knew, for example, what 'jump up' and 'wave de flag' meant (I had done both, from what I was told), I knew of some political affairs and I knew all the jokes about the regional air carrier, LIAT (Leeward Island Air Transport): 'Leave the Island Any Time' or 'Luggage In Another Terminal'. This tacit knowledge meant that I knew about the things my informants (formal and informal) spoke about; not always, but more often than not. It also meant that I was a little 'closer' to the region than someone who had never been (or had never seen the Caribbean that I saw as a veritable non-tourist).

As in the case of many fieldwork settings, friendships developed. The real problem, however, came after the fieldwork was completed. I faced a difficult situation of what to do with these friendships I had developed. It this post-fieldwork stage of relationship management that I now wish to address.

## Post-fieldwork relationship management

Like others before me, I faced the daunting task of writing everything up after the fieldwork. What complicated this was my full-time career as a market research consultant (a direction taken ostensibly to pay the bills, but also to broaden my skill base) and thus was not able to do any work related to my PhD during regular office hours. In a way, this did not impede the actual fieldwork, as most of my key respondents and members of the networks I 'infiltrated' also worked full-time; thus my experiences within these networks were largely relegated to evenings and weekends. Once I was charged with the task of beginning the analysis of the reams of data, however, I faced a difficult decision: to what extent would it be logistically feasible to maintain relationships with people during rather precious times when I should, in reality, be writing about them so I can finish my dissertation? In my eyes at the time, it was a problem of time management.

The decision I made is one which I regret to this day: because it was convenient, I opted to devote most evenings and weekends to my dissertation as opposed to socialising and maintaining friendships with people whom I had come to know during my fieldwork. I say 'convenient' because, at the time, I had convinced myself that it really was a question of time management, but I recall thinking, rather embarrassingly I realise now, that if I broke off contact I would not have to worry about new conversations and/or new data 'corrupting' what I already had (in my own defence, a genuine concern). By breaking contact, I would not have to worry about how I would talk to someone that I was just writing about. I would not have known how to answer the question 'So, what are you writing about me?', if it indeed would have come up. Looking back, I doubt it would have. My dilemma brought to mind Brettell's (1996) *When They Read What We Write*: now that I was finished with the actual fieldwork, what would happen? In many respects, I felt at the time that the 'others' becoming too close for comfort, although they did not know it.

I was not prepared for the decision I had to make. In the end, I severed all ties. Over ten years later, I remain unhappy with this decision. In fact, I was not happy with the decision almost immediately, but I rationalised in my head that it had to be done. I was, and remain to this day, troubled by how I handled my interpersonal relations with key informants. I have not had contact with any of them, nor have I seen any other members of the networks within which I was attached. Granted, some of them would have long forgotten about me, and if I were being honest the faces of some of them in my own mind are today slightly blurry. In fact, looking at my fieldnotes, where of course I followed standard ethnographic practice and used pseudonyms, I struggle to remember proper names (the small piece of paper that links pseudonyms with proper names is buried in a box of papers in my home office). These people remain anonymous ghosts whose emotions and lives were captured and shaped by a budding anthropologist with little experience and foresight in people skills.

## Conclusion

This chapter is not meant (entirely) to be a *mea culpa*, but in some ways it must be in order to bring forward the importance of the issue. Fieldwork requires significant skills, many of which, as junior scholars, we barely have a grasp of when we summon them at critical times. It requires the ability to think on one's feet, plan for eventualities and hiccups and, especially with ethnographic fieldwork, patience and fortitude.

Proper fieldwork goes beyond the cursory skills of actually conducting interviews and 'making sense' of the data at the back end; the shoulder activities, as I like to call them, that frame these core activities probably exert influence more on a researcher's ontological positioning than perhaps anything else. Maintaining post-fieldwork relationships is an example of a shoulder activity in fieldwork that can speak about the integrity of the research, even though the previously collected data remain unaffected. Granted, not all relationships sparked during fieldwork are required to be carried over into the post-fieldwork period, but hopefully this chapter has at least made some aware of the possibility.

In the early stages of my PhD, I was somewhat uninspired by most academic treatments of ethnographic fieldwork. Most were strong on theoretical and methodological treatments, and some even spoke about how to negotiate one's 'self' within the field (a concept I still struggle with to this day). The vast majority were relatively light on specific practicalities relating to post-fieldwork relationships with informants or research subjects. Volumes such as Sanjek's *Fieldnotes* (1990) and R.F. Ellen's (1984) 'general conduct' guide for ethnographic research gave excellent practical advice, but neither offered useful assistance in the managing of post-fieldwork relationships. To be fair, however, there is good reason for this: fieldwork is a very personal undertaking, where mistakes will be made, triumphs celebrated quietly and friendships (potentially) formed. Detailed guidelines, apart from those of an ethical nature, could never be passed off as universal when fieldwork means different things to different people. Looking back, I am happy with the outcome of the research as I believe I gained a good understanding of migrants and their travels back home (a subject which became quite popular in the early part of this decade, and continues to this day), but the decision I made to sever ties with a small number of friends is something which I would prefer to change given the opportunity.

# References

Agar, M.H. (1996) *The Professional Stranger*, 2nd edn. New York: Academic Press.

Basch, L., Glick Schiller, N. and Szanton Blanc, C. (1994) *Nations Unbound: Transnational Projects and the Deterritorialized Nation-state*. New York: Gordon and Breach.

Becker, H. (1996) 'The Epistemology of Qualitative Research', in R. Jessor, A. Colby and R.A. Shweder (eds), *Ethnography and Human Development: Context and Meaning in Social Inquiry*. Chicago: University of Chicago Press.

Bernard, H.R. (1996) *Research Methods in Anthropology: Qualitative and Quantitative Approaches*, 4th edn. Lanham, MD: AltaMira Press.

Brettell, C.B. (ed.) (1996) *When They Read What We Write: The Politics of Ethnography*. Westport: Bergin & Garvey.

Coffey, A. (1999) *The Ethnographic Self: Fieldwork and the Representation of Identity*. London: Sage.

Ellen, R.F. (ed.) (1984) *Ethnographic Research: A Guide to General Conduct*. London: Academic Press

Evans-Pritchard, E.E. (1937) *Witchcraft, Oracles and Magic among the Azande*. London: Oxford University Press.

Evans-Pritchard, E.E. (1940) 'The Nuer of the Southern Sudan', in M. Fortes and E.E. Evans-Pritchard (eds), *African Political Systems*. London: Oxford University Press.

Hastrup, K. (2005) 'Social Anthropology: Towards a Pragmatic Enlightenment?', *Social Anthropology* 13(2):133–49.

Hollinshead, K. (2004) 'A Primer in Ontological Craft: The Creative Capture of People and Places through Qualitative Research', in J. Phillimore and L. Goodson (eds), *Qualitative Research in Tourism*. London: Routledge.

Sanjek, R. (ed.) (1990) *Fieldnotes: The Makings of Anthropology*. Ithaca: Cornell University Press.

# 23 Concluding thoughts

## Where does fieldwork end and tourism begin?

*C. Michael Hall*

Fieldwork is a structured temporal and geographical space marked by empirical research on a selected set of subjects. However, fieldwork, like much tourism, also bears some of the hallmarks of a ludic experience in that it requires temporary changes in location as well as psychology and can even be regarded as a form of play – at least in comparison with laboratory or office work and as an escape from those environments (see Hall, Chapter 1, this volume). Play is 'a well defined quality of action which is different from "ordinary life"' (Huizinga 1980: 4) or 'real life' (1980: 8), but it is not, contrary to popular thinking, simply the opposite of seriousness. Instead, all play 'absorbs us in a ludic moment. A freedom delimited in time and space. We become serious within a non-serious situation, or vice versa. A certain amount of tension is inevitable, but serves to feed the fire of creativity, when anything may be possible. It may be tense, because after all "who knows what's going to happen?" but above all, it is fun' (Sawkins 2002). The notion of fieldwork as play is also picked up by Arizona State University geographer Casey Allen:

> I often refer to fieldwork as 'play', because playing usually connotes fun. And fieldwork is certainly FUN! You may already be familiar with fieldwork. Maybe you've already conducted fieldwork (even though you may not have known it)! (Most) geographers see 'the field' anywhere and everywhere: the forest, a foreign country, the CBD of a city, the corn fields of Iowa, a classroom, the city plaza, rooftops, a river, the road, movies, even life itself! Being in the field – playing in the field – with a full-fledged Geographer is a fabulous treat. Tag along with a Geographer doing fieldwork and see for yourself!
>
> (Allen n.d.)

Madison (2005) understood playfulness as being extremely important for ethnographic ethics and performity in fieldwork, stating: 'As ethnographers, we may be both playful and unplayful while recognizing and understanding when the subjects of the world we enter feel they can be both playful and/or unplayful with us and the worlds we represent' (Madison 2005: 104).

Boon (1982: x) described his attitude towards fieldwork as 'playful, because I find the concept an ideal and action that should be simultaneously be debunked and preserved'. Interestingly such issues are also raised by Wolcott (2005: 17) in discussing the art of fieldwork when he responds to the statement by Charles Wagley that 'Fieldwork is a creative endeavor', and notes that 'there is an implied playfulness' in the terms 'imagination and intuition' as they are applied to scientific endeavours such as fieldwork. Wolcott also quotes Imre Lakatos to support his case: 'The direction of science is determined primarily by human creative imagination and not by the universe of facts which surround us' (Lakatos 1978: 99, cited in Wolcott 2005). Many people undertaking work in the field will have great empathy.

Unfortunately this notion of fieldwork as play, while I know it is shared with a number of colleagues and students, is unfortunately not something that can be discussed very easily out in the open. After all, especially for those of us who work in tourism studies (about which we are often told in a most Pooh-like voice that we do not study serious things anyway), travelling in relation to our research work is often seen by research committees and deans as being to do with going on a holiday or being at play in a popular and more demeaning sense as not being worthy of study, with one of the author's favourite quotes being from an Associate Research Dean when discussing funding applications from tourism staff, 'why do you need to travel? Why can't you just study the tourists *here?*'

Of course, even despite the creative and performative importance of the notion of fieldwork as play, it is important to note that fieldwork should not be regarded as leisure. 'Fieldwork inevitably involves a lot more than just sitting around watching things and asking questions' (Ellen 1984: 102). Indeed, Shaffir and Stebbins (1991: 1) observe that 'fieldwork must certainly rank with the more disagreeable activities that humanity has fashioned for itself. It is usually inconvenient, to say the least, sometimes physically uncomfortable, frequently embarrassing, and, to a degree, always tense'. Such sentiments are perhaps tied up in the title of Pollard's (2009) article on the difficulties faced by doctoral students undertaking ethnographic fieldwork, 'Field of screams'! Pollard (2009) describes a range of feelings as experienced by 16 interviewees: alone, ashamed, bereaved, betrayed, depressed, desperate, disappointed, disturbed, embarrassed, fearful, frustrated, guilty, harassed, homeless, paranoid, regretful, silenced, stressed, trapped, uncomfortable, unprepared, unsupported and unwell.

To a great extent this volume has been a reaction to such sentiments. It is not perfect. But it is hoped that the articles will at least help get readers thinking about the issues that they face in the field (Pollard has an excellent range of questions with respect to prospective fieldworkers that relate very strongly to many of the issues posed in the present volume).

For Hastrup and Hervik, the social science fieldwork experience is attempting to explore 'the flow of intersubjective human experience' (1994: 9). Nevertheless, the researcher constructs the field whether it be 'exotic', 'local' or in 'cyberspace' and therefore where and how those flows are studied. Yet, as many of the chapters in this volume have highlighted, there are very substantial formal and informal pressures that shape our fieldwork, with a number of the institutional frames for it often being regarded as somewhat unrealistic or at least out of step with what happens 'out there'. At the end of the day a research output is required. Therefore, to over-determine fieldwork practices is to undermine and diminish their strength. Nevertheless, this must still be done with the following in mind: 'Genuine respect for local people and customs, flexibility in the research design, a sense of humour, and a willingness to share one's own experiences and knowledge with research participants, are all critical if cross-cultural and cross-gendered understanding is to be enhanced through the research process' (Scheyvens and Leslie 2000: 129).

As many of the chapters in this volume have indicated, fieldwork is as much about emotion as it is about the formal research process that you encounter in most textbooks. In fact the biggest challenge to fieldwork is really one of self and dealing with emotions and experiences. This has been beautifully put by Woodthorpe (2007: 8–9):

> Rather than it being a case of whether the researcher does or does not reflect upon their role and emotions within their research, it is the extent to which that researcher acknowledges this that imparts credibility to a piece of analysis. What we need to consider is what insight into our informants' beliefs and experiences, and indeed our research question itself, can be developed from our emotional response to our data. It is an arrogant researcher who will dismiss their emotions and feelings and render them invisible in their analysis; to pretend that they are gener-ating research from a distanced neutral standpoint. In contrast, it is the naïve researcher that will be so obsessed with accuracy and unsustainable academic standards that they are blinded to the emotionality of the human world. However, it is the misguided researcher who spends so much time being 'reflexive' that they fail to fully attend to the world within which their project is taking place. It is a case of 'hitting the right note' and incorporating all these issues into one credible piece of . . . research.

The concluding thoughts on this volume drew relationships between play and fieldwork. This was not done lightly. To play means to risk something that we may hold dear (Sawkins 2002), which may be our own reputation, our hard-earned savings and/or our relationships with our loved ones. These are all things that are concerns when we engage in fieldwork and research, especially as graduate students. But good fieldwork is as much about finding something in ourselves as it is about who and what we are studying; as in the tense moment of risk, when we do not quite know the outcome of our efforts, something 'real' within us may be observed.

## References

Allen, C.D. (n.d.) *The Importance of Fieldwork: A Simple Primer*, Adapted by Casey D. Allen from the original by Ronald I. Dorn. Online. Available HTTP: <http://www.public.asu.edu/~callen5/me/musings/fieldwork.html> (accessed 10 January 2010).

Boon, J.A. (1982) *Other Tribes, Other Scribes: Symbolic Anthropology in the Comparative Study of Cultures, Histories, Religions, and Texts*. New York: Cambridge University Press.

Ellen, R.F. (1984) *Ethnographic Research: A Guide to Good Conduct*. London: Academic Press.

Hastrup, K. and Hervik, P. (1994) 'Introduction', in K. Hastrup and P. Hervik (eds), *Social Experience and Anthropological Knowledge*. London: Routledge.

Huizinga, J. (1980) *Homo Ludens: A Study of the Play Element in Culture*. London: Routledge and Kegan Paul.

Lakatos, I. (1978) *The Methodology of Scientific Research Programmes, Philosophical Papers*, Vol. 1. London: Cambridge University Press.

Madison, D.S. (2005) *Critical Ethnography: Method, Ethics, Performance*. Thousand Oaks: Sage.

Pollard, A. (2009) 'Field of Screams: Difficulty and Ethnographic Fieldwork', *Anthropology Matters* 11(2). Online. Available HTTP: <http://www.anthropologymatters.com/index.php?journal=anth_matters&page=article&op=view&path[]=10> (accessed 10 January 2010).

Sawkins, P. (2002) 'Playful Attraction: Examining the Nature of Japanese Cruising', *Reconstruction* 2(4). Online. Available HTTP: <http://reconstruction.eserver.org/024/sawkins.htm> (accessed 18 January 2010).

Scheyvens, R. and Leslie, H. (2000) 'Gender, Ethics and Empowerment: Dilemmas of Development Fieldwork', *Women's Studies International Forum* 23(1): 119–30.

Shaffir, W. and Stebbins, R. (eds) (1991) *Experiencing Fieldwork: An Inside View of Qualitative Research*. Newbury Park: Sage.

Wolcott, H.F. (2005) *The Art of Fieldwork*, 2nd edn. Walnut Creek: AltaMira Press.

Woodthorpe, K. (2007) 'My life after death: Connecting the field, the findings and the feelings', *Anthropology Matters* 9(1). Online. Available HTTP: <http://www.anthropologymatters.com/index.php?journal=anth_matters&page=article&op=view &path[]=54> (accessed 18 January 2010).

# Index